Costa Rica

the Bradt Travel Guide

Larissa Banting

édition
1

www.bradtguides.com

Bradt Travel Guides Ltd, UK
The Globe Pequot Press Inc, USA

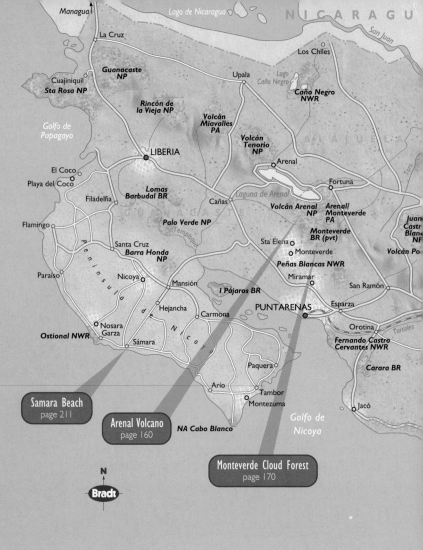

Managua

Lago de Nicaragua

NICARAGUA

La Cruz

San Juan

Los Chiles

Guanacaste
NP

Upala

Lago
Caño Negro

Cuajiniquil
Sta Rosa NP

Rincón de
la Vieja NP

Volcán
Miavalles
PA

Caño Negro
NWR

Golfo de
Papagayo

Volcán
Tenorio
NP

Arenal

LIBERIA

Fortuna

El Coco
Playa del Coco

Filadelfia

Lomas
Barbudal BR

Cañas

Laguna de Arenal

Volcán Arenal
NP

Arenal/
Monteverde
PA

Juan
Castr
Blan
NF

Flamingo

Palo Verde NP

Monteverde
BR (pvt)

Volcán Po

Santa Cruz

Sta Elena

Barra Honda
NP

Monteverde

Paraiso

Nicoya

Mansión

Peñas Blancas NWR

Miramar

San Ramón

I Pájaros BR

Hejancha

PUNTARENAS

Esparza

Carmona

Orotina

Nosara
Garza

Ostional NWR

Sámara

Fernando Castro
Cervantes NWR

Paquera

Carara BR

 Arío

Tambor

Golfo de
Nicoya

Jacó

Montezuma

Samara Beach
page 211

Arenal Volcano
page 160

NA Cabo Blanco

Monteverde Cloud Forest
page 170

N

Bradt

PACIFIC OCEAN

0 ——————— 50km
0 ——————— 30 miles

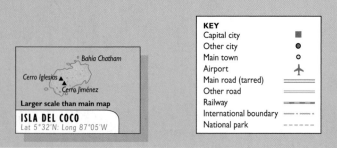

Bahía Chatham

Cerro Iglesias ▲
Cerro Jiménez

Larger scale than main map

ISLA DEL COCO
Lat 5°32'N; Long 87°05'W

KEY
Capital city   ■
Other city   ●
Main town   ○
Airport   ✈
Main road (tarred)
Other road
Railway
International boundary
National park

Barra
del Colorado
NWR

Puerto
Viejo

Tortuguero
NP

Tortuguero Canals
page 135

Caribbean Sea

Braulio
Carrillo
NP

Guápimo

Puerto Viejo
page 144

Volcán
Turrialba NP

Siguirres

Matina

Moín

LIMON

HEREDIA

Volcán
Irazú NP

Barbilla
BR

JUELA

SAN JOSÉ

CARTAGO

Ignacio

Macizo de La Muerte-
Tapantí NP

Cahuita

Cahuita NP

Hitoy-Cerere
BR

Bibrí

an Pablo

Santa María

Cerro de
La Muerte

Sixaola

Chirripó
NP

International
La Amistad
NP

Quepos

**Manuel Antonio
NP**

San Isidro

**Manuel Antonio
National Park**
page 247

General

Cortés

Tóncoles

Paso Real

San Vito

P
A
N
A
M
A

Piedras
Blancas NP

**Golfito
NWR**

Golfo
Dulce

Neily

Península de Osa

Corcovado
NP

Golfito

Puerto
Jiménez

David

Osa Peninsula
page 256

Costa Rica
Don't
miss…

Arenal Volcano
Arenal Baldi Termae thermal
baths and resort
(VL) page 160

**Drinking coffee
on the plantations**
Harvesting coffee
(AM/TIPS) page 113

Turtle watching
Turtles on Dominical Beach
(VRM) page 25

Sunset on a Pacific beach
Twilight over Playa Conchal
(FC) page 193

Hiking in Monteverde Cloud Forest
2,500 plant species and over 100 species of mammal
(CE/TIPS) page 170

top	Rainbow over San José (VL) page 85
above left	Poas Volcano crater (VL) page 109
above right	Waterfall at Cinchona, near Vara Blanca (VL)
below	Playa Langosta (FC) page 201

Author

Larissa Banting has lived and worked in Costa Rica since 2002 as an English teacher, travel consultant and travel writer. Prior to moving to Costa Rica, she was the dance writer for a weekly alternative paper in addition to writing for various travel and dance magazines. A graduate of Canada's York University with a specialisation in dance ethnology, two of her research papers on folk dance in Canada have been published in different academic journals. *Costa Rica: The Bradt Travel Guide* is her first book.

FEEDBACK REQUEST

Once the secret of backpackers and eco-tourists, Costa Rica is now a favourite destination for travellers of all interests, ages and economic classes – there is something for everyone here to experience and enjoy. Although I live in Costa Rica and travel throughout it on an almost weekly basis, it's impossible for one person to experience all this small but diverse country has to offer. Part of the thrill of travel is meeting other tourists and learning about their experiences. Have you discovered a delicious new spot for dinner, a thrilling adventure tour, a funky beach *cabina*? I'd love to hear your feedback about your journey to Costa Rica as well as your thoughts on this guide – has it been helpful? What would you like to see changed? Your information will help make future editions of the guide even better. Please send your comments to Larissa Banting at Bradt Travel Guides, 23 High Street, Chalfont St Peter, Bucks SL9 9QE, England; e info@bradtguides.com.

PUBLISHER'S FOREWORD *Hilary Bradt*

The first Bradt travel guide was written in 1974 by George and Hilary Bradt on a river barge floating down a tributary of the Amazon. In the 1980s and '90s the focus shifted away from hiking to broader-based guides covering new destinations – usually the first to be published about these places. In the 21st century Bradt continues to publish such ground-breaking guides, as well as others to established holiday destinations, incorporating in-depth information on culture and natural history with the nuts and bolts of where to stay and what to see.

Bradt authors support responsible travel, and provide advice not only on minimum impact but also on how to give something back through local charities. In this way a true synergy is achieved between the traveller and local communities.

* * *

Costa Rica featured in the third Bradt Guide (to Central America) and back in the 1970s it seemed a haven of good government and environmental management in a turbulent region. Central America has settled down since then and Costa Rica is now deservedly Latin America's most popular destination for ecotourists. We've been asked to do a new guide to the country for many years and I've always said that we're waiting for the perfect author. Now we've found one: Larissa Banting is a resident of Costa Rica who knows the country inside out. It was worth the wait.

First published September 2006

Bradt Travel Guides Ltd, 23 High Street, Chalfont St Peter, Bucks SL9 9QE, England.
www.bradtguides.com
Published in the USA by The Globe Pequot Press Inc, 246 Goose Lane,
PO Box 480, Guilford, Connecticut 06475-0480

Text copyright © 2006 Larissa Banting
Maps copyright © 2006 Bradt Travel Guides Ltd
Illustrations © 2006 individual photographers and artists (see below)

British Library Cataloguing in Publication Data
A catalogue record for this book is available from the British Library
ISBN-10: 1 84162 134 X   ISBN-13: 978 1 84162 134 0

Photographs Vicky Longland (VL), Jonathan Green (JG), Diana Holder (DH),
Chris Talbot (CT), Fernando Carcamo (FC), Larissa Banting (LB), Villas Río Mar (VRM), TIPS:
Chad Ehlers (CE), David W Hamilton (DWH), Donata Pizzi (DP), Aris Mihich (AM), Charles
Mahaux (CM), Roberto Rinaldi (RR), Reinhard Dirscherl (RD)
Front cover Red-eyed leaf frog, *Agalychnis callidryas* (Kevin Schafer/NHPA)
Back cover Oxcart wheel detail (VL), Male golden-headed quetzal, *Pharomachrus auriceps*
(DWH/TIPS)
Title page Golden-hooded tanager, *Tangara larvata* (VL), Tree ferns in mist (VL), Cattle drive in
Guanacaste (LB)
Illustrations Carole Vincer   **Maps** Alan Whitaker, ITMB

Typeset from the author's disc by Wakewing
Printed and bound in Italy by Legoprint SpA, Trento

917.286
BAN

Acknowledgements

There is an African saying that it takes a village to raise a child – I believe that it takes a community to write a book. There are so many people to thank for their help in making this guide a reality. None of this would have been possible without the incredible love and support of my husband, Roberto Leiva – thank you for your belief in me and for sharing your outstanding knowledge and insight of your beautiful country. My unending gratitude to my family: my late mother for teaching me to 'absorb other cultures, but don't forget your own', my aunt for nurturing my writing from an early age, my late godfather for giving me books instead of toys and fanning my fire for reading, my sister for her unwavering support and my late father whose spirit of adventure made 'no one told me I couldn't do it' his favourite phrase and instilled in me the belief that anything is possible.

My community in Costa Rica has been instrumental in the writing of this book – thanks to Vicky Longland for her wonderful contributions on the Caribbean, Orosí Valley and interesting bits of info as well as her gorgeous photos which have truly captured the magic of this country. To Abigail Leaver, Blondell Thomas, Yi Mora, Randy Gritz, Charlotte Leaver and Zhanna MacMillan for their invaluable assistance with fact checking, research and editing. Gracias to Carrie Smith, Casey Halloran and Tony Silva of Costa Rican Vacations for starting me on this path – their insightful feedback has contributed greatly. And many thanks to the countless folks in the Costa Rican tourism industry for their information, hospitality and kindness – you are the spirit of *Pura Vida*.

A massive thank you to everyone at Bradt, whose support and patience has been incredible – despite technical difficulties, earthquakes and other catastrophes, they've been kind and gentle to this novice book writer. My gratitude to Hilary Bradt for giving me the opportunity to share my love of Costa Rica with others, to Tricia Hayne for saying 'yes' and to Adrian Phillips for having the patience of Job. Jim Rice and Emma Thomson are also to be commended for their assistance in the editing process, which felt as challenging to me as climbing Mount Chirripó. And thanks to everyone behind the scenes for making sure the maps, photos and typesetting were engaging to the eye.

Thanks to the hundreds of travellers I've known over the years for their reflections on Costa Rica – hearing the good, the bad and the ugly from other voices has helped me stay objective.

And finally, *muchas gracias* to the *Ticos* for their warm hospitality, joy and eagerness to share their delightful land with all who travel the 'rich coast'.

Contents

Introduction

Bienvenido! Welcome to the land of 'Pura Vida', a place where the sun shines bright, the people are friendly and the landscape is breathtaking – in other words, welcome to Paradise!

I first came to Costa Rica as part of a film crew and fell in love with this small country from the moment I stepped off the plane. Coming from the snow-swept prairies of western Canada, I found the lushness and warmth of Costa Rica to be a salve to body, mind and soul. The *Ticos* (as Costa Ricans are affectionately called), who are as warm and welcoming as their beautiful environment, made me feel at home, despite language barriers. Meeting my future husband sealed the deal and soon, I was selling off my *mukluks* and mittens, heading due south for a new life. It's a move I have celebrated every day since.

After marrying on the Caribbean beach where we met (yes, we are true romantics), I started working with a small travel agency. This experience not only gave me the opportunity to explore every corner of Costa Rica but to learn first-hand from my hundreds of clients what made their stay here special (or not). This insight, coupled with my husband's 17 years' experience as a white-water rafting and tour guide, is what I offer to you now in the hope it helps you discover the many treasures of this 'rich coast'.

Thank you for choosing this book and I sincerely hope your travels through this land of peace are magical and memorable.

LIST OF MAPS

Part One

GENERAL INFORMATION

Official name Republic of Costa Rica

Location Central America, 10°N, 84°W; to the north is Nicaragua, to the south Panamá, west is bordered by the North Pacific Ocean and the east coast by the Caribbean Sea

Area 51,100km²

Status Democratic republic

Government Democracy

Capital San José

Population 4.1 million

Life expectancy Female 79.74 years, male 74.43 years

Official language Spanish

Religion Roman Catholicism is the official religion although all religions are respected and able to worship freely

Currency Costa Rican colon (CRC)

Exchange rate (as of 1 August 2006) US$1 = 516 colones, £1 = 977 colones, €1 = 662 colones

Major industries Tourism, electronics, coffee, bananas, palm oil, sugar, food processing, textiles and clothing, construction materials, fertiliser, plastic products

Major trading partners USA, Germany, Italy, Japan, Guatemala, Mexico

International telephone code +506

Time GMT –4 hours (Central Standard time by North American time zones)

Electricity supply 110 volts AC, 60 Hz (same as North America)

Flag The official flag has five horizontal bands of blue (top), white, red (double width), white and blue, with the coat of arms in a white disk on the red band and the words AMERICA CENTRAL and REPUBLICA COSTA RICA just above the coat of arms. The more commonly seen flag has just the five bands and no coat of arms.

Public holidays 1 January – New Year's Day, March or April – Semana Santa (Easter Week), 11 April – Juan Santamaría Day, 1 May – Labour Day, 25 July – Guanacaste Day, 2 August – Virgin of Los Angeles, 15 August – Mother's Day, 15 September – Independence Day, 12 October – Cultures Day (Columbus Day), 25 December – Christmas Day

National flower Guaria Morada (*Cattleya skinneri*)

National tree Guanacaste (*Enterolobiom cyclocarpum*)

National bird Yiguirro (*Turdus grayii*)

Background Information

The name 'Costa Rica' literally means 'Rich Coast' in Spanish and despite lacking mountains of gold, silver, oil or other material riches, this tiny land has shown the rest of the world that peace is the greatest treasure of all. The only country in the western hemisphere without an army, Costa Rica has been called the 'Switzerland of the Americas' for its visionary belief that weapons and war are not the answer. Blessed with an abundance of nature, this meeting place of the Americas is the most biodiverse place on earth, accounting for 6% of the planet's flora and fauna within a landmass that accounts for only 0.01% of terra firma's territory. Thanks to far-sighted governments, 26% of Costa Rica is protected in national parks, nature reserves, protected areas and private refuges, ensuring the preservation of these natural treasures for future generations to enjoy.

Costa Rica is located in Central America with Nicaragua to the north, Panamá to the south, with the Pacific Ocean and Caribbean Sea bordering the entire west and east coasts respectively. Just 10°N from the Equator, the climate is surprisingly diverse, on account of the many mountain ranges running through the country but travellers should make sure, no matter where they are staying, to slather on the sunscreen.

GEOGRAPHY AND CLIMATE

Costa Rica's landmass is 51,100km² making it about the size of West Virginia, Nova Scotia or twice the size of Wales. Despite its small size, the country boasts a dozen distinct microclimates scattered throughout – travelling an hour or two brings you from hot, dusty plains into cool, lush rainforests.

Mountain ranges or *cordilleras* run like a backbone down the length of Costa Rica, part of the giant Andean–Sierra range that runs through the length of the western Americas. Three of the ranges have active volcanoes, spewing steam and spitting lava as a reminder that Costa Rica is the baby of the continent, with only three million years under its belt. In the north is Cordillera de Guanacaste, home to the volcanoes of Rincón de Vieja and Miravalles. Continuing down is Cordillera de Tilaran with the famous Arenal volcano and on to Cordillera Central, where the volcanoes of Irazú, Poas, Barva and Turrialba flank the Central Valley. A number of other dormant volcanoes are found in these ranges, including Tenorio, Orosí, Santamaría, Cacho Negro and Platanar while over 200 extinct volcanoes are scattered both on land and in the sea.

The fourth and only non-volcanic range, Cordillera de Talamanca, is the highest and oldest in the country, housing Cerro Chirripó, the tallest mountain in Costa Rica at a height of 3,819m. On a clear day, one can see the Pacific Ocean and Caribbean Sea from its peak.

At the centre of the country, physically, socially and economically, is the Meseta Central (Central Valley), home to half of Costa Rica's population. Flanked by the Talamanca and Central cordilleras, the valley has rich volcanic soil and predictable rainy seasons, making it the ideal spot for farming. San José (1,160m), the nation's capital, is at the centre of the valley and with its temperatures constantly hovering around 20°C, it's been called 'The City of Eternal Spring'. Areas in upper elevations are renowned for their coffee and dairy products while the Orosí Valley grows plants for export.

Heading northwest, the Tilaran area around the manmade Lake Arenal resembles Switzerland, with lush green meadows. A bit further on, up one of the worst roads in the country, are the cool, misty forests of Monteverde, sitting high in the clouds at 1,440m. Westward, the topography changes dramatically upon entering the Nicoya Peninsula and Guanacaste province, where cattle ranching is king. Daytime temperatures can reach a searing 38°C, cooling off to 20°C at night.

Moving southward to the central Pacific region, the landscape changes again to verdant rainforests, home to palm oil plantations. Further south, the remote Osa Peninsula is a tangle of wild, wet jungles. Rains start a month earlier here than the central Pacific region and many resorts close during the peak of the rainy season in September and October.

The Caribbean coast has a maze of canals to the north and lush, thick jungles to the south. Rain falls here year round, with October normally the driest month so humidity levels are higher here than in the rest of the country, although the climate is comfortable, thanks to temperatures averaging 25°C. Bananas is the major industry here and plantations dot the landscape from Limón down to Cahuita.

For the rest of the country, there are two seasons in Costa Rica – rainy ('winter') from May to November, and dry ('summer') from December to April. Although a rainy season may conjure up images of monsoons, it's not as bad as one would think, as usually the early part of the day is hot, sunny and bright until cloud rolls in after lunch, which is likely to release a downpour at some point during the afternoon lasting a couple of hours, but which quickly tapers off by dinner. *Veranillo* (little summer) is a brief respite lasting a couple of weeks in late June or early July. The dry season is mostly sunny and anything more than a shower is rare during this time. In the south Pacific, the rainy season starts a month earlier while the northern areas aren't as affected by the seasons.

Tropical weather is basically the result of the combination of solar radiation and air circulation. Strong heat at the Equator gets air in motion establishing the pattern of winds experienced worldwide. The most common of these in Costa Rica are the *vientos alisios* (northeasterly trade winds), which blow with considerable force between December and April, and are responsible for carrying the moisture that sustains the entire cloudforest ecosystem.

Costa Rica's year-round climate is pleasant with naturally occurring breezes cooling most of the coastal areas. Temperatures in the highlands and the mountains are warm by day and brisk at night, giving the 'eternal spring' feeling. The average annual temperatures range from 31.7°C on the coast to 16.7°C inland. There is little variation in temperatures from season to season, however March and April can get a lot warmer in the Guanacaste region, as the dry ground screams out for rain. December and January usher in the brisk Papagayo winds from the north and the Central Valley area can get chilly (by Costa Rican standards), with daytime temperatures dipping to 16°C.

Being a relatively young landmass, Costa Rica is still experiencing 'growing pains', with volcanoes erupting from time to time when the earth vents off steam. Lying on the boundary between Coco's Plate and the Caribbean Plate, Costa Rica is at ground zero for seismic activity when these two huge plates collide into each other deep below the earth. Thousands of tremors are recorded every year in Costa Rica, although many are so insignificant they are never felt. Some are short, sharp jolts while others are long and rolling. The good news is that geologists believe the frequency of earthquakes releases the pressure so 'the Big One' is kept at bay. The largest earthquake on land in Costa Rica occurred on 22 April 1991 off the coast of Limón on the Caribbean. Registering a mighty 7.4 on the Richter scale, it left 27 dead, over 400 injured, 13,000 homeless and almost 3,300 buildings destroyed in the province of Limón. Part of Limón's coast disappeared due to areas permanently rising 1.5m, exposing coral reefs and changing the shoreline.

An earthquake measuring 6.4 on the Richter scale occurred in the early morning hours of 20 November 2004, with its epicentre only 10km from the town of Parrita, near Quepos. Having been in Quepos at the time, I can attest that it was a bit surreal and felt like an amusement park ride. Over 100 aftershocks were felt for the next 24 hours (sharp, short jolts) and it definitely had everyone on edge, as this had been the biggest experienced in the area in over a decade. As a result of the quake, plates and glasses were broken as far away as San José (although my husband, amazingly, slept through it). Considering the size of the quake, the ensuing damage was surprisingly minimal – there were seven deaths attributed to heart attacks. Buildings damaged or destroyed were mostly shacks around Parrita that had been slapped together with spit and prayer to begin with, while the hotels in Manuel Antonio, for example, suffered some exterior cracking but nothing structural. Building codes in Costa Rica have strict anti-seismic requirements, ensuring buildings are capable of withstanding greater quakes than the country is likely to ever experience.

If you do experience a quake, get to an open area, away from overhead electric lines. If in a building, stand under a doorframe (the strongest part of a building) and if you are driving, pull over off the road, as paved surfaces tend to heave and crack.

When speaking of earthquakes now, tsunamis are always included in the discussion, after the destruction wreaked upon Indonesia and the surrounding area in 2004. Scientists believe that the geographical position of Costa Rica is such that it should not be in any danger of experiencing a powerful tsunami and if one were to occur, there are adequate pre-warning systems in place to evacuate affected areas in time.

As Costa Rica is situated on an isthmus, it rarely suffers the ravages of hurricanes and tropical storms like its neighbours to the north.

HISTORY

PRE-COLUMBIAN Little is known about pre-Columbian Costa Rica as there are few archaeological monuments and no proof of a written language has been discovered. Archaeologists have been able to determine that the area of Costa Rica was used as a trading route for the Maya, Almec, Aztec and Incas prior to 1000BC. Between 1000BC and AD1400 the city of Guayabo (near present-day Turrialba) was built and archaeological digs have unearthed aqueducts, causeways and various artefacts. Scientists estimate there were up to 15,000 inhabitants of Guayabo and bits of jade, pottery and gold jewellery point to a much more developed society than other pre-Columbian settlements in the area. Large, perfectly spherical stones have been discovered in the southern zones, some weighing over several tonnes. How they were made, where they came from and what they were used for are still all mysteries, although researcher Ivar Zapp has theorised that they were ancient navigation markers used by sailors.

COLONIAL ERA In 1502, on his fourth voyage to the New World, Christopher Columbus anchored his storm-ravaged boats in the Bay of Cariari, near present-day Limón. He named the country Costa Rica, 'the Rich Coast', because he was so impressed by the many gold ornaments and decorations worn by the friendly locals. Even with the lure of untold wealth, colonisation was slow to happen and it took nearly 60 years for the Spanish settlers to make a dent in the tangled jungle. Those first settlers must have thought Columbus had played a cruel joke in the naming of this new land, as they encountered floods, swamps, swarms of ravenous insects and hostile natives, but no gold.

The indigenous population was practically eradicated due to diseases introduced by the Europeans and the few survivors headed for the hills in the Talamanca region. Only the Chorotegas of Nicoya were left somewhat untouched, although they were forced into slavery by the settlers – before long, their numbers all but disappeared as well. With no gold, no indigenous people to subjugate and no crops to export, Costa Rica remained a forgotten backwater for many years.

The 18th century saw the establishment of settlements such as Heredia, San José and Alajuela but it was not until the introduction of coffee in 1808 that the country really began to develop. Coffee brought wealth, a class structure, a more outward-looking perspective, and, most importantly, independence. On 15 September 1821, Central America declared independence from Spain – it was a month before the news reached Costa Rica. In 1848, the country declared itself an independent state, no longer part of the Central American Federation.

However, the ensuing years of the 19th century saw power struggles among members of the coffee-growing elite with the military. After a 12-year rule by military strongman, General Guardia, the country's first democratic elections were held in 1889 and have continued virtually uninterrupted ever since.

MINOR KEITH AND THE RAILWAY

Coffee was big business in the mid-1800s and it was imperative to reach the European markets faster than the five-month delivery out of Puntarenas and via Cape Horn. The government decided to build a railway to the Caribbean coast to facilitate faster exports.

Beginning in 1871, the project soon foundered. In the first 40km of track laying, almost 4,000 workers died from accidents, malaria or yellow fever. It took a 23-year-old American former pig farmer, Minor Keith, to succeed. Keith replaced Costa Rican labourers with first Chinese and Italian and later Jamaican workers who turned out to be the most resistant to disease and near inhuman conditions. The crowded Chinese cemetery in Limón bears witness to their suffering.

Sheer determination, confidence and occasionally his gun barrel kept the work going – for nearly 20 years. In 1884, Keith succeeded in renegotiating British bank loans that had crippled progress and a grateful Costa Rican government gave him a concession of 800,000 acres of land along the tracks, which he put to use in cultivating bananas. They flourished and helped finance the railway construction, feed his workforce and determine a nation's future.

The railway had to climb to 3,800ft before falling to the Central Valley. Lacking accurate surveys, the tracks were rerouted several times, marshes drained, tunnels bored and jungles opened. Only in 1890 did a steam locomotive finally make the trip from Limón to San José. By then, however, coffee's supremacy had given over to Keith's stroke of genius or luck with bananas.

In 1899, he merged his banana company into the United Fruit Company (La Yunai) that became one of the world's biggest multinational companies, transforming Costa Rica into a true banana republic. Minor Keith ended up in style, married the president's daughter and became the proverbial Banana King.

Some people just never give up. Nashville-born career-changing William Walker went from doctor to lawyer to potential emperor. Luckily for the Costa Ricans, he failed because Central America was his proposed empire.

William Walker, slight of stature, with sky-high delusions of colonial grandeur, believed it 'the manifest destiny' of the United States to colonise other nations and establish slavery, creating a confederacy of southern states attached to the US and ensure the nation's commercial supremacy. In 1855, he successfully invaded Nicaragua before heading for Costa Rica.

Alarmed by the threat to his substantial shipping interests in the region, fellow American Cornelius Vanderbildt forwarded funds for the *Tico* 'national campaign' to repel Walker. A makeshift army of 9,000 wielding farm tools reforged as weapons marched towards the now folkloric Battle of Guanacaste at Rivas. Popular legend has it that drummer boy Juan Santamaría rushed Walker's stronghold to torch the thatch roof only to die in a hail of bullets. He saved his country, however, Walker was defeated and Santamaría has a national holiday and airport named after him.

Although the *Ticos* won the day, they lost a more insidious battle. Walker's troops brought cholera that left a mortal legacy killing almost a quarter of Costa Ricans in 1856 and 1857.

Winning wars is a bittersweet sacrifice.

MODERN ERA Civil war raised its ugly head in 1948 after an election in which ex-president Rafael Angel Calderón refused to hand over power to ballot-winner Otilio Ulate. Thousands of angry voters joined the National Liberation Army, led by José 'Pepe' Figueres, taking their protests to the streets. After a month of warfare Figueres emerged victorious and formed an interim government, promising to give the presidency to Ulate in 18 months.

The first act of Figueres's interim government was to abolish the army on 1 December 1949. Figueres then nationalised the banking system and public utilities, gave women and blacks the vote and declared it mandatory that all citizens 18 years of age and over vote in the elections every four years. Figueres kept his promise and stepped aside for Ulate – a beloved hero of the people, 'Don Pepe' was elected to the presidency twice more in his lifetime.

During the 1980s, war raged in Nicaragua and Costa Rica was succumbing to US pressure to support the Contras. President Oscar Arias was elected in 1986 and brokered the Central American peace plan. Despite US President Ronald Reagan calling the plan 'fatally flawed' and the CIA trying to derail it, Arias succeeded and all five Central American presidents signed the accord in which they committed to fundamentally reform their political systems. Arias received the Nobel Peace Prize the following year for his attempts to spread Costa Rica's culture of peace to its warring neighbours. As Arias said in a speech to the US Congress shortly after the plan was signed: 'the Costa Rican people are convinced that the risks we run in the struggle for peace will always be less than the irreparable cost of war.'

Succeeding Arias, Rafael Angel Calderon Fournier, son of a former president, was elected and sworn into office in 1990, 50 years to the day his father was inaugurated. His father's great nemesis, Pepe Figueres, died the same year and Calderon junior had to declare a national day of mourning. Even more ironic was the outcome of the 1994 election where José Maria Figueres, Don Pepe's son, took the reins of power from Calderon.

In February 1998, the Social Christian Unity Party's Miguel Angel Rodríguez won the presidency with almost exactly 50% of the vote. A conservative businessman who made the economy his priority, he went on to privatise state companies and encourage foreign investments in an effort to create jobs.

By the time the February 2002 elections came around, however, the *Ticos* were mumbling about lack of government transparency and shady deals between political mates. These grass-roots misgivings resulted in a 'no win' election, and pollsters returned to the ballot box in April 2002. Rodríguez's successor, Abel Pacheco of the conservative Social Christian Unity Party, was elected. He began his term promising to eliminate the public debt within four years and launched a platform banning new oil drilling and mining and proposed legislation guaranteeing citizens the right to a healthy environment. It didn't take long before the sheen paled – a campaign finance scandal clouded his presidency, leading some opponents to demand his resignation.

The year 2004 will be remembered as the year of political scandal. Ex-president José Maria Figueres admitted to receiving over US$900,000 from French telecommunications firm ALCATEL for consulting services after he left office. The revelations led Figueres to resign as chief executive of the World Economic Forum. The timing coincided with two other high-profile corruption scandals involving ex-presidents – Miguel Angel Rodriguez was put under house arrest for allegedly taking further payments from ALCATEL, while Rafael Angel Calderon was charged with accepting an illegal commission on medical equipment. Although *Ticos* are embarrassed by the actions of these former presidents, they are justly proud that no Costa Rican, no matter what their status or family history, is immune from the long arm of justice.

The 2006 presidential race was so close that a recount was ordered, delaying the announcement of a winner by a month as every single ballot was hand counted. In the end, Oscar Arias won by a slim margin. His support for the controversial free-trade agreement with the United States (CAFTA) lost him the backing of a large number of *Ticos* who strongly oppose the agreement's passage. The one thing that all Costa Ricans share, however, is the hope that Arias will be a more effective leader than the last few lack-lustre *presidentes*.

GOVERNMENT AND POLITICS

The longest-established democratic nation in Central America, the Costa Rican constitution guarantees all citizens and foreigners equality before the law, the freedom of speech, the right of petition and assembly, the right to own property and the right to *habeas corpus*.

The government is divided into three different branches that have separation of power. The **Executive Branch** has the president, two vice-presidents and a cabinet of 17 *diputados* (deputies). The **Legislative Assembly**, which has legislative powers, comprises 57 members elected by proportional representation. The Assembly can override presidential decisions with a two-thirds majority. They also appoint a **Supreme Court**, which selects judges for civil and penal courts as well as the **Supreme Electoral Tribunal**, an independent body that oversees each election and has far-reaching powers (for example, during election campaigns, control of the police force is given to the Tribunal to ensure the constitution is upheld).

While *Ticos* take their civic duty seriously and are passionate about the electoral process, their proclivity for peace has ensured that no election has ever been marred by violence since 1948. International election-watchers have also lauded Costa Rica for its transparent and efficient elections (other, much larger nations could learn a lot from this tiny nation).

OXCARTS

These colourful two-wheeled carts are the national symbol of Costa Rica, representing both the importance of agriculture and the cheerful countenance of *Ticos*. Until recently, these *carretas de bueyes* transported coffee from the Central Valley, through the mountains to the port at Puntarenas for shipping.

No-one is exactly sure where the tradition of painting the carts and yokes started – some believe it was a way to impress the ladies and others say it was owners painting their initials and then elaborating. If you go to the artisan town of Sarchí, which was a stopping point on the original route, they swear the craftsmen who fixed the carts started to create designs to mark their handiwork. The cart route may be long gone but visitors can still watch the artists build and paint the carts. Most are smaller souvenir versions that tourists can pack in their suitcases.

Oxcarts are still used for hauling wood and even passengers, especially in rural areas. The second Sunday of March marks Oxcart Driver's Day and hundreds of oxcarts parade through the San José town of San Antonio de Escazú, where the animals are blessed and the carts are judged with awards for the best decorations.

ECONOMY

Costa Rica is considered to be the most stable country in Central America and among the elite of Latin America. Not having to spend most of its GNP on military expenditure, as other countries do, Costa Rica has been able to offer its citizens universal healthcare, a strong social net and free public education. State-owned telephone and electrical companies have ensured affordable communications and power in almost every part of the land, no matter how remote the area. The result is a high literacy rate (97%), an impressive public healthcare system (Costa Rican men have a longer lifespan than their US counterparts) and the most affluent country in Central America, with the largest middle class in the region. While there is poverty, the government is consciously trying to reduce the numbers. As it stands, Costa Rica does not suffer the extremes in living standards found in other parts of Latin America, where citizens are either 'haves' or 'have nots'. This stability, together with an educated workforce and proactive investment policies, has attracted much foreign money, the lifeblood for this developing nation.

Costa Rica was once described as 'a nation of clerks, lawyers and oxen', a true observation to this day as agriculture remains one of the cornerstones of the economy. Pineapples, bananas, coffee, cattle and palm oil are the biggest exports and seemingly every part of the country has ranches, plantations, farms or nurseries for ornamental plants (another popular export).

In recent years, however, tourism has become the number one industry in Costa Rica, with over 1.5 million visitors entering the country in 2004. Realising that eco-tourism is Costa Rica's calling card, the government is working with the tourism sector and developers to ensure that 'the goose that laid the golden egg' isn't strangled by its own popularity.

PEOPLE

The *Ticos* are a mixed group. Though the majority of the country's four million inhabitants are descendants of Spanish immigrants, many families originated from other parts of Europe, Asia, Africa and Central America. Visitors may be surprised at how fair many Costa Ricans in the Central Valley are, a result of European bloodlines. In the lowlands, more people are *mestizo*, a mixture of European and indigenous blood, whereas the majority along the Caribbean coast are of African lineage. Indigenous peoples inhabit much of the Talamanca mountain range and a full 1% of the entire population is of Asian origin.

Costa Ricans are very family oriented and it's not uncommon for children to live with their parents until they are married and then many married couples live with their parents or in-laws for as long as possible, until a growing number of offspring force them to move out. It's common practice for families to build on the same property and when a child marries, they build an addition to the house or, if space allows, a separate building to the side, back or even front of the parents' house. Needless to say, this leads to cramped living and only encourages the family interference that *Ticos* are well known for.

Ticos are very affectionate people and polite public displays of affection between couples are a common sight. Costa Ricans will greet each other with hugs and a kiss on the cheek and it's common for them to address each other, even total strangers, as *mi amor* (my love), *corazon* (heart), or other such endearments.

This being a Latin American country, machismo is alive and well and living in Costa Rica. Males are mostly chauvinistic and women are expected to do all housework, cook the meals and serve them to their husband and family regardless of their other duties (young *Tico* men I know have their mothers make and pack lunches for them and then they bring home the Tupperware lunch containers for their mothers to wash, despite having a working sink with soap in the lunch room at work). This belief that men are to be waited on hand and foot by women is still prevalent and it may be a few generations before there is more equality on the home front.

Despite the machismo, women hold many high positions in government and business – after the last election, Costa Rica had the highest number of women in elected government positions in the western hemisphere.

As a rule men don't participate in childcare, at least not until children are older and then their role is mostly as the disciplinarian. Men who show their feminine/sensitive sides are teased and labelled as 'wimps' so few dare to. These traditions are slowly evolving and more progressive thinking is taking their place. As they say, *poco a poco* (little by little) as *Ticos* are not quick to embrace change.

Generally, *Ticos* are pretty laid back and are not very goal oriented – as long as there is food on the table and the rent is paid, they are content. This passivity can drive foreigners crazy, especially those who are used to a fast-paced, 'grab the brass ring' society. Being forthright is not a *Tico* trait and they would rather skirt an issue than give a direct answer that might possibly offend someone. Rather than say 'no', they will drag things out *ad nauseam* until the other party finally gives up in frustration. But their friendliness and genuine interest in others compensates for their idiosyncrasies.

LANGUAGE

The national language is Spanish, although those working in tourism usually also speak English. It's been said that Costa Rica is one of the best countries in which to study Spanish as the accent is not as pronounced as in other countries – for example, the Spaniards lisp their *c*s and *z*s. Costa Ricans are known for the use of diminutives, adding the suffix *tico* to many words in order to create a diminutive (from where the nickname *Ticos* originates). For example, instead of saying *chico* (small) they use the word *chiquitico,* which means the same thing but sounds more endearing.

Another unique *tiquismo* is calling others, even those they don't know, as they see them. A skinny fellow will be nicknamed *flaco,* a fat girl *gorda,* an Asian would be *chino* and a black man *negro.* While these terms would be unacceptable or racist in other countries, they are a totally innocent custom among *Ticos.*

Globalisation and the growth of the tourism industry have seen English becoming more widely used; however, the majority of English speakers belong to the higher classes who can afford private education, whilst most lower classes know only very few basic words.

For those who want to learn Spanish, there are a number of excellent schools in various locations across the country that offer a good combination of exotic living and language learning (see *Language schools* in *Appendix 1*, page 274).

TIQUICA *Tiquicia* (also the *Tico* nickname for Costa Rica) are the things that make *Ticos* tick – their stories, slang and beloved cultural icons.

EL CADEJOS The story of *El Cadejos* (The Devil Dog) begins with Joaquin, the irreverent son of a Cartago family during colonial times. Every night, Joaquin would chase around the towns, doing whatever he pleased. His father, tired of his son's insolent ways, put a curse on him, turning him into a wild dog. Since that time, the wild black dog with the glowing red eyes and rattling chains has scared travellers on dark roads throughout the land.

DIA DE LOS INOCENTES If you're in Costa Rica on 28 December, be on your toes as its *Dia de los Inocentes* (Day of the Innocents), the *Tico* equivalent of April Fool's Day. Practical jokes and pranks prevail, and you just never know if you're being set up. The date was originally a Church holiday, commemorating the day King Herod slaughtered all the newborns, but the holy family, warned by an angel, had tricked the king by sneaking away to Egypt.

In past times, tricks would be accompanied by the rhyme, *'paso por inocente, comiendo pan caliente'* ('there goes an innocent eating hot bread'). Although the custom is not as popular as it once was, it is still a source of 'innocent' fun and games.

SLANG No matter where you travel in the world, you'll always run across words they never taught you in language class and Costa Rica is no exception. If you find yourself scratching your *cabeza (*head) over words you're hearing on the street, it's probably because the speakers are using *pachuco* (slang).

The most common is *mae* ('my'), which is the equivalent of 'man' or 'dude'. It's often peppered throughout the speech of young *Ticos*, who use it both as a term of acquaintance as well as a general expression. Another word is *tuanis* (twa-nees) meaning 'nice' or 'very good' and which originates from the Caribbean form of patois for 'too nice'.

Undoubtedly, the most *Tico* expression of them all is *Pura vida* (poo-ra vee-da) which translates as 'pure life' and sums up the optimistic approach of Costa Ricans to life in general. Usually it's used to answer the question 'How are you?' but it can also be used for 'OK' or 'fine'. Expect to hear and see this expression everywhere and before long you'll most likely be using it yourself.

With the good, there is the bad and *hi'jueputa* (ee-why-poota), meaning 'son of a whore', is used to express anger or surprise but can also be quite insulting – best leave this one to the *Ticos*.

RELIGION

Religion, or to be more exact, the Catholic Church, has a strong influence on Costa Rica's culture as over 80% of the population is Catholic, although many don't consider themselves practising. Evangelical and fundamentalist churches have been gaining in popularity recently and there are also a number of Mormons in the Central Valley. There is a small but active Jewish community as well as tiny enclaves of Muslims and Buddhists. Being fairly open-minded people and the least secular of all Latin Americans, *Ticos* respect others' religious beliefs and all are free to worship as they choose.

EDUCATION

A highly educated country, Costa Rica has the most literate population in Central America. Many of the country's founders, including the first president, José Maria Castro, were former teachers. Implementing both free and obligatory education in 1869, the country became one of the first in the world to make education a priority. By 1920, 50% of the population was literate and by the 1970s, 89% of the population was able to read and write.

Since the 1970s, the government has invested more than 28% of the national budget on primary and secondary education. President Figueres (1994–98) advocated a computer in each of the nation's 4,000+ schools and obligatory English classes as a measure to keep pace with the tourism and technology boom.

Elementary and high schools can be found in every community. Elementary school starts with kindergarten for six year olds and has a total of six year levels while high school has five levels. To obtain a diploma, students of both public and private schools are required to pass government tests on all subjects (Bachillerato Tests). If a student fails one of the tests, they have one chance to retake the test – if they fail a second time, they must repeat the year regardless of their school grades.

Although a good primary and secondary education is provided free of charge, fundamental educational values like reading and researching outside the classroom are not inculcated. Few Costa Ricans are taught to think, much less act, 'outside the box'. Few Costa Ricans will sit and read a book and most *Ticos* are content to just sit on the porch and watch the world pass by.

Although the first university was not founded until 1940, Costa Rica now boasts four state-funded universities and over the last decade the number of private post-secondary schools has increased dramatically owing to high admission standards of the state-funded, more prestigious universities. Additionally, state-funded schools require two years of general studies, making them less attractive to those students who want the 'fast track' to graduation.

The University of Costa Rica (UCR), the oldest and largest university in the country, has 35,000 students, the majority of whom attend on scholarships, although full tuition is only US$200 a semester. The main campus is in the northeastern San José community of San Pedro but the UCR also has regional centres in Alajuela, Turrialba, Puntarenas and Cartago. The National University in Heredia offers a variety of liberal arts, sciences and professional studies to 13,000 students. Cartago's Technical Institute of Costa Rica (ITCR) specialises in science and technology, as well as agriculture, industry and mining. The State Correspondence University, founded in 1978, is modelled on the United Kingdom's Open University and has 32 regional centres offering 15 different degree courses in health, education, business administration and the liberal arts.

Ticos have a high respect for education and night-school courses are extremely popular.

CULTURE

LITERATURE Being neither a nation of great readers nor a land filled with the history and strife of other Latin countries, Costa Rica has failed to give rise to outstanding writers, like Colombia's Gabriel García Márquez or Chile's Isabel

Allende. Costa Rican prose includes stories, novels, historical chronicles and essays, often reflecting the social, cultural and political changes that have influenced the nation.

Tico writers Carmen Lyra and Carlos Luis Fallas, members of the socialist and communist movements in the 1940s, wrote on themes such as the sufferings of the banana plantation workers under the stifling grasp of imperialistic companies, as in Lyra's *Bananos y hombres* and Fallas's *Mamita Yunai*. Julieta Pinto's *El Edo de los Pasos* is an outstanding novel about the 1948 civil war and worth a read.

Contemporary *Tico* prose has been somewhat lacklustre, with Alfonso Chase being the one bright spot of irreverent wit and keen observation.

2

Natural History

Mother nature has blessed Costa Rica with more biodiversity than any other place on earth. As the meeting point of North and South America, and with only 119km separating the Caribbean Sea and Pacific Ocean at its narrowest point, this tiny country is a giant mosaic of genuses and species. Thankfully, the people of Costa Rica have recognised the treasure trove they call home and have created an extensive system of national parks, biological reserves, forest reserves and wildlife refuges, protecting over 25% of the country – in fact, no other country in the world protects a greater proportion of its territory.

Costa Rica lies totally within a tropical zone yet its variations in elevation, rainfall, topography and temperature have created 12 distinct microclimates, ranging from mangroves to dry tropical forests. A short drive can take one from a humid rainforest to the cool highlands of the mountains and this rich diversity in flora and fauna is a siren's call to biologists who return time and time again to unlock the mysteries of the 'Rich Coast'.

FLORA

Over 9,000 species of 'higher plants' are found in Costa Rica, including more species of ferns than in all of North America combined. Over 30 species of heliconias (members of the banana family which include the colourful bird of paradise) grow throughout the land while 2,000 species of *bromeliads* (such as the pineapple) are found in almost every microclimate. When flying overland, the layer upon layer of impossibly lush green is what strikes one at first and makes garden lovers' hearts skip a beat. Against this velvety backdrop of trees, leaves and ferns explodes a riot of colour, flowering plants such as fiery-red hot lips, purple jacaranda, anthuriums in a paint box of shades, begonias and flame-of-the-forest tree.

Originally, Costa Rica was a giant forest, with 99% of the country covered by trees. Humans and their quest for wood have changed the landscape drastically and the last century has reduced the forest cover to only 25% of the land. The national parks and reserves hold approximately 75% of the country's total flora and fauna, including many species that have disappeared from neighbouring lands.

MICROCLIMATES
Tropical rainforests Remnants from the Cretaceous period, tropical rainforests are the land that time forgot and walking through these towering plants, it's easy to imagine dinosaurs supping on the leaves from slender trees that blanket the sky. Found in a narrow band encircling the Equator, these forests have the perfect conditions – rain, heat, sunlight – for a constant growth cycle. In fact, over half of the earth's living things are found in these areas.

Although images of thick jungle are conjured up, the rainforest is actually fairly sparse at ground level, as only 10% of sunlight is able to penetrate the dense canopy.

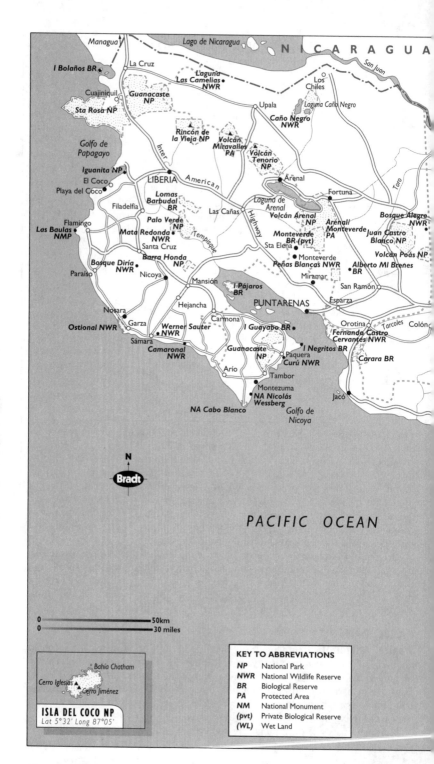

Managua

Lago de Nicaragua

NICARAGUA

San Juan

I Bolaños BR

La Cruz

Los Chiles

Laguna Las Camelias NWR

Cuajiniquil

Guanacaste NP

Upala

Laguna Caño Negro

Sta Rosa NP

Caño Negro NWR

Golfo de Papagoyo

Rincón de la Vieja NP

Volcán Miravalles PA

Volcán Tenorio NP

Iguanita NP

El Coco

LIBERIA

American

Arenal

Fortuna

Toro

Playa del Coco

Lomas Barbudal BR

Laguna de Arenal

Bosque Alegre NWR

Filadelfia

Las Cañas

Volcán Arenal

Palo Verde NP

Flamingo

Arenal/ Monteverde PA

Volcán Árenal

Monteverde BR (pvt)

Juan Castro Blanco NP

Las Baulas NMP

Mata Redonda NWR

Santa Cruz

Sta Elena

Tempisque

Volcán Poás NP

Barra Honda NP

Monteverde

Alberto MI Brenes BR

Bosque Diría NWR

Nicoya

Mansión

Peñas Blancas NWR

Miramar

San Ramón

Paraiso

Hejancha

I Pájaros BR

PUNTARENAS

Esparza

Nosara

Carmona

Orotina

Tarcoles

Colón

Garza

Werner Sauter NWR

I Guayabo BR

Fernando Castro Cervantes NWR

Ostional NWR

Sámara

Camaronal NWR

Guanacaste NP

I Negritos BR

Corara BR

Curú NWR

Paquera

Ario

Tambor

Montezuma

Jacó

NA Nicolás Wessberg

NA Cabo Blanco

Golfo de Nicoya

N

Bradt

PACIFIC OCEAN

0 ——————— 50km
0 ——————— 30 miles

Bahia Chatham

Cerro Iglesias

Cerro Jiménez

ISLA DEL COCO NP
Lat 5°32' Long 87°05'

KEY TO ABBREVIATIONS

NP	National Park
NWR	National Wildlife Reserve
BR	Biological Reserve
PA	Protected Area
NM	National Monument
(pvt)	Private Biological Reserve
(WL)	Wet Land

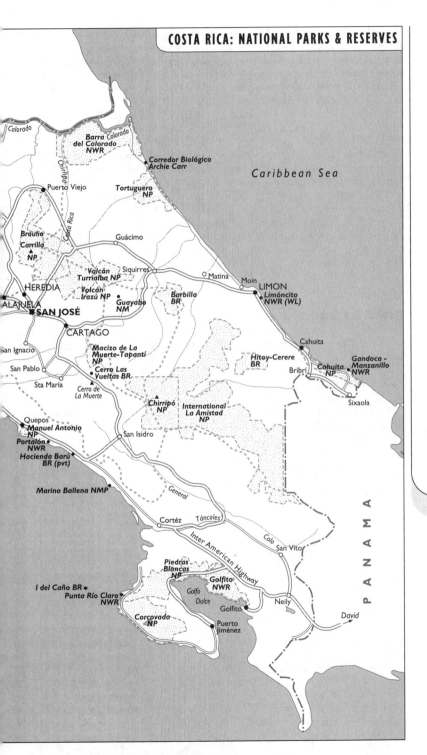

COSTA RICA: NATIONAL PARKS & RESERVES

Colorado

Barra Colorado del Colorado NWR

Chirripó

Puerto Viejo

Corredor Biológico Archie Carr

Tortuguero NP

Costa Rica

Guácimo

Caribbean Sea

Braulio Carrillo NP

Siquirres

HEREDIA

Volcán Turrialba NP

Volcán Irazú NP

ALAJUELA

SAN JOSÉ

Guayabo NM

Matina

Moín

LIMON

Barbilla BR

Limóncito NWR (WL)

CARTAGO

San Ignacio

Macizo de La Muerte-Tapantí NP

Cahuita

Cerro Las Vueltas BR

San Pablo

Sta María

Cerro de La Muerte

Hitoy-Cerere BR

Cahuita NP

Gandoca - Manzanillo NWR

Bribrí

Chirripó NP

International La Amistad NP

Sixaola

Quepos

Manuel Antonio NP

Portalón NWR

San Isidro

Hacienda Barú BR (pvt)

Marino Ballena NMP

General

Cortéz

Táncoles

Colo

San Vito

Inter American Highway

Piedras Blancas NP

I del Caño BR

Golfito NWR

Punta Río Claro NWR

Golfo Dulce

Neily

Golfito

Corcovado NP

Puerto Jiménez

David

P A N A M A

Natural History FLORA

2

17

Plants here have adapted to maximise the little light they receive – leaves arrange themselves so they avoid shade from each other, some have deep purple colouring on their undersides to reflect light back through the leaf and 'walking palm trees' actually move locations on their spindly, leg-like roots in search of pockets of light. Fungi and mould thrive in the humid environment, where plants decompose at accelerated rates (a leaf on the rainforest floor will be reclaimed by the earth in less than a month).

Standing in the midst of the cathedral of trees, one is amazed at how dark it is in the heart of the rainforest. Every tree is host to clinging vines or ferns or *bromeliads* or epiphytes (plants that root on other plants but do not have a parasitic relationship) and one lone tree can play host to 20 different plant species. Rich too is the variety of fauna here, with brilliant blue Morpho butterflies, emerald-green tree python, scarlet macaws, monkeys and big cats all at home in the lush hush.

These majestic rainforests harbour many secrets and scientists are still discovering new species on a regular basis. Over 2,000 plant species have been identified has having cancer-fighting properties and many commercial drugs rely on natural ingredients found in the world's rainforests. However, extreme preservation tactics are called for as the present rate of destruction will see the rainforests disappear completely within the next 35 years.

Tropical rainforests are found in the areas of Tortuguero, Braulio Carrillo, Osa Peninsula and Manuel Antonio.

Tropical dry forest Dry forests once blanketed the lowlands of the Pacific coast, from Mexico to Panamá, until the Spaniards arrived and started to clear the forest using fire. The ensuing savannas became home to crops and herds of cattle – today, less than 2% of tropical dry forest remains in Costa Rica, making it the most endangered of the country's microclimates. Trees here have short, stout trunks and far-reaching, flat-topped branches. Below are found short, open-canopied trees and shrubs with sharp thorns.

During the dry season, the dry forest undergoes a magical transformation – while the rest of the landscape is burnt brown from the searing sun and heat, the deciduous trees bloom in an explosion of colour. The juxtaposition of the brilliant flowers of yellow *corteza amarilla*, purple jacaranda, pink and white meadow oak and flame-of-the-forest against the parched brown hills is awe-inspiring – despite the drought and heat, beauty emerges and flourishes.

Tropical dry forests are found in the northwest province of Guanacaste.

Mangroves Situated on the shorelines, mangroves are the buffer zone between land and sea. These halophytes live in salt water and not only survive but thrive where no other tree is able. The mud in mangrove areas is acidic and lacks oxygen; as its grain is so fine, air is unable to penetrate it. Rather than send their roots downwards, mangrove trees have aerial roots, giving the trees the appearance of floating on the water.

Mangroves are a safe haven for young marine life that live hidden amongst the tangled roots from surf-presiding predators. Oysters, sponges and even an endemic species of mangrove tree crab (*Aratus pisonii*) thrive amongst the thick maze of spidery roots. Along with birds and sealife is a variety of insects so visitors should be sure to wear insect repellent.

Boat tours through the mangroves can be arranged in Manuel Antonio, Tortuguero, Golfo Dulce and Tamarindo.

As with all things in nature, the rule of thumb is 'look but don't touch', not only to protect yourself from possible harm (many trees and plants have spines, thorns or secretions that can be irritable to the skin) but to also protect the plants from possible destruction.

FAUNA

As Carl Sagan used to say, 'Millions and millions of years ago…' (well, three million to be exact), the isthmus which is now Central America rose from the sea, forming a bridge between the two landmasses now known as the Americas. A few hearty mammals like the porcupine, armadillo, agouti, anteater, sloth and spider monkey headed north to more temperate zones – the vast majority, however, headed south from North America in a veritable invasion which vastly changed the landscape and the hardy northern mammals quickly dominated the scene. Costa Rica's unique positioning, range of microclimates and incredible array of plants offered a safe haven to species that had either disappeared elsewhere or died out altogether.

MAMMALS Surprisingly, there are only 200 species of mammals in Costa Rica, the most popular of which amongst tourists are the four types of **monkeys**, all hailing from South America: howler monkeys (*Alouatta* spp), spider monkeys (*Ateles* spp), capuchin monkeys (*Cebus* spp) and squirrel monkeys (*Saimiri* spp). Found throughout most of the country (except for the squirrel or *titi* monkey which is endemic to Manuel Antonio), monkeys are not shy about making their presence known. The roar of the howler monkey is said to be the loudest animal sound on earth and once you've heard it, you will never forget it – imagine the sound of a dinosaur waking up and you get the idea. Roughly the size of a medium-sized dog, howlers are the most common and largest monkey in Central America and despite their impressive vocalisations, they are not aggressive. They are most active in the early morning and at dusk – and you're more likely to hear them long before you see them so keep an ear open.

Spider monkeys were once the most common monkeys on the continent but human intrusion has vastly affected their numbers. Long and loose limbed, these orange-coloured simians are the acrobats of the treetops, using their incredibly long tails to hang from branches.

The most inquisitive and intelligent of Costa Rican monkeys is the capuchin or white-faced found in the national parks at Santa Rosa and Manuel Antonio. Entire families will descend upon a tree, looking for food and are sometimes cheeky enough to steal items from unattended beach bags (during filming of the movie *Spy Kids II* at Manuel Antonio, close guard had to be kept on the camera equipment to prevent it going missing to furry little fingers). If you go to the beach, watch your stuff!

The smallest monkey in Costa Rica is the squirrel, reaching only 25–35cm with a tail up to 45cm in length. They travel in groups of up to 40 and tend to forage on the forest floor where they are safe from raptors. *Titis* are highly endangered, with present numbers approximated at only 1,500–4,000 individuals – in 1983, their numbers were well over 200,000. Two foundations are making aggressive efforts to turn the tide for these petite primates – ASCOMOTI (*www.ascomoti.org*) and Kids Saving the Rainforest (*www.kidssavingtherainforest.org*). Both of these non-profit organisations are headquartered in Manuel Antonio and have the backing of many area businesses that make ongoing donations – please help the *titi* by supporting these businesses and/or making a small donation directly.

If you spot a monkey, PLEASE DON'T FEED IT! These creatures are at risk from environmental destruction and encroachment – the last thing they need is to battle human disease or sickness from eating food they weren't meant to consume. If you see tourists trying to coax monkeys with food, please remind them that the monkeys have no problem finding their own food.

Costa Rica is home to two species of **deer** – the slightly humpbacked red brocket deer (*Mazama americana*) found in the rainforests and the common white-

SLOW BUT STEADY PROGRESS FOR SLOTHS

Peering into a cluttered hanging wicker-basket seat, it takes time for my eyes to adjust that I am looking at a large lady sloth (*Bradypus variegatus*) tucked up in her blanket. Buttercup snoozes on; at some 14 years of age she is used to the gasps and coos of admiration and takes her stardom status in true slothful fashion – laid back.

The 1991 earthquake that hit the Caribbean coast flattened Luis and Judy Arroyos's home near Cahuita. They rebuilt it as a bed and breakfast, offering tropical tours into their patch of jungle and island domain until a neighbour brought them an injured three-toed baby sloth. This was Buttercup and she changed their careers. As word got out more injured and abandoned sloths kept arriving and the Aviarios Sloth Rescue Centre was born. Nothing much was known about sloth behaviour before the centre opened up. Many of the resident sloths are burned by overhead electric wires, hit by cars or mistreated in captivity. Where possible, suitable animals are reintroduced into the forest nearby.

Two young orphans have been successfully put back and several sick or wounded adults have been returned to health and their natural homes. Others like old Max, a confiscated pet, has no interest in life in the canopy. He's so picky he refuses all food unless hand fed to him. He lives in the sloth house with the 40 or so other orphans and patients clinging to their cuddly teddy bears and dining on specially prepared sloth cuisine of fruits, proteins and vegetables.

Surviving on private donations, visitors and an adopt-a-sloth programme, the centre has made some cutting-edge advances in sloth behaviour and breeding habits and a definitive report of the Arroyos's findings is to be published that should help sloth programmes worldwide.

---

tailed deer (*Odocoileus virginianus*), a cousin of the North American species, often seen in the Guanacaste region.

Raccoons (*Procyon* spp)are widely found across the country, usually trying to steal some of your dinner at an open-air restaurant. The northern raccoons look almost identical to North American raccoons, albeit a bit smaller in size. There is a darker-coloured crab-eating raccoon found only along the Pacific coast as well.

Coatimundi (*Nausa* spp) are members of the raccoon family and pretty fearless with humans. Ranging in colour from yellow to deep brown, they have white-ringed tails, black circles around their eyes and white-tipped noses. They are equally at home on the ground or in trees and are scavengers who will boldly approach people for a titbit. Be aware of their sharp claws, though!

The more passive **kinkajou** (*Potos flavus*) is another member of the raccoon family and totally nocturnal. It's usually found hanging by its tail, munching on insects and honey or sleeping by day. Apparently, if you pick up this small, fuzzy creature, its first instinct is to cuddle into you and fall asleep (all together now ahh … !).

Sloths are perhaps one of the strangest creatures on this big blue marble and are guaranteed to cause a traffic jam with camera-wielding tourists. About the size of a dog, they have a small head, flat nose, a sweet smile, seemingly no ears and long arms ending in curved claws. Moving at a blistering speed of one mile per four hours, sloths have the slowest metabolisms in the mammal kingdom. Food takes up to a week to move through their digestive tracts and evolution has sacrificed muscle mass (speed) to maximise body size in proportion to weight.

Two types of sloth are found in Costa Rica – the three-fingered sloth (*Bradypus* spp), which is active during the day, and the nocturnal Hoffman's two-fingered sloth (*Choloepus hoffman*). Both are covered in algae and host an entire world of moths and insects in their fur. Although sloths look a little dopey and sweet, if you meet one up close, avoid touching it – those claws are like razors (plus the green algae and crawling insects aren't so conducive to cuddling).

Tapirs (*Tapirus terrestris*) are the largest land mammals in Central America and are a strange-looking combination of horse, elephant, rhinoceros and pig. Hunted to the brink of extinction, the last remaining tapirs are generally found in Corcovado National Park where they are protected, although poachers are threatening to eradicate the last of these gentle creatures. Roughly 300 tapirs are in Corcovado and few travellers are lucky enough to spot one, as these defenceless mammals have become extremely wary of humans.

Peccaries (*Tayassu* spp) are another animal that are dangerously close to being hunted to extinction and these wild pigs, the main prey of jaguars, also call Corcovado home. There are two types of peccaries in Costa Rica – the collared peccary so named for the ochre-coloured band running from its nose to shoulders, and the white-lipped peccary, the larger of the two. Usually peccaries will flee if they stumble upon humans but should you run across an aggressive male, climb a tree.

Bats account for half the mammals in Costa Rica and it's not unusual to spy a few of the furry creatures hanging from rafters or swooping around at night. Despite vampire folklore, bats are not out to suck your blood and most are fruit eaters. There is a vampire bat, however, that swoops down to suck the blood of livestock and these little fanged fiends transmit rabies and other diseases to domestic farm animals. Luckily, humans are not on the dining menu.

Six species of endangered **wild cats** are found in Costa Rica, including spotted ocelots, the smaller oncilla and the small margay, which is the size of a house cat. Pumas are rarely seen while the jaguarundi is the rarest of them all. The largest cat in Central America is the jaguar (*Panthera onca*), worshipped as a god by pre-Columbian tribes but reduced to scarce numbers now living in reserves at Corcovado National Park, Tortuguero, Santa Rosa, Río Macho Forest Reserve and the Cordillera de Talamanca. Although some progress has been made recently in the increase of jaguar numbers, they are dangerously close to becoming extinct in Corcovado, largely because of poaching of peccaries, their main food source. The Corcovado Foundation (*www.corcovadofoundation.org*) has been successful in raising funds to increase the number of rangers in the park, who have been able to reduce poaching in the area.

BIRDS (For information on birdwatching, see page 69.) The most numerous vertebrates in Costa Rica are birds, with 878 recorded species, equal to one-tenth of the world's total bird population. Costa Rica is birdwatching paradise found and numerous lodges throughout the country specialise in birding tours. Birding Escapes is one such specialist and their excellent website (*www.birdwatchingcostarica.com*) lists all birds and species found in Costa Rica.

Parrots and **macaws**, symbols so closely associated with the tropics and jungles, are found in Costa Rica, with 16 parrot species, six parakeet species and two species of macaws. Once prolific throughout Central and South America, there are currently more macaws in captivity than in the wild and they are precariously close to disappearing. The best places to observe macaws are at Carara Biological Reserve, Corcovado National Park and sometimes at the national parks in Manuel Antonio, Palo Verde and Santa Rosa.

Toucans are another bird synonymous with the jungle and the six species found in Costa Rica make regular appearances, to the delight of birders and tourists alike. Their bright yellow bills are easily spotted amongst the greenery as they forage for fruit.

There are 50 species of **raptors**, birds with sharp talons and piercing beaks that prey on live animals (usually rodents or lizards although the harpy eagle will take down monkeys or sloths). Other birds of prey include common black hawk, osprey,

Standing on the dusty roadside deep in the valley of San Gerardo de Dota staring up into a leggy *aguacatillo* tree, we wonder whether Gary, host at nearby El Toucanete Lodge, is quite right when he assures us that you can almost set your watch by the appearance of that most alluring of neo-tropical jewels – the resplendent quetzal (*Pharomachrus mocinno*). Our morning eyes gradually become used to the tree's tones and textures and suddenly with a twitch of an endless hanging tail plume a male in breeding plumage shows us his best. Despite a green punk crest with bright emerald shoulders and back contrasting with a livid red chest and white undertail, his stillness on the branch merges him into the speckled lights of early morning.

Ranging from southern Mexico to western Panamá, they were fabled in Aztec times when damaging a quetzal led to the death sentence. The birds were captured and subsequently released, but not before the selective removal of a number of tail feathers for use in ceremonial costumes, the exclusive use of nobility and the priesthood.

Perching motionless for hours deep in the rainforest, they were thought a figment of colourful Mayan imagination until an English naturalist spotted one in 1861, identified it and promptly shot it! They were remorselessly hunted after that to provide feather adornments for fashionable Victorian hats.

The quetzals breed between March and June and the males are not above the domestic chore of egg sitting and will spend the day, with tails dangling like epiphytic fern leaves from the hollowed hole in a rotten tree before being relieved by the female in the evening.

'Our' male takes a sudden upward swoop to pluck a ripe *aguacatillo* fruit before moving to the depths of a branch beyond our sight, and we walk on awed by the Mayan myth and his ridiculous tail.

laughing falcon, crested caracara and numerous other hawks. There are also 17 species of owls, which are usually heard but not seen on account of their nocturnal hunting.

Hummingbirds are among the most fascinating birds found in Costa Rica and the 51 species are all stunningly beautiful. Beating their wings at 100 beats per minute, the flurry sounds like a hum (hence the name). They don't just fly, they dart from flower to flower and then hover over a petal as they extract nectar with their straw-like tongues. Found throughout the country, the best place to see a variety of species really close up is at the La Paz Waterfall Gardens (*www.waterfallgardens.com*), near the Poas Volcano where they have a hummingbird garden. If you stand still, these quicksilver birds buzz about, passing so close you can feel the breeze of their wings. Hummingbirds have the highest metabolic rate in the bird world, consuming 850 times their body weight daily in order to keep their tiny hearts beating at 1,200 beats per minute.

AMPHIBIANS AND REPTILES Close to 225 species of reptiles and 160 species of amphibians are to be found in Costa Rica. The most ferocious are the **crocodiles** and **caimans** (their smaller cousins), which don't chew their food but tear and swallow, allowing their strong stomach acids to break down their meal. The American crocodile was hunted to the brink of extinction in the 1960s but, thanks to conservation programmes, can be seen basking on riverbanks in large numbers on the Pacific coast (the Tarcoles Bridge is an excellent croc spot and there are usually 20 or so crocs in the river below). Although they are fish eaters, they will attack unsuspecting livestock that wander too close to the riverbanks. In 2004, a murderer escaping from Panamá was being chased by Costa Rican police and dived into a river to avoid being caught – where he was promptly attacked and killed by a crocodile (karmic justice, methinks). If you are in an area noted for crocodiles, be careful! At less than 2m long, caimans are the smallest of the crocodile family. Found on both coasts, they are most commonly spotted at Tortuguero and Palo Verde.

Iguanas and lizards Small **geckoes** are ubiquitous so don't be surprised to find a few scurrying along your hotel room wall. Their distinctive 'clucking' noise is heard when they have eaten an insect and they are not to be feared (they are actually pretty cute little creatures). These skittish lizards should be welcomed, as they munch on mosquitoes, flies and other insects one wouldn't want in one's sleeping quarters.

Iguanas are a common sight and while they do look a great deal more menacing, they are strictly vegetarians and will run away upon your approach. There are two species of iguanas in Costa Rica – the green iguana, which is larger and green, and the spiny-tailed, which is smaller and either grey or tan coloured. Called 'tree chickens' by locals, iguana meat is eaten throughout Central America but isn't very popular in Costa Rica (thankfully!) although it can be found in larger central markets.

The Jesus Christ lizard (*Basilicus basilicus*) isn't a religious reptile but is so named for its unusual method of escaping predators – running across water on their long feet and spindly legs. Found throughout the Pacific lowlands, look for them in the national parks at Tortuguero, Corcovado, Palo Verde and Santa Rosa.

Snakes There are 137 species of snakes in Costa Rica but only 22 species are poisonous. Before you start exchanging your plane ticket for the Arctic, be assured that the likelihood of running into a viper is next to nil (to my knowledge, only one tourist has ever run into a poisonous snake when he went into the jungle, alone, at night – something that is NOT recommended). Snakes are elusive and not fond of

RAPTOR MIGRATIONS – ON THE AVIAN AUTOPISTA

By the time our birding group reached the 10m observation platform deep in the Keköldi Indigenous Reserve near Puerto Viejo in the southern Caribbean, the eye-stretching strings of hawks had shifted over west with the afternoon thermals and were almost out of sight. Lucky for us that a forest window during the hike in had given us inspiring views as hundreds of raptors spiralled in soaring kettles, mixed species taking advantage of the thermals on their resolute (up to two-month) flight south from North America, some going as far as the Argentinian pampas: turkey vultures, broad-wing and Swainson's hawks and Mississippi kites while barn swallows trustingly shared the 'flight paths' some way below. Keköldi is one of three world hotspots for massive raptor migrations (along with Veracruz in Mexico and Eilat in Israel) as the birds use the 'bottleneck' of a narrow isthmus to share the only path south to their wintering grounds. By the time of our visit, an impressive two million mixed-species migrants had already passed through. The observation platform is staffed during the migrations by local and international volunteers of the Raptor Migration Monitoring Project. Started in 2000, the project's objective is to collect data that will establish numbers and behaviour patterns and teams spend up to 11 exhausting hours per day monitoring raptors during the August to December or February to May migrations. This birding en masse was a humbling experience as we pondered their increasing struggle to find essential roosting spots in increasingly deforested areas and reduced habitat. Every year for them is a true leap, or flight, into the unknown.

people while poisonous snakes are usually active at night. Visitors are likely to spy small snakes, such as the brilliant green vine snake, slithering across jungle paths or perhaps a boa resting on a tree branch. Although they are not poisonous, boas can be very aggressive if confronted and their large teeth are not to be trifled with.

There is a highly venomous rattlesnake found in Guanacaste and parts of the Central Valley – its rattling tail should alert you should you stumble into its territory. The most aggressive snake is the fer de lance, which accounts for almost 90% of all snakebites in Costa Rica (agricultural workers are the majority of snakebite victims, especially those working in sugarcane fields). Highly aggressive, it will attack with little provocation. Its lethal venom dissolves nerve tissue and destroys blood cells. A night hunter, it coils itself on the ground during the day so be careful to not step off the path when hiking.

Even more lethal are coral snakes, their small bodies wrapped in rings of red, yellow and black. Costa Rica produces a large amount of anti-venom and as all the poisonous snakes in the country have the same venom (except for the coral snake), there are only two types of anti-venom necessary.

In order to protect yourself from possible harm, never walk barefoot in the forest, wear high rubber or leather boots, never use your hands or feet to lift rocks or logs nor to inspect a hole – use a long rod or branch instead. If you do come across a snake, keep your distance and avoid making any sudden movements.

THE ORGANISATION FOR TROPICAL STUDIES (OTS)

Being a non-scientific nature lover, I thoroughly approved of sitting in a comfortable air-conditioned bus to visit Ometepe Island on Lake Nicaragua for a nature photography course. Everything was laid on: hotel, food, transport, instructor and help at the border crossing. The BioCurso (as they are called by OTS) was a great success. All we had to do was absorb the professional advice of our instructor, practise his words of wisdom and benefit from the evening lectures about topics of interest in the region. After four days I returned impressed by an affordable outing that combined immaculate planning with professional instruction and very agreeable company.

This is all part of the OTS's effort to publicise and educate the general public about things tropical. OTS offers the short BioCursos and week-long boot camps to scientifically interesting sites in topics that range from whale watching and bird migrations, to orchid care. Its mission, however, is quite serious – to educate students, future leaders and policy makers about the responsible use of natural resources in the tropics and to increase public awareness of the tropics.

The OTS, created in 1963, has become a shining beacon on an enlightened path for tropical environmental research and protection through education. Involving universities from the US, Australia and Latin America, students and scientists can follow graduate-level courses in natural sciences. More than 200 graduate-level courses have produced over 3,600 graduates and professionals and in any year, some 300 scientists from 25 countries work on OTS sites and projects. The brand-new Simons Centre recently inaugurated on the UCR campus provides a permanent home for OTS programmes in education, research and conservation with lecture rooms and a comprehensive library in tropical ecology and environmental studies.

OTS runs three field stations: La Selva in the Caribbean lowlands is a premier facility for rainforest research; Las Cruces in the pre-montane wet forest on the Pacific watershed; and Palo Verde in the tropical dry forest of the Pacific coastal plain. For more information, contact OTS (✆ 524 0607; www.ots.duke.edu).

The tiny amphibian that helped put Monteverde on the map and gave its name to at least one hotel and handicraft shop has gone.

It reads like a mystery thriller. Back in 1987, various amphibian species in the Monteverde area began dying off at an alarming rate. Though their upland cloudforest habitat has been a reserve for decades, the massive drop in populations around the region saw 20 out of 50 recorded species fall off the ecological map.

The unique golden jewel in the reptilian crown, the **golden toad** (*Bufo periglenes*; *sapo dorado* in Spanish), numbered amongst them. From hundreds found in 1986, most had gone just three years later, most likely because they too inhabited the protected Monteverde Cloud Forest Preserve. It has not been seen since 1989 and is officially 'extinct' according to the Species Survival Commission of the World Conservation Union.

Even more mysterious is the similar decline of upper-elevation populations in Australia and the rest of Latin America.

How can this happen? Why some species of frog and not others? Why so fast and so dramatically?

Reasons vary from a rare fungal disease, decreased humidity brought on by deforestation in the region, volcanic fallout, unfavourable weather conditions that dried up the tadpole pools, to global climate change that has caused a pronounced drop the world over.

Like the canaries carried down contaminated coalmines, amphibians act as early-warning systems to change and are affected by increased pollution in the air. Herpetologist Karen Lips, analysing 50 dying frogs in Panamá, found a microscopic surface fungus that effectively suffocated the skin-breathing amphibians, and which has subsequently been found in Australia and North American zoos.

Not much is known about Monteverde's golden toad. The critically short breeding season from April to June used to bring huge numbers of the toads to seasonal pools where the luminous orange males would seek out the black, yellow and red mottled females. Outnumbering the females by 8:1, unsuccessful males would clasp each other in 'toad balls' or try to mate with an already paired female in determined efforts to reproduce. Otherwise, they would hide for most of the year deep in the forest litter.

Whatever the cause, until further research is carried out on the extent of the extinctions, all most of us can do is keep observing and delighting in the brightly leaping flashes of colour of other froggy species while they last.

Frogs and toads Think of Costa Rica and tiny, colourful toads are usually pictured in the mind's eye. Several species of poison-arrow frogs are endemic to the country and are so named because the indigenous people used to dip their arrowheads in the frog's toxic secretions. Highly poisonous to predators, the frogs' toxins are their defence and their neon-coloured bodies announce to all to look but don't touch. Confident little fellows, these tiny frogs can be found darting about on the ground during the daytime, at ease with the knowledge only the most foolish of predators would dare attack. Keep an eye open for flashes of neon green, ruby red, blazing yellow – these tiny toads are stunning to behold (if you do hold them, though, make sure to wash your hands well and never lick the secretions as they are toxic).

Turtles Turtle watching has become a tourist draw, as six of the world's eight species nest on the beaches of Costa Rica. Tortuguero is a famous spot for the green turtle (*Chelonia mydas*) and is the largest nesting spot in the Caribbean. Over 5,000 green turtles swim from as far away as Mexico and Venezuela to lay their eggs in the ancient nesting spots on Tortugeuro's coast. June through November is nesting season and peak months are August and September.

Tens of thousands of Olive Ridley (*Lepidochelys olivacea*) turtles lug themselves en masse to Playa Nacite and Ostional Wildlife Refuge every July through December. The largest turtle in the world, the leatherback (*Dermochelys coriacea*), prefers Playa Grande and Tamarindo between October and April. Other turtles found occasionally on the Pacific coast include hawksbills and loggerheads (although there are more on the Caribbean coast). Terrestrial turtles are found in the Caribbean lowlands and the red turtle is particular to the northern Pacific lowlands.

Most major nesting beaches are now protected but continued development of highly prized beach property threatens the calm that these animals need to lay their eggs. Conservation efforts have greatly aided in increasing dwindling turtle populations but environmental pressures have seen a recent decline in the numbers returning to nest. For further information, see box *Marine turtles*, opposite, and *Turtle watching* on pages 80–1.

MARINE LIFE (For information on dolphin and whale watching, see page 72.) Although Costa Rica is the great 'meeting spot' of the Americas, the isthmus acts as a great barrier between the Pacific Ocean and Caribbean Sea. The Pacific is much colder, more turbulent, more nutrient-rich, and supports large populations of open-water fish like tuna, mackerel, jacks and billfish. In contrast, the Caribbean is much more stable, shallow and nutrient-poor, encouraging the growth of coral reefs, sea grasses and mangroves. Isla del Coco is especially rich in sealife and was a favoured diving spot of Jacques Cousteau – here, hammerhead and great white sharks slip silently through dark waters.

INSECTS AND SPIDERS 'What about the bugs?' is the most common question asked by travellers to Costa Rica. Yes, there are insects (ant species alone number in the thousands) and spiders and a number of creepy crawlies that range in size from the head of a pin to a man's shoe. Some, like the iridescent blue morpho butterflies, are dreamy while others, like the large rhinoceros beetle, look fierce.

LEAF-CUTTER ANTS – FOCUS ON FUNGUS

Any visit to Costa Rica would not be complete without pausing along some forest trail to watch the scurrying line of leaf-cutter ants (*Atta cephalotes*) along their carefully cleaned pathway or climbing over a seemingly insurmountable stone or fallen trunk in their way, weighed down with a comparatively huge leaf or petal piece, that may have been cut way deep in the forest.

Crumbly earth on the forest floor is the giveaway for their nests. Tunnels in the older colonies can delve 6m down with galleries and chambers to accommodate the population of several millions. The carefully carried greenery is not for food, but is masticated to make compost used to cultivate a tiny white fungus that is the staple diet for the ants. When a new queen leaves her home to start a new colony, she takes a piece of the fungus with her – like a dowry – to begin a new larder. So specialised is the symbiotic relationship of ant to fungus that it no longer produces spores to reproduce, depending solely on the ants to ensure propagation. A queen's colony has three castes: the tiny *minimas* that do housekeeping and tend the fungus gardens; the *medias*, the most visible leaf-cutters marching the trails to deliver their cargo; and the imposing *majors* that protect the trails and will attack to the death with ferocious jaws.

Tricia Hayne

Turtles live largely in water, coming ashore only to nest, and unlike their landlubber cousins they are unable to retract either their heads or their flippers into their shell for protection.

Turtles do not nest until they are at least 25 years old, when they lay their eggs deep in the sand. The eggs take around 60 days to hatch, at which time the hatchlings make their way towards the sea, attracted by the play of moonlight on the waves. The green turtle, the most likely of the five species to be seen by visitors, lays between 300 and 540 eggs per season in the wild, nesting every three or four years, with the eggs hatching from May to September. In captivity, these figures increase, with up to 1,700 eggs in total laid over several batches in a season. In their first year, the hatchlings grow up to 2.7kg, and they can be expected to weigh up to 24kg by the time they are three or four. Green turtles may live to be centuries old, and can weigh in excess of 200kg. Turtles are cold-blooded animals, requiring warm water to survive. In fact, water temperature affects the sex of the hatchlings – at 28°C a balance between male and female is to be expected; cooler than that and males will dominate; hotter and there will be a predominance of females.

The world's eight species of marine turtle are all protected under the Convention on International Trade in Endangered Species (CITES).

The most colourful are the 1,000 species of **butterflies** (10% of the world's population), which are found throughout the country. Fascinating in their range of colouring and camouflage, butterflies and moths have even adapted to mimic other animals, such as the owl-eye butterflies (*Caligo memnon*) whose wing patterns depict large circles similar to the eyes of an owl – ensuring birds (who find butterflies particularly tasty) keep a healthy distance. Butterfly farms are numerous across Costa Rica and are an excellent opportunity to see a wide variety of species in one location. **Spiders** in Costa Rica come in all shapes, colours and sizes, ranging from your standard harmless house spiders to giant tarantulas and golden orb spiders.

Some **insects** are bothersome to humans, especially mosquitoes, chiggers and ticks. A good repellent is recommended as is wearing long sleeves and trousers. Sand flies and 'no-seeums' are particularly vicious on beaches at sunset – if you must head to the water's edge at this time, I suggest the Cactus Juice brand of repellent, the only one I've found effective against these nasty little critters. Bees here are Africanised, so they are very aggressive and will swarm if their nest is disturbed. If you happen to provoke these bees, run in a zigzag and head for a body of water. Bullet ants are particularly nasty – they are large black ants with massive mandibles. It's been said that five or six bites from these ants is enough to kill a man – my husband was bitten by one and he said it was the most painful experience of his life (and he's been in a lot of scrapes as an adventure guide), equivalent to what he imagines a bullet wound would feel like. Bullet ants are found in the jungle so do be wary about leaning up against trees.

Scorpions are common, especially in hot areas. Their sting is sharp but generally harmless – people who are allergic, however, will need to seek medical help. Various caterpillars are toxic and should not be touched.

A good practice is to check toilet seats (for spiders) prior to use and to bang your shoes together before putting them on (as scorpions and spiders seek out closed dark spaces). I always double check what's under the sheets before getting into bed, especially if in a remote area.

THE ZOMBIE SPIDERS OF COSTA RICA

Perhaps one of the strangest phenomena of the forest is the mind-controlling wasps and their zombie spiders. The *Plesiometa argyra*, a harmless species of orb spider, happily spins its perfectly round web and feasts upon the hapless insects that become entangled within it. But when an as-yet-unnamed wasp stings the spider, the eight-legged spinner becomes temporarily paralysed while the wasp lays its eggs on the tip of the spider's abdomen and flies off. The spider regains movement and carries on for the next two weeks, unaware that wasp larvae have hatched and are sucking out its juices through tiny punctures in its abdomen.

Then things get weird. The night before the larvae kill their host, the spider inexplicably builds a web unlike anything it has made before. Rather than constructing its flat, round web, it creates a short, squat web more akin to a hammock. Once the web is complete, the larvae kill the spider and cocoon themselves in the web where they are protected from ants, wind and rain.

The University of Costa Rica's Dr William G. Eberhard was the first to observe this strange behaviour and hypothesises that the larvae secrete a fast-acting chemical which forces the spider to change its usual five-step web-building process to only a two-step procedure, which creates the perfect habitat for the larvae. If the larvae are removed before they kill the spider, the spider usually recovers within a few days. But what the chemical is and how it works remains a mystery.

3

Practical Information

WHEN TO VISIT

'HIGH SEASON' v 'LOW SEASON' Generally, 'high season' corresponds with the Costa Rican summer (the dry season) and the northern hemisphere's winter (late November through mid-April). The 'low season' is during the rainy season or 'green season', starting late April with the rains becoming heavy in September and October. Although the months of September and October can be exceptionally wet (though some travellers don't mind at all), the beginning and end of the green season are, I think, some of the best months to travel here – prices are lower, the foliage is green and there are fewer tourists. Most hotels will have price discounts in May, June, August, September and October (July has become a busy travel month so many hotels now increase their rates then).

The Caribbean has its own weather pattern and sees rain throughout the year, although October is traditionally its driest month and consequently the best time to visit.

If it can be avoided, do not travel during Christmas week or *Semana Santa* (Easter week) as these are the two busiest, most expensive travel weeks in Costa Rica as all the locals take those weeks off and head to the beach. Hotels are sold out months in advance, despite charging higher prices and imposing minimum-stay policies for those weeks. Beaches are crowded and dirty (many *Ticos* will just camp on the beach) and, unfortunately, *Ticos* seem to have no qualms about littering and leave their rubbish wherever it may fall.

HIGHLIGHTS

Although Costa Rica is a small country, its biodiversity is amazing. With one of the most widespread park systems in the world, Costa Rica is a nature lover's paradise and eco-tourism is what first put the land of 'Pura Vida' on the map. Here are but a few visitor highlights from different areas around the country.

SAN JOSÉ The capital city is located in north central Costa Rica. It is a delicious mix of two cultures – North and Latin American – that intertwine to give it a unique cosmopolitan flavour. Home to numerous museums, restaurants and theatres, it is a culture vulture's dream. The crown jewel, however, is the National Theatre located in the centre of the city, built in 1890 and modelled on Italy's famed La Scala. The exterior boasts columns and images of Calderon de la Barca and Beethoven while inside are numerous oil paintings, marble staircases, golden ceilings and floors built with rich local wood. From the National Theatre you can walk to the Central Market, or visit the Legislative Assembly, National Library or the Gold Museum (see *Chapter 5*, page 93, for more details).

CENTRAL VALLEY The Braulio Carrillo National Park is home to the Barva Volcano (2,906m) while Poas Volcano National Park houses the volcano of the same name (2,704m), which is still active and boasts a dwarf cloudforest near the crater of the last major eruption in 1989. You can walk up to the lip of the Poas Volcano; be sure to arrive before 10.00 for a view into the crater before the clouds roll in. Both parks have lush vegetation and are excellent day hikes.

CARTAGO Founded in 1563 and the national capital until 1820, Cartago is one of the oldest settlements in Costa Rica. One of the main attractions is Las Ruinas where you can visit the ruins of a very old and beautiful church and its gardens. The main attraction, however, is the Basilica de Nuestra Señora de los Angeles, the largest and most opulent cathedral in the country and home to the Virgin patron of Costa Rica, La Negrita, an image of the virgin discovered on 2 August 1635. Homage to Mother Mary is paid yearly on this date when tens of thousands of pilgrims from all over the country walk to the basilica to pray before her.

OROSÍ VALLEY A few minutes from the centre of Cartago is Lankester Gardens, with its multitude of gorgeous orchids and other tropical plants. Further on is the valley of the Orosí River with incredible views and the small village of Ujarrás, famous for its ruins of a 17th-century church. The Tapanti National Wildlife Refuge is a treasure for bird lovers. The town of Turrialba is near the Pacuare River, one of the fastest-flowing in the country and extremely popular for kayaking and white-water rafting. Nearby is the Guayabo National Park, the most important archaeological site in the country.

TORTUGUERO A series of canals connect sleepy villages together, excellent for wildlife viewing all year round, but the real attractions here are the three species of turtles – leatherback, green and hawksbill – which nest in the area.

PUERTO LIMÓN A delightful town to visit, especially Parque Vargas with its tropical trees, flowers, birds and beautiful ocean views. Further down the coast is the funky town of Cahuita, with its Creole culture and national park with two long white-sand beaches, joined by a small coral reef. Further south is Puerto Viejo, with reggae rhythms, crystal-clear waters and great surf waves. Heading south, Manzanillo is the last town on the coast, renowned for the Gandoca Natural Reserve, home to a 200m coral reef excellent for scuba diving.

SOUTH PACIFIC Surfing's the thing in the south Pacific, and the beaches at Zancudo and Pavones are world class. The town of San Vito, founded in 1950 by Italian immigrants, is home to the Wilson Botanical Gardens with a variety of tropical species. At the southernmost tip of the country is Corcovado National Park, with the largest biological diversity of all the coastal rainforests in Central America, in which animals such as the scarlet macaw make their home.

CHIRRIPÓ Chirripó National Park is home to the tallest mountain in Costa Rica, Mount Chirripó (3,819m), a challenging hike.

BALLENA MARINE NATIONAL PARK This national park has a 4,500ha coral reef surrounding the Isla Ballena, home to aquatic birds, green iguanas and spectacular alligators.

MANUEL ANTONIO This beautiful clifftop beach town neighbours Manuel Antonio National Park, one of the smallest in the country although one of the most popular with its tropical rainforests, white-sand beaches, crystal-clear waters, fantastic reefs and incredible fauna. Nearby is the town of Quepos, a paradise for sport fishing.

MONTEVERDE Founded in 1951 by a community of Quakers, the draw here is the beautifully preserved cloudforest and its many birds. In 1972, the Bosque Nuboso Monteverde Biological Reserve was created as the main research point for the Tropical Science Centre of San José and the Monteverde Conservation League. The Santa Elena Natural Reserve created in 1992 is home to 400 different species of birds, especially during the migration period between March and April. Highlights include the Bajo del Tigre Hike, Sendero Tranquilo Reserve hikes, Cerro Amigo (1,842m), the Butterfly Garden, the Hummingbird Gallery, the Handmade Cheese Factory and the Cooperativa Artesanal where you can buy handmade clothes and other articles.

LA FORTUNA Home of the famous Arenal Volcano, one of the most active in the world. This volcano was dormant until 1968 when it awoke with fury destroying everything around it. It continues to maintain a stable activity with eruptions (mostly at night) in which lava is clearly visible. Near to the volcano are Arenal Lake and the small town of Tilaran where traditional rodeo shows are held. Natural hot springs are found scattered throughout the area and are almost as popular a draw as the mighty volcano, thanks to their soothing waters that lack any sulphur odour.

CAÑAS A small town that is the entry point to the Palo Verde National Park, an important bird sanctuary and home to diverse species of animals. Close by is the Lomas Barbudal Biological Reserve, famous for the enormous variety of insects inhabiting this coastal area, including 250 different species of bees.

NICOYA PENINSULA One of the most popular areas of the country with its heavenly beaches and natural reserves, such as Palo Verde National Park and Barra Honda National Park, famous for its impressive caves. Nicoya is the main town of the peninsula and its inhabitants descend from the Chorotegas who welcomed the first Spaniards in 1523. The church and Central Park, built in the 17th century, are charming. From Nicoya you can visit a myriad beaches including Samara, Nosara, Pelada and Guiones.

GUAITIL Home of the famous Chorotega-style pottery.

TAMARINDO One of the most popular beaches and an ideal place for surfing. The Baulas National Marine Park is famous as a site for turtle nesting (October to March).

LIBERIA The largest and most important city in the north of Costa Rica and an excellent starting point when visiting the natural parks in the area, such as the Santa Rosa National Park where up to 8,000 turtles arrive to lay eggs annually.

LOS CHILES A small town located only 3km from the Nicaraguan border and the entry point for the Caño Negro Wildlife Refuge. From there you can cross through San Carlos and reach Puerto Viejo de Sarapiqui, famous for its Barra del Colorado National Wildlife Reserve and tropical rainforest.

SUGGESTED ITINERARIES

The single biggest mistake travellers make is trying to do too much in too short a time. Looking at a map of Costa Rica is deceiving, as travel distances are usually no more than 200km (often considerably less) between major tourist destinations, but the lack of proper highways makes driving slow going. If coming for a week, I would suggest that you visit three areas maximum – otherwise, you are going to spend the majority of your holiday time travelling.

Here are some examples of itineraries to the most popular areas in Costa Rica that will give the maximum enjoyment with the minimum of travel time. For details of sport and other activities, see *Chapter 4*.

ITINERARY ONE – SAN JOSÉ/ARENAL/TAMARINDO ADVENTURE (8 DAYS)
Day 1 Arrive in San José late afternoon. Transfer to hotel in San José.
Day 2 Morning transfer via Interbus to Arenal. Check into hotel early afternoon. Take guided hike to observation point late afternoon, then to Tabacon Hot Springs for dinner and soak.
Day 3 Morning canyoning tour. Afternoon horseride to waterfall. Dinner and soak at Baldi Hot Springs.
Day 4 Morning transfer to Tamarindo via Interbus. Afternoon relaxing on beach.
Day 5 All-day combination canopy tour to Rincón de la Vieja.
Day 6 Morning canopy tour followed by sunset sailing trip.
Day 7 Morning mangrove tour. Fly to San José in afternoon.
Day 8 Transfer to airport, fly home.

ITINERARY TWO – SAN JOSÉ/TORTUGUERO/MONTEVERDE/MANUEL ANTONIO NATURE TOUR (10 DAYS)
Day 1 Arrive in San José. Transfer to hotel.
Day 2 Transfer to Tortuguero. Evening turtle tour.
Day 3 Tour of canals.
Day 4 Fly to San José. Transfer to Monteverde via private minibus.
Day 5 Tour of cloudforest. Afternoon exploring town.
Day 6 Canopy tour in the morning and horseback riding in the afternoon.
Day 7 Transfer to Manuel Antonio via Interbus. Afternoon relaxing on beach.
Day 8 Morning tour of Manuel Antonio National Park. Sunset sailing tour.
Day 9 Morning tour of mangroves. Late afternoon tour of butterfly garden.
Day 10 Early-morning flight to San José. Fly home in afternoon.

ITINERARY THREE – VOLCANO TOUR (8 DAYS)
Day 1 Arrive at San José. Transfer to local hotel
Day 2 Transfer to Rincón de la Vieja volcano.
Day 3 Hiking tour of Rincón de la Vieja.
Day 4 Transfer via private minibus to Arenal. Hanging bridges tour.
Day 5 Horseride to observation point. Trip to caves. Evening relaxing in hot springs.
Day 6 Transfer to La Paz Waterfall Garden. Stay at Peace Lodge.
Day 7 Tour to Poas Volcano and coffee plantation.
Day 8 Transfer to San José, fly home.

ITINERARY FOUR – COSTA RICA JUNGLE TOUR (14 DAYS)
Day 1 Arrive in San José. Transfer to hotel.
Day 2 White-water rafting at Pacuare River. Overnight at jungle lodge.
Day 3 Continue rafting tour. Transfer to Puerto Viejo.
Day 4 Relaxing in Puerto Viejo.
Day 5 Tour to Bri Bri village.
Day 6 Hiking Cahuita National Park.
Day 7 Transfer to San José via Interbus. Fly to Quepos. Transfer to Manuel Antonio.
Day 8 Tour Manuel Antonio National Park in morning. Relax in afternoon.
Day 9 Tour of mangroves in morning, canopy tour in afternoon.

Day 10 Fly to Puerto Jimenez via NatureAir. Transfer to lodge in Osa.
Day 11 Dolphin boat tour.
Day 12 Hike Corcovado.
Day 13 Relaxing.
Day 14 Fly to San José. Fly home.

TOUR OPERATORS

UK

Bales Worldwide Bales Hse, Junction Rd, Dorking, Surrey RH4 3HL; ℡ 0870 752 0780; f 01306 740048; e enquiries@balesworldwide.comBales; www.balesworldwide.com

Exodus Travels Grange Mills, Weir Rd, London SW12 0NE; ℡ 870 240 5550; f 020 8673 0779; e sales@exodus.co.uk; www.exodus.co.uk

Geodyssey ℡ 020 7281 7788; e enquiries@ geodyssey.co.uk; www.geodyssey.co.uk

Journey Latin America 12 & 13 Heathfield Terrace, Chiswick, London W4 4JE; ℡ 020 8747 8315; f 020 8742 1312; e tours@journeylatinamerica.co.uk; www.journeylatinamerica.co.uk

Sunvil Latin America Sunvil House, Upper Sq, Old Isleworth, Middx TW7 7BJ; ℡ 020 8758 4774; e latinamerica@sunvil.co.uk; www.sunvil.co.uk

Worlds Apart 15 Clarance Parade, Cheltenham GL50 3PA; ℡ 01242 226 578; e info@ worldsaparttravel.co.uk; www.worldsaparttravel.co.uk

GERMANY

Exodus Travels Huttenstrasse 17, 40215 Dusseldorf; ℡ (0211) 99 49 02; f (0211) 38 22 88;

e marketing@explorer-fernreisen.com

US

Apple Vacations www.applevacations.com (various agents throughout US)

Caravan Tours 401 North Michigan Av, Chicago, IL 60611; ℡ 312 321 9800; f 312 321 9845; www.caravantours.com

IN COSTA RICA

ABA Costa Rica Exotica Natural ℡ 350 3670; f 239 0587; www.travellingcostarica.com

ABC Tours ℡ 290 5442; f 290 3386; www.abc-costa-rica.co.cr/EN/

Absolute Tropical Extravaganza ℡ 297 0664; f 297 0549; www.ecoscapetours.com

Agencia Camino Travel ℡ 234 2530; f 225 6143; www.caminotravel.com

Agencia Gray Line Costa Rica ℡ 220 2126; f 220 2393; www.graylinecostarica.com/index.html

Agencia Miki Travel ℡ 257 8166; f 221 3681; www.mikitravel.net

Asuaire Travel ℡ 220 1882; f 220 1546; www.asuaire.com

Aventuras Tierra Verde SA ℡ 249 2354; f 249 1000; www.adventure-costarica.com

Costa Rica Natural Travel ℡ 262 0632; f 262 0653; www.costaricatravel.co.cr

Costa Rica Nature Escape ℡ 257 8064; f 257 8065; www.crnature.com

Costa Rica OnTrack ℡ 256 0121; f 256 0120; www.costaricaontrack.com

Costa Rican Vacations ℡ 296 7715; www.vacationscostarica.com

Costa Rica's Temptations ℡ 239 9999; f 239 9990; www.crinfo.com

Destination Costa Rica ℡ 257 5700; f 257 5717; www.destinationcr.com

Expediciones Tropicales ℡ 257 4171; f 257 4133; www.costaricainfo.com

Latitudes The Adventure Co ℡ 203 7576; f 203 0095; www.latitudesadventure.com

Travel Excellence ℡ 258 1046; f 258 0795; www.travelexcellence.com

Vesa Tours ℡ 239 6767; f 239 6868; www.vesatours.com

RED TAPE

Citizens of Australia, Canada, Ireland, New Zealand, South Africa, the UK and the USA need valid passports to enter Costa Rica and to re-enter their home countries. Costa Rica does not allow entrance if the holder's passport expires in less than six months – returning home with an expired passport is illegal and may result in a fine.

Citizens of the aforementioned countries do not need visas to enter Costa Rica. For detailed information on visa regulations, check on entrance requirements at the nearest Costa Rican embassy or consulate before your departure.

Entering as a tourist or student does not include the right to work or study, which require a permit and visa respectively.

If you lose your passport, immediately notify the local police and the nearest embassy or consulate of your home government. In an emergency, ask for immediate temporary travelling papers that will allow you to enter your home country.

When you travel, make sure your passport is always with you, as the police sometimes stop buses and demand proof that you are a legal tourist. We recommend making two photocopies of the pages of your passport with your photo and entry stamp and any other important documents, and carry one set of copies, separate from the originals, leaving another set at home.

When arriving in Costa Rica, you must declare certain items from abroad and pay a duty on the value of those articles if they exceed the allowance established by Costa Rica's customs service. Check with the nearest Costa Rican embassy for details. Note that goods and gifts purchased at duty-free shops abroad are not exempt from duty or sales tax; 'duty-free' merely means that you need not pay a tax in the country of purchase. Upon returning home, you must similarly declare all articles acquired abroad and pay a duty on the value of articles in excess of your home country's allowance.

Visitors leaving Costa Rica have to pay the official airport tax/exit fee of US$26, payable at the airport prior to checking in (travellers' cheques are not accepted).

Ⓔ EMBASSIES

COSTA RICAN EMBASSIES ABROAD

Australia 11th Fl, 30 Clarence St, NSW 2000, Sydney; ✆ 612 9261 1177; f 612 9261 2953. *Open Mon–Fri 10.00–17.00.*

Canada 325 Dalhousie St, Suite 407, Ottawa, Ontario KIN 7G2; ✆ 613 562 2855; f 613 562 2582; e embcrica@travel-net.com; www.costaricaembassy.com. *Open Mon–Fri 09.00–17.00.*

South Africa PO Box 68140, Bryanston 2021; ✆ 11 705 3434; f 11 705 1222. *Open daily 08.00–18.00.*

UK Flat 1, 14 Lancaster Gate, London W2 3LH; ✆ 020 7706 8844; f 020 7706 8655; www.embcrlon.demon.co.uk. *Open Mon–Fri 09.00–16.00.*

US 2114 S St NW, Washington, DC 20008; ✆ 202 234 2945; f 202 265 4795; www.costarica-embassy.org. *Open Mon–Fri 09.00–17.00.* Consulate: 2112 S St NW, Washington, DC 20008; ✆ 202 328 6628; f 202 265 4795. *Open Mon–Fri 10.00–13.00.*

EMBASSIES IN COSTA RICA

Australia, Ireland and **New Zealand** do not have embassies in Costa Rica but can be contacted via the UK embassy.

Canada Oficentro Ejecutivo, Edificio #5 detrás de la Contraloría, Sabana Sur, San José (mail only: Apdo 351-1007, Centro Colón, San José); ✆ 296 4149; f 296 4270; e canadacr@co.cr; www.sanJosé.gc.ca. *Open Mon–Thu 08.00–16.30, Fri 08.00–13.30.*

France Indoor Club 200m sur, 25m oestes, Curridabat; ✆ 234 4167; e sjfrance@racsa.co.cr; www.ambafrance-cr.org. *Open Mon–Fri 08.30–12.00.*

Germany 300m oeste de ICE, Torre de La Sabana, 8 piso, Sabana Norte; ✆ 232 5533; e info@san-jose.diplo.de; www.costa-rica.diplo.de. *Open Mon–Fri 09.00–12.00.*

Holland Oficentro Ejecutivo, Edificio #3 detrás de la Contraloría, Sabana Sur, San José ✆ 296 1490; e nethemb@racsa.co.cr; www.nethemb.or.cr. *Open Mon–Fri 09.00–12.00.*

Italy 25m oeste de la Restaurante Río, Los Yoses;

234 2326; e ambasciata.sanjose@estire.it; www.ambitcr.com. *Open Mon–Fri 09.00–12.00.*
Sweden 100m este de La Pozuelo, La Uruca; 232 8549; emergencies: 846 0307; e erodriguez@font.co.cr (no website). *Open Mon–Fri 09.00–12.00.*
Switzerland Edificio Centro Colon, Paseo Colón, San José; 233 0052; e vertretung@sjc.rep.admin.ch; www.eda.admin.ch/sanjose. *Open Mon–Fri 09.00–12.00.*

UK Centro Colón (11th Fl), San José (mail only: Apdo 815-1007, San José); 258 2025; f 233 9938; e britemb@co.cr; www.britishembassycr.com. *Open Mon–Thu 08.00–16.00, Fri 08.00–13.00.*
US Ca 120, Av Central, Pavas, San José (mail only: Apdo 920-1200, San José); 220 3939; after hours 220 3127; f 220 2305; www.usembassy.or.cr. Call for detailed hours of services.

GETTING THERE AND AWAY

Approximately 20 international airlines fly regularly to Costa Rica with the majority of flights landing at Juan Santamaría International Airport (airport code SJO) in San José. A number of flights also fly in to the Daniel Oduber International Airport (airport code LIR) in Liberia, the closest international airport to the beaches of the north Pacific.

Make your reservation as early as possible – two months or more in advance is best – and reconfirm your reservation a few days before departure. Owing to heightened security measures, it's advisable to arrive at the airport at least three hours before the scheduled flight. Midweek and low-season flights are generally the least expensive.

Iberia flies from Madrid, Spain, with direct connections to San José four days a week and **Air Madrid** has direct flights from Madrid three times a week.

Alitalia flies from Italy to Miami, Caracas and Santo Domingo, and **Taca** provides passengers with a connecting flight to San José from various points in the US, Mexico City, Havana as well as all Central America and parts of South America.

Condor provides services from Frankfurt, Germany, via Miami to San José three times a week.

Martinair flies from Amsterdam via Orlando daily.

No British or Irish airlines provide services to Costa Rica.

American Airlines, **United Airlines**, **Continental Airlines** and **Delta Airlines** fly from the US to San José and Liberia.

Air Canada has direct flights between Toronto and San José.

HEALTH

Hopefully, you won't need it but if you do, the healthcare in Costa Rica is excellent. The country boasts a modern and renowned public medical health system, under the administration of the Caja Costarricense de Seguro Social (CCSS). Internationally administered private hospital facilities provide an alternative to the public system when desired. Medical services in rural areas are usually very basic.

If you take prescription medication, have your doctor give you a spare prescription with a note suggesting an alternative medication if your first choice isn't available.

There are several options for purchasing medical assistance for your trip. The International Association for Medical Assistance to Travelers (IAMAT, see below for contact details) has free membership, lists English-speaking doctors, immunisation requirements and sanitation. If your regular insurance policy does not cover travel abroad, you may wish to purchase additional coverage. Most UK travel insurance policies include cover for medical assistance.

There are several ultra-modern hospitals with English-speaking doctors in the greater San José area. Below are some contact numbers. For emergency assistance in Costa Rica, dial 911.

✚ PRIVATE CLINICS

Clinica Americana Downtown San José; ☎ 222 1010
Clinica Biblica Downtown San José; ☎ 257 5252, 0466
Clinica Catolica Guadalupe; ☎ 225 5055

Hospital CIMA Escazú; ☎ 208 1000
KOP Medical Clinic San Rafael de Escazú; ☎ 228 4119

Make sure to have a list with the names of who should be contacted if you have a medical emergency, as well as any information on allergies or other conditions.

IMMUNISATIONS Although there are no required vaccinations to enter Costa Rica, travellers should make sure that they are up to date with the most common vaccines such as **hepatitis A** (eg: Avaxim, Havrix Monodose – two doses given at least six months apart which lasts for 20 years in adults), typhoid, diphtheria and tetanus. Although polio vaccine is no longer recommended for the Americas, a combined diphtheria, tetanus and polio (Revaxis) vaccine is currently available, and lasts for ten years.

TRAVEL CLINICS AND HEALTH INFORMATION A full list of current travel clinic websites worldwide is available from the International Society of Travel Medicine

A deep-vein thrombosis (DVT) is a blood clot that forms in the deep leg veins. This is very different from irritating but harmless superficial phlebitis. DVT causes swelling and redness of one leg, usually with heat and pain in one calf and sometimes the thigh. A DVT is only dangerous if a clot breaks away and travels to the lungs (pulmonary embolus). Symptoms of a pulmonary embolus (PE) include chest pain that is worse on breathing in deeply, shortness of breath, and sometimes coughing up small amounts of blood. The symptoms commonly start three to ten days after a long flight. Anyone who thinks that they might have a DVT needs to see a doctor immediately who will arrange a scan. Warfarin tablets (to thin the blood) are then taken for at least six months.

PREVENTION OF DVT Several conditions make the problem more likely. Immobility is the key, and factors like reduced oxygen in cabin air and dehydration may also contribute. To reduce the risk of thrombosis on a long journey:

* Exercise before and after the flight
* Keep mobile before and during the flight; move around every couple of hours
* During the flight drink plenty of water or juices
* Avoid taking sleeping pills and excessive tea, coffee and alcohol
* Perform exercises that mimic walking and tense the calf muscles
* Consider wearing flight socks or support stockings (see www.legshealth.com)
* Taking a meal of oily fish (mackerel, trout, salmon, sardines, etc) in the 24 hours before departure reduces blood clotability and thus DVT risk
* The jury is still out on whether it is worth taking an aspirin before flying, but this can be discussed with your GP.

If you think you are at increased risk of a clot, ask your doctor if it is safe to travel.

on www.istm.org. For other journey preparation information, consult www.tripprep.com. Information about various medications may be found on www.emedicine.com, and for information on preventing malaria, see www.preventingmalaria.info.

UK

Berkeley Travel Clinic 32 Berkeley St, London W1J 8EL (near Green Park tube station); ☎ 020 7629 6233
British Airways Travel Clinic and Immunisation Service There are 2 BA clinics in London, both on ☎ 0845 600 2236; www.ba.com/travelclinics. *Appointments only Mon–Fri 09.00–16.30* at 101 Cheapside, London EC2V 6DT; or walk-in service *Mon–Fri 09.30–17.30, Sat 10.00–16.00* at 213 Piccadilly, London W1J 9HQ. Apart from providing inoculations and malaria prevention, they sell a variety of health-related goods.
Cambridge Travel Clinic 48a Mill Rd, Cambridge CB1 2AS; ☎ 01223 367362; e enquiries@ cambridgetravelclinic.co.uk; www.cambridgetravelclinic.co.uk. *Open Tue–Fri 12.00–19.00, Sat 10.00–16.00.*

Edinburgh Travel Clinic Regional Infectious Diseases Unit, Ward 41 OPD, Western General Hospital, Crewe Rd South, Edinburgh EH4 2UX; ☎ 0131 537 2822; www.link.med.ed.ac.uk/ridu. Travel helpline (0906 589 0380) open weekdays 09.00–12.00. Provides inoculations and antimalarial prophylaxis and advises on travel-related health risks.
Fleet Street Travel Clinic 29 Fleet St, London EC4Y 1AA; ☎ 020 7353 5678; www.fleetstreetclinic.com. Vaccinations, travel products and latest advice.
Hospital for Tropical Diseases Travel Clinic Mortimer Market Bldg, Capper St (off Tottenham Ct Rd), London WC1E 6AU; ☎ 020 7388 9600; www.thehtd.org. Offers consultations and advice, and is able to provide all necessary drugs and vaccines for travellers. Runs a healthline (0906 133 7733) for

country-specific information and health hazards. Also stocks nets, water purification equipment and personal protection measures.
Interhealth Worldwide Partnership Hse, 157 Waterloo Rd, London SE1 8US; ✆ 020 7902 9000; www.interhealth.org.uk. Competitively priced, one-stop travel-health service. All profits go to their affiliated company, InterHealth, which provides healthcare for overseas workers on Christian projects.
MASTA (Medical Advisory Service for Travellers Abroad) London School of Hygiene and Tropical Medicine, Keppel St, London WCI 7HT; ✆ 0906 550 1402; www.masta.org. Individually tailored health briefs available for a fee, with up-to-date information on how to stay healthy, inoculations and what to bring. There are currently 30 MASTA pre-travel clinics in Britain. Call 0870 241 6843 or check online for the nearest. Clinics also sell malaria prophylaxis memory cards, treatment kits, bednets, net treatment kits.
NHS travel website www.fitfortravel.scot.nhs.uk.

Provides country-by-country advice on immunisation and malaria, plus details of recent developments, and a list of relevant health organisations.
Nomad Travel Store/Clinic 3–4 Wellington Terrace, Turnpike Lane, London N8 0PX; ✆ 020 8889 7014; travel-health line (office hours only) 0906 863 3414; e sales@nomadtravel.co.uk; www.nomadtravel.co.uk. Also at 40 Bernard St, London WCIN 1LJ; ✆ 020 7833 4114; 52 Grosvenor Gardens, London SW1W 0AG; ✆ 020 7823 5823; and 43 Queens Rd, Bristol BS8 1QH; ✆ 0117 922 6567. For health advice, equipment such as mosquito nets, and other anti-bug devices, and an excellent range of travel gear.
Trailfinders Travel Clinic 194 Kensington High St, London W8 7RG; ✆ 020 7938 3999; www.trailfinders.com/clinic.htm
Travelpharm The Travelpharm website, www.travelpharm.com, offers up-to-date guidance on travel-related health and has a range of medications available through their online mini-pharmacy.

Irish Republic

Tropical Medical Bureau Grafton St Medical Centre, Grafton Bldgs, 34 Grafton St, Dublin 2; ✆ 1 671 9200; www.tmb.ie. A useful website specific to

tropical destinations. Also check website for other bureaux locations throughout Ireland.

USA

Centers for Disease Control 1600 Clifton Rd, Atlanta, GA 30333; ✆ 800 311 3435; travellers' health hotline 888 232 3299; www.cdc.gov/travel. The central source of travel information in the USA. The invaluable *Health Information for International Travel*, published annually, is available from the Division of Quarantine at this address.
Connaught Laboratories PO Box 187, Swiftwater, PA 18370; ✆ 800 822 2463. They will send a free list

of specialist tropical-medicine physicians in your state.
IAMAT (International Association for Medical Assistance to Travelers) 1623 Military Rd, 279, Niagara Falls, NY 14304-1745; ✆ 716 754 4883; e info@iamat.org; www.iamat.org. A non-profit organisation that provides lists of English-speaking doctors abroad.
International Medicine Center 920 Frostwood Drive, Suite 670, Houston, TX 77024; ✆ 713 550 2000; www.traveldoc.com

Canada

IAMAT Suite 1, 1287 St Clair Av W, Toronto, Ontario

M6E 1B8; ✆ 416 652 0137; www.iamat.org

Australia, New Zealand, Singapore

TMVC ✆ 1300 65 88 44; www.tmvc.com.au. TMVC has a total of 31 clinics in Australia, New Zealand and Singapore including:
Auckland Canterbury Arcade, 170 Queen St, Auckland; ✆ 9 373 3531
Brisbane 6th fl, 247 Adelaide St, Brisbane, QLD 4000; ✆ 7 3221 9066

Melbourne 2nd fl, 393 Little Bourke St, Melbourne, VIC 3000; ✆ 3 9602 5788
Sydney 7th fl, Dymocks Bldg, 428 George St, Sydney, NSW 2000; ✆ 2 9221 7133
IAMAT PO Box 5049, Christchurch 5, New Zealand; www.iamat.org

South Africa and Namibia

SAA-Netcare Travel Clinics P Bag X34, Benmore 2010; www.travelclinic.co.za. Clinics throughout South Africa.
TMVC 113 D F Malan Drive, Roosevelt Park,

Johannesburg; ✆ 011 888 7488; www.tmvc.com.au. Consult website for details of 9 other clinics in South Africa and Namibia.

IAMAT 57 Chemin des Voirets, 1212 Grand Lancy, Geneva; www.iamat.org

FIRST-AID KIT A first-aid kit for Costa Rica should contain all the basics for travel anywhere in the world. Adjust the quantities of individual items to reflect conditions and availability of replacement items (eg: pack additional mosquito repellent). Other suggestions as follows:

- antiseptic wash
- blister patches
- bandages and plasters
- sachets of rehydration mix
- painkillers
- antifungal cream
- travel-sickness tablets
- lots of mosquito repellent
- antibiotics
- cold-cure sachets
- throat lozenges
- eye and ear drops
- indigestion tablets
- iodine or alcohol wipes
- your own prescription medicine

DRINKING WATER The local authorities state that the water in Costa Rica is perfectly potable, but I recommend that you stick to the bottled variety for drinking (you can brush your teeth with tap water anywhere in the country without worries). Costa Rica is NOT Mexico and 'Montezuma's Revenge' is not a problem here but there MAY be bacteria in the water in some areas that disagree with you so do be cautious of what you eat and drink.

SOME MEDICAL PROBLEMS

Malaria Malaria is rare in Costa Rica but there are cases occasionally on the Caribbean coast and the northern zones. Malaria pills can be taken prior to and during your trip but they are hard on the body, especially the liver, so I personally don't recommend taking them unless you are planning on being in a remote or high-risk area but check with your health professional. The list of antimalarials includes:

- Chloroquine (Nivaquine, Avloclor)
- Proguanil or chloroguanide (Paludrine)
- Mefloquine (Lariam)
- Doxycycline (Doxy, Vibra-tabs, Doxine)
- Pyrimethamine and dapsone (Maloprim)
- Hydroxychloroquine (Plaquenil)
- Quinine (Q 300, Quinoc)
- Pyrimethamine and sulfadoxine (Fansidar)

These pills do not give 100% protection from contracting malaria so it is important to be diligent in preventing mosquito bites (eg. wearing repellent, long-sleeved shirts and long trousers). It is vitally important that you do not miss a dose and that you continue to take the medication upon arrival home – some upwards of four weeks – regardless if you feel well or not.

Malaria is transmitted by the *Anopheles* mosquito and the incubation period ranges from six to eight days to several months. Early symptoms include fever,

Practical Information HEALTH 3

chills, aches and fatigue followed by high fever and sweating, sometimes with vomiting and diarrhoea. If you have any symptoms, see your doctor as there is the risk of becoming infected even up to a year after visiting a malarial area.

Dengue Dengue is the most problematic disease in Costa Rica, with 2005 having the largest outbreak for 20 years. Transmitted by the *Aedes aegypti* mosquito, which bites during the day, it is most prevalent during the rainy season. Areas where dengue occurs include the Caribbean coast, central Pacific and occasionally in the poorer areas of San José, although travellers aren't at great risk. Be sure to wear a good insect repellent with DEET, avoid areas with stagnant water and wear long trousers and long-sleeved shirts.

Leishmaniasis Leishmaniasis is transmitted by the bite of an infected sand fly. The bite allows the parasite to enter the body, where it stays for anything up to six months without symptoms. Eventually the parasite creates a sore, which often begins as a pimple before swelling in size. Sores of up to 2.5cm in diameter are not uncommon and these often weep to develop a crusty surface. It is possible to treat leishmaniasis successfully via a series of injections.

Chagas's disease (American trypanosomiasis) This infection is spread by a bug commonly found in the cracks and crevices of poorly constructed housing. Chagas's disease is not considered severe in the early stage of infection but can cause death, particularly in infants. Chronic symptoms are rare but can develop some 20 years after infection, decreasing the average life expectancy by an average of nine years by weakening the immune system. Blood tests can determine infection but to minimise the risk avoid sleeping in thatch-and-mud housing and use insecticides to reduce the risk of transmission. Acute symptoms only occur in about 1% of cases and chronic Chagas's is uncommon in Costa Rica. There is currently no vaccine or recommended drug available to prevent the disease.

Rabies Many animal species can be infected with this fatal viral infection, including dogs, cats and monkeys. Any bite, scratch or lick over an open wound from any warm-blooded animal in Costa Rica should be thoroughly cleaned immediately, using soap and hot water to scrub the area before wiping it with an alcohol or iodine solution. This will stop the rabies virus entering the body and will guard against secondary wound infections, such as tetanus. Those who think they have been exposed to rabies should seek medical attention immediately. Travellers without immunisation who are bitten will need both RIG (rabies immunoglobulin) and a full course of injections. This will prevent the onset of rabies symptoms but can be expensive (RIG alone can cost around US$800 a dose excluding the cost of the six or seven doses of vaccine needed). Pre-exposure vaccination is a sensible precaution for travellers who plan to visit remote areas. Furthermore, by taking at least two doses of rabies vaccine before exposure then you won't need the expensive RIG and the number of post-exposure doses of vaccine will be reduced.

Traveller's diarrhoea (TD) The medical world disagrees about the causes of TD. Some say that it is due to a contaminant, probably in water and possibly in food, while others say that travel itself and a change of diet are the causes. Certainly the latter seems to be supported by the fact that visitors to the UK or US from the Third World often fall ill when they arrive, despite the disparities in the levels of hygiene. However, one thing is agreed – if you travel you are certain to get it sooner or later; it is just a matter of time. TD is unpleasant, with symptoms that vary in severity from person to person. Generally symptoms will settle within 48 hours and should not require treatment beyond replacing lost fluids and salts and sugar as outlined below. Any blood or slime in the stool or a fever should alert you to the fact that antibiotics are required. Likewise if the TD fails to settle with basic replacement therapy medical help should be sought.

Travellers should stick to the bottled water that can be found in most shops and restaurants in larger towns. While there is no foolproof method of avoidance, common sense should prevail when it comes to eating and drinking. Opt for freshly cooked food served in a clean environment rather than street stalls surrounded by dogs and flies. Eat where the locals eat and order a traditional staple rather than a culinary oddity prepared with tourists in mind that may have been hanging around for a while.

Medical advice for the treatment of TD is largely that of rest and plenty of liquids. The most dangerous side effect is dehydration and care should be taken to replace lost body salts. Avoiding food for 24–48 hours can help speed recovery. Refraining from alcohol and caffeine for several days will also help prevent cramping.

Sun and heat The reported incidence of skin cancer continues to soar worldwide, as the number of pale-skinned travellers who expose themselves more and more to the sun escalates. Melanoma is responsible for nearly three-quarters of all skin cancer deaths and is increasing in frequency. Unlike other skin growths it is always malignant and caused by DNA cell changes. The most common cause of DNA damage is ultraviolet radiation from sunlight, and Caucasians are 20 times more likely to develop melanoma than those with darker skin. In simple terms the fairer the skin the more susceptible the individual, and people with a large number of moles or freckles are at increased risk. Covering up with loose, baggy clothes and applying plenty of suncream will help protect you. Wear a hat when possible and keep out of the harsh midday sun. Those who are determined to sunbathe should apply an adequate sun lotion with protective SPF and build up exposure time gently from a starting point of 15–20 minutes a day. If you overdo the sunshine and begin to feel the effects of heatstroke it is important to drink plenty of fluids. Rest in the shade and keep the body cool with wet towels.

Fungal infections Moisture encourages fungal infections to thrive and these are more common in hot, tropical climates. Infections are generally concentrated around the groin area, between the toes and on the scalp and are more likely to occur where the body is warm and damp. Wearing loose-fitting clothes in natural fabrics that breathe and avoiding artificial fibres, especially in socks and underwear, will help.

WOMEN TRAVELLERS Women travelling in unsanitary conditions are vulnerable to urinary tract and bladder infections, common and very uncomfortable bacterial conditions that cause a burning sensation and painful (sometimes frequent) urination. Over-the-counter medicines can sometimes alleviate symptoms, but if they persist, see a doctor.

Vaginal yeast infections may flare up in hot and humid climates. Wearing loosely fitting trousers or a skirt and cotton underwear will help, as will over-the-counter remedies.

In terms of safety, Costa Rica is a typically 'macho' Latin American nation, and women (single or otherwise) can expect a near-constant stream of catcalls, hisses, whistles and car horns, especially in San José. The best advice is to ignore the unwanted attention. Of course, the more provocatively you dress, the more likely you are to receive attention so try not to 'dress for success'. Women should also be careful walking alone at night, both in San José and in other more remote destinations.

COSMETIC SURGERY Cosmetic surgery and cosmetic/restorative dentistry is Costa Rica's hidden treasure, but not a well-kept secret. Each year thousands of men and women take advantage of the low-cost, high-quality care provided by Costa Rica's highly trained cosmetic surgeons and dentists. In fact, a 1991 survey conducted by the University of Costa Rica found that 14.25% of all visitors to Costa Rica come to receive some sort of medical care – most often cosmetic surgery and dental work.

Central American Institute of Cardiology
http://www.edenia.com/medical/me14001.htm
Clinica Laser Visual
www.edenia.com/medical/me14001.htm. Comprehensive eyecare, optical vision, ophthalmology, laser eye surgery.
Dental Retreat in Costa Rica
http://www.edenia.com/medical/anfuba.htm. A secluded Spanish-style mansion.
Hospital Clínica Biblica Medical consultation offices; ☎ 221 3922; f 257 5252; http://www.edenia.com/medical/biblica.htm

Hospital Clínica Católica ☎ 246 3000; f 283 6171; www.clinicacatolica.com
La Florecilla ☎ 249 4161; f 249 4162; http://www.edenia.com/medical/new-you.htm. Luxurious post-operative recovery retreat.
Las Cumbres Inn Surgical Retreat ☎ 228 1011; f 228 7955; www.surgery-retreat.com
Rosenstock-Lieberman Clinic ☎ 223 9933; www.cosmetic-cr.com. Cosmetic surgery.
The Strawberry Farm ☎ 382 1081; http://www.edenia.com/medical/me11007.htm. Country recovery retreat.

SAFETY

Generally, Costa Rica is a very safe place. Violent crime against tourists is a rarity here and in most cases avoidable as long as you use common sense. Do NOT do anything in Costa Rica that you would not do in your home country. Do NOT buy drugs, party late with strangers, walk alone late at night in San José, get into a car with a stranger, flaunt cash or wear fancy jewellery. The most common crimes against tourists are pickpocketing and breaking into rental cars. If you get a flat tyre, or experience a minor roadside emergency do NOT stop and accept assistance from strangers. Instead, drive to the nearest petrol station or public place to change it. If you go looking for trouble, no matter where you are in the world, it will find you. Have fun but don't be reckless and your holiday should be free of any complications.

San José is a big city, and North American and European visitors bring expensive cameras and other things that tempt. Here are a few tips for avoiding petty theft.

- Make a photocopy of your passport and leave the original, your airline ticket and the bulk of your money in your hotel safe.
- Change money in your hotel and ask for part of it in small notes.
- Gentlemen, carry your cash, credit card and passport copy in your front pocket. Ladies, grip your purse tightly against your side. Never let a purse dangle from your shoulder.
- Carry backpacks on your front.
- Never change money in the street or flash big wads of notes.
- Avoid seedy areas of town – ask your hotel. If you find yourself in one – leave immediately!

Riptides are fast, unseen rivers of water flowing from the beach back into the ocean. Although they aren't visible, they are powerful and can be deadly. Swimmers usually don't know they're in a riptide until they realise how far from shore they suddenly are. When they try to swim back to shore and can't, they try swimming harder, which only exhausts them and can lead to drowning.

If you are caught in one, DON'T SWIM TO SHORE. Instead, swim to the right or left, parallel to the shore until you no longer feel the strong current. Swim a bit further and then into shore. Take your time, don't panic and don't try to fight the current – it will only exhaust you.

- Don't wear anything other than costume jewellery. Men, get a cheap watch for the trip.
- If you are going out at night, take a taxi.
- Don't leave money or valuables lying around your hotel room. Use the safe or check them in at the reception desk.
- Cars do not give pedestrians the right of way. Walk defensively and be very careful when crossing streets.

NOTES FOR DISABLED TRAVELLERS

With Gordon Rattray (www.able-travel.com)

I've heard it said that the harder you have to work to get there, the greater the reward will be when you eventually do. This is certainly true if you have mobility problems and wish to explore Costa Rica. Although access is improving and there is now a law mandating equal opportunities for the disabled, there is still a long way to go – to date, few hotels and public buses are accessible by wheelchair. And since Costa Rica has many other more pressing financial problems, it is unlikely to become a priority in the near future.

Carolyn Underwood, who has lived in Costa Rica for 14 years, has this to say to disabled visitors:

Costa Rica is rather a hands-on, physically involved vacation. It is not an easy country to get around, especially with the roads in such abominable condition. The terrain is rough as the tiny country is resplendent with volcanoes and tropical, dry, and cloud rainforests. It is a wonderful place to come, but it takes work to be here and enjoy all that is available.

GETTING AROUND

On foot In San José some pavements have sloped drop-offs onto the street. Furthermore, they are often crowded, narrow and difficult to navigate due to numerous cracks and pot-holes. Public streets and highways are generally in poor condition, again with many pot-holes. Newer buildings will have wide doorways and lifts to higher floors, but despite attempts by the government to bring everywhere into line, most older buildings remain inaccessible.

By car The Association of Costa Rican Special Taxis (℡ *296 6443 or 396 8986*) has a fleet of 40 wheelchair-accessible vans able to fit up to 15 people. If you use normal local taxis, the driver will usually be happy to help with transfers, but will not be trained in this skill. You must thoroughly explain your needs and stay in control of the situation.

3

Roads are often bumpy, so if you are prone to skin damage you need to take extra care by placing your own pressure-relieving cushion on top of the original car seat and if necessary, padding around knees and elbows.

It is possible to hire self-drive vehicles, but I know of no company providing cars that are adapted for disabled drivers. If you're not staying in San José, you will need to use a 4x4 vehicle, which will be higher than a normal car, making transfers more difficult.

By bus There was legislation in Costa Rica stating that all buses had to have a degree of access within eight years. This time period expired in 2006, and, unfortunately, only some companies in the San José area are in compliance.

Travelling cross-country by bus is not for the faint-hearted. The buses are often crowded and getting off and on can be a hectic affair. You will need to ask for help from fellow passengers to lift you to your seat and it is unlikely that there will be an accessible toilet. If you can cope with these difficulties then this is a more affordable option than hiring a car.

By air San José's Juan Santa María International Airport has jet-ways, wheelchair-accessible ramps, lifts, toilets and preferential lines for non-ambulant travellers. I am also assured that aisle chairs are used, allowing a dignified exit from the plane. However, domestic flights to smaller airfields might not be so trouble-free. Here, entering and exiting the aircraft may be a manhandling affair, and staff probably won't be highly trained or experienced.

ACCOMMODATION Many of Costa Rica's newest hotels have a degree of accessibility, and the more upmarket the accommodation is, the greater the chance that the rooms and bathrooms will be spacious, and that conveniences like bedside telephones will be present. That said, it is still extremely difficult to find an establishment that is fully equipped with grab handles, roll-under sinks and roll-in showers. The budget disabled traveller will struggle to find ideal lodgings, although with some research and effort, and probably some improvisation, this should be possible. Where this is not the case, you should be prepared to be lifted, or do your ablutions in the bedroom.

ACTIVITIES Most national parks and attractions lack paved trails, ramps and accessible toilets. The Rainforest Aerial Tram (⧽ *257 5961*), Poas Volcano National Park and the National Institute of Biodiversity's Biopark located in Santo Domingo de Heredia are some exceptions.

In general, no tourist highlights can be deemed easy, but none are impossible. You may need to be helped, lifted and carried over obstacles and steps, but there will usually be plenty of willing hands to do this. The most difficult aspect of these situations is being the centre of attention, and remaining in control of how you are assisted is again important. Always offer a tip, although sometimes this is not accepted.

HEALTH Doctors will know about 'everyday' illnesses, but you must understand and be able to explain your own particular medical requirements. It is wise to take all necessary medication and equipment with you and to pack this in your hand luggage during flights in case your main luggage gets lost.

Costa Rica can be hot. If this is a problem for you, be careful to book accommodation with fans or air conditioning. A useful cooling aid is a plant-spray bottle.

SECURITY The usual security precautions apply, but it is also worthwhile remembering that, as a disabled person, you are even more vulnerable. Stay aware of who is around you and where your bags are, especially during car transfers. These activities often draw a crowd, and the confusion creates easy pickings for an opportunist thief.

SPECIALIST OPERATORS There are, as yet, few operators who specialise in running disability trips in Costa Rica. Having said that, most travel companies will listen to your needs and try to create an itinerary suitable for you. For the independent traveller, it is possible to limit potential surprises by contacting local operators and establishments by email in advance.

One local agency that specialises in tours for travellers with disabilities and restricted mobility is **Vaya Con Silla de Ruedas** (\f *454 2810, 391 5045; www.gowithwheelchairs.com*) It has a ramp and elevator-equipped van and knowledgeable bilingual guides. It charges very reasonable prices and can provide anything from simple airport transfers to complete multi-day tours.

The **Costa Rica Deaf Travel Corporation** (\ *289 4812*) is a local travel agency specialising in making group and individual travel arrangements for deaf tourists. The company has deaf tour guides in ASL, English sign language, German sign language and international sign language. Costa Rica Deaf Travel was founded in 1998 and has established a relationship with the National Association of the Deaf in the US (NAD), the World Recreation Association of the Deaf (WRAD) and the Gallaudet University, bringing groups of students of biology and Spanish to learn about Costa Rica's culture, language and biodiversity.

Accessible Journeys (*www.disabilitytravel.com*) is a US-based travel agent, which offers an itinerary for disabled people and wheelchair users.

International Institute of Creative Development (\ *771 7482; www.empowermentaccess.com*) designs personalised itineraries for physically challenged travellers.

Moss Rehab ResourceNet (*www.mossresourcenet.org*) is a great source of information, tips and resources relating to accessible travel. You'll find links to a number of travel agents who specialise in planning trips for disabled travellers here and through **Access-Able Travel Source** (*www.access-able.com*), another excellent online source.

FURTHER INFORMATION For more information on any of the above topics, a helpful contact is Tim Lytle (e *info@therealcostarica.com; www.therealcostarica.com*).

GAY AND LESBIAN TRAVELLERS

Although Costa Rica is the most liberal of Central American countries, it is still Catholic, conservative and macho and public displays of same-sex affection are rare and considered somewhat shocking (in 1998, the Archbishop of San José publicly denounced homosexuality). However, Costa Rica receives a regular stream of gay and lesbian tourists who are generally treated with respect and generally do not experience any harassment. Manuel Antonio is the favoured beach spot and there are a number of hotels that cater specifically for a homosexual clientele.

The Gay Costa Rica website (*www.gaycostarica.com*) has a wide range of information. A local tour agency specialising in gay and lesbian travel is **Tiquicia Travel** (\ *236 7446; www.tiquiciatravel.com*).

The International Gay & Lesbian Travel Association (IGLTA) (*www.iglta.org*) links travellers up with gay-friendly hoteliers, tour operators, and airline and cruise-line representatives.

As prices for weddings in Europe and North America continue to skyrocket, many couples are choosing to marry in more affordable and exotic spots, such as Costa Rica. Pacific beaches are the most popular locations for weddings, thanks to their stunning sunsets, while butterfly gardens and waterfalls are also popular, followed by boutique hotels high in the mountains.

For a legal marriage, the couple must either be married in a Catholic church or have a lawyer present during the ceremony. Catholic wedding masses can only be performed in a church, so beach weddings are not possible. A good wedding lawyer will have the couple fill out an affidavit in which they swear they are legally free to marry, thus alleviating the need to have birth certificates and civil status certificates translated into Spanish and authorised by the Costa Rican consulate. There is no minimum stay policy or any need for a blood test. If eloping, the wedding planner can arrange for two witnesses to be present. After the wedding, the papers are sent to the Civil Registry, then to the embassy for authentication (ie: the British, US or Canadian) and then to the couple. The entire process can take up to four months for the papers to snake their way through the bureaucracy.

Hiring a wedding planner in Costa Rica is highly recommended, as finding reliable and professional vendors is always a challenge. Beach towns are very limited in their services (ie: no flower shops, bakeries for wedding cakes) so most wedding-related goods and services are brought in from San José. Some of the larger hotels offer wedding planning by in-house staff members, although I've heard complaints from brides about lack of communication and language barriers. There are two full-service wedding planning companies owned by North Americans living in Costa Rica: **Weddings Costa Rica** (☎ 203 5272; www.weddingscostarica.net) and **Pura Vida Weddings** (www.weddingsincostarica.com) and these would be your best bet for organising a stress-free wedding.

SENIOR CITIZENS

Be sure to mention the fact that you're a senior citizen when you first make your travel reservations because many airlines and hotels offer senior citizen discounts. While it's not common policy in Costa Rica to offer such discounts, don't be shy about asking for one anyway – you never know. Always carry some kind of identification, such as a driving licence, that shows your date of birth.

Owing to its temperate climate, stable government, low cost of living and friendly *pensionado* programme, Costa Rica is popular with retirees from North America. There are excellent medical facilities in San José and plenty of community organisations to help retirees feel at home. If you would like to learn more about applying for residency and retiring in Costa Rica, contact the **Association of Residents of Costa Rica** in San José (☎ 221 2053; www.arcr.net).

FAMILIES

Hotels in Costa Rica often give discounts for children under 12 years old, and children under three or four years old are usually allowed to stay for free. Discounts for children and the cut-off ages vary according to hotel so don't assume that your kids can stay in your room for free.

Many hotels, villas and *cabinas* come equipped with kitchenettes or full kitchen facilities. These can be a real money-saver for those travelling with children, and I've listed many of these accommodations in the destination chapters that follow.

Hotels offering regular, dependable babysitting services are few and far between. If you will require babysitting, make sure your hotel offers it, and be sure to ask whether the babysitters are bilingual, as usually they aren't. While not a problem for infants and toddlers, it can cause problems with older children.

STUDENTS AND YOUNG TRAVELLERS

Students qualify for an **International Student ID Card,** which can offer substantial savings on plane tickets, lodging and entrance fees. It also provides basic health and life insurance and a 24-hour helpline. The **International Teacher Identity Card** (ITIC) offers teachers insurance coverage as well as limited discounts. For travellers who are 25 years old or under but who are not students, the **International Youth Travel Card** (IYTC; formerly the GO 25 Card) also offers many of the same benefits. ITIC cards are valid for roughly $1^1/_2$ academic years; IYTC cards are valid for one year from the date of issue. Each of these identity cards costs US$22 or equivalent, and are available from **STA Travel** (*www.statravel.com*), the biggest student travel agency in the world. (*Note:* In 2002, STA Travel bought competitors **Council Travel** and **USIT Campus** after they went bankrupt. It's still operating some offices under the Council name, but it's owned by STA.)

Contacts are as follows: STA Travel in Australia and New Zealand; Travel CUTS (✆ *414 614 2887; www.travelcuts.com*) in Canada and the US; USIT (✆ *01 602 1600; www.usitnow.ie*) in the Republic of Ireland and Northern Ireland; SASTS in South Africa; Campus Travel and STA Travel in the UK; and Council Travel and STA Travel in the US. For a listing of issuing agencies or for more information, contact the International Student Travel Confederation (ISTC), Herengracht 479, 1017 BS Amsterdam, The Netherlands (✆ *31 20 421 28 00;* f *31 20 421 28 10;* e *istcinfo@istc.org; www.istc.org*).

Costa Rica has a network of hostels and budget hotels around the country affiliated with the International Youth Hostel Federation. Check out **Hostelling International Costa Rica** (*www.hicr.org*), or ask at the **Toruma Youth Hostel** Avenida Central, between calles 29 and 31, San José (✆ *234 8186;* ✆/f *224 4085*). Member hotels give discounts to youth and affiliated travellers, with participating hotels in Monteverde, La Fortuna, San Isidro, Jacó Beach, Liberia, Tamarindo, Puerto Viejo, Golfito, Puerto Jiménez and Rincón de la Vieja National Park.

In San José, there are two student travel agencies: **OTEC** Edificio Ferencz, 2nd floor, Calle 3 between Avenidas 1 and 3, 275m north of the National Theater (✆ *257 0166; www.otec.co.cr*) and **Sin Límites** Calle 35 and Avenida Central, 200m east of the Kentucky Fried Chicken in Los Yoses (✆ *280 5182*). If you don't already have an International Student ID Card, stop by the OTEC or Sin Límites office with proof of student status, two passport photos and a passport or other identification that shows you are under 25 years old and for about US$22, you can get an ID card.

WHAT TO TAKE

When travelling, a good rule of thumb is 'the less, the better' as being bogged down with a load of luggage only makes the journey more difficult. Plan what you're going to wear according to where you're exploring – the mountain areas are always cooler and evenings can be downright chilly so a lightweight fleece, long-sleeve shirt and long trousers are recommended (if climbing Mount Chirripó, be prepared for freezing temperatures at night). The Central Valley is usually warm in the day but cools off at night, requiring a lightweight jacket or jumper. The Caribbean, central/south Pacific and Osa Peninsula are very humid and hot so lightweight clothing made of technologically advanced wicking fabrics (such as CoolMax, Dryskin, Powerdry, Dri-Tech) are highly recommended, especially if you plan on hiking, as these will keep you drier and more comfortable. If spending time at the beach areas, shorts and T-shirts are perfect anytime of the day.

In general, avoid 100% cotton clothing when travelling in the tropics, as it is a fabric that does not dry quickly (remember that most areas here are extremely humid and electric clothing driers are few and far between) – look instead for a cotton/polyester blend or, preferably, wicking fabrics. Highly recommended is hiking/adventure clothing found in specialist outdoor stores – a pair of lightweight trousers with zip-off legs (trousers and shorts in one) is one of the best purchases you can make for your trip as it will play double-duty, weighs almost nothing and takes up virtually no space in a suitcase. Good walking shoes are recommended as are a pair of flip-flops for the beach and sport sandals/running shoes for any activities or tours. If you plan on horseback riding, a pair of long trousers is a necessity to prevent chafing. A lightweight sun hat (such as a Tilley) is also recommended.

A good practice is to always have tissues or toilet paper on hand, as not every bathroom will have it. Most hotels will have soap and towels but if you're really 'roughing it', it's wise to bring your own as well as a clean sheet as some places have dodgy beds. Although toiletries are found in virtually every *pulpería* throughout the land, women are advised to bring along their own supply of tampons as sanitary pads are more commonly used by *Ticas*. Insect repellant is an essential as is suncream (after-bite and sunburn cream are also recommended). Unless you are camping, don't bother packing mosquito netting.

Electricity is 110 volts AC, 60Hz (same as in North America) and usually two-pin. It's easier to bring an adaptor than buy one in Costa Rica. Power surges happen on a seemingly hourly basis so be sure to unplug your appliances when not in use – sensitive equipment (such as computers or high-end digital cameras) should have a surge protector. A battery-powered or wind-up travel alarm clock is recommended. If travelling with a group or family, a set of walkie-talkies can be a godsend and are recommended if staying at hotels with no phones in the rooms.

A regular driver's licence is all you need to rent a vehicle. I recommend making photocopies of the photo/info and date-stamp pages of your passport, keeping these with you at all times and locking away your original passport in the safe.

Bring along a Spanish dictionary/phrasebook – although English is widely spoken in larger hotels and tourist areas, learning even a few rudimentary phrases in Spanish will make your adventure more interesting (and easier). Like they say, 'When in Rome ...'

ELECTRICITY

Costa Rica uses the US standards of 110 volts AC, 60Hz. Three-pin earthed plugs are very uncommon, so if you have equipment that needs this type of plug, be sure to bring an adapter or buy one at an electrical store.

$ MONEY

The national currency is the **colon**, named in honour of Christopher Columbus. High devaluation has seen the colon take a beating in recent years and at the time of writing, July 2006, the exchange rate was 515 colones to one US dollar. Most businesses involved with tourism set their prices in US dollars and both currencies are readily accepted by hotels, restaurants, tour companies and souvenir shops. If driving, make sure to have some colon coins with you for toll-booths. Bills come in 1,000 colones, 2,000 colones, 5,000 colones and 10,000 colones, all of which are brightly coloured and fairly artistic. You will undoubtedly find your pockets weighed down by large amounts of coins (which are heavy and big), ranging from the almost worthless 1 colon to 5 colones, 10 colones, 25 colones, 100 colones and 500 colones.

Carry a supply of **US dollars** with you when you are travelling in Costa Rica. As the local currency is on a fixed devaluation schedule with the US dollar, you will almost always get the best rate of exchange.

As most vendors give discounts for using cash, **credit cards** can prove expensive by comparison, as credit-card merchant companies charge high percentages on transactions in Costa Rica and many vendors will subsequently tack on an additional 4–13% fee if you do pay by credit card. Some vendors do not accept credit cards, while many take only Visa.

Although accepted by most large establishments, you will usually be charged an exchange commission fee of 2–5% for using **travellers' cheques**. Many smaller businesses will not accept travellers' cheques at all.

When you arrive, you may **exchange** your money at any local bank or most of the upmarket hotels (if you are one of their guests). Note that you will get a better exchange rate at banks. As US currency is widely used and accepted, it is recommended that you bring US dollar bills and travellers' cheques as many places will not accept pounds sterling, euro or Canadian dollars.

BUDGETING Allow US$20–25 per day for additional meals/beverages not included in your trip price, and US$60–125 for tips (tips for guides, cooks and porters are at your discretion). Be sure to have US$26 in cash or on your credit card for the airport departure tax.

Car-rental costs are high here as insurance is state-run, vehicles have a high import tax and there simply aren't a lot of vehicles in the country. Be prepared to pay a damage deposit of US$1,500 and upwards of US$100 a day for car rental and insurance.

Costa Rica has an extensive, inexpensive bus system that will take you to beaches, national parks, cities, small villages and other Central American countries at a nominal cost. Sit back, relax and watch the passing panorama while someone else deals with the driving!

Budget travel in Costa Rica is less expensive than the United States, Canada or Europe but it is not as inexpensive as you might think for a Central American country, as both the cost and standard of living are higher here.

Shoestring: US$20–35 per person per day

Accommodation It's much easier to stay within this budget range if you have a travel companion to share lodging costs. Low-cost places to stay range from US$15–30 per person per night. You should expect a very clean, safe room in prime locations, such as on the beach or within walking distance of a national park, volcano or other attraction. You might want to consider making reservations for a few nights' lodging in this price range if there is a particular place you really want to stay, but you should almost never have trouble finding a room.

Transport The local bus (all the way across the country takes about seven hours and costs US$7) will probably be your main form of transportation. There will be room in the budget for an occasional minibus journey (faster, more comfortable, more convenient and more likely to have an English-speaking driver), taxi and even internal flight.

1 litre of bottled water	850 colones
Bottle of beer	450 colones
Loaf of bread	350 colones
Street snack	500 colones (though these are not recommended)
Mars Bar	450 colones
Postcard	150 colones
T-shirt	5,000 colones
Camera film (24 pictures)	3,800 colones
1 litre of unleaded petrol	526 colones

Food Most of your breakfasts and lunches will be in small family-run restaurants called *sodas*, but there is room in the budget for a couple of beers or a glass of wine with a nice dinner at a beachfront restaurant every once in a while.

Activities Most of what you do will involve walking, which is the best way to explore the rainforests, cloudforests, tropical dry forests and beaches. There is room in the budget for guides (which are highly recommended), horserides, boat trips, tours of coffee farms, and entrance fees to botanical gardens and private reserves. If you have never tried it before, take a suggestion from the super budget category and offer to help pick coffee, work on a fishing boat, round up cattle, or anything else you see going on where you might be useful.

Moderate: US$35–80 per person per day
Accommodation It is much easier to travel solo in this budget category than in the lower-price ranges. Hotels are the biggest cost for solo travellers as the cost for a single room is generally about the same as a double, and a triple or quad is usually not much more. A couple travelling in this price range will probably spend around US$40–90 a night for lodging. In this price range it will also be necessary to make reservations during the high season and it is recommended to make reservations during the green season.

Transport Public buses, taxis and minibuses, such as Grayline or Interbus.

Activities Surfing, horseriding, nature hikes, guided tours through mangroves and river rafting.

Expensive: US$85–195 per person per day
Accommodation Reservations are absolutely essential at all times for travel in this price range. A couple travelling will usually spend from US$100–150 per night for lodging.

Transport Private minibus transfers, Grayline, Interbus transfers, commuter flights and rental cars are all possibilities.

Activities Sailing day trips, sport fishing.

Luxury: US$200+ per person per day
Luxury travel in Costa Rica costs almost exactly the same amount as luxury travel anywhere else. Although your *Tico* golf caddy or busboy might be making less than US$2 per hour, the resorts are owned by American, Canadian or European corporations whose executives and

shareholders wouldn't accept Costa Rican wages or returns on their investments. There is currently a lively debate taking place in Costa Rica about the pros and cons of international resort development.

Your travel agent or tour company websites can give you a description of what to expect when travelling in this budget category. If you would like to save some money while travelling in this price range you should consider a trip during the green season.

TIPPING Generally, tip like you would in your own country. Restaurants automatically add a 10% service charge plus 13% tax by law so your bill is automatically 23% higher. If you receive exceptional service, leave an additional 10%. For porters, 250 colones (about 50 cents) per bag is a fair gratuity. For tour guides, follow the guidelines for each company or again, tip like you would in your own country for similar services. Taxi drivers are usually not tipped but if you feel like doing so, the driver will be most appreciative.

GETTING AROUND

BUSES Costa Rica's public bus system is excellent, cheap and quite frequent, even in remote areas. Getting anywhere by bus with a lot of baggage can be a problem – many people travel light, leaving the bulk of their baggage somewhere secure (a San José hotel, for example) while on the road. The most expensive journey in the country (from Puerto Jiménez on the Osa Peninsula, to San José) costs US$7, while fares in the mid- to long-distance range are US$2.50–5. Tickets on most mid- to long-distance and popular routes are issued with a date and a seat number and you are expected to sit in the seat indicated. Make sure the date is correct – even if the mistake is not yours, you cannot change your ticket or get a refund. You cannot purchase return bus tickets on Costa Rican buses, which can be quite inconvenient if heading to very popular destinations like Monteverde, Jacó and Manuel Antonio at busy times – you'll need to jump off the bus as soon as you arrive and buy your return ticket immediately to assure yourself a seat.

On the most popular buses, like the service to Golfito, it's advisable to book in advance though you may be lucky and get on without a reservation. Services to popular tourist areas in high season – especially Monteverde – get booked up very quickly so buy your ticket several days ahead of travel. For information on bus timetables check www.yellowweb.co.cr/crbuses.html.

Though most Costa Rican buses are fairly decent, the best of the bunch – arguably the best in Central America – is **Ticabus** (✆ *221 8954; www.ticabus.com*) which runs the border routes from San José to Panamá and Nicaragua. They have comfortable seats, adequate baggage space, air conditioning and very courteous drivers.

San José is the hub for virtually all bus services in the country and it's often impossible to travel from one place to another without backtracking to the capital. Different companies have semi-monopolies on various regions.

Another option is the semi-private buses operated by **Interbus** (✆ *283 5573; www.interbusonline.com*) and **Grayline** (✆ *220 2126; www.graylinecostarica.com*) offering door-to-door service from points throughout the country on air-conditioned micro-buses. These trips must be pre-booked and paid. Most fares will cost about US$25 (ie: San José to Arenal) and is definitely more comfortable and faster than public buses.

TAXIS Taxis are available for both short- and long-distance trips, although they are pricey if travelling outside of San José. Look for licensed cabs, which are red with a yellow triangle painted on the door. By law, they are required to use the *maria* (meter) and if they don't turn it on, ask them to *'ponga la maria por favor'*. If they refuse, ask them to stop and hail another cab. Note that they usually won't use the *maria* for trips outside of San José so agree upon a price beforehand. The fare from San José to the airport, for example, is around US$13, although the official airport taxis (which are orange and operate out of the airport), cost more. You can either hail a cab on the street or call ahead for one.

Taxi companies in San José are **CoopeTico** (✆ *235 9966, 224 7979*), **Alfaro** (✆ *221 8466*), **Taxis Coopeguraria** (✆ *227 9300*) or **Taxis Unidos Aeropuerto** (✆ *221 6865*) if going to the airport.

There are unofficial taxis called *piratas* (pirates), which may be just a guy in a car or a car that looks like an official taxi (although the home paint job is usually a dead giveaway). Most of the time, they won't have a *maria* or if they do, it's most likely rigged. They may be cheaper but if they see you're a tourist, don't bet on it. If travelling late at night, do not use a *pirata* – a *Tico* friend of mine coming home from his late-night DJ job was held up at knifepoint by the driver. Better to pay the extra dollar or two for safety's sake.

Taxis are usually *piratas* once you get outside of San José and prices tend to be higher than in the city (like the time I was charged 1,600 colones in Manuel Antonio to be driven just 300m as the driver's argument was he had to come in from Quepos).

Make sure you have small notes and if you receive good service, a tip is a nice (and unexpected) gesture (see *Tipping* above).

RENTAL CARS Exploring the country by car is a great way to see the sights at your leisure but it can be stressful and driving defensively is strongly recommended. You must have a passport and be at least 21 years old to drive in Costa Rica and a foreign driving licence is valid for three months. Make sure you always have your passport or a copy of your passport and entry stamp with you and to wear your seat belt, as it has recently become law.

Be careful driving everywhere but especially in San José where traffic can get rather fierce, and be aware of pot-holes. If travelling in more remote areas, check with the locals on the road conditions before venturing out, as many roads disappear during the rainy season. Avoid driving from town to town at night, as unfamiliarity with the roads combined with poor driving conditions can be extremely stressful and potentially dangerous. Roads are often unmarked, unlit and some bridges lack railings. Pavements are virtually non-existent outside of the cities so be aware of pedestrians, cyclists and animals on the highways (in Guanacaste, it's not unusual to be stuck behind a cattle drive). Many bridges are one-way only and the side that has the *ceda* (yield sign) must give way to cars coming the other way. When driving through the mountains, be extremely careful as drivers will often pass on a double-yellow line around a blind corner. With the second-highest mortality rate from traffic accidents in the world, Costa Ricans are notoriously bad drivers. While laid back and relaxed in daily life, they become impatient speed demons when sat behind the wheel of a car (my theory is that they vent all their pent-up emotions when driving, like a pressure valve of the psyche taken to the national level). Take it easy and don't follow their lead.

You have to exercise caution when renting a car in Costa Rica – companies have been known to claim for damage they insist you caused to their vehicle. By far the best policy is to rent a car through a Costa Rican travel agent or tour operator.

Car rental in Costa Rica is expensive. Expect to pay about US$400 per week for a regular (non-4x4) vehicle, including insurance, and up to US$500 for a 4x4. I do not recommend that you rent anything other than a 4x4 on account of the poor road conditions throughout the country and because some routes, such as Monteverde, are accessible only with a 4x4. If you're renting a vehicle, it's worth the peace of mind to pay the bit extra for a 4x4 that will allow you better access and which is less likely to be damaged.

Your Visa or MasterCard will be charged a damage deposit (usually US$1,000–1,500) on picking up your vehicle – if returned in safe condition, the damage deposit will be refunded back to your card. As most rental car companies are centred in San José, pickups and dropoffs will occur there – otherwise, you will be charged a fee for dropping off in another town (Adobe Rental Car has free dropoff to major tourist towns). In my experience, the best rental car company, for service and quality of vehicles, is Adobe Rental Car. Highly recommended!

Adobe ☏ 258 4242; www.adobe.com
Dollar Rent A Car ☏ 443 2950; www.dollarcostarica.com

Economy Rent A Car ☏ 442 5100; www.economyrentacar.com

The speed limit on the highways is either 75km/h or 90km/h as marked on the roadside or on signs. If you're caught speeding you could find yourself paying a fine of US$12 to US$150. If stopped by a *transito* (transit cop), be courteous. If they are hinting for a bribe, insist on being given a ticket *('Deme el parte')*.

Fuel is positively cheap by European standards but expensive by North American – expect to pay about US$40 a tank on a medium-sized vehicle or about US$60 for a big 4x4.

Never leave your car in an unguarded area and never leave anything of value inside. If you park on the street in San José, you'll undoubtedly be approached by a *wachiman*, a fellow in a reflective vest carrying a large stick. He'll watch your car for you and will expect a few coins when you return (I usually give 600 colones or so).

TRAINS Since the 1991 earthquake, there has been no train service in Costa Rica, as the lines were severely damaged and the repair costs simply too prohibitive. In 2006, the city of San José started offering train service during peak traffic hours to

Driving in Costa Rica is an adventure sport in its own right and you'll need all the help you can get. If you see a large tree branch on the road, it is most likely a warning that a disabled vehicle is ahead. If oncoming cars are flashing their headlights, there is a *transito* or even an accident ahead of you. A good practice is to drive with your lights on at all times, as they do in Canada or Scandinavia – the more visible you are, the safer you are.

Be aware of pot-holes, which are stunning in their size and number. Hitting a bad pot-hole can seriously damage your car or leave you with a flat tyre so watch the cars ahead of you and if they're swerving, they're dodging pot-holes.

If you do get a flat tyre, drive to the first *bomba* (gas station) you see and change it there. I know of tourists who've had a nice young man stop to help them and steal their purses out of the car. If you have a breakdown, call the rental car company and they will send out a tow truck.

If you're involved in an accident, DO NOT MOVE YOUR CAR until the *transitos* and INS (the insurance officials) arrive, as they must take photos and measurements first. Do not allow the other driver to leave the scene, move their car or try to make a deal with you. Take down the name, licence and *cedula* (identification number) of any witnesses. Call the police (☎ *222 9330*). In case of injury, call the Red Cross (☎ *128 or 911*). Call your rental car company as well.

Note that *transitos* can only issue a summons or a ticket – they are not allowed to accept any payment. Instructions for fine payment at the bank are written on the ticket. Neither can they impound the vehicle or take away your driving licence.

Best to drive with caution and within the speed limit.

---

ease congestion. The route presently runs from the east side (near the University of Costa Rica) to the west (Sabana area) with runs to Cartago in the plans.

CYCLING Costa Rica's terrain makes cycling a pleasure – indeed, it's easier to dodge the pot-holes and wandering cattle on a bike than in a car – and the range of places to stay and eat means you don't need to carry a tent. There is very little traffic outside the Valle Central, and Costa Rican drivers tend to be courteous to cyclists. Be warned, however, that if you cycle up to Monteverde, one of the most popular routes in the country, you're in for a slow trip – besides being steep, there's not much traction on the loose gravel roads.

San José's best cycle shop is Bicimania, at the corner of Paseo Colón and C 26. They have all the parts you might need, can fix your bike, and may even be able to give you a bicycle carton for the plane.

AIRLINES Costa Rica's two domestic air carriers offer fairly economical scheduled services between San José and many beach destinations and provincial towns. Sansa is the state-owned domestic airline and NatureAir is its commercial competitor. Both fly small twin-propeller aircraft, servicing the same destinations. Of the two, NatureAir (which flies from Tobias Bolaños Airport in Pavas, 7km west of San José) is more reliable, and more frequent on some runs. Sansa (which flies from Juan Santamaría Airport, 17km northwest of San José) is cheaper but less reliable – make your reservations as far as possible in advance and even then be advised that a booking means almost nothing until the seat is actually paid for. Reconfirm your flight in advance of the day of departure and once more on the day of departure, if possible, as schedules are likely to change at short notice. Both Sansa and NatureAir have different timetables in the dry and rainy seasons and change their flight schedules each year, so check their websites (see below) for up-to-date information.

Important note: the baggage limit on internal flights is only 12kg (24lb) per person. Furthermore, during the green season it is advisable to take morning flights whenever possible as afternoon flights are susceptible to cancellation on account of bad weather.

Sansa ↷ 221 9414; www.flysansa.com   **NatureAir** ↷ 220 3054; www.natureair.com

ACCOMMODATION

Visitors will find everything from hostels to homestays and eco-lodges to elegant five-star hotels in every corner of the country. Generally, prices are highest during the high season (December to April) and drop by roughly 20% during the green season (May to November). The holiday weeks of Easter and Christmas are peak travel times and hotels increase rates and impose minimum-stay policies on account of the overwhelming demand for rooms. At the time of writing, Costa Rica was facing a room shortage, as the number of tourists has steadily been increasing yet the number of hotel rooms in the country has not kept pace. Therefore, it is HIGHLY recommended that travellers pre-book hotel reservations, especially in medium- to upper-range hotels.

Accommodation prices are quoted in US dollars, because of the daily devaluation of the colon. By law, hotels must charge 13% sales tax and 3.39% room tax (prices are usually posted at the pre-tax rate).

Budget accommodation encompasses hostels, small *cabinas*, rooms and rural homestays, ranging in price from US$8 to US$25. Backpackers can log on to www.costarica.backpackers.com for information on where to stay. **International Hostelling** (↷ 234 8186; *www.youth-hostels-in.com/costarica-hostels.htm*) has 23 affiliated hotels in Costa Rica – look on their website for more information or call their head office in the Toruma Hostel in San José. Rates range from US$10–18 per night. Language schools often offer homestays as part of their courses. For those who would like to homestay on their own can contact **Bell's Home Hospitality** (↷ 225 4752; *www.homestay.thebells.org*) who will connect you with a suitable host family. Rates are around US$64 per double with private bath and dinner.

Rural co-operatives offering a 'true *Tico*' experience are another option for those who want to travel off the beaten path but stay on a budget. Tours are in remote areas, usually staying in basic accommodation, allowing guests to experience first-hand the lifestyle of the people in that community. Not only is community tourism opening up new areas to visitors, it's making a positive impact on the communities, giving them new avenues to augment their often limited resources. COOPRENA RL is a network that assists and markets rural co-operatives through their agency **Simbiosis Tours** (↷ 248 2538; *www.turismoruralcr.com*). They have lodges in the Osa Peninusla, Arenal and Monteverde, for example, and opportunities to stay with indigenous groups and on working farms. **Cultourica** (↷ 249 1271; *www.cultourica.com*) specialises in ecological tourism. **Real Places, Real People** (↷ 810 4444; e *info@realplaces.net*) offers single- or multi-day tours to a variety of farming and indigenous communities.

Eco-tourism is the hot ticket in Costa Rica and numerous hotels have jumped on the bandwagon, even when the only 'eco' thing about them is their concern for economics. In an effort to discern the real green hotels from those who only think of greenbacks, the Costa Rican Tourism Board (ICT) has created the Certificate for Sustainable Tourism, awarded to hotels after a rigorous assessment is

GALLO PINTO (RICE AND BEANS) – BREAKFAST

Ingredients:
Butter
1 onion, finely chopped
450g (1lb) cooked beans
2 cups white rice, cooked
Salt and pepper
Salsa Lizano

In a large frying pan melt the butter and fry the onion until golden and transparent. Add the beans and continue frying. Add the rice and cook over low heat until the mixture is dry. Season to taste with Salsa Lizano.

SOPA DE FRIJOLES NEGROS (BLACK-BEAN SOUP)

Ingredients:
450g (1lb) black beans
1 tablespoon of cooking oil
$1/2$ cup diced onion
2 cloves of garlic (chopped)
1 chopped green or red bell pepper
$1/2$ cup chopped celery
$1/2$ cup fresh coriander (use fresh only!)
Salt and pepper to taste.

Rinse beans, cover with water and soak overnight.
Next day cook with at least 7 cups of water for 3 hours.
Add more water if necessary. When almost soft, add the rest of the ingredients.

Hints for serving:
Add fresh lemon juice, tabasco, sour cream, chives or green onions to enhance flavour.

conducted in which marks are given for eco-friendly buildings, responsible use of resources and involvement and care of the community. Rankings are out of a possible five 'leaves' and hotels sporting the ICT Green Leaf sign are certified. To learn more, contact the ICT (✆ 257 2264; *www.turismo-sostenible.co.cr*).

The Costa Rican Hotel Association (✆ 248 0990; f 222 6716; *www.costaricanhotels.com*) is a good source of information on medium to upper-end hotels. For further information on camping, see pages 69–70.

✖ EATING

The cheapest places to eat in Costa Rica, and where most workers eat lunch, their main meal, are the ubiquitous *sodas*, halfway between the North American diner and the British greasy café. *Sodas* offer filling set *platos del día* (daily specials) and *casados*, for about US$3. Most menus will have a vegetarian option, and asking for dishes to be served without meat is perfectly acceptable.

The greater San José area has a wide variety of dining. Dining options are more limited in the beach towns, although there are some exceptional restaurants in Tamarindo ('Pachanga') Manuel Antonio ('Marlin') and Santa Teresa (the restaurant at 'Flor Blanca'). In general, the seafood is amazing and you can't go wrong with a dinner of *mahi-mahi* (Dorado) or tuna. In San José, Asian, Italian, French and international cuisine are all readily available. Some of our favourites in San José:

Or add one or two eggs, cook for another three minutes and serve with flour or corn tortillas.

ENSALADA DE REPOLLO (CABBAGE SALAD)

Ingredients:
1 whole cabbage
3 ripe tomatoes
Vinegar or lemon
Salt

Dice whole cabbage very fine. Dice tomatoes in small squares. Combine cabbage and tomatoes, sprinkle mixture with vinegar or fresh lemon juice. Add salt to taste.

ARROZ CON LECHE (RICE PUDDING)

Ingredients:
225g ($\frac{1}{2}$ lb) of uncooked rice
4 cups milk
4 cups sugar
1 tablespoon vanilla
$\frac{1}{2}$ teaspoon powder cinnamon (or sticks)
$\frac{1}{2}$ teaspoon powder cloves or 6 whole cloves
$\frac{1}{2}$ teaspoon of nutmeg
112g (1 stick) of butter
Raisins (optional)

Cook rice with 8 cups of water for 45 minutes until rice is almost mushy (add more water if needed or milk for smoother texture). When soft add all other ingredients. Stir together and let it simmer for 30 minutes on low heat. Serve hot or refrigerate and serve cold. A very popular dish.

Tin Jo – Asian and Thai dishes, located just off Avenida 2 in downtown San José
Ceviche del Rey – Award-winning Peruvian food in Santa Ana
Moby Dick – Incredible sushi at incredibly affordable prices in San Pedro near Jazz Café (Main Avenue)
Isle de France – Authentic French cuisine in the Hotel Le Bergerac in Los Yoses (San Pedro)
La Princesa Marina – Very affordable local-style seafood restaurant near the Parque La Sabana
Café Mundo – Hip, international cuisine and trendy atmosphere in Barrio Amon.

Because Costa Ricans start the day early, they are less likely to hang about late in restaurants in the evening and establishments are usually empty or closed by 22.00–22.30. Waiters tend to leave you alone (almost to the point of ignoring you) unless they are called for. Non-smoking sections are uncommon, to say the least, except in the most expensive establishments; if you're looking for a smoke-free environment, try the vegetarian *sodas*.

COSTA RICAN FOOD

Ticos call their cuisine *comida típica* (native food). Simple it may be, but tasty nonetheless, especially when it comes to interesting regional variations on the

Caribbean coast (Creole cooking) and in Guanacaste (where there are vestiges of the ancient indigenous peoples' love of maize, or corn).

Dishes you'll find all over Costa Rica usually include rice, beans and some kind of meat or fish, often served as part of a special plate with coleslaw salad, in which case it is called a *casado* (literally, 'married person'). The ubiquitous *gallo pinto* ('painted rooster') is a breakfast combination of red and white beans with rice, sometimes served with *huevos revueltos* (scrambled eggs). You should also try *ceviche* (raw fish marinated in lime juice with coriander and peppers), *pargo* (red snapper), *corvina* (sea bass), and fresh fruit.

Costa Rica offers a cornucopia of fresh fruits and vegetables and the best place to buy fresh produce is the local markets. Each town has a weekly market, usually on a Saturday or Sunday morning, held in the town square or on the street. They usually open around 06.00 and run until noon, although the freshest products are found at the beginning of the day. Prices are very reasonable and it's a great way to interact with the locals.

MEALS Costa Rican cuisine is very simple, boring almost to some. Carbohydrates are paramount to the *Tico* diet and it's not unusual to have bread, pasta, rice and potatoes in one meal (needless to say, the Atkins diet was a bust in Costa Rica). The most common Costa Rican dish is the *casado*, consisting of rice, beans, fried sweet plantains, a piece of meat or fish and a *picadillo* (vegetables diced and cooked with condiments, sometimes with ground beef, a portion of salad and, if you get the real deal, a fried egg on top). The name of this dish is a *Tico* joke, as once married, a husband receives the same thing all the time, both in the *casado* dish and in the marriage.

Gallo pinto is also a local favourite and a staple of any *Tico* diet. A mixture of rice and beans fried with seasonings like red peppers, onions and the indispensable dash of *Salsa Lizano*, a famous local sauce made from tamarind. *Gallo pinto* is usually eaten for breakfast along with a few eggs, bread, *natilla* (sour cream) and, of course, a steaming cup of coffee.

Other popular dishes are *arroz con pollo* (rice and chicken), *mondongo* soup (made with tripe) or *olla de carne* in which meat and vegetables such as potato, chayote, plantain, corn and carrots, are cooked for hours until a delicious and nutritious broth is formed.

The Caribbean has a unique cooking style, utilising coconut milk in dishes like rice and beans, *pan bon* (a heavy cake-type bread), and the delicious *ron don* (a soup of vegetables and fish or whatever they can 'run down'). Seasoned *patties*, turnover-type pasties filled with spicy ground meat, are also a Caribbean treat. In the Pacific port town of Puntarenas, you'll find almost all of their dishes are seafood based, with specialities like *arroz con mariscos* (rice with seafood) and *corvina al ajillo* (fish fillets cooked in garlic butter).

Ticos have an incredibly sweet tooth, love of rice and fondness for milk. Not surprisingly, their favourite dessert dishes are *arroz con leche* (like rice pudding) and *tres leches* (a cake soaked in a mixture of condensed, evaporated and regular milk).

DRINKING

Mellow-tasting Costa Rican coffee is among the best in the world and it's usual to end a meal with a small cup – the coffee is traditionally served in a jug with a separate jug of heated milk. The best blends are graded for export, but you can buy them in stores and many are served at some cafés. Also good are *refrescos*, cool drinks made with *leche* (milk) or *agua* (water), fruit and ice, all whipped up in a blender. You can buy them at stalls or in cartons, though the latter tend to be sugary. You'll find herb teas throughout the country and those served in Limón are especially good. In Guanacaste you can get the distinctive corn-based drinks *horchata* and *pinolillo,* made with milk and sugar and with a grainy consistency.

Sugar finds its way into all kinds of drinks, even water. *Agua dulce*, another popular *campesino* (farmer) drink, is boiled water with brown sugar – energy for field workers. Roadside stalls also sell *pipas*, green coconuts with the tops chopped off so you can drink the refreshing cool milk through a straw.

In addition to the many imported American beers, Costa Rica has a few local brands, which are excellent. Most popular is Imperial (American-style light draught), followed by Bavaria (sweeter, more substantial and slightly nutty). Heineken is brewed under licence here and is pretty close to the original brewed in Holland. Of the local low-alcohol beers, Bavaria Light is a good option.

There is an indigenous hard-liquor drink, *guaro*, of which Cacique is the most popular brand. It's a bit rough, but good with fresh watermelon juice. For an after-dinner drink, try Café Rica, a rich liqueur made with the local coffee.

NIGHTLIFE

Ticos love to party and the number of bars, discos and restaurants is testament to their lust for nightlife (note – a 'nightclub' is a strip bar so be careful to not use this term for a disco or bar). Football (soccer) is the second religion in Costa Rica and bars with big-screen televisions are usually packed on Wednesday nights, when the local professional teams have matches. The drinking age is 18 and most bars in urban areas will ask for identification from young-looking people.

Most typical *Tico* bars serve small servings of snacks called *bocas* (the Spanish word for 'mouth') featuring local dishes such as *patacones con frijoles molidos* (fried plantains with refried beans), *ceviche* (raw fished cooked in lemon), *frijoles blancos con cerdo* (white beans cooked with pork) and the all-time favourite, *chicharrones* (fried pork rinds). *Bocas* are a great way to taste *Tico* foods and their low prices are easy on the purse.

One of the most popular spots in San José for partying is **El Pueblo**, located in the north area of the city. It's a mix of bars, clubs, restaurants and shops in a picturesque 'old town' setting with cobblestone streets and colonial-style architecture. Here you find souvenir shops, art galleries, restaurants and thumping clubs with everything from hip-hop to Latin to Top 40 hits. Clubs usually get rocking around 23.00 and close in the wee hours of the morning. Note: thieves have been known to target tourists at El Pueblo so do be wary.

The university crowd hangs out on Calle de Amarguro (literally 'Road of Bitterness') in San Pedro where weekends see the street packed with wall-to-wall people going to the seemingly endless bars. More upmarket partygoers head to Escazú on the west side of the city, where the shopping parade at Trejos Montealegre has a number of popular clubs. Those who seek jazz can find it at the **Jazz Cafe** (❄ *253 8933*) on the main drag in San Pedro.

Being casual dressers, *Ticos* don't dress up to go clubbing or out for dinner as they do in more cosmopolitan cities so feel free to wear jeans.

PUBLIC HOLIDAYS AND FESTIVALS

Costa Rica is a Catholic country and its holidays are mostly Church-related. Most businesses, including banks, close on official holidays. The country closes down entirely during the biggest holiday time, Easter Holy Week, but only during Holy Thursday, Friday and Saturday – on Holy Sunday, some services might be available, but don't count on it in remote parts of the country. Buses stop running on Holy Thursday and Good Friday while banks and offices are closed. Easter is a perfect opportunity to see colourful religious processions, including Passion parades that recreate Christ's Stations of the Cross. Entire towns get involved, dressing up as Roman centurions and other characters. Note: alcohol sales are prohibited from Holy Thursday until midnight on Good Friday, although tourist hotels are exempt.

Individual towns also celebrate their patron saint's day and highlights usually include a procession, bullfights, rodeos, dancing, and other parades. Fireworks and firecrackers are a popular part of local fiestas and Church celebrations.

PUBLIC HOLIDAYS This is the list of the main and official holidays in Costa Rica.

1 January	New Year's Day
19 March	St Joseph's Day, patron saint of San José and San José province
Easter	Holy Week, Semana Santa. Dates vary annually but businesses will often close for the entire week preceding Easter weekend.
11 April	Juan Santamaría Day. Public holiday to commemorate the national hero who fought at the Battle of Rivas against the American invader William Walker in 1856.
1 May	Labour Day. Dia de los Trabajadores.
29 June	St Peter and St Paul's Day
25 July	Guanacaste Day. Marks the annexation of Guanacaste from Nicaragua in 1824.
2 August	Virgin de los Angeles Day. Patron saint of Costa Rica.
15 August	Mother's Day and Assumption Day
15 September	Independence Day, with big patriotic parades, celebrates Costa Rica's independence from Spain in 1821
12 October	Cultures Day (Columbus Day)
2 November	All Souls' Day
8 December	Immaculate Conception of the Virgin Mary
25 December	Christmas Day

FESTIVALS Arts festivals abound, attracting performers from all over the world. If you're in the country, don't miss the opportunity to take in a show.

The International Arts and Music Festival (✆ 221 2154; e ilerojas@ costarricense.cr) is held in March and features all disciplines. Performances take place not only in theatres but open-air venues, galleries and even resorts in different parts of the country. Tickets are extremely reasonable.

The Monteverde Music Festival (✆ 645 5053; www.mvinstitute.org) has music and nature in sweet harmony together. Held annually in February and March (peak toucan and quetzal birding season), national and international musicians perform in this beautiful but remote cloudforest, raising funds for the local school music programme.

The South Caribbean Music Festival (✆ 750 0062; www.playachiquita.com/ festival.htm) gets groovin' at the Playa Chiquita Lodge in Puerto Viejo from March to May, with proceeds supporting various programmes in the area.

SHOPPING

Shop for replicas of pre-Columbian jewellery, pottery, miniature oxcarts, jewellery made of semi-precious stones, hand-painted feathers, woodcarvings and leather goods. Don't expect to find the array of inexpensive, high-quality handmade articles available in some Central American countries, such as Guatemala or even Nicaragua, as Costa Rica does not have a rich handicraft tradition. For local treats such as coffee, rum, coffee liqueur, macadamia nuts and hearts of palm, try shopping at grocery stores or roadside *pulperias* – the prices are usually much better than in gift shops, and you'll find a wider selection. Coffee is cheap (and world class) in Costa Rica and easily accessible as a law requires that a portion of the annual crop remains in the country for domestic consumption (Cafe Britt and Doka Estate/Three Generations are my two favourite brands and both companies now offer a delivery service to North America while arrangements can be made to ship to Europe.

San José has some of the best options for shopping (though it may seem at first glance that every other shop is a shoe shop or a photography studio). At weekends, vendors set up shop in Plaza de la Cultura to sell T-shirts, leather goods, jewellery and handicrafts. The stalls on the west end of the Plaza de la Democracia have similar goods. The crowded Central Market has practically everything – from fresh produce to souvenirs. Across the street is the Flower Market, which has more handicraft items. The National Artisans Market sells reproductions of pre-Columbian gold jewellery and woodcarvings, and the souvenir marketplace at La Casona offers a substantial supply of affordable gifts.

ARTS AND ENTERTAINMENT

Although art is not the first thing people think about in association with Costa Rica, this small country has a thriving arts and entertainment scene – San José is said to have the most theatres per capita in the world. In addition to a thriving thespian scene, there are festivals (see *Festivals* above), galleries and live music to suit all tastes.

In general, theatres and art galleries are found in San José although there is an amateur theatre group in Dominical that presents shows once a year or so as well as small art galleries featuring local artists in Tamarindo, Monteverde and Manuel Antonio.

MUSIC Music lovers can relish the sweet sounds of *marimba*, the bouncy rhythm of *cumbia* or chill out to jazz, all in the same day. For symphony lovers, the **National Symphony Orchestra** (✆ 236 6669) hosts guest conductors and artists from all over the globe and is a world-class organisation in its own right. The March to November season has performances at the historic National Theatre every Friday evening and Sunday morning at a cost of only a few dollars.

The jazz/new age/Latin trio **Editus** put Costa Rican music on the map after winning two Grammy awards for their work on the Ruben Blades albums, *Timepos* (1999) and *XXX (*2003). Keep an eye open for their performances around the country or check out San José's **Jazz Café**, where they have regular gigs.

Other notable *Tico* groups are **Marfil** (big band with reggae, Latin music), **Manuel Obregon** (piano), **Mal Pais** (jazz), **Gandhi** (Latin rock), **Kadeho** (Latin rock), **Xpunkha** (*Tico* street punk), **Mekatelyu** (reggae) and **Peregrino Gris** (Celtic). Latin music lovers will want to check out Salsa legends **Los BrillanTicos** and *cumbia* giants **Kalua** and **Calle 8**. Calypso legend **Walter Ferguson** doesn't perform much now that he's in his mid-eighties but his two discs capture the unique essence of Limonese music.

Better souvenir shops, record stores and bookshops usually have displays of CDs by Costa Rican musicians. Log on to www.papayamusic.com for updates and to purchase CDs by *Tico* artists.

Fernando Carcamo

Photographs are the lasting, tangible record of your vacation and we often revisit them to remind us of how and what we felt during the journey. If you are going to bring some type of photographic equipment along here are some things to consider.

CARING FOR YOUR EQUIPMENT The advent and proliferation of digital cameras has radically revolutionised how we capture images. It is now easily possible to bring back hundreds – if not thousands – of photos of our trips. In the past just the cost of acquiring and developing film (not to mention the challenges in caring for it during your trip) made it inconvenient to take more than a couple of hundred photos of a trip. There are some new challenges to keep in mind.

Digital cameras are often much more fragile than their film counterparts. They damage easily and are practically impossible to repair (or have repaired) while you're on the road. Make sure to care for it by keeping it free of dirt, dust, sand, liquids, and excessive heat and humidity. Constant shaking of the camera can also cause it to seize or lock up. You have to remember to treat your camera as a delicate item like your glasses or your contact lenses. When not in use keep it in its case at all times and remember to put it back when you're done. Regular cleaning (with any soft cloth) is also a good idea.

If you are going to use a film camera make sure you bring plenty of film: you must assume that should you run out it will not be available for purchase. Though it often is, the price of rolls is substantially higher, and it may not be as fresh as what you would find in your local camera store. Make sure to have all your film hand-inspected when x-ray equipment is being used. Pack it in a way that will make it easy for you to separate it from the rest of your luggage and give it to the inspection officer. Give yourself extra time as you can often be made to wait longer whenever you have such special requests!

MEDIA AND COMMUNICATIONS

Numerous newspapers, websites and chat rooms can keep you up to date with the latest goings-on in Costa Rica.

NEWPAPERS AND MAGAZINES The best English-language paper is the *Tico Times* (\ *258 1558*), published every Friday and covering news, culture, sports, business, politics – everything. Highly recommended!

Costa Rica Outdoors (\ *282 6743*) is a colourful, glossy bi-monthly magazine specialising in fishing, sports and tourism. *La Nación* is the largest daily newspaper in Spanish while *Al Dia* is a smaller daily, *Diario Extra* is the most sensational and *La Republica* is geared towards business.

Online news AM Costa Rica: daily news in English (*www.amcostarica.com*) has daily news in English covering tourism, sports, government, crime, current events, agriculture, boating, retirement issues, weather and travel.

The *Tico Times* On Line (*www.ticotimes.net*) offers most of the weekly print edition online as well as daily news stories. **Inside Costa Rica** (*www.insidecostarica.net*) has links to stories about Costa Rica printed in other publications from around the world. *La Nación* (*www.nacion.com*) is the online daily newspaper in Spanish. **Costa Rica Living** (*www.costaricaliving.org*) has a chat line to exchange information on living in Costa Rica, a job and business ideas bulletin board as well as a chat line for those learning Spanish.

LENSES The obvious choice is a camera with sufficient telephoto capabilities to bring far objects (wildlife mainly) up close. Don't forget, however, that the ability to capture a large group or scene at close range is also important so a camera or lens with wide angle capabilities is essential as well. Many higher end 'prosumer' digital cameras come with versatile lenses with impressive wide angle to telephoto ranges. A 28–300mm (SLR equivalent) lens is most ideal.

MEMORY The price of memory drops constantly; take advantage of it by buying extra memory cards with large capacity. For each week away plan on having at least 1 gigabyte of storage. Many internet cafes can record the images from you camera onto CDs or DVDs. Take advantage of that to clear and reuse your memory cards.

OTHER THINGS TO KEEP IN MIND Light, framing and composition are things that help you reach the next photographic level but you should not think about them so much that it'll keep you from capturing the memories of your journey. Remember that the photos will hold special meaning to you pretty much regardless of the results you obtained. You stand a better chance of capturing that great image by photographing often and spontaneously. Also don't underestimate what a great read your camera manual can be! It's the perfect book companion on the plane and while waiting at the airport. Understanding how your camera works (and how all those features you paid for but haven't taken the time to use) will give you immediate improved results.

BE CONSIDERATE The world is camera shy (chances are you too as well). Be mindful, respectful and sensitive. Always ask permission, approach your subject in a friendly manner, and respect their wishes.

Fernando Carcamo is Costa Rica's foremost wedding (and sunset) photographer. His website is www.weddings.co.cr and he may be reached at fernando@weddings.co.cr

RADIO There are over 100 radio stations in Costa Rica but for English radio, the pickings are slim – classic rock at 107.9 FM, jazz on 95.5 FM or Radio Dos at 99.5 FM with traffic reports, news and a mixed bag of music from the 1960s to today. Flip around the dial and you'll hear everything from *cumbia* (all day, all night and blaring from your taxi driver's stereo) to *mariachi* (blaring from your bus driver's stereo) to the religious station (blaring in the taxis that aren't playing *cumbia*). It's a musical adventure and a fun part of any driving trip.

TELEVISION With the advent of cable and satellite dishes, many North American channels and programmes (even some from the UK) are seen in Costa Rica. Most are subtitled but others are badly dubbed (Donald Trump speaking Spanish – need I say more). TV *novelas* (soap operas) from all over Latin America are popular on prime-time and it's not unusual for some shows to garner the same fanatical fervour as football matches (God help the hapless fool who tried to call anyone during the finale of *Beti la Fea* – 'Betty the Ugly One'). Costa Rica isn't noted for its television industry, save for the wacky variety/game show *A Todo Dar* ('We Give you All') which is seen throughout Latin America.

TELEPHONE Telecommunications are under the auspices of ICE (Instituto Costarricense de Electricidad), the state monopoly governing power and telephones.

To use your cellular telephone within Costa Rica, please check with your local cellular provider to see if they are able to offer coverage in Costa Rica.

The best place to make an international call is from your hotel. All phone booths are connected to the international system, and you can connect directly to operators in the UK, Europe, the US, Canada to call collect or use your credit card. The numbers are listed in the telephone directory, or ask at your hotel.

Most public phones do not accept coins and the best thing to have is a phonecard. There are two types: a 'chip' card that allows you to replenish funds, or a scratch-off phonecard in denominations of 500 and 1,000 colones. I recommend you buy one of these phonecards when you arrive; they are available at most grocery shops, pharmacies and the airport.

From within Costa Rica, you can call anywhere in the country directly. To call Costa Rica from North America or Europe, you must dial 011 506 and then the number.

Emergency contact numbers The emergency number throughout the entire country is 911, although it's faster if you dial the ambulance, police or fire department directly.

Ambulance ☎ 128
Fire department ☎ 118
Police ☎ 222 1365, 221 5337
Transit police ☎ 222 9330, 222 8245

San José hospitals

Clínica Bíblica (south central) ☎ 257 0466, 257 5252
Calderón Guardia Hospital (east) ☎ 257 7922
Hospital CIMA (west) ☎ 231 2781
San Juan de Dios (west) ☎ 257 6282
Mexico Hospital (west) ☎ 232 0299
Clínica Católica (northeast) ☎ 283 6616

Hospitals in central provinces

Max Peralta Hospital (Cartago) ☎ 550 1911
San Rafael Hospital (Alajuela) ☎ 440 1333
San Vicente de Paul Hospital (Heredia) ☎ 261 0091

Other hospital telephone numbers

Puntarenas ☎ 663 0033
Limón ☎ 758 2222
Liberia ☎ 666 0011
Quepos ☎ 777 0922
San Carlos ☎ 460 1176
Turrialba ☎ 556 1133
Golfito ☎ 775 1001
Ciudad Neily ☎ 783 4111

Credit cards Try 175 for international collect call and the calling number on the back of your credit card. Your credit-card company should accept your collect call. If you have no luck with this or can't find your card try the following numbers.

Visa International ☎ 800 847 2911
Visa Costa Rica (Spanish) ☎ 224 2631, 224 2731
MasterCard and American Express International ☎ 800 458 2733, 305 272 3027

MasterCard and American Express Costa Rica ☎ 257 4744, 257 0155 (ask for *extranjeros*)
Western Union ☎ 800 777 7777

BUSINESS

Costa Rica remains one of the safest and most attractive countries for foreign investment in Latin America, thanks to its stable government, highly educated workforce and one of the most open economies in the region. Interest rates have dropped steadily over the last few years, thanks largely in part to a large reserve of foreign currency resulting from the tourism sector.

No longer dependent upon coffee and bananas, Costa Rica's economy has diversified greatly in the last decade – over 3,000 types of products, such as microchips, pineapples, textiles, ornamental plants and medical equipment, are exported to 130 countries. The boom in tourism shows no sign of abating, especially when recent unfortunate events in other parts of the world have travellers seeking a tropical destination that is politically and environmentally safe.

Eager to do business with other regions, Costa Rica has free-trade agreements with Canada, Chile, Mexico, the Caribbean and Central America, with an agreement with the US (CAFTA) awaiting passage through the US Congress at the time of writing. Bilateral investment agreements have also been signed with Great Britain, Germany, France, Taiwan, Spain and Canada.

Free zones, which offer businesses tax exemptions and various incentives, have attracted companies from all over the world, including large multinationals such as Intel, which has built its third-largest microchip factory in the world on the outskirts of San José. Panasonic has a large factory nearby as does Conair.

For those who want to start a business or invest in Costa Rica, there are boundless opportunities but the streets are not lined with gold – success takes time, careful planning and a lot of triple-checking of details. A number of people here have recently lost their entire life savings in high-yield investment schemes gone awry. Short rule – if something sounds too good to be true, IT IS. Use your common sense, listen to your intuition and get yourself a good lawyer. A legitimate company must be registered with and monitored by the country's financial regulation institutions. Look before you leap and do your homework as it could save you a lot of heartache (and headaches) down the road.

LIVING IN COSTA RICA

Inevitably, visitors to Costa Rica find themselves basking in the sun, toes in the sand, cold Imperial in hand, thinking how easy it would be to live in this paradise – 'sunshine syndrome' as it's called by those in the know. The natural beauty, tranquillity and lower cost of living are extremely enticing and over 100,000 foreigners have followed that dream. If you are serious about relocating, contact the **Residents' Association of Costa Rica** (✆ *233 8068;* ✆ *255 0061; www.arcr.net*) before calling the removal company. They suggest living here for six months before making any concrete plans, as the difference in culture, slow-moving bureaucracy and overall underdevelopment can burst the bubble quickly for a lot of people.

Rules of residency are being reconsidered by the government at the time of writing, but for now, residents fall into four categories:

a) *pensionados* (retirees), who must prove a minimum monthly pension of US$600
b) *rentistsas* (investors), who must receive US$1,000 a month for five years from investments outside of Costa Rica or deposit at least US$60,000 in a Costa Rican bank approved by the government
c) *inversionistas* (large investors), who must invest a minimum of US$50,000 in an export or tourism business, US$100,000 in a reforestation project or US$200,000 in other government-approved businesses and reside in Costa Rica for six months each year
d) *representantes* (company directors), who must be directors of a company that meets certain requirements (ie: employing a certain number of local workers).

There are thousands of 'perpetual tourists' who leave the country every 90 days to renew their tourist visas, although many don't even bother with that technicality and live here illegally year round. If caught, perpetual tourists can be deported and not allowed back into the country for ten years.

Another sobering reality is that the average monthly salary here is US$300 and upper-management jobs make US$2,000 tops. Teaching English nets about US$4 an hour and odd jobs usually found in other parts of the world (such as waitering) aren't as easy to snag here, because of strict employment laws (a number of restaurants in Tamarindo were recently slapped with fines for hiring illegal North American and European waiting staff). Even large multinationals, such as Firestone, Intel or Motorola, pay wages far below what their offices in North America or Europe would pay for the same type of work.

Living here is wonderful – and exasperating at times, so it's definitely not for everyone. Some things are much easier (can't say I miss Canadian winters) and some things are so much more difficult (banking, getting a phone, anything involving a phone call with a government employee). If you are seriously considering relocation, take the six months to find out if this is really the right place for you.

CULTURAL ETIQUETTE

Ticos are gentle, incredibly accommodating, friendly and very polite. Being one of the most open and liberal countries in Latin America, there isn't much that is taboo and visitors most likely won't have any negative experiences as long as they treat others with the same kindness and respect shown by their generous hosts.

In the land of peace, civility is everything. *Ticos* are justly proud of their peaceful heritage and do not glorify war, guns or violence (Arnold Schwarzennegger movies – not a big hit). They avoid confrontation and would rather sit on the fence than make a decision that might offend. While they may comment on how the government is making a mess of things or criticise some other aspect of the country, they are incredibly offended by foreigners (especially tourists) doing the same. Never put down Costa Rica and never wax on about how much better your home country is as these are surefire ways to turn that polite *Tico* smile upside down.

Respect for older people is of utmost importance – whether it's the president or a street vendor, always place *Don* or *Doña* before an older person's name. For example, call your friend's father Don Alberto and not just Alberto. *Tico* society is classless – in earlier years, even the wealthy coffee barons were not considered 'above station'. All people in Costa Rica are treated with the same amount of respect.

When greeting someone you know, young or old, kiss the person once, on the right cheek (except if it's two men greeting each other – a firm handshake is expected).

Costa Ricans are always very conscious about looking presentable and tidy when they go out. Although they dress very casually in comparison with other countries, beachwear should be kept at the beach. Flip-flops, shorts or hiking gear worn in San José pegs you as a tourist – *Josefinos* (people who live in San José) wear jeans or slacks and shoes appropriate for the city. Nudity at the beach is not permitted and whilst thong bathing suits may be the rage in Brazil, they are frowned upon here.

Be polite, open and accepting of things *a lo Tico* ('the *Tico* way') and you'll bask in the warmth of this land and its people.

GIVING SOMETHING BACK

If you're looking for a holiday that has a positive impact on the country and its people, consider volunteering for a worthwhile cause. Speaking Spanish is not necessarily a requirement but an eagerness to learn and serve others is. Some organisations may pay a small stipend and most require you to pay your own way. The following is a selected list of associations that organise volunteer vacations.

APREFLOFAS www.preseveplanet.org. Environmental education, wildlife conservation; 3-month commitment necessary.

Associacion ANAI 224 3570; f 253 7524; www.anaicr.org. Conservation projects for birds of prey and leatherback turtles and runs an experimental farm for college graduates.

Caribbean Conservation Corporation 297 5510 f 297 6576; www.cccturtle.org. Protects turtle-nesting areas and participants assist with research and tagging turtles. All meals inc for 15 days in either Jul or Aug at a cost of US$1,890.

The Dolphin Foundation of Costa Rica 847 3131; f 786 7636; www.divinedolphin.com. Marine mammal conservation.

Cruz Roja 233 7033; www.cruzroja.or.cr. Costa Rican branch of the Red Cross, providing medical and humanitarian aid, disaster relief, HIV/AIDS prevention.

La Flor de Paraiso Agroecological Farm /f 534 8003; www.La-Flor.org. Organic farm art, environmental education, medicinal plants.

Genesis II Cloud Forest Reserve /f 381 0739; www.genesis-two.com. Private cloudforest reserve focused on reforestation, canopy tour training, experimental farming. 4-week placement for a donation of US$150 per week and participants should be physically fit.

Habitat for Humanity 296 8120; f 232 8679; www.habitatcostarica.org. International programme providing construction of low-cost housing, 3–6-month commitment, intermediate Spanish necessary.

Humanitarian Foundation 837 5205; e gnystrom@racsa.co.cr. National programme to assist at-risk groups, including indigenous people, orphans, street kids and the elderly.

The McKee Project /f 293 6461; www.mckeeproject.org. A spaying/neutering programme for street animals; needs support workers and vets.

National Parks 192 when in Costa Rica. Assist with park maintenance and stay in the parks across the country.

FCO TRAVEL ADVICE
know before you go
fco.gov.uk/travel

Bradt Travel Guides is a partner to the 'know before you go' campaign, masterminded by the UK Foreign and Commonwealth Office to promote the importance of finding out about a destination before you travel. By combining the up-to-date advice of the FCO with the in-depth knowledge of Bradt authors, you'll ensure that your trip will be as trouble-free as possible.

www.fco.gov.uk/travel

4

Sport and Other Activities

If getting out and about in the great outdoors is your cup of tea, Costa Rica is the place for you. Beaches, oceans, lakes, mountains and cities offer an amazing array of leisure activities that fit any budget.

BIRDWATCHING

A big draw for any nature lover is Costa Rica's stunning wealth of bird species and even non-twitchers hope to catch a glimpse of the country's signature species, the resplendent quetzal (*Pharomacrus mocinno*) with streaming green tail coverts sported by the showy males in breeding season. Specialist birding groups are brought in from abroad but local trips are organised through the English-speaking Birding Club of Costa Rica (e *costaricabirding@hotmail.com*) and its Spanish-speaking equivalent, Asociación Ornitológica de Costa Rica (*www.zeledonia.org*) which offers monthly talks, carries a full species list and can recommend guides. The research stations run by the Organisation for Tropical Studies (*www.ots.ac.cr*) are a haven for birders. La Selva Biological Station near Sarapiquí with its comprehensive trail system is a must-visit part of any birdwatcher's itinerary. Also one of the centres for the Audubon Christmas Bird Counts, it boasts second place for the number of species seen in the Americas (in 2003 the Rain Forest Aerial Tram Braulio Carrillo National Park topped the international charts with a mind-boggling 400 species seen). Patience and good binoculars should also yield good views of the weird and wonderful three-wattled bellbird (*Procnias tricarujnculata*) especially around Arenal, or the elusive bare-necked umbrella bird (*Cephalopterus glabricollis*), a resident of La Selva and other Caribbean slopes.

CAMPING

In theory beach camping is the right of all who want to sleep under canvas by the lapping waves; recent conflicts with overcrowded beach sites, garbage and swanky resort developers trying to 'raise the tone' of their particular patch of beach have caused some stand-offs and the whole issue is under discussion. To avoid eviction, head for a designated campsite and pay the pittance needed for a pitch and access to bathrooms and water. Space can be limited, especially near the beach at peak seasons, ie: Easter (when all *Ticos* seem to discover some boy-scout urge to sleep in a tent), when reservations are recommended. The national parks vary but most offer at least basic camping grounds and get you right into the heart of spectacular countryside. If camping is permitted, the protected reserves and national parks will charge an entrance fee of around US$2 per person. Since restrictions in numbers apply in some of the more popular parks, you need to get permission to pitch a tent, so contacting the nearest MINAE office (Ministry of the Environment, *www.minae.or.cr*) before you even get close to the park is a necessary although often

Inland from the Pacific town of Dominical, the Tinamaste Mountains drop sharply with sheer cliffs and the Diamante (Diamond) Falls sparkle most of the year, a visible landmark from the coastal road. Easy to spot they may be, but the steep struggle to the falls keeps them isolated from the crowds, and well worth the sweat and toil necessary to get there. A deep gash of a cave hewn by nature from a cliff behind a waterfall has been 'furnished' with broad stone platforms and hardy visitors can spend a stony night's rest behind the veil of falling water. The area is owned by the Tree of Life organisation (c/o Jon Chapman; ↘ 771 6200; e info@treeoflifetours.com), a non-profit Christian group that takes troubled young people to stay at the waterfall. The physical effort required with often lonely introspection has helped these youngsters towards spiritual renewal and social reintegration. The cave boasts bedding, candles, cooking facilities and latrines; no electricity or jacuzzis here. It may have been exhaustion but our overnight stay was surprisingly comfortable. Part of a series of falls, the main Diamante cascade offers majestic views of the Pacific coastline up towards Manuel Antonio so with breath recovered after the hike, we relished a sharp freshwater bathe in the pool. We ate our simple meal early and as dusk fell gathered to stargaze by the precipitous drop-off (thankfully fenced) just by our sleeping quarters. Like roosting birds, we were ready to seek out our petrified perches and settle for sleep with the splash of water and croaking of the occasional frog.

Casa de Piedra is four hours south of San José via the San Isidro del General road towards Dominical. From Platanillo – 2.5km with signs to the Diamante waterfall and Camp Santo Cristo.

frustrating requirement. For example, permission to camp at Sirena in the Corcovado National Park entails making reservations directly at the MINAE rangers' office in Puerto Jimenez, which can mean hanging around for a few days if the park is full.

Please note that camper van and motor homes are not available for hire here and there are no caravan sites.

See www.costaricahomepages.com for a concise list of all the national parks with their facilities.

CANOPY TOURS

Roughly 25% of all visitors to Costa Rica opt to fly through the trees like a modern-day Tarzan. Canopy or 'zip line' tours are found throughout almost every corner of the country and are a thrilling way to see the forest through the trees. Steel cables, up to hundreds of metres in length, run from tree to tree from which participants, wearing a modified climbing harness and using cables and pulleys, fly along the cables to a series of platforms. The experience is exhilarating, scary and liberating all at once.

In Monteverde, the longest cable in the country is at **Skytrek** (↘ 654 5238). In Manuel Antonio, check out **Canopy Safari** (↘ 777 0100) or in Jacó **Chiclets Canopy** (↘ 643 1880).

The Original Canopy Tour (*www.canopytour.com*) was the first company to build a commercial tree tour and they have a number of operations around the country. In 2004, there was an attempt by the owner of the Original Canopy Tour to claim intellectual property on the canopy tour idea and while the courts flip-flopped on the legal decision, a few competing canopy tours were damaged and shut down by the OCT crew. The matter is still snaking its way through the courts but the brouhaha has seen more strident safety issues being implemented.

Regardless of which company you choose, double check your equipment and make sure your cables are hooked up properly – hurtling across a metal cable is, after all, an adventure sport and there are inherent dangers.

CASINOS

Care to woo Lady Luck? Casinos are common in San José and larger tourist centres at the beaches, such as Jacó, Playas del Coco, Flamingo, Tamarindo and Tambor. Electronic slot machines and table games such as rummy (like '21' but with extra payout for three of a kind and straights but no bonus for blackjack), *tute* (like Caribbean stud poker) and *canasta* (numbered ping-pong balls are whirled about in a basket-like roulette) are featured, along with video poker and sportsbook betting.

Many offer free transportation within San José and some have free cocktails for gamblers. The larger hotels in the city all have casinos, including the Radisson Europa, Holiday Inn, Gran Hotel, Hotel Cariari, San José Palacio, Hotel Presidente, Hotel Corobici, Hotel del Rey and Herradura Hotel.

CYCLING

The breathtaking landscapes make all the huffing and puffing well worth the effort that cycling requires here. Roads outside of the cities aren't usually paved and pot-holes are always a danger. Bike paths or lanes don't exist so extreme caution should be used at all times – along with a good helmet and reflective vest.

Ticos are fond of cycling and the weekends see the hills above Santa Ana, Heredia, Coronado and San Marcos filled with mountain bikers. Every November, the best of the best compete in one of the most gruelling races, the three-day **Ruta de los Conquistadores Race** (*www.adventurerace.com/ruta1.html*), which runs coast to coast through challenging back roads. December sees the **Vuelta de Costa Rica Race** hit the trails.

There are a number of excellent organised cycle tours around Costa Rica. Most routes include the Orosí Valley and the Arenal Volcano area, depending on participants' fitness levels. Contact **Coast to Coast Adventures** (✆ *280 8054; www.ctocadventures.com*) for a complete rundown of tours offered. **Bike Arenal** (✆ *479 9454; www.bikearenal.com*) specialises in half-day and multi-day tours around the Arenal Volcano area but also has nine-day tours into the Osa Peninsula. Regardless of where and how long your tour is, make sure you are in good biking condition prior to your arrival as the heat and elevation can make things a lot more challenging.

DIVING

Admittedly, Costa Rica doesn't hold a candle to Australia or Belize for crystalline waters or verdant coral reefs but divers of all levels will find the diving challenging and rewarding. Cahuita National Park down to Manzanillo on the Caribbean has the largest coral reef in the country, with 35 species of coral to explore. The best time to dive is October through November. Over on the Pacific side, there may not be colourful coral but the magnitude of marine life is staggering. To the north near Ocotal, Catalina and Murcielago islands are the big draws while the far south, in the Osa Peninsula, offers exceptional diving in Golfo Dulce and Isla del Caño.

If you have the diving ability, experience, time and money, head to the Mecca of diving, Cocos Island (Isla del Coco), for a once-in-a-lifetime adventure. Located

500km from the southwest tip of Costa Rica, the 36-hour boat trip takes divers to one of the most remote and mythological spots on the map. Stories of buried treasure have lured many a prospector and pirate here, and writer Robert Louis Stevenson used the uninhabited island as the setting for his famous book, *Treasure Island*. Cocos Island has been rated number one in the world by dive magazines, with manatees, manta rays and eight shark species swimming amongst hundreds of colourful, exotic fish. Contact Undersea Hunter (*www.underseahunter.com*).

Courses are offered through resorts and dive shops for all levels of divers, usually at much lower prices than in other parts of the world. A four-day PADI open-water course costs around US$300. Contact **Ocotal Resort** (☎ *670 0321*), **Agua Rica** in Tamarindo (☎ *653 0094*) or **Aguila de Osa** in the Osa Peninsula (☎ *296 2190*).

DOLPHIN AND WHALE WATCHING

You could say it's no fluke Costa Rica is a prime spot for watching these marine mammals, as roughly half of the world's 80 dolphin, porpoise and whale species are found in its waters.

The Caribbean is home to three species of dolphins – the bottlenose, Atlantic spotted and the freshwater *Tucuxi* (which is endemic to the area) – all of which are commonly found in the waters off the south Caribbean Gandoca-Manzanillo National Wildlife Refuge. Near Manzanillo, just outside of Punta Mona, orcas and sperm whales can be seen. Contact **Aquamor Adventures** (☎ *759 0612*).

On the Pacific side, from the Murcielago Islands down to Caño Island, there is a greater number of dolphins including spinner, bottlenose, rough-toothed, Risso's, pan tropic, spotted and common as well as orca, humpback, sperm, blue and pilot whales.

FISHING

According to the International Game Fish Association, close to 100 world-record catches have been raised from Costa Rica's waters, including 20 all-tackle, 54 line-test and 21 fly-fishing marks (don't even get started on the ones that got away). Hooking at least one fish a day is practically guaranteed. Note that catch and release is the law when it comes to game fish and reputable boat operators abide by the rules, thus ensuring there's great fishing for all.

INLAND FISHING Lake Arenal has great fishing year round and *guapote* (rainbow bass) is the main catch. Related to South American peacock bass, *guapote* have feathered dorsal and caudal fins and brilliant rainbow hues (as well as a mean set of teeth). Use the same bait as for largemouth, spinner baits and surface lures.

Caño Negro Lagoon, bordering Lake Nicaragua, has trout, rainbow bass and a variety of tropical species such as *machaca* and *tepemechin*. This area has some of the best tarpon and snook fishing in the world.

Fly fishing in mountain lakes as well as rivers and along both coastlines offers lots of challenge and reward. **Fly Fish Costa Rica** (*www.flyfishcostarica.com*) are the specialists; most boat operators also offer fly-fishing packages.

CARIBBEAN COAST Tarpon and shook reign supreme and some of the best fishing is near the mouth of the Río Colorado. A number of fishing lodges are in this area of the northern Caribbean, with others to the south in Samay Lagoon, Tortuguero, Parisimina and Manzanillo. Fishing is great year round although October to April is the best time.

NORTH PACIFIC The islands of Catalina and Murcielogo have wahoo, rooster, cubera and amberjack. A bit further south, from Ocotal down to Flamingo, sailfish are plentiful year round and tuna, bonito, blue and rainbow runners are a good bet. Best time to fish here is after May and before January, when the Papagayo wind blows in from the north. Check out **Blue Marlin Services** (☏ 670 0707) operating out of the Cocos area.

CENTRAL PACIFIC Billfish are the main attraction, with December to April being the prime season. Marlin are plentiful in October, sailfish December to April, while tuna are found year round but is most prominent from June to September. **Bluefin Fishing** (☏ 777 1676; *www.bluefinsportfishing.com*) is one of the best in the country.

SOUTH PACIFIC Marlin is the prize fish here and is caught year round from Golfito and further south. Sailfish is plentiful from November to March but overall, the area is renowned for its year-round abundance of a variety of fish, including tuna, wahoo, grouper, cubera, barracuda, corvine, snook, jack crevalle and amberjack. **Crocodile Bay Lodge** (☏ 735 5632) was built specifically for fishing.

Jerry Ruhlow is an encyclopaedia of Costa Rican fishing and his travel company, **Costa Rica Outdoors** (*www.costaricaoutdoors.com*) is highly recommended to anyone wanting a sport fishing holiday.

GOLF *Note: all prices listed are per round of golf*

Although golf was first introduced to Costa Rica in 1944, it wasn't until the 1970s that the first course was built – the Cariari Country Club, near San José, which is still one of the most challenging courses in Central America (those dog-legs!). For the next two decades, it was the only place to play golf until other courses started springing up, and now golfers can choose from a number of excellent places to tee off.

Guanacaste is home to the best courses in all of Central America, which include the **Garra de Leon Golf Course** (☏ 654 4123) at the Paradisus Playa Conchal resort. Designed by Robert Trent Jones III, this par-72, 18-hole seaside course will bring out your inner Tiger Woods (or have you throwing your woods into the water traps). The course is now open only to guests of the resort (rates are US$150).

A bit further south is the course at **Hacienda Pinilla** (☏ 680 7000), another par-72, 18-hole course on what was once a cattle ranch. Designed by Mike Young, the course hugs the coastline and features wide-open fairways. Rates are US$150 for non-hotel guests.

Those staying at the **Four Seasons Resort** (☏ 696 0000) have the privilege of playing the new Arnold Palmer-designed 18-hole course. Rates are US$185 (cart included) and club rental runs to US$55. The course is exclusively for those staying at the resort.

The area of Tambor in the Nicoya Peninsula has two small nine-hole courses open to the public – **Tango Mar Resort** (☏ 683 0001), US$25 for green fees, US$20 each for rental of clubs and a cart, and **Barcelo Los Delfines** (☏ 683 0333), US$20 for green fees and US$25 for carts.

Los Suenos Marriot (☏ 630 9000) is the southernmost course in the country, just outside of Jacó. The Ted Robinson course features an 18-hole, par-72 course. Rates for the public are US$140 and US$40 for rental clubs.

In the San José area, check out **Valle del Sol** (☏ 282 9222) in sunny Santa Ana. This 18-hole course is a great deal, at only US$80 including cart and unlimited golf for the day. Rental clubs are US$20–35.

No matter where you choose to play golf, remember to drink plenty of water and that the afternoon sun and heat is intense – best to tee off in the early morning.

HIKING

Recently arrived in Costa Rica, I was lucky enough to find an informal group of hikers who organised a wonderful array of treks. Every month, we ventured into the hills overlooking Heredia or Escazú for strenuous day hikes normally rewarded with fabulous panoramas over Central Valley or at least, if cloud kept the views, a deserved beer or two at some village *soda* (general store/café). At least half the outings were overnight trips that took us further afield deep into the remoter corners of the national parks, up the volcanoes and mountains, along forest trails or trudging upriver to isolated waterfalls and a dip in refreshingly chilly pools. We would stay in rustic but comfortable lodgings taking over a veranda for early-evening *bocas* (snacks) and drinks as we went over the rigours of the day and generally put the world to rights. It was a wonderful way to learn about yet another little-known corner of a country abundant in special corners, at low cost and in good company. Sadly, that group has largely disbanded, and since trails are often poorly marked and maps are notoriously unreliable it is paramount for hikers to venture forth with a reliable guide.

If you are tied to the Central Valley, Warner Rojas of **Pico Tours** (✆ *288 2118;* e *picotours@racsa.co.cr*) takes out groups most weekends into the hills around Escazú and Aserrí and the walks are graded according to length and difficulty. A tireless supporter and eco-warrior of his patch, he provides (bilingual) knowledgeable insights into the history, ecology and conservation of the area. He also offers hikes to other areas and can be contracted as a private guide. Since he is a trained forest firefighter and in the local rescue squad, he inspires confidence should you be nervous about finding your way home. I will always remember a gruelling but totally enjoyable two-day slog from the top of Turrialba Volcano down through the dramatic Braulio Carrillo National Park forests to the Caribbean flatlands near Guápiles with Warner. He carried our entire evening meal that first day: weighty potatoes, carrots, beans and *chayotes* with rice, which he converted into an exquisite and filling stew at the campsite – for 14 of us! If that's boot camp, then keep it coming.

HORSERIDING

Horses are still used as a source of transportation, especially out in the *campo* (country). Driving along a dusty road, it's not unusual to see high-stepping *criollos* taking riders to their next destination. Giant horse parades called *topes* see the entire town lining the street, cold drinks in hand, cheering on the hundreds of riders all decked out in their finest as they compete for a variety of prizes.

Seeing the countryside from atop a horse allows you to travel into areas not easily accessed by foot or car. **Caballos Valientes** (*www.horsetrekcr.com*) offers day trips for all levels of riders as well as interesting multi-day trips for experienced riders. Situated in the Central Pacific farming community of Salitrales, the owners Eduardo and Valentine try to minimise their impact on the remote forests and rivers by allowing only 50 riders per year – trips are limited to only four people at a time.

Horseback Ride Costa Rica (✆ *232 3113; www.horsebackridecostarica.com*) is owned and operated by biologist/nature guide Ingrid Ayub, who marries her passion for riding with her knowledge of Costa Rica. The company's trademark is an eight-day trek that takes riders through coffee plantations, into the backwoods, down mountains and into the rainforest to arrive at the beach in Manuel Antonio. A three-day trek stays in the areas of coffee plantations and forests. Future plans include a coast-to-coast trek, all on horseback.

Stables throughout the country offer day trips. Please note that it is illegal to ride horses on the beaches of Tamarindo (riding on any beach dirties the sand and water and should be discouraged). There are transfers via horseback between Monteverde and Arenal which should never be attempted during the rainy season (May to November) as steep and rocky trails become a mud bog which no horse should ever be forced to navigate.

MOTORCYCLING

If sightseeing on a motorbike gets your engine revving, grab a bike but be forewarned – driving a bike on Costa Rican roads is dangerous and requires quick reflexes, nerves of steel and a whole lot of defensive driving. Drivers here are notoriously bad and don't give motorbikes much respect (most bikers ride dirt bikes that they weave dangerously through city traffic).

Maria Alexandra Tours (✆ 289 5552; *www.mariaalexandra.com/harley*) rents Harley-Davidson XLH Sportster 883 and FXD Dyna Super Glides by the day or week and offers guided day tour and multi-day tours to all parts of the country. **Costa Rica Motorcycle Tours & Rentals** (✆ 225 6000; *www.motoexpedition.com*) rents BMW F650cc and KTM 640 LC4 bikes and also has guided multi-day tours as well as self-guided tours across the country.

ORCHIDS AND BOTANICAL GARDENS

Orchids have inspired collectors to go to extreme lengths to find these rare beauties – luckily, aficionados won't have to look too hard as over 4,500 species have been identified in Costa Rica. Orchids are everywhere, decorating the most humble of abodes in the cities to growing wild in the woods and it seems only fitting that the lovely purple Guaria Morada (*Cattleya skinneri*) is the national flower. Costa Rican orchid farms ship a large portion of the world's commercial orchids and some, such as **Orchimex de Costa Rica** (*www.orchimex.com*), offer guided tours through their operations.

Jardin de Orquideas (*Ca el Coyol;* ✆ 487 7178; *open Mon–Fri 12.30–15.00*), 1km southeast of the Fiesta de Maiz Restaurant in La Garita de Alajuela, has a lovely orchid garden open to the public. **Lankaster Botanical Gardens** (*Paraiso de Cartago;* ✆ 552 3247; *open daily 08.30–16.30*), southwest of San José, has winding paths through colourful gardens. **Wilson Botanical Gardens** (*Las Cruces Biological Station;* ✆ 240 6696; *www.ots.ac.cr*) is situated in the southern zone near San Vito. Walk through an explosion of colourful tropical flowers and plants, including orchids, in this fascinating research centre. Guests can stay overnight, with three meals and a guided tour, for US$70 per person.

RAFTING

Whether you're a beginner or an Olympic-level paddler, Costa Rica's rivers run the gamut from Class I to Class V (ONLY for the professionals – do not attempt them unless you have a great deal of experience). The water is warm but be wary, as some rivers are contaminated with parasites so try to avoid ingesting mouthfuls of water. Rafting is an adventure sport, so do pay close attention during the safety talk – accidents have happened and while reputable operators take every precaution possible, it is man versus nature and not a ride at Disney World.

Wear a bathing suit under longer shorts, a T-shirt, shoes that won't fall off (trainers or Teva sport sandals are perfect) and sunblock (don't use on the back of your legs, however, as you'll slide off the raft). Bring an extra set of dry clothes to change into, a towel and some soap to shower off at the end. When the guide tells you to paddle, paddle and paddle hard – this is a team effort and everyone in the boat has to do their part (also, paddling will help you stay in the boat).

Most rafting companies operate out of San José, putting in just outside of the Caribbean slope town of Turrialba. Day trips include the Reventazon, with the Florida section (Class II–III) which has lovely scenery and is pretty mellow, or Pascua (Class IV) that is challenging and best left for those with experience. This river has a couple of dams on it that have affected the quality of the water and the rapids – Olympic kayakers used to train here before the damn dam.

The Sarapiqui is great for families, with warm clean water, monkeys and lots of birds. La Virgen de Sarapiqui (Class II–III) is about a two-hour trip and the Lower Sarapiqui is perfect for a gentle floating trip. **Aventuras del Sarapiqui** (✆ 766 6768; *www.sarapiqui.com*) has rafting and canoeing trips as well as a kayaking school.

Pacuare River has been named one of the top four rivers in the world for white-water rafting. Challenging, beautiful and clean, it is the run every rafter and kayaker dreams of. Spring water rushes down from the mountains above, crashing through virgin jungle, pocketed by the odd indigenous settlement. The 29km run can be done in a day but opting for a two-day tour allows for more time to enjoy the waterfalls and scenery. Operators **Coast to Coast Adventures** (*www.ctocadventures.com*) have a lovely jungle lodge at the halfway point where weary paddlers can lay their heads. There is no electricity and water is fed from an underground spring – access to the Nido del Tigre (as the tent camp is called) is via river or hiking trail. Remote and beautiful! Other recommended operators include **Aventuras Naturales** (✆ 225 3939; *www.toenjoynature.com*) and, the biggest rafting operation in the country, **Rios Tropicales** (✆ 233 6455; *www.riostropicales.com*).

La Fortuna's Río Toro is a seasonal, technical river with day tours offered by **Desafio** (✆ 479 9464; *www.desafiocostarica.com*).

Sevegre, near Manuel Antonio, has Class III–IV stretches while the seasonal Naranjo is a little gentler. **Iguana Tours** (✆ 777 1262; *www.iguanatours.com*) runs both and also has ocean and mangrove kayaking.

Most of these companies will allow experienced kayakers to run the rivers in hard-shell kayaks or 'Duckies', the inflatable white-water kayaks. If you're seeking more challenging runs than those offered commercially, contact any of these companies about arranging private tours.

SAILING

Unlike Florida's waters or the Caribbean Islands, recreational charter sailing has barely started in Costa Rica. Unreliable charts, unmarked rocks and the infamous Papagayo wind that can rip a sail to shreds in minutes – or, no winds at all – mean bareboat multi-day charters are not available and the choice of crewed trips is limited.

If you arrive in your own boat, the ports of entry into Costa Rica are Playas de Coco, Puntarenas, Los Sueños, Golfito and Limón but don't expect full marina facilities. Most cruisers bypass the mainland en route to Cocos Island and beyond. There are no commercial sailboat outfits operating on the Caribbean coast.

You can go out for half-day, full-day and sunset cruises with several companies along the Pacific.

In Garza, **Sunset Sails** (☎ 682 0509; m 840 2231; e lpeters885@aol.com; cost US$70 pp), run by Lisa Peters offers half- and full-day tours on a pretty 35ft catamaran for up to 12 people, and can be contracted for overnight charters through the islands for up to four people. Free pickup from area hotels. Cost includes all drinks, gourmet *bocas* and barbecue lunch. Includes fishing and snorkelling equipment, towels and a hot-water shower. As with other 'cats' easy access into the water is a plus from sea-level ladders off the rear hull, suitable for the less agile. Under-14 age limit applies. In Tamarindo, **Mandingo Sailing** (☎ 831 8875; cost US$50 pp) has a beautiful replica of a 19th-century New England schooner. Lazy sunset tours are offered daily, including drinks and yummy homemade snacks. Family owned and operated **Blue Dolphin Sailing** (☎ 653 0867; www.sailbluedolphin.com) has a 40ft catamaran available for snorkelling or sunset tours. Both include drinks and appetisers. Also available for private charters or special events. Once a month, they offer a Full Moon Sail, a unique experience to sail under the light of a full moon.

In Flamingo, **Lazy Lizard Catamaran Sailing** (☎ 654 4192; e brisas22001@ yahoo.com; www.sailingcostarica.com; cost US$75 pp) has a 35ft catamaran that goes out from 14.00–18.00 with free pickup from the Tamarindo/Flamingo area, with onboard guide, free snacks, fruit platter and drinks. With two sea kayaks and snorkel gear for up to 25 passengers.

Samonique III (☎ 388 7870; e samonique50@hotmail.com; www.costarica-sailing.com) works out of Flamingo with half- and full-day cruises and will customise cruises for multi-day trips. In Quepos, both **Planet Dolphin** (☎ 777 2137) and **Sunset Sails** (☎ 777 1304) offer sunset and snorkelling tours. At the time of writing, Kerry (☎ 390 8940) was gearing up to bring in a number of boats for charter work.

SURFING

The surfing here is the best-known 'secret' in the world. Although Costa Rican waters lack the monstrous tubes found in Australia or Hawaii, both coasts offer amazing rides for beginners and pros alike. No need for wetsuits, thanks to the bathtub-like water, and the danger of great white sharks is non-existent. Surfing paradise found!

NORTH PACIFIC May to November are the best months, as the Papagayo winds blow offshore from January to April and can reduce the ocean to choppy whitecaps. Ollie's Point, a fast right-break and the legendary Witch's Rock are both accessible by boat and various surf shops in Tamarindo offer daily trips. Playa Grande is a beach break and nearby Tamarindo has a fast tubing section at the river mouth – the main beach is a favoured spot for surf schools on account of its consistent and gentle waves. A bit further south are Langosta, Avellanas and Negra beaches, all great options for those wanting a more technical ride. Continuing south is Nosara, a yet-to-be-discovered beach that is popular with the locals.

CENTRAL PACIFIC Waves are good year round, with consistent breaks at Malpais, Hermosa and Dominical (although Hermosa's huge, fast waves are best left to the more experienced – definitely not a spot for swimming!). Jacó is also a decent spot. There is a bit of surfing around Manuel Antonio although conditions are inconsistent and don't offer any great rides.

SOUTH PACIFIC At the right time, this area has some of the most perfect waves mother ocean has to offer. Pavones and Matapalo are legendary and have attracted

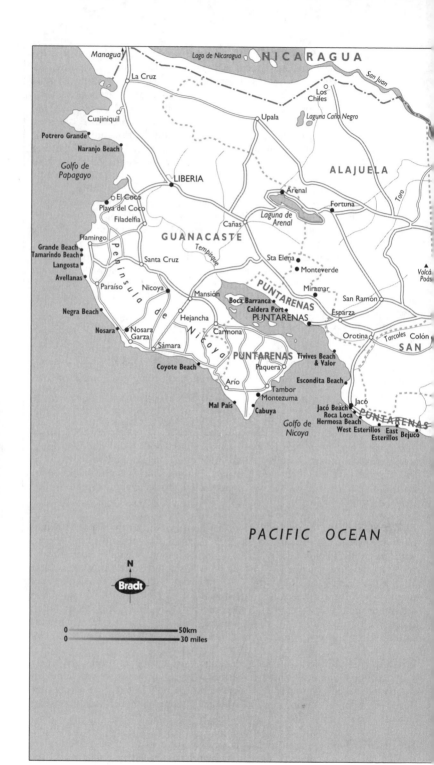

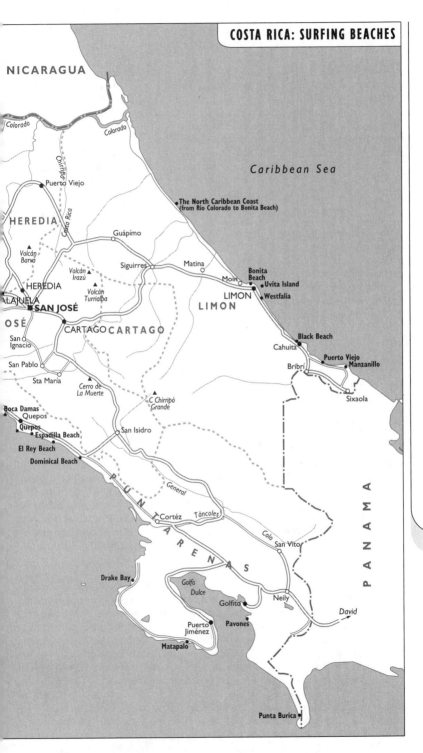

COSTA RICA: SURFING BEACHES

NICARAGUA

Colorado

Colorado

Caribbean Sea

Chirripó

Puerto Viejo

Costa Rica

HEREDIA

The North Caribbean Coast
(from Río Colorado to Bonita Beach)

Guápimo

Volcán
Barva

Siguirres

Matina

Moín

Bonita
Beach

Volcán
Irazú

HEREDIA

Volcán
Turrialba

Uvita Island

Westfalia

ALAJUELA

SAN JOSÉ

LIMON

LIMON

OSÉ

CARTAGO CARTAGO

San
Ignacio

Black Beach

Cahuita

San Pablo

Puerto Viejo

Manzanillo

Sta María

Cerro de
La Muerte

Bribrí

C Chirripó
Grande

Sixaola

Boca Damas
Quepos

Quepos

Espadilla Beach

San Isidro

El Rey Beach

Dominical Beach

P
U
N
T
A

General

Cortéz

Táncoles

Colo

San Vito

P
A
N
A
M
A

Drake Bay

Golfo
Dulce

Neily

David

Golfito

Puerto
Jiménez

Pavones

Matapalo

Punta Burica

a permanent surf community to these once-sleepy fishing villages. Playa Zancudo has a nice beach break and some action can be found in Drake Bay.

CARIBBEAN COAST Ranked one of the best waves in the world by surfing magazines, Puerto Viejo's legendary Salsa Brava is the holy grail for advanced surfers who flood the area from January to April in search of the hollowest wave in the land. A bit further south is Playa Cocles, a much gentler beach for those who aren't quite ready for Salsa Brava (be warned – there is a strong riptide and many swimmers have drowned at this beach). Cahuita has an interesting beach break at Playa Negra but be wary of sharks. North of Limón is the fast and barrelling wave at Playa Bonita. Tortuguero's river mouths are shark infested and not advised.

Check out www.crsurf.com for the latest on surfing in Costa Rica.

TURTLE WATCHING

Many visitors co-ordinate their trips to Costa Rica with one of the turtle-nesting or hatchling seasons. Some who witness these prehistoric creatures labouring up the beach or the tiny turtles' racing to the comparative safety of the ocean describe the experience as unforgettable and even life altering.

Six species in two families are found in Costa Rica: *Chelonia mydas* and *agazzisii* (green), *Eretmochelys imbricata* (hawksbill), *Dermochelys coriacea* (leatherback) on both Pacific and Caribbean coasts and *Lepidochelys* (Olive Ridley) only on the Pacific side. The *Caretta caretta* (loggerhead) doesn't breed and has been only occasionally seen in the Caribbean.

GREEN The second-largest turtle species at about 1m long and 150kg has long foreflippers and a short rounded head with different colour variations between coasts. Up to 8,000 breed from July to October in Tortuguero, the females coming in to nest five to six times. On the Pacific side they nest at Playa Cabuyal near Papagayo Gulf and Playa Minas near Brasilito.

LEATHERBACK This giant can reach one tonne in weight and measure over 2m and is the only turtle to have an inside skeleton covered by the leathery skin. It can withstand icy waters and dive to an astounding depth of 1,300m. The females' breeding cycle goes from 15 to 50 years preferring steep beaches at night, visiting up to four times each season; her eggs incubate in 60–70 days. Nesting occurs on the Pacific coast from October to March at Playa Grande, Playa Langosta near Tamarindo and Playa Naranjo in Santa Rosa National Park. In the Caribbean, they arrive from Playa Matina, north of Limón, to Tortuguero, from March to May.

OLIVE RIDLEY This smallest of the turtles measures about 60–75cm and weighs 35–40kg. Spectacular mass arrivals, *arribadas*, exclusive to Ridleys take place between June and December at Playa Nancite in Santa Rosa National Park, and Ostional. Up to 120,000 may nest in 4–8-day periods, arriving usually during the last quarter moon with a rising tide and onshore wind. The females plough their noses up through the sand almost as if they are sniffing their way to their chosen nest site. Taking about 50 minutes to dig their nest and lay eggs, up to 30% of the eggs can be destroyed during the same or a later *arribada* as females dig up previous nests and inadvertently kill earlier embryos. Other predators are humans, raccoons, opossums, vultures, crabs, frigate birds and sharks, so the Ridley's ploy is safety in numbers. Over 30 million eggs are laid during the *arribadas*, of which only 1% survive. Legal collection is permitted as an effort in community involvement to ensure conservation. Overseen by ADIO (Ostional Development Association) and

CRICKET, SUCH A LATIN GAME

Mad dogs and Englishmen head down to Puerto Viejo on the Caribbean coast these days. Cricket is making a comeback in Costa Rica with teams in San José and the southern Caribbean. The game's possible *Tico* survival is thanks to a lingering cricketing tradition in the country and the enthusiasm of some expatriates. Jamaican labourers on the Atlantic railway introduced cricket in the 1880s. It was welcome relief from their back-breaking exertions and reinforced their separate cultural identity. In its heyday from 1910 to 1939 there were 45 teams in three Caribbean leagues with club teams that toured in Jamaica.

League matches were played on Sundays and Mondays and public holidays. Teams used the train to reach their games and so the leagues grew up along the tracks. Leaving at dawn to play in the morning cool, lunch would be offered of rice, peas and chicken with leatherback or green turtle when in season. The game would finish at 16.00 with iced tea, sandwiches and biscuits. Teams usually stayed over with their hosts and carried their hangovers next morning on the first train.

At the height of its popularity, international teams from Panamá and even the West Indies played, with one memorable visit by the West Indian team to Limón in 1930 that included the legendary Learie Constantine and George Headley en route to Australia with a Panamá Canal stopover.

The last balls were bowled with the advent of World War II when the game abruptly declined. The pitch in Limón was built over for a hospital and after the war, football's better-publicised popularity, and later, with Pele's charisma, won over the young, and the spread of a more Latin-American culture saw cricket decline along the Caribbean coast … until now, that is.

the University of Costa Rica, locals have a quota of egg numbers for each *arribada*. The savoured eggs are bagged with an ADIO seal before sale to mostly male customers convinced of their aphrodisiac properties.

HAWKSBILL The most endangered of the turtles because its thick shell is prized for jewellery. Measuring 70–90cm and weighing 70kg, the hawksbill come into Tortuguero where they tend to nest singly somewhat earlier than the greens.

WINDSURFING

The western end of the manmade lake at Arenal is regarded as one of *the* spots for windsurfing in the world, as the winds here are constant and fast. Conditions are equally optimal for the latest rage that is kite surfing. At Lake Arenal, **Hotel Tilawa** (✆ 695 5050; *www.hotel-tilawa.com*) and **Rock River Lodge** (✆ 692 1180; *www.rockriverlodge.com*), rent equipment for both sports and offer lessons. Outfitter **Tico Wind** (*www.ticowind.com*) offers windsurfing from December to April, complete with equipment rentals, lessons and tours. They also run a centre in the north at **Ecoplaya Resort** (✆ 676 1063) in the northwestern area of Salinas Bay. **Kite Centre 2000** (✆ 826 5221; *www.suntoursandfun.com*) has a kite-surfing operation in the same area year round.

Part Two

THE GUIDE

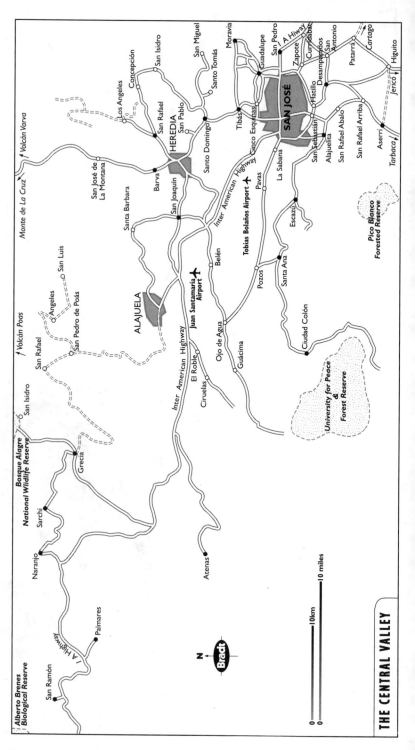

THE CENTRAL VALLEY

Alberto Brenes
Biological Reserve

San Ramón

Palmares

I A Highway

Naranjo

Sarchi

Bosque Alagre
National Wildlife Reserve

San Isidro

Grecia

Atenas

Ciruelas

El Roble

Ojo de Agua

Guácima

San Rafael

Angeles

San Luis

San Pedro de Poás

Volcán Poás

Inter American Highway

ALAJUELA

Juan Santamaría
Airport

Belén

Pozos

Santa Ana

Ciudad Colón

University for Peace
&
Forest Reserve

San José
de La Montana

Santa Barbara

Barva

San Joaquin

Volcán Varva

Monte de La Cruz

Los Angeles

San Rafael

San Pablo

HEREDIA

Concepción

San Isidro

San Miguel

Santo Tomás

Santo Domingo

Cinco Esquinas

Tibás

Inter American Highway

Tobias Bolaños Airport

Pavas

La Sabana

Escazú

Pico Blanco
Forested Reserve

Moravia

Guadalupe

San Pedro

I A Hiway

Zapote

Curridabat

Desamparados

San
Antonio

Patarra

Cartago

Higuito

Jericó

Tarbaca

Aserrí

San Rafael Arriba

San Rafael Abalo

Alajuelita

San Sebastián

Hatillo

SAN JOSÉ

N

Bradt

10km

10 miles

0

0

5

San José

Despite the bad press this capital city has received, travellers shouldn't fear it nor try to 'get out of Dodge' as soon as their flight touches down at Juan Santamaría International Airport. If I had a colon for every time I've heard 'I don't want to spend any time in San José', I'd be able to buy a Coke (have you seen the devaluation of the currency?). I think San José just needs a good publicist – and I'm here to start the positive press junket.

Yes, it's a noisy city where the streets have no names and those that do no-one knows what or where they are. Sure, it's the centre of business and commerce is bustling in every nook and cranny downtown has to offer (even on the buses someone is hawking something). OK, I admit that they drive like maniacs, crossing the street should be classified as an adventure sport, maps are useless for trying to navigate the endless maze of streets, the air is smoggy and the place is crowded – but, it's San José, the capital city where people from all over the world live, work and play, where sushi restaurants cosy up to Peruvian and Italian eateries. Its galleries, grand theatres, massive churches and crowded markets, humble adobe homes and modern condos, are all bundled together in a heady blend of shabby and chic. San José is beautiful and banal, a driver's hell and a pedestrian's paradise (along the ten-block mall, that is). It may be a big city but walk around a couple of blocks and the small-town feel that still pervades will charm you.

HISTORY

The city's humble beginnings as a cluster of shacks that gained village status in 1737 gave no indication of the stature it would shortly acquire. Ousted Creole and Spanish smugglers, banished from the colonial capital of Cartago, set up shop in Villa Nueva de la Boca del Monte del Valle de Abra – or San José, named after the area's patron saint. Their keen business sense helped the town quickly grow to equal the population of Cartago (5,000 souls in the 1820s). Grasping onto a monopoly of the country's tobacco business and capitalising on the new coffee trade, San José soon became the belle of the ball with beautiful buildings and lovely parks.

When Central America gained independence from Spain in 1821, the four villages of Costa Rica (conservative Cartago and Heredia, liberal Alajuela and San José) struggled to gain the upper hand, erupting in a showdown between the two factions on 5 April 1823 in the Ochomogo Hills. Cartago was captured and San José became the new capital.

But uneasiness and bickering between the towns caused San José to offer a concessionary gesture of rotating the capital between Cartago and San José every four years. The other villages still weren't satisfied, created a league and attacked San José on 26 September 1837 in what became known as La Guerra de la Liga (The War of the League), which they lost and San José has remained the capital ever since.

The coffee boom a few years later propelled the city from backwater village to a city of the belle époque. Wealthy coffee families wanted to recreate a bit of Europe in their city so brick roads were laid down and electricity was introduced, making San José the third city in the world to have public lighting and public telephones were installed well before other, more 'international' cities.

The post-war years of the late 1940s saw the city burst at the seams as thousands moved from the country to the town. Smaller villages on the outskirts were swallowed by the ever-growing San José and buildings were razed to make room for more modern structures – unfortunately, few of the architecturally interesting structures were spared and downtown San José is today mostly cement, box-like buildings. Nevertheless, the city's constant spring-like climate and surrounding mountains make it one of the most comfortable cities in Central America and it is truly the most cosmopolitan of the area.

GETTING THERE AND AWAY

If arriving via plane at the Juan Santamaría International Airport (✆ 443 2942), you can take a bus from in front of the airport – the Tuasa buses are red and the Station Wagon buses are beige and yellow. Both end up in downtown San José on Paseo Colón. If taking a cab, go with the official orange Aerotaxis at the exit of the airport. Depending on where you are travelling to, rates will range from US$12–20, which you pay up front. There are also pirate taxis that will make themselves well known to you (their incessant 'taxi, taxi, lady you need a taxi' will tip you off) but best to avoid them as they aren't always the most scrupulous nor are their vehicles in the best shape. If a transfer company or hotel is meeting you, your driver will have a sign with your name on it. As no-one is allowed inside the airport, there is a huge throng of people outside of the doors waving signs. Take your time and look carefully. Be aware that some pirate taxi drivers are now telling tourists that their pickup isn't coming for them so they should just go with the taxi – don't believe them!

If you're renting a car, it's easiest if they pick you up at the airport, as negotiating San José traffic is not for the faint of heart.

SAN JOSÉ – DOWNTOWN

WHERE TO STAY Prices are based on high-season rates (December–April) for double occupancy and do not include the 16.39% room tax unless otherwise stated.

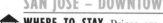
Expensive (US$70 and up)

⌂ **Hotel Aurola Holiday Inn** (200 rooms) Av 5, Ca 5; ✆ 222 2424; f 255 1171; e aurola@ racsa.co.cr; www.aurola-holidayinn.com. The tallest hotel in Costa Rica, this is a typical Holiday Inn – basic, hotel chain rooms and nothing out of the ordinary (except for the views from the upper floors). There is a restaurant on the 17th floor with international food and a casino. Guests have access to a pool, sauna, small gymnasium and jacuzzi. There is another restaurant, snack bar and a bar. In addition to rooms there are different suites, many suited to business travellers. Personally, there are far more interesting hotels in the area to choose from. Wheelchair access. Rates US$125–650.

⌂ **Hotel Barcelo San José Palacio** (222 rooms) General Cañas Highway, La Uruca; ✆ 220 2034; f 220 2036; www.barcelo.com. One of the largest hotels in San José, this is a surprisingly luxurious hotel for the price. Rooms are large as are the bathrooms, reminiscent of large American 4-star chain hotels. The suites are an excellent deal, with 2 rooms and bathrooms, kitchenette, dining and living room. There's a pool, small gardens, casino, bar, 2 restaurants and gift shops. Wheelchair access. Recommended. Rates US$120–395.

⌂ **Hotel Grano de Oro** (32 rooms) Ca 30, Av 2/4; ✆ 255 3322; f 221 2782; e granoro@racsa.co.cr; www.hotelgranodeoro.com. A tropical Victorian mansion turned boutique hotel, this is a stunner and easily my favourite hotel in San José. Period photos line the walls, harking back to a simpler time. Gleaming hardwood surrounds and beautifully painted tiles brighten up the floors. The rooftop jacuzzi is the perfect spot to unwind and the excellent restaurant with its open patio is spectacular. Guests can choose from suites or rooms and each is decorated differently from the next, although all have wrought-iron beds, rich damask coverings, original artwork and reproduction Victorian furnishings. Rooms in the original house can be noisy, as footsteps from above travel below but that has been the only complaint I've ever heard. Service is top notch. Highly recommended. *Rates US$90–250.*

⌂ **Gran Hotel Costa Rica** (94 rooms) Av 2, Ca 1/3; ✆ 221 4000; f 221 3501; e granhcr@racsa.co.cr; www.grandhotelcr.com. They say the 3 most important things in real estate are location, location and location — Gran Hotel has it in spades, being just steps from the Teatro Nacional and right on the pedestrian boulevard. The rooms are pedestrian, sterile almost, and don't live up to the splendour of the hotel's exterior. Rooms are large for the most part but basic. There is a 24hr casino, 24hr room service and the restaurant downstairs is a prime people-watching spot. Wheelchair access. B/fast inc. *Rates US$85–130.*

⌂ **Hotel Presidente** (110 rooms) Av Central, Ca 7/9 on the pedestrian mall; ✆ 257 8525; f 221 1205; www.hotel-presidente.com. Recently renovated and redecorated, this is an excellent choice for those who want to be central in a safe, clean hotel. Security is tight (although a friend had her video camera stolen from the lobby while checking in so remember to keep an eye on your things), the staff are attentive and rooms are neat and very clean, with AC, safety box, phones and cable TV. The master suite on the top floor has an 8-person jacuzzi with an amazing view of the city, 2 bedrooms and bathrooms, living room, dining room and bar. The hotel's restaurant/bar, the News Café, is a prime spot for people watching. There is a small sauna and whirlpool on the top floor for guests as well as a casino. B/fast buffet inc. *Rates US$75–250.*

Mid-range (US$30–70)

⌂ **Hotel Best Western San José Downtown** (70 rooms) Av 7, Ca 6/8; ✆ 255 4766; f 255 4613; www.bestwesterncostarica.com. Typical chain hotel rooms, with carpeting, AC, cable TV and safety boxes. Pleasant pool, b/fast and airport transfer included. The area, however, is one of the worst in San José

⌂ **Hotel Best Western Irazú** (32 rooms) General Cañas Highway, La Uruca; ✆ 232 4811; f 231 6485; www.bestwesterncostarica.com. Big chain hotel close to the airport with AC, swimming pool, tennis court, bar, casino and 24hr Denny's restaurant. If you're overnight to or from the airport, this is a good option. Free airport shuttle. B/fast inc. Wheelchair access. *Rate US$92.*

⌂ **Hotel Britannia** (24 rooms) Ca 3, Av 11; ✆ 223 6667; f 223 6411; www.hotelbritanniacostarica.com. A former plantation house painted bright pink, this hotel sets itself apart from other restored homes by the attention to detail and luxury of its furnishings. Rooms are large and airy and very well appointed with Victorian reproductions. There is a 4-storey addition at the back of the hotel, recommended for light sleepers. Older rooms have fans while new ones have AC. There is TV, phones and an intimate restaurant in what was once the wine cellar. Wheelchair access. Recommended. *Rates US$89–117.*

⌂ **Hotel del Rey** (104 rooms) Av 1, Ca 9; ✆ 257 7800; f 221 0096; e info@hoteldelrey.com. In the heart of downtown San José, this grand old dame is a historic building — if the walls could talk! The hotel's bar, the Blue Marlin, is an infamous hooker hangout popular with rowdy fishermen looking to hook up more than just marlin. Rooms have king-size beds, carpeting, hot water, cable TV and there is a 24hr casino and restaurant. Street-side rooms are noisy. Wheelchair access. No kids. *Rate US$85.*

⌂ **Hotel Don Carlos** (36 rooms) Ca 9, Av 9; ✆ 221 6707; f 255 0828; www.doncarloshotel.com. A former president's mansion, this hotel harks back to the days of the coffee barons. There is an orchid garden, pleasant atrium to enjoy b/fast in, huge gift shop. original artwork on the walls (all for sale) and a veritable jungle of orchids, ferns and tropical plants throughout, giving guests the feeling of being far from downtown. There is also a large jacuzzi tub to relax in after a hard day of sightseeing. Rooms vary greatly in size and most don't have AC so be sure to enquire. Also included are free local calls, safes in all rooms, internet and b/fast buffet. Recommended. *Rates US$70–80.*

and guests should not walk around after dark (drunks, junkies, beggars — you get the picture). To be honest, I'm not sure why anyone would choose to stay here as the area is quite dangerous (a friend of my husband worked here and was mugged en route to work). *Rate US$67.*

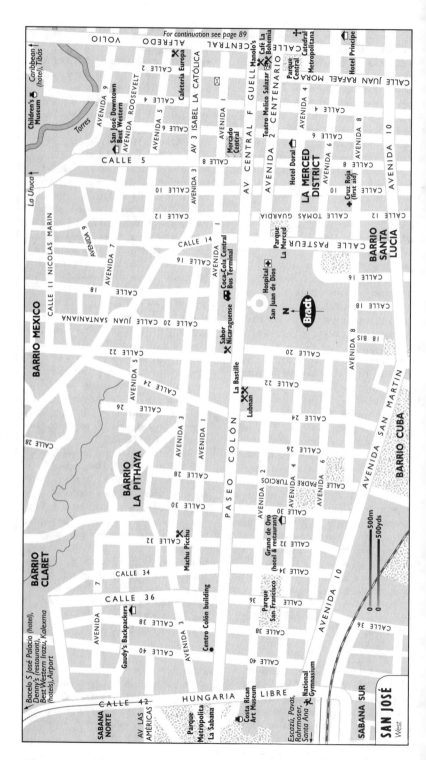

For continuation see page 89

SAN JOSÉ
West

500m
500yds

San José DOWNTOWN

SAN JOSÉ
East

↑ Guadalupe, Moravia, Coronado

Los Yoses, San Pedro, Curridabat, Cartago →

Zapote →

Desamparados, Mojuelita, Aserrí →

Plaza González Víquez →

↑ Ram Luna

↑ La Sabana

Torres

BARRIO OTOYA

BARRIO AMON

BARRIO LA CALIFORNIA

SOLEDAD DISTRICT

LA MERCED DISTRICT

Kap's Place

Bolívar Zoo

JR's House of Ribs

Vesuvio

Hemingway Inn

Café Mundo

Mecca Galería & Restaurant

Bakea

Castillo

Foreign Ministry

Don Carlos

Tranquillo Backpackers

Joluva Guesthouse

Dunn Inn

Britannia

Kekoldi

INS Building Jade Museum

Parque España

Hospital Calderón Guardia

National Library

National Cultural Centre

Parque Nacional

National Museum

Hotel del Mar Restaurant

Election Tribunal

Snake Zoo

Shakti

PICADO

Plaza de la Democracia

National Assembly

Café de la Posada

Court buildings

Casa Ridgeway

Don Wang

Tin-Jo

Hotel Presidente & News Café

El Balcon de Europa

Gold Museum

Café Teatro Nacional

National Theatre

Restaurante Do

La Vaconia

Vishnu

Aurola Holiday Inn

Parque Morazan

Church

Gran Hotel Costa Rica & La Cafeteando

Café La Bohemia

Manolo's

Teatro Melico Salazar

Parque Central

Catedral Metropolitana

Hotel Príncipe

Restaurante Nuestra Tierra

Cafetería Europa

Mercado Central

Hotel Doral

Cruz Roja (first aid)

AVENIDA 13
AVENIDA 15
AVENIDA 11
AVENIDA 9
AVENIDA 7
AVENIDA 5
AVENIDA 13
AVENIDA 11
AVENIDA 9
AVENIDA 3
AVENIDA 1
AVENIDA 1
AVENIDA 3
AVENIDA 9
AVENIDA 17
AVENIDA 11
AVENIDA 9
AVENIDA 7
AVENIDA 5
AVENIDA 1
AVENIDA CENTRAL
AVENIDA 2
AVENIDA 4
AVENIDA 6
AVENIDA 8
AVENIDA 10
AVENIDA 12
AVENIDA 14

CALLE 23
CALLE 33
CALLE 31
CALLE 29
CALLE 27
CALLE 25
CALLE 23 BIS
CALLE 21
CALLE 19
CALLE 17
CALLE 15
CALLE 13
CALLE 11
CALLE 9
CALLE 7
CALLE 5
CALLE 3
CALLE 1
CALLE CENTRAL
CALLE 2
CALLE 4
CALLE 6
CALLE 8
CALLE 10
CALLE 31
CALLE 33
CALLE 10
CALLE 8
AV 10 TER

CALLE ISMAEL MURILLO

CALLE JOSÉ MARÍA CAÑAS

AV DE LAS DAMAS

ALFREDO VOLIO

PASEO RUBEN DARIO

PASEO DE LOS ESTUDIANTES

CALLE JUAN RAFAEL MORA

CALLE CENTENARIO

CALLE FERNANDEZ GUELL

CASTRO MADIZ

SIMÓN BOLIVAR

SAN MARTIN

REPÚBLICA DE CHILE

PASEO SARMIENTO

AV CENTRAL GUELL

AV 3 ISABEL LA CATÓLICA

AVENIDA ROOSEVELT

N

Bradt

0   500m
0   500yds

For continuation see page 88

5

89

🏠 **Hotel Kekoldi** (10 rooms) Av 9, Ca 5/7; ☎ 248 0804; f 248 0767; e reservations@kekoldi.com; www.kekoldi.com. A funky art deco building in Barrio Amon, each room has a large bathroom with hot water, cable TV, safety box and phone. The internal garden is a nice spot to read a book. Free internet and b/fast buffet is inc. Rates US$63–85.

🏠 **Joluva Guesthouse** (7 rooms) Ca 3, Av 9/11; ☎ 223 7961; f 257 7668; e joluva@racsa.co.cr; www.joluva.com. Renovated house catering to gay and lesbian travellers. Rooms are on the small side and a bit dark, as they all open onto the central court. All but one room have private bathrooms with hot water, all have cable TV and b/fast is inc. The hotchpotch of décor is disappointing to look at, but the house still retains a number of its features, such as antique tiled floorings. Rate US$50.

🏠 **Hotel Vesuvio** (20 rooms) Av 11, Ca 13/15; ☎/f 248 9442; www.hotelvesuvio.com. Very clean, carpeted rooms have private bathrooms with hot water, cable TV, safety boxes, ceiling fan and phone. There is a charming little restaurant and nice patio. B/fast inc. Rate US$50.

🏠 **Hotel Dunn Inn** (24 rooms) Av 11, Ca 5; ☎ 222 3232; f 221 4596; www.hoteldunninn.com. A renovated mansion from 1929, the hotel features lots of hardwood, stained glass and original artwork. Rooms are spacious and comfortable and come with ceiling fan, bathroom with hot water, cable TV, minibar, clock radio and phones. Common areas are decorated with greenery and the restaurant serves up delicious fare. There is an easy atmosphere here and guests feel at home instantly. Recommended. Rates US$47–80.

🏠 **Hemingway Inn** (17 rooms) Ca 9, Av 9, Barrio Amon; ☎ 257 8630; f 221 1804; www.hemingwayinn.com. A Spanish-style home from the 1920s, the exterior is charming but the hotel

Budget (under US$30)

🏠 **Hotel Casa Ridgeway** (15 rooms) Ca 15, Av 6; ☎/f 233 6168; e friends@racsa.co.cr. Shared bathrooms with hot water, small, clean and quiet with wheelchair access. B/fast inc. Recommended. Rate US$25 inc tax.

🏠 **Hotel Caribbean** (14 rooms) Ca Central, 100m south of Gran Terminal del Caribe Bus Station; ☎ 248 0472; e info@hotelcaribbean.cr.com. New, clean, with private bathrooms (2 rooms share) and hot water. Dbl US$20 includes cable TV and taxes.

🏠 **Hotel Principe** (35 rooms) Av 6. Ca Central/2; ☎ 222 7983; f 222 7205. All rooms with private bathrooms and hot water. Rate US$16.

inside doesn't live up to the wrapping as rooms are dark. Service is hit and miss. Private bathrooms with hot water, ceiling fans, phones. B/fast inc. Rates US$42–52.

🏠 **Hotel Castillo** (23 rooms) Av 9, Ca 9/11; ☎ 221 5141; e hotelcastillo@racsa.co.cr. A remodelled Spanish-style mansion, rooms have hard wood or tiles, TV, views, private bathrooms and hot water but lack any sense of style and the renovation has lost all charm the house might have once had. There are rooms, suites and kitchenettes available. The hotel's restaurant, La Palma, is noted for its steaks. Rates US$58–78.

🏠 **Hotel Doral** (42 rooms) Av 4, Ca 6/8; ☎ 233 9410; f 233 4827. Very basic rooms with tiled floors, TV, ceiling fan, hot water in private bathrooms, safety box and there is a small restaurant. Rate US$46.

🏠 **Hotel Kap's Place** (17 rooms) Ca 19, Av 11/13; ☎ 221 1169; f 256 4850; www.kapsplace.com. Run by a charming Tica, Kap's Place is neat as a pin and each room has been lovingly decorated with unique painted touches (such as turtles swimming along the walls). All rooms share common cooking, living and dining areas as well as a bright and cheery patio. Karla, the owner, is busy raising her family but is never too busy for her guests and she really goes out of her way to make each one feel like they are at home — 'mi casa es tu casa'. Recommended for quiet folks who are interested in experiencing a Tico home. Recommended. Rates US$38–50.

🏠 **Hotel Kalexma** (10 rooms) 50m west, 25m south of Juan Pablo II overpass in La Uruca; ☎ 290 2624; f 231 0638; www.kalexma.com. 6 rooms have private bathrooms, 4 have shared facilities and all have hot water. 3 of the rooms have TV and there are 2 TV lounges. Kitchen facilities. B/fast inc. Also has a Spanish-language school. Rates US$25–35.

🏠 **Tranquilo Backpackers** Ca 7, Av 9/11; ☎ 223 3189; www.tranquilobackpackers.com. The Rolls-Royce of hostels. Excellent (and free) pancakes, fun and funky décor, very safe and clean. Free internet, luggage storage. There is a communal kitchen as well as sushi, curry and pasta nights. Friendly environment and hot showers. Dorm beds US$8, dbl US$19.

🏠 **Hostel Gaudy's Backpackers** Av 5, Ca 36/38; ☎/f 258 2937; e gaudys@backpackers.co.cr. Dormitory rooms with shared bathrooms or private rooms with private bathrooms. Clean, safe and has wheelchair access. Dorms US$7, private room US$20.

WHERE TO EAT This being a cosmopolitan city with international influences, diners can find a cornucopia of flavours to tempt their taste buds. Remember that service tends to be very slow and the 10% tip is already included in the bill by law. If you do receive excellent service (don't hold your breath), feel free to add a bit more.

✗ **Café Teatro Nacional** Lobby of National Theatre; ℡ 221 1329. A wonderful spot for a brief respite from the bustle outside and a chance to bask in the glory that is the National Theatre. Sipping a delicious cup of coffee at a marble café table as you watch the pedestrian traffic outside is like a mini-holiday to Rome or Paris (but with better weather and lower prices). There are few cafés or eateries to be found anywhere on the planet that are as luxuriously decorated and steeped in such history. Highly recommended. *Open Mon–Fri 09.00–17.00, Sat–Sun 09.00–16.00. Meals average US$15.*

✗ **Cafeteando** Gran Hotel Costa Rica; ℡ 221 4011. A pleasant spot for people watching. *Open 24hrs a day. Average price per meal US$12.*

✗ **News Café** Hotel Presidente; ℡ 222 3022. Surprisingly good food and service in one of the prime spots to watch the world walk by on the mall. *Average price per meal US$15. Open daily 06.00–22.00.*

✗ **La Vasconia** Av 1, Ca 3/5; ℡ 223 4857. Offers typical *Tico* fare and a must-see for football fans as the walls are covered with team photos dating from 1905. *Average price per meal US$3. Open 10.00–01.00 daily.*

✗ **Restaurante Do** Av 1, Ca 7; ℡ 258 0208. Japanese sushi bar. *Closed Sun.*

✗ **Del Mar Restaurante** Av 1, Ca 9; ℡ 221 7272. The infamous Café del Rey, noted for its prostitute-laden bar, serves up American-style food 24hrs a day in this, its restaurant (hey, those girls work up an appetite). *Average meal US$20.*

✗ **El Balcon de Europa** Av Central, Ca 9; ℡ 221 4841. The oldest restaurant in San José (since 1905), this is a classic spot for Italian cuisine served in a pleasant atmosphere. *Average meal US$12. Open 11.00–22.00; closed Sat.*

✗ **Restaurante Nuestra Tierra** Av 2, Ca 15, across from the Nacional Museum; ℡ 258 6500; Av 9, Ca 3; ℡ 2582983. Typical *Tico* food in a setting that resembles a typical *Tico* house. Seating is on long, wooden benches with bunches of onions hanging on the walls and waiters are dressed like *campensinos*. Food is extremely tasty, with roasted chicken, *chicharrones* and handmade tortillas in huge quantities. Highly recommended. *Average meal US$10. Open 24hrs daily.*

✗ **Café de la Posada** Pedestrian walkway across from the National Museum; ℡ 257 9414. One of the best deals for lunch in town. Specialities are perfectly spiced Argentine *empanadas* and pastries. *Meals average US$6. Open Mon–Fri 09.00–19.00, Sat 10.00–19.00*

✗ **Café La Bohemia** Next to Melico Salazar Theatre, Av 2, Ca Central; ℡ 253 6348. High ceilings and dark wood give the café an old-world feel. Situated on the corner, across from the park and Metropolitan Church (the amplified droning of the priest's daily prayers is a bit wracking on the nerves if you are trying to enjoy a quiet moment over coffee and a book), the location is prime for watching the busy traffic go by. Excellent crêpes and the service is wonderfully attentive. *Average price per meal US$6. Open Mon–Sat 08.00–22.00.*

✗ **Cafeteria Europa** Av 3/5, Ca Central; ℡ 222 1222. European-style café serving customers 24hrs a day. *Meals average US$8.*

✗ **Manolo's** Av Central, Ca Central/2; ℡ 221 2041. On pedestrian bd. A classic *Tico* eatery with some of the best black bean soup anywhere. Renowned for its *churros*, long, tube-like doughnuts. *Average price per meal US$ 4. Open 24hrs daily.*

✗ **Vishnu** Av 1, Ca 1/3; ℡ 256 6063. Quality vegetarian restaurant chain with somewhat sparse atmosphere but food more than makes up for it. Excellent value! *Avrege price per meal US$4. Open Mon–Sat 07.00–21.30, Sun 09.00–19.30.*

✗ **Shakti** Av 8, Ca 13; ℡ 222 4475. Another vegetarian offering (seems Hindu names and vegetarian are synonymous here). Yummy fruit shakes, veggie burgers and salads. *Average price per meal US$9. Open Mon–Fri 08.00–19.00, Sat 10.00–17.00.*

✗ **Tin-Jo** Av 6/8, Ca 11; ℡ 221 7605, www.tinjo.com. Nestled in a restored plantation house decorated with eclectic Asian artefacts, this is one of the best restaurants in the country. Varied menu offers exquisite Thai, east Indian, Indonesian, Japanese and Chinese foods that never fail to send the senses on a sublime trip to the Orient. Service, atmosphere and food all score top marks – the perfect restaurant in my book! Highly recommended. Note: the neighbourhood is a bit sketchy so take a taxi. *Average price per meal US$15. Open Mon–Thu 11.30–15.00, 17.30–22.00, Fri–Sat 11.30–15.00, 17.30–23.00, Sun 11.30–22.00.*

✗ **Don Wang** Next door to Tin-Jo; ✆ 223 5925. Perhaps the best Chinese restaurant in Costa Rica and one of the few to enjoy authentic dim sum. *Average meal US$17. Open Mon 08.00–15.00, 18.00–23.00, Tue–Sat 08.00–23.00, Sun 08.00–22.00.*

✗ **Café Mundo** Av 9, Ca 15, Barrio Amon; ✆ 222 6190. Another antique home transformed into trendy eatery, this is the spot where the 'in-crowd' of hip Josefinos hangs out, intermingled with guidebook-clutching tourists. The fabric wallpaper with cabbage roses on the high walls against dark hardwood floors captures the building's turn-of-the-century elegance. The menu has international cuisine, such as Caesar salad, wood-oven pizza, crab cakes (my favourite) and pasta. In my opinion, I feel the quality of food has slipped a bit over the last few years (perhaps coasting a bit on its popularity) but it is still worth a visit, if only to sip a cocktail on the large veranda. *Average meal US$15. Open Mon–Thu 11.30–22.00, Fri 11.30–23.00, Sat 17.00–23.00.*

✗ **JR's House of Ribs** Av 11, Ca 7; ✆ 223 0523. Got a hankering for an American-style steakhouse? This is the place for you, with Fred Flintstone-sized ribs. *Average meal US$30. Open Mon–Fri 12.00–14.30, 18.00–22.00, Sat 12.00–23.00, Sun 12.00–17.00.*

✗ **Bakea** Av 7, Ca 11; ✆ 221 1051. Intriguing fusion of French cuisine with international flavours professionally served up in an antique home creatively transformed into chic eatery. Portions are small but allow for more room to experience their delicious cuisine. One of San José's best bets. *Average meal US$30. Open Mon 12.00–16.00, Tue–Fri 12.00–midnight, Sat 18.00–midnight.*

✗ **Mecca Galeria & Restaurante** Av 11, Ca 15; ✆ 222 8957. Artsy setting for delicious tapas and creative cuisine with flavours from around the world. Perfect spot for a laid-back nosh with a happenin' groove. *Average meal US$19. Open Mon–Sat 17.00–midnight.*

✗ **Machu Picchu** Av 1/3, Ca 32; ✆ 222 7384. This is a case of 'don't judge the book by the cover' – despite its location and hotchpotch décor, this restaurant serves up the same delicious Peruvian cuisine as its upmarket sister in San Pedro. Wonderful *causa limena* (mashed potatoes stuffed with seafood) and potent *pisco sours* (although *nothing* is as potent as that hot sauce). *Average price per meal US$20. Open Mon–Sat 11.00–15.00, 18.00–01.00.*

✗ **El Grano de Oro** Av 2/4, Ca 30; ✆ 255 3322. In the hotel of the same name. In a word – outstanding. Creative international cuisine beautifully presented and expertly served (the fish in macadamian nut crust is divine!). The patio is an oasis of calm, the perfect place to linger over one of the many excellent wines offered. Not surprisingly, this is one of the most popular fine-dining spots and the limited number of tables require reservations to avoid disappointment. Most interesting is that all the restaurant's profits fund a home for young single mothers – gourmet dining with a social conscience. *Average price per meal US$34. Open daily 06.00–22.00.*

✗ **Lubnan** Paseo Colón, Ca 22/24; ✆ 257 6071. One of the first Lebanese restaurants in the country, Lubnan serves up Middle Eastern delights at decent prices. The restaurant at the front is acceptable while the bar at the back is where the hipsters gravitate (pillows on the floor, wood stump stools at the bar, hookah pipes). Belly dancers entertain on the weekends, the waiters wear fez caps and the Lebanese culture club is upstairs so this is definitely the 'real deal'. Unfortunately, the service is horrible! Reservations made are ignored, the waiters aren't allowed to move about when the belly dancer is performing and the bartender is snarky. If you can put up with the appalling waiting staff (I guess they're called that for the amount of time they make you wait), the food is actually worth it (the appetiser sampler is massive!). *Average price per meal US$12. Open Tue–Sat 11.00–15.00, 18.00–01.00.*

✗ **La Bastille** Corner of Ca 22 and Paseo Colón; ✆ 255 4994; www.la-bastille-restaurante.com Funky spot with interesting artwork and very good French cuisine are ample reasons to storm this Bastille! *Average price per meal US$15. Open Mon–Sat 12.00–14.00, 18.30–22.30.*

✗ **Sabor Nicaraguense** Corner of Ca 20 and Paseo Colón; ✆ 248 2547. Clean, bright and cheery with Nicaraguan fare at giveaway prices. Recommended for a filling, delicious cheap lunch. *Average price per meal US$5. Open 07.00–21.00.*

✗ **Denny's** Next to Hotel Best Western Iraz; ✆ 231 3500. Part of the American chain, Denny's is open 24hrs a day and is a favoured late-night munchies spot for partiers heading home from a late night at the bar. Pancakes, hamburgers, steaks – all straightforward diner-type food and served in heaping portions. *Average price per meal US$9. Open 24hrs daily.*

✗ **Ram Luna** Aserri; ✆ 230 3060. Excellent views, nicely decorated, varied menu with the emphasis on Tico food. The entire restaurant is geared to the tourist crowd and has regular performances by folkloric dancers and singers. Fun night in *tiquicia*! *Average price per meal US$20. Open Tue–Fri 16.00–23.00, Sat 12.00–23.00, Sun 12.00–22.00*

ENTERTAINMENT AND NIGHTLIFE As a large, metropolitan city, San José has no shortage of nightspots for those who want to dance and drink. The minimum entry age is 18 and bars usually don't get hopping until after 23.00, closing in the wee hours of the morning (usually whenever people start to head for home). Establishments are categorised as follows.

Latin dance clubs

Salsa 54 Av 1/3, Ca 3; ☎ 233 3814
Castro's Av 13, Ca 22; ☎ 256 8789. Really rough neighbourhood but awesome dancing.

El Tobogan 200m north, 100m east of La Republica; ☎ 223 8920. Live bands and great dancing!
Ebony 56 El Pueblo; ☎ 223 2195

Bars/discos

Café 83 Sur Av 2, Ca 25; ☎ 221 2369. Hip-hop, soul and R&B.
La Plaza El Pueblo; ☎ 233 5516

Gravity El Pueblo
Friend's Disco El Pueblo; ☎ 233 5283
Twister Club El Pueblo; ☎ 222 5746

Reggae, hip-hop

Ebony 56 El Pueblo; ☎ 223 2195
Cocoloco El Pueblo; ☎ 222 8782. Latin/reggae music.
Ivory El Pueblo; ☎ 233 9964. Reggae.

La Caribeña ☎ 253 9276. Reggae.
Tarrico's El Pueblo. Hip-hop.
Manhattan El Pueblo; ☎ 233 2309. Hip-hop.

Live music

El Cuartel de la Boca del Monte Av 1, Ca 21/23; ☎ 221 0327
Jazz Café Main road in San Pedro; ☎ 253 8933
Goya Bar & Restaurant Av 1, Ca 5/7; ☎ 256 5815

Luna Roja Av 9/11, Ca 1; ☎ 222 5944
La Casa de la Urraca Tibas; ☎ 235 5719
El Trapiche La Uruca; ☎ 223 4708
Malibu La Uruca; ☎ 258 1155

Gay bars

Avispa Av 8/10, Ca 1; ☎ 223 5343. Features monthly women-only nights.
Club Oh Av 14/16, Ca 2; ☎ 256 6332

El Bochinche Av 10/12, Ca 11; ☎ 221 0500. *Open Wed–Sat.*

WHAT TO SEE AND DO Most of San José can be explored on foot, as the majority of museums and points of interest are within an eight-block radius. The **Pedestrian Boulevard** runs down the centre of downtown for ten blocks, parallel to Paseo Colón. Here you'll find enough shoe shops to keep even Imelda Marcos happy, casinos, *soda* restaurants, beggars, hawkers, fruit stands, the **Gold Museum** and the **Teatro Nacional**. If you have a day to explore, here is an easy route around the main sights of San José that will show you the very best of the city.

Have a coffee at the café in the **Teatro Nacional** (*Av 2, Ca 3/5*). Take the guided tour through this impressive building, inspired by La Scala in Italy. When the prima donna Adelina Patti toured the continent in 1890, she couldn't perform in San José owing to the lack of a proper theatre. The coffee barons pooled together their resources and on 19 October 1897 the Paris Opera and Ballet inaugurated the Teatro Nacional with a performance of *Faust*. The exterior is classic Renaissance while the interior is marble, gilt and lush frescoes. The ceiling of the inner lobby has a mural depicting coffee being harvested and shipped – the old five colon banknotes featured the same scene. The main floor can be raised to meet the level of the stage to allow the transformation into a ballroom. The horseshoe-shaped theatre has box seats and velvet armrests, although the 'cheap seats' up top are crowded and can be stuffy. Performance tickets are very affordable and if you have the opportunity to enjoy a concert, do so as sitting in this theatre is truly an incredible experience.

After the theatre tour, walk down the street to the **Plaza de la Cultura** (*Av Central, Ca 1/5*) and check out the booths selling souvenirs. Here, you'll also see the bronze statue of **Don 'Pepe' Figuerres**, three-time president and beloved leader who abolished the army. Next is the **Bellavista Fortress**, which was the former army barracks (bullet holes from the civil war of 1948 are still visible in the outer walls) but now houses the **National Museum**. Head across the street for lunch at **Nuestra Tierra** for a real taste of *tiquicia*.

Head back towards the Teatro Nacional and visit the **Gold Museum** under the plaza. Continue east on the boulevard and turn left at the **Banco Central** to check out the impressive statues of *campensinos* by *Tico* sculptor Francisco Zuniga. One block north is the **Correo Central** (Post Office), an ornate building in the Baroque style. Here you'll find the **Postal Museum**, **Tourist Information Office** and the **Café de Correo**, where you can rest and enjoy a cup of Java.

Continue and head west along Avenue Central to the **Central Market**, a maze of stalls selling everything from magic herbs to rabbits to souvenir T-shirts. Built in 1881, it's dark, noisy and a real experience! There are some excellent little *sodas* here where lunch can be had for a song. Be careful here of pickpockets and purse snatchers.

If you prefer to get out of town, the **Costa Rica Highlight Tour** (℡ *297 0664*) is highly recommended as it gives a slice of the best of the country in one day. A full-day trip, it takes you to a coffee plantation, waterfalls, hummingbird garden, the Poas Volcano, a jungle lodge and a boat ride down a river full of wildlife. B/fast, lunch, transportation and bilingual guides are included for US$79, children 5–11 years US$45.

Other day tours include the **Calypso Catamaran Tour** (℡ *256 2727; www.calypsotours.co*m), which takes guests to a deserted island for a day and includes transportation, meals, soft drinks, marimba music and guide. A great opportunity to spend time at the beach if you're otherwise stuck in the Central Valley. Cost of tour US$99.

Most rafting companies operate out of San José (see *Chapter 4, Rafting*, page 75) and you can take either one- or two-day rafting tours.

ART GALLERIES The following galleries feature classic and contemporary Costa Rican artists.

The National Gallery Costa Rica Science & Culture Centre, end of Ca 4; ℡ 258 4929; www.museocr.com

Contemporary Art and Design Museum of Costa Rica Av 3/5, Ca 11/15; ℡ 257 9370; f 257 8702

Museum of Costa Rican Art Housed in the former airport in Sabana Park; ℡ 222 7155;

www.musarco.go.cr

Klaus Steinmatz 25m south of Plaza Rolex, Escazú; ℡ 289 5403

Sophia Wannamaker CR-North American Cultural Centre, Av Central, Ca 37, Barrio Dent; ℡ 207 7554; www.cccncr.com

THEATRE San José has an abundance of theatres, offering bedroom farces to Shakespearian tragedies. All performances are in Spanish, except for the Little Theatre Group, the longest-running English-language theatre in Latin America. Performances are held four times a year at the **Blanche Brown Theatre** (℡ *355 1623*) in Escazú. **The National Theatre Company** (℡ *257 8304*) is internationally acclaimed and produces a wide range of programming, encompassing classics, Shakespeare, drama as well as original works by Costa Rican playwrights. There are numerous small theatres around San José running a variety of productions on a nightly basis. Best bet is to check out the 'Weekend Calendar' of the *Tico Times* or the 'Viva' section in *La Nacíon* for plays and times. Here are but a few of the most popular venues.

Auditorio Nacional Museo de los Niños; ☏ 222 7647
Teatro Fanal/1887 Av 3, Ca 11 y 7; ☏ 257 5524
Teatro Melico Salazar Av segunda, diagonal a la Catedral Metropolitana; ☏ 221 4952

Teatro UCR Bellas Artes Facultad de Bellas Artes, UCR, San Pedro; ☏ 207 4095
Teatro Abya Yala Torres del Colegio de Costa Rica. Complejo Fanal; ☏ 241 1519, 240 6071

MUSEUMS San José has a number of excellent museums, many close enough to each other that you could visit a few all in o ne day.

Museo de Oro Precolombino (Museum of Pre-Columbian Gold) under the Plaza de la Cultura in downtown San José (☏ *243 4202; www.museodelbancocentral.org; open Tue–Sun 10.00–16.30*). This impressive underground building creates a mysterious and dark background for the gleaming beauty of the golden pieces, which seemingly float thanks to being suspended by transparent strings. These pre-Columbian jewels have wonderfully eccentric representations of animals, such as frogs, snakes, insects, crocodiles, lobsters, birds and even sharks.

Museo Nacional (National Museum) (*Av Central, Ca 17;* ☏ *257 1433; www.museocostarica.com; open Tue–Sat 08.30–16.30, Sun 09.00–16.00*), is housed in the former fortress built in 1870 (bullet holes from the 1948 civil war are still visible). The archaeological room offers several indigenous artefacts made of stone and clay. The colonial room has period furniture and religious art brought by the Spaniards during the time of the conquest. Another section of the museum is dedicated to temporary exhibits.

Museo de arte contemporaneo (Contemporary Art Museum) (*Av 3/5, Ca 11/15;* ☏ *257 9370; open Tue–Sat 10.00–17.00*) is located in what used to be the National Liquor factory. This former factory has been transformed into an artistic and graceful set of buildings and grounds. Exhibits vary and the small and medium-sized auditoriums offer dance and theatre presentations.

Museo de Ciencias Naturales La Salle (Museum of Natural Science) (*southwest corner of La Sabana Park;* ☏ *232 1306; www.ulasalle.ed.cr; open Mon–Sat 07.30–16.00, Sun 09.00–17.00*). Over 65,000 specimens of mineralogy, palaeontology, zoology and archaeology.

Insect Museum (*basement of the University of Costa Rica Music School;* ☏ *207 5318; open Mon–Fri 13.00–13.45*). Contains over 500 insects of Central and South America, including beautiful butterflies.

EAST OF SAN JOSÉ – LOS YOSES, SAN PEDRO, CURRIDABAT

The east end of San José is home to universities and older, genteel neighbourhoods. Students rub shoulders with the well-heeled in one big mix of culture that has something for every taste and pocketbook.

GETTING THERE AND AWAY From San José, take Avenue 2 east past the National Museum – Los Yoses begins where the road merges with Avenue Central by Kentucky Fried Chicken. Follow the road to Mall San Pedro and go halfway around the La Hispanidad traffic circle; at the other side is San Pedro. Keep following the main road and at Plaza del Sol Shopping Centre begins Curridabat.

WHERE TO STAY All prices are based on double occupancy high-season rates (December–April) unless otherwise noted. Prices are in US dollars and do not include the 16.39% hotel tax.

Boutique Hotel Jade (30 rooms) 200m north of Autos Subaru; ☎ 224 2455; f 224 2166; www.hotelboutiquejade.com. European-run hotel beautifully decorated and well maintained with tastefully decorated bright and airy rooms – the entire place has a European 'chicness' about it. Amenities include a swimming pool, cable TV, phones, minibar, hot water and b/fast. Hotel Jade is home to the outstanding Jurgen's Restaurant, one of the best spots in town for a great dinner. *Rates US$97–115.*

Casa Agua Buena (22 rooms) Lourdes de San Pedro; ☎ 280-3548; e rastern@racsa.co.cr; www.aguabuena.org. 3 old, converted houses provide a semi-communal living arrangement for those on a budget in San José for a week or a month. There is a common kitchen, living and dining areas, cable TV and washing machine. The houses are operated by the human rights organisation of the same name, which works primarily with people living with HIV/AIDS in Costa Rica and other Central American countries. *Rates US$80 per week, US$250 per month.*

Hotel 1492–Jade y Oro (10 rooms) Av 1/3, Ca 31; ☎ 256 5913; f 280 6206; www.hotel1492.com. This elegant Spanish mansion turned small hotel makes guests feel at home. Rooms are comfortably furnished, with sgl or queen beds and showers with hot water. The small garden offers a quiet spot for reflecting on the day's events or reading. B/fast is inc. *Rates US$70–90.*

Hotel Don Fadrique (20 rooms) Corner of Av 8, Ca 37, next to Club Aleman; ☎ 225 8186; f 224 9746; www.hoteldonfadrique.com. Another former mansion, this cosy hotel features a large internal patio with gardens and a fountain where the inc b/fast is served. Rooms have queen beds, bathrooms, hot water, cable TV and security boxes. What really sets this place apart is the commitment to art, as every room has original artwork by Costa Rican artists – wandering around the hotel is like walking into an art gallery. *Rate US$70.*

Hotel Milvia (9 rooms) 200m east, 100m north of Munoz and Nanne; ☎ 225 4543; f 225 7801; www.novanet.co.cr/milvia. The grande dame of the neighbourhood, this 1930s' Caribbean-styled mansion has been carefully restored to its former glory, creating an oasis of art and architecture in the middle of the busy city. Antiques co-mingle with modern paintings for an artsy blending of eras. Each large room features a king-size bed, private bathroom, cable TV and telephone. The upstairs reading room has internet access and the beautifully manicured garden beckons one to relax with a good book and a cool drink. Attentive service makes each guest feel at ease and truly welcome. B/fast inc. An excellent choice for a mid-range hotel. *Rate US$69.*

Hotel Le Bergerac (26 rooms) Ca 35; ☎ 234 7850; www.bergerachotel.com. Charming hotel on a quiet side street with rooms opening onto a lush inner garden. Rooms are spacious with handmade wooden furniture and gleaming hardwood floors. All rooms have access to the gardens and some have private patios. The wonderful French restaurant, L'Ile de France, is housed in the hotel and the b/fasts (inc with the rooms) are delicious. Excellent customer service, quiet surroundings and wonderful food make this hotel an excellent choice for a San José base. *Rates US$68–110.*

Apartotel Los Yoses (23 rooms) Main road across from Mall San Pedro; ☎ 225 0033; f 225 5595; www.apartotel.com. An apartment-hotel complex, each room is a small suite, complete with full kitchen, living room, dining room, hot water and high-speed internet connection. Despite being on one of the busiest roads in Costa Rica, the rooms are surprisingly quiet. A small pool and sundeck adds to the hotel's appeal. A good option for those who want their budget to stretch but still have access to amenities. *Rates US$58–115.*

Theologos Apartahotel (3 rooms) South of Mas X Menos 725m south of Ferreteria El Mar; ☎ 225 6565; e jtheologos@hotmail.com. 3 furnished suites have hot water, private bathroom, full kitchen, internet, cable TV, maid service, secure parking. Lovely gardens and original artwork (Jim Theologos, the owner, is a well-known painter) make for an interesting location to hang your hat for an extended period. *Rates US$52, US$240 weekly, US$640 for 4 weeks.*

Hotel Las Orquideas (15 rooms) Av Central, 75m west of Automercado; ☎ 283 0095; f 234 8203; www.casaorquideas.8k.com. Simple accommodation in an old mansion. Rooms have private bathrooms, hot water, cable TV. B/fast inc. *Rate US$45.*

D'Galah Hotel & Spa (25 rooms) North of University of Costa Rica campus; ☎ 280 0614;

f 280 8092; **e** dgalah@racsa.co.cr. Modern apartment complex with rooms and some suites. Rooms have hot water, cable TV and kitchenettes but are noisy because of the busy street in front. There is a pool, small gym, sauna, jacuzzi, spa and nice gardens. For the price, it's a good option if you need to be near the university. B/fast inc. *Rate US$35.*

🏠 **B&B Madeleine's** (7 rooms) Residencial Malaga west of Sabanilla Church; **📞** 283 0158; **f** 280 4764; **e** bbmady@racsa.co.cr. 4 furnished rooms in 2 houses within a gated community. Quiet and family run, some rooms have a shared bathroom and a shared kitchen. There is a TV in the lounge and secure parking. *Rates US$20–25.*

🏠 **Hostel Toruma** (18 rooms) Av Central, across from KFC in Los Yoses; **📞** 224 4085; **f** 234 8186; www.hosteltoruma.com. The first hostel in Costa Rica to be a member of Hostelling International, this is the grande dame for those seeking budget accommodation. Located in the home of former president (José Figueres Ferrer) built at the beginning of the 19th century, it's likely to be one of the most stately hostels you'll ever encounter (at least from the outside). Rooms are basic, either in a dormitory with bunk beds or private rooms with sgl or dbl beds. All have shared bathrooms. Its location makes it easily accessible to downtown or the university area. Free internet, shared kitchen, living area. *Rate US$10.*

✖ WHERE TO EAT

✖ **Bagelmans** **📞** 224 2432. On the main road, upmarket deli with excellent bagels (the closest to New York you'll get in Costa Rica). The atmosphere is relaxed and they have a drive-through and delivery service as well. *Average price per meal US$6. Open daily 07.00–21.00.*

✖ **Il Ritorno** Inside Casa Italia, south of KFC, Ca 31; **📞** 225 0543. Excellent Italian food. For those who want to splurge with a culinary trip to boot, this is the place to do it. *Average meal US$12. Open Mon–Sat 12.00–14.30, 18.00–22.00.*

✖ **Restaurant L'Ile de France** Hotel Le Bergerac, south of Av Central, Ca 35; **📞** 283 5812. All the flavours of exquisite French cooking are presented in an elegant setting by attentive waiters for a true Gallic experience (but without the Parisian attitude). Highly recommended. *Meals average US$35. Open Mon–Sat 18.00–22.00.*

✖ **Pasteleria y Cafeteria Giacomin** Next to Automercado; **📞** 234 2551. The best bakery in the country (in my opinion) with delectable European-style cakes, pastries, ice cream and other such indulgences. *Average meal US$6. Open Mon–Fri 08.00–12.00, 14.00–19.00, Sat 08.00–12.00, 14.00–18.00.*

✖ **Café Ruisenor** Av Central, Ca 41, east of Automercado; **📞** 225 2562. A pleasant spot for a brief respite from the noisy traffic outside. Excellent European food and desserts make this a perfect luncheon spot. *Meals average US$17. Open Mon–Fri 07.00–20.00, Sat 10.00–18.00.*

✖ **La Trattoria** Behind Automercado; **📞** 224 7065. Delicious pizza, pastas and homemade sauces served in an inviting atmosphere. *Average meal US$12. Open Mon–Thu 12.00–22.00, Fri–Sat 12.00–23.00, Sun 12.00–16.30.*

✖ **Jurgen's Grill** In Hotel Boutique Jade, Ca 39; **📞** 283 2239. German chef Jurgen Mormels works culinary magic in his beautifully designed restaurant. The menu is French but with an emphasis on fresh and light offerings. Service is attentive yet not overbearing, décor is sleek yet engaging and the presentation has elevated food on a plate to works of art. An impressive wine cellar complements the well-executed menu. *Average meal US$35. Open Mon–Fri 12.00–14.00, 18.00–22.00, Sat 18.00–23.00.*

✖ **Donde Carlos** Av 10, Ca 43; **📞** 225 0819. A new entry to the restaurant scene with a refreshing take on the Costa Rican grill. Impressive wine list, relaxed ambience – overall good value in a pleasant dining environment. *Average meal US$14. Open Mon–Thu 12.00–15.00, 18.30–22.30, Fri 12.00–15.00, 18.30–23.00, Sun 12.00–19.00.*

✖ Fast-food chains are sprouting up all over San José and 2 of the better ones are **Subway** (**📞** 283 6651) and **Quiznos** (**📞** 281 0705), both on the main road approaching the Mall. *Average price per meal US$6.*

✖ **Restaurant and Pub Olio** Av 5, Ca 33/35; **📞** 281 0541. Situated in an old corner building, the interior is an appealing mix of antique brick and wood fused with funky works of art and ambient lighting (a rarity in Costa Rica!). Primarily a tapas bar, the kitchen's offerings are delectable and just as creative as the restaurant's décor. The preferred hangout for young professionals and the artsy university crowd. Highly recommended. *Average meal US$15–20. Open Mon–Fri 11.30–01.00, Sat 16.00–midnight.*

✖ **Café Expresivo** Av 9, Ca 29/31; **📞** 224 1202. Hey, daddy-o, looking for a laid-back café to check out local performers? Very artsy café/gallery features performers (mostly singers) throughout the week. Cool place to hang with the local artsies (food is so-so but great atmosphere). *Average meal US$12. Open daily 16.00–midnight.*

✖ **Whapin'** Av 13, Ca 35/37; ↘ 283 1480. Funky little bar/restaurant with some of the best Caribbean food this side of Cahuita. Live music occasionally. *Average meal US$10. Open Sat–Thu 11.30–14.30, 18.00–22.00, Fri 18.00–23.00.*

✖ **Parrillada El Churrasco** Av 9/11, Ca 31; ↘ 225 0778. An institution in these parts, this Argentinian steakhouse has excellent food served by friendly and professional wait staff in an elegant (but not stuffy) atmosphere. If you are a meat lover, you owe it to yourself to try the Argentine method for cooking beef, as the results are incredibly delicious, allowing the full flavour of a great piece of meat to be savoured. Highly recommended as a splurge. *Average meal US$20. Open Mon –Sat 12.00–14.30, 18.30–22.30, Sun 12.00–16.00, 19.00–22.00.*

✖ **Café El Farolito** Av 13, Ca 33; ↘ 225 6875. A quaint spot for coffee and desserts. Also has a variety of macrobiotic products. *Average US$4.*

✖ **Café Sabor y Suenos** Av 13, Ca 31/33; ↘ 257 4148. Tucked away in a residential neighbourhood, this former house turned trendy café/bar has a limited but delicious menu of International cuisine. The walls are hung with original pieces of art and there's an open-air patio in the back where live music is featured on Thu and Fri nights. A fun spot for dinner. *Meals average US$8. Open Mon–Fri 12.00–15.00, 18.00–22.00, Sat 16.00–22.00.*

✖ **Antojitos Restaurant** ↘ 225 9525. Across from Mall San Pedro. Part of the chain of Mexican restaurants, the food is good and atmosphere festive. *Meals average US$15. Open Sun–Thu 11.00–midnight, Fri–Sat 11.00–00.30.*

✖ **Le Chandelier** 50m west, 100m south of ICE; ↘ 225 3980. Those who crave gourmet French food should head over to Le Chandelier. The stately restaurant, appointed in rich tones of dark woods, sets the stage for chef Claude Dubois's masterful creations which marry the best of French cuisine with local flavours such as veal in a tamarindo sauce or Long Island duck in a pepper and passion fruit sauce. Dubois's fame has extended to the grocery aisles, where his gourmet line of ready-made food products is available at Automercados (excellent sauces and sausages). Pricey but worth it. *Meals average US$40. Open Mon–Fri 11.30–14.00, 18.30–22.30, Sat 18.30–23.00.*

✖ **Spoon** 125m west of ICE; ↘ 224 0328. This uniquely Costa Rican coffee shop has great ambience and even better food. Service is fast and the extensive menu offers everything from *empanadas* to *gallo pinto* to a delectable *Torte Chileno*. Yum! *Average meal US$10. Open daily 07.00–22.00.*

✖ **Il Pomodoro** Behind Outlet Mall; ↘ 283 1010. A veritable institution in San Pedro, Il Pomodoro serves up some of the best wood-oven pizza on the east side of San José. This is a newer, larger location than the original (which is still near the UCR) and the handsome brick building sets a comfortable atmosphere for delicious Italian fare (although softer lighting would make it so much better). Good, straight-ahead Italian cooking using fresh ingredients. *Meals average US$16. Open Sun–Thu 11.30–23.00, Fri–Sat 11.30–midnight.*

✖ **Restaurante Vegetariano San Pedro** Next door to Il Pomodoro; ↘ 224 1163. If you're looking for great vegetarian food, this is the place. Creative menu and relaxed ambience make it a popular student hangout. *Meals average US$7. Open Mon–Fri 10.00–18.00.*

✖ **Tico Burguesas** On the main road across from Banco Popular; ↘ 283 6840. Hamburgers and other fast food with a *Tico* flair are offered in this 24hr restaurant. *Average price per meal US$1.*

✖ **Rostipollos** Inside Calle Real Shopping Centre; ↘ 253 2784. One of the most successful chain restaurants in Costa Rica and for good reason — roasted chickens over coffee wood, great tortillas and prompt service in nicely appointed surroundings. Careful — one visit and you're likely to become an addict. Great value for money. *Average meal US$6. Open daily 11.00–22.00.*

✖ **Moby Dick** On main road, just past Ca Real; ↘ 224 7613. Excellent sushi, Japanese and Korean food (I've had friends swear it's the best sushi they've had *anywhere* in the western hemisphere). Atmosphere is a touch sterile (because of the blinding fluorescent lights) but the food and affordable prices more than make up for any shortcomings. Highly recommended. *Average meal US$11. Open Mon–Sat 10.30–15.00, 17.30–22.30, Sun 12.00–22.00.*

✖ **Machu Picchu** 150m north of traffic circle; ↘ 222 7384. Situated in an old house turned Peruvian eatery, their backyard patio offers the perfect spot to indulge in delicious (but strong!) *pisco* sours, *ceviche* (fish or seafood 'cooked' in lime juice) and exquisite *causa limenas* (mashed potatoes stuffed with seafood). Watch out — that innocent-looking hot sauce is a killer so use the smallest dot for seasoning. One of the best Peruvian restaurants you'll find in Costa Rica. *Meals average US$18.*

Open Mon–Sat 11.00–15.00, 18.00–22.00, Sun 11.00–16.00.

ENTERTAINMENT AND NIGHTLIFE As with any city, bars open and shut their doors faster than you can say *'cerveza'* so I'm only noting those establishments that have been around long enough to prove their staying power (and popularity). On the main street in Los Yoses, **Bar El Yos** (↘ *280 1139*), next to Hotel Las Orquideas, is a happening spot with the younger, hip crowd with live music sometimes. Across the street is **El Río Bar & Restaurant** (↘ *225 8371*), which has outdoor seating, bands at weekends and a fun, party atmosphere.

Across from Mall San Pedro are a number of bars, some of which change hands seemingly every month. **Raices** (↘ *280 4964*) across from Mall San Pedro, is *the* place for reggae and roots in San José. For those about to rock, head to **Vyrus** (↘ *280 5890*) 200m west of the ICE building where classic rock rules.

Heading into San Pedro, **Anochecer** (↘ *234 1410*) by the petrol station, is a small, funky spot with sand floors and a tropical feel. It's a popular hangout amongst the artsy students, especially when it's live *Trova* music night. Across the main road is the only jazz club in the country (thank God it's a good one!), **Jazz Café** (↘ *253 8933*). The long brick building is beautifully crafted to create a dim, smoky (but not too smoky) jazz club. Live music every night, excellent atmosphere and some decent eats. Grammy award-winners Editus play here along with visiting artists. Highly recommended.

A new addition to the scene, **.G** (pronounced 'punto G') (↘ *280 3726*), next to Mas X Menos supermarket, is an upmarket gay bar that is straight-friendly featuring Spanish, Lebanese and Hindu food. Eclectic and cool!

I'll just say this about **Calle de la Amargura** (Street of Bitterness) – the entire place is door-to-door bars filled with university students working off steam. If you want a party crowd, this is the spot. Just be wary with the purse and wallet.

If you're in Curridabat, I highly recommend **K&S Brewery & Restaurant** (↘ *283 7583*) south of POPS in Centro Comercial Cristal, the only place I know of in Costa Rica that brews its own beer on the premises. The large restaurant area and bar overlooks the giant vats of German-style brew – which is excellent and with good food to accompany it. Live performances during the week.

WHAT TO SEE AND DO The big draw here is the **University of Costa Rica**, with its sprawling campus and parks of welcome green grass and trees amongst the smog-congested streets surrounding it. The grounds are a great place to get away for a jog or power walk – weekends see the park full of t'ai chi groups enjoying the peace of the gardens. The **Insect Museum** (↘ *207 5318; closed weekends*) in the Music School basement is a treasure of six- and eight-legged creatures. Dance shows are held on a regular basis at the **Teatro Montes de Oca** (↘ *207 4595*), usually by the school's dance students who are well trained in modern/contemporary styles.

A variety of cultural centres are found in the area, including the **Spanish Cultural Centre** (↘ *257 2919; e ccultucr@racsa.co.cr*) near Farolito Restaurant in Barrio Escalante, which hosts cross-cultural events and dinners throughout the month. The **Instituto de Mexico** (the Mexican Cultural Centre) in Los Yoses (*Av 10, Ca 43;* ↘ *283 2333; e cultamex@racsa.co.cr; closed weekends*) has art exhibits and cultural events. The largest centre is the **Costa Rican–North American Cultural Centre** (*Barrio Dent;* ↘ *207 7500; e cultural@cccncr.com*). In addition to language classes in English and Spanish, there is a reference library, the **Eugene O'Neill Theatre** for music, dance and drama (often with performances by artists

5

from the USA), the **Sophia Wanamaker Gallery** displaying international visual artists' works and the **Mark Twain Library and Information Centre** (e *bibmarktwain@cccncr.com; closed Sun*), with a full library.

If art is your thing, be sure to check out the many excellent galleries, most with Costa Rican and Central American artists. **Galeria 11-12** (*Av 11, Ca 33/35, Barrio Escalante;* ✆ *280 8441; www.galeria11-12.com*). **Galeria Mata** (*200m south, 25m east of Banco Nacional in San Pedro;* ✆ *253 6473*) is a fine art market, as is nearby **Galeria Santana** (*100m south, 150m east of Banco Nacional;* ✆ *280 1295*). **Kandinsky Art Gallery** (*Calle Real Shopping Centre;* ✆ *234 0478*) is regarded as having one of the finest collections in the country.

WEST OF SAN JOSÉ – LA SABANA, ROHRMOSER, PAVAS

The huge La Sabana Park is the heart of this area and *Josefinos* flock to it at weekends for open-air aerobics, jogging, kite flying and even a bit of fishing in the giant pond. Rohrmoser is where many old-monied families live while Pavas is the more industrial/lower-income area of the west. Many of the hotels listed are within a short drive of the international airport and close to downtown.

WHERE TO STAY Prices are based on high-season rates (December–April) for double occupancy and do not include the 16.39% room tax unless otherwise noted.

Hotel TRYP Corobici (203 rooms) Across from Sabana Park at corner of highway; ✆ 232 8122; f 231 5834; www.trypcorobici.solmelia.com. A large hotel run by the Spanish Melia group, this is a hotel geared towards the business traveller. There is a variety of suites available and all rooms have safety box, minibar, radio, cable TV and phones. There is a business centre as well as a swimming pool, spa, sauna, jacuzzi, casino, 2 restaurants and a bar. B/fast inc. *Rates US$135–350.*

Hotel Casa Roland (14 rooms) End of Rohrmoser Bd; ✆ 231 6571; f 290 5462. Quiet hotel with nicely appointed rooms, cable TV, internet and pool with patio. B/fast inc. *Rate US$62.*

✖ WHERE TO EAT

✖ **Fuji** Hotel TRYP, Corobici; ✆ 232 8122, ext 191. Very high-end Japanese food and sushi. Pricey. *Average price per meal US$40. Open daily 12.00–15.00, 18.30–23.00.*

✖ **El Chicote** Across from La Sabana Park, 400m west of ICE; ✆ 232 0936. The best steakhouse in Costa Rica, with huge pieces of meat cooked to perfection. The room is warmly decorated with wood and plants and the waiters are all very formal. *Average meal US$30. Open daily 11.00–23.00.*

✖ **Deli Pasta** 75m north of Canal 7; ✆ 220 4439. Part of the Argentinian chain of restaurants, the emphasis is on Italian food and wood-oven pizza. Great value for money and although it is a 'family' restaurant, the atmosphere is decidedly grown up. *Average meal US$20. Open daily 11.30–22.30.*

✖ **La Princesa Marina** 200m south of Canal 7; ✆ 232 0481. Part of the chain of seafood restaurants where the food is tasty, portions are massive and prices ridiculously low. Don't expect anything fancy – this is strictly diner-type food at bargain prices. *Average meal US$11. Open Mon–Thu 11.00–22.30, Sun 11.00–21.00.*

✖ **Bangkok** On the road towards Los Anonos; ✆ 296 6110. A converted house serving up Thai and Indonesian cuisine (the only place in the country other than Tin Jo). Ambience is nice, food is good and pricing is moderate. *Average meal US$15. Open Mon–Thu 12.00–15.00, 18.00–22.00, Fri 12.00–15.00, 18.00–23.00, Sat 11.00–23.00, Sun 12.00–20.00.*

✖ **Pita Rica/Little Israel** Across from the Shell station in Pavas; ✆ 290 2083. For all things kosher, this is the place. Great pita bread, hummus and deli treats. *Meals average US$4. Open Mon–Fri 11.00–17.00.*

✖ **Pollo Cervecero** 300m east of the US embassy; ✆ 232 2727. Popular *Tico* spot for *bocas* and beer after work. Great *chicharrones* and bargain prices. *Average meal US$10. Open daily 11.00–midnight.*

✖ **El Fogoncito** Across from Plaza Mayor on the main road in Rohrmoser; ✆ 290 0910. Great Mexican food with extremely attentive service. *Average meal US$15. Open daily 11.00–midnight.*

✕ Little Seoul 50m north of Plaza Mayor; ☎ 232 5551. Outstanding Japanese and Korean food. Great sushi, teppanaki and tempura. Highly recommended. *Average meal US$12. Open Wed–Mon 12.00–15.00, 18.00–22.30.*

ESCAZÚ

A dichotomy, Escazú is the most upmarket town in the country but also the most traditional, with white and blue adobe houses still dotting downtown. *Boyeros* bump up against BMWs as old world meets the rich and famous. Escazú is also noted for its witches (it was once said that any woman who lives here long enough becomes one), which is the symbol for this sprawling town. If you wander off the main roads, it's incredibly easy to get lost here, as roads twist and turn and end without rhyme or reason (perhaps they are enchanted).

GETTING THERE AND AWAY

By car Take the Prospero Fernandez Highway until the Escazú turn-off. From Sabana, you can also reach Escazú by taking the road parallel to the Prospero Fernandez Highway, past Pops and crossing the Los Anonos Bridge.

By bus Catch the bus at Avenida 1/3, Calle 14/16.

⬦ WHERE TO STAY All prices are based on double occupancy high-season rates (December–April) unless otherwise noted. Prices are in US dollars and do not include the 16.39% hotel tax.

⌂ Hotel Camino Real Intercontinental (261 rooms) In front of MultiPlaza off Prospero Fernando Highway; ☎ 289 7000; f 289 8980; www.iccostarica.gruporeal.com. Elegant large hotel with 15 rooms catering to business travellers. Décor is classy, service impeccable and there is a host of facilities, including a beauty salon, outdoor tennis court, lovely pool with swim-up bar, business centre, 3 restaurants and a bar. Full amenities in each room, including minibar, phone, cable TV, AC, hot water and bathtub. B/fast inc. *Rates US$262 and up.*

⌂ Hotel Courtyard Marriott (122 rooms) Plaza Itzkatzu off Prospero Fernando Highway; ☎ 228 5400; f 288 0808; www.marriott.com. Part of the Marriott chain of hotels aimed at more budget-conscious travellers. Rooms are typical of a Marriott Courtyard anywhere else in the world and have all the standard amenities such as hot water, phone and cable TV. There is also a gym, pool and wheelchair access. Being just off a highway, the hotel is recommended for either business travellers or those overnighting just prior to or after flights. *Rate US$119.*

⌂ Hotel San Gildar (27 rooms) On the main road near the US Ambassador's residence; ☎ 289 9843; f 228 6454; www.sangildar.com. Charming small hotel that is close to all of Escazú's delights yet quiet and relaxing. Rooms have hardwood floors and

are spacious and comfortable. The inner courtyard has a pool and restaurant that serves excellent *Tico* and international fare. Wheelchair access. Guests also have use of the fitness club nearby. Service is very attentive, décor is artistic and overall, excellent value for money. B/fast inc. *Rate US$98.*

⌂ Apartotel Maria Alexandra (14 apts) San Rafael de Escazú; ☎ 228 1507; f 289 5912. 1- and 2-bedroom apts and 2-storey townhouses on a quiet side street just off the main road. Fully equipped kitchen, laundry room, AC, cable TV and telephone. There is a pool and a restaurant. A great option for longer-term visits. *Rates start at US$80.*

⌂ B&B Casa de las Tias (5 rooms) San Rafael; ☎ 289 5517; f 289 7353; www.hotels.co.cr/casatias.html. Charming, charming, charming! A huge Victorian-style house set in the country. The entire house is filled with colourful artwork from Central and South America as well as beautiful antiques. Owners Xavier and Pilar Vela are vivacious and gracious hosts and go out of their way to make their guests feel like family. B/fast inc. *Rates US$75–89.*

⌂ Hotel Costa Verde Inn (14 rooms) Central Escazú; ☎ 228 4080; www.costaverdeinn.com. Peaceful surroundings and fresh air make you quickly forget that you're a short drive from bustling Escazú. Wood and stone are used judiciously throughout this converted home. There are lush gardens, a tiny pool, tennis courts, a large living room with a fireplace (to ward off the chill at night) and a lovely patio. Rooms are spacious and decorated with Guatemalan

✕ WHERE TO EAT

✕ **El Novillo Alegre** 100m before the Los Anonos Bridge; ☏ 288 4995. This small restaurant has outstanding Argentinian BBQ. Massive portions of beautifully cooked meat with delicious *chimmichurra* sauce. Highly recommended. *Average meal US$20. Open Mon–Fri 12.00–14.30, 19.00–22.30, Sat–Sun 12.00–16.30.*

✕ **Bagelmen's** Near Rolex Plaza; ☏ 228 4460, 289 4616 for deliveries. Great bagels, sandwiches and soups (although a bit pricey). *Average meal US$6. Open daily 07.00–21.00.*

✕ **Häagen Dazs Café** Near Rolex Plaza; ☏ 228 4260. I'm nuts about Häagen Dazs and this place made my moving to Costa Rica a whole lot easier. It's the Rolls-Royce of ice creams. *Average meal US$6. Open daily 11.00–21.00.*

✕ **Café de Artistas** South from Rolex Plaza; ☏ 288 5082. Funky bistro setting with different artists' work on the walls keeps the artist theme going with menu items named after Picasso, Van Gogh, etc. Sun brunch is wonderful (and filling). Daily specials are always fresh and tasty. *Average meal US$10. Open Mon–Sat 08.00–18.00, Sun 08.00–16.00.*

✕ **Embrujo Limeño** Maria Alexandra Hotel; ☏ 228 4876. Cosy dining room with outstanding Peruvian food. *Average meal US$16. Open daily 07.00–23.00.*

✕ **Cerutti** Just past ScotiaBank heading towards Central Escazú; ☏ 228 4511. Elegant Italian restaurant in posh surroundings with personalised service. The swankest Italian restaurant in Costa Rica, with prices to match. *Average meal US$45. Open Wed–Mon 12.00–14.30, 18.30–23.00; closed Tue.*

✕ **Samurai** Heading towards Central Escazú; ☏ 228 4124. Big Japanese restaurant with all-you-can-eat-sushi on Tue nights (which is when I usually go). Food is good but service is s-l-o-w. *Average meal US$15. Open Mon–Fri 12.00–15.00, 18.00–23.00, Sat–Sun 12.00–23.00.*

✕ **Goyi** Plaza Real, Central Escazú; ☏ 289 5590. In this small, nondescript plaza you'll find good Japanese food at great prices. Atmosphere is open and the fluorescent lighting a big harsh but the attentive service and sushi make up for ambience shortcomings. *Average meal US$12. Open Tue–Thu

11.30–14.00, 17.30–22.00, Sat–Sun 12.00–22.00.

✕ **Mirador Valle Azul** In the hills above San Antonio; ☏ 254 6281. Although the view is the big draw here, the international cuisine and live music on weekends make it worth the journey. Pricey. *Average meal US$34. Open Tue–Fri 16.00–23.00, Sat –Sun 11.00–23.00.*

✕ **Mirador Tiquicia** High in the hills of San Antonio; ☏ 289 5839. A true *Tico* classic, serving up typical cuisine. The view is amazing (but it does get a bit chilly at night so bring a jacket). Folkloric music and dance are often presented for a full night of *tiquicia* (all things Costa Rican). Best to call ahead as the trek is steep and it mostly caters to groups. *Average meal US$16. Open Tue–Fri 17.00–01.00, Sat 12.00–01.00, Sun 12.00–18.00.*

✕ **Henry's Beach Café & Grill** Centro Comerical, San Rafael; ☏ 289 6250. It's a sports bar with a twist, serving up Creole/Cajun food. Henry, the owner, honed his culinary skills in New York and the food here is better than you'd ever expect from a crowded bar with big-screen TVs. At night, it's the 'in' spot to see and be seen. *Average meal US$10. Open Mon–Thu 11.30–midnight, Fri–Sat 11.30–02.00.*

✕ **Antojitos** On the road past Centro Comercial, San Rafael; ☏ 289 9700. Part of the popular chain of moderately priced Mexican restaurants. *Average meal US$17. Open daily 11.00–00.30.*

✕ **Sensu** Plaza Los Laureles; ☏ 228 2443. Excellent sushi bar with intriguing twists on the sushi theme, incorporating many local ingredients (such as Turrialba cheese in their *Tico* sushi creations). Zen-influenced décor hits all the right notes for a sophisticated dining experience. *Average meal US$15. Open Mon–Thu 12.00–15.30, 18.00–23.00, Fri 12.00–15.30, 18.00–midnight, Sat 12.00–midnight, Sun 12.00–22.00.*

✕ **Pizzeria Il Pomodoro** 50m west of the US ambassador's house; ☏ 289 7470. Tucked away from the busy road is this oasis of simple, homemade Italian cuisine. Reasonably priced and tasty! *Average meal US$10. Open Tue–Thu 11.30–23.00, Fri–Sat 11.30–midnight, Sun 11.30–22.00.*

✗ Tre Fratelli Paco Centro; ☎ 289 4389. Great Italian cuisine offered in an ambient setting. Huge menu features an entire selection of healthy, low-fat options. *Average meal US$15. Open 12.00–23.00 daily.*

✗ Il Panino Paco Centro; ☎ 228 3126. The sleek, modern design and ambient lighting create an upmarket lounge atmosphere that has attracted the BMW crowd of Escazú in droves. This is the place where the hip and monied hang out. The homemade *paninis*, desserts, varied cocktail menu (great *mojitos*) and coffee that is roasted on the premises are all delicious. *Average meal US$16. Open Mon–Wed 08.00–midnight, Thu–Sun 08.00–02.00.*

✗ Restaurant Lotus Just past Paco on the road to Santa Ana; ☎ 228 8105. Newly constructed huge restaurant with excellent and varied Chinese cuisine. Ambience is pretty minimal (why is it every Chinese restaurant in this country is poorly decorated and lit with fluorescent lights?) but the food more than makes up for it. Cantonese dishes are the strong suit here but spicy Szechwan is also impressive. *Average meal US$16. Open Mon–Fri 11.00–15.00, 18.00–22.00, Sat–Sun 11.00–22.00.*

✗ Le Monastere Above Paco, high in the hills of Escazú; ☎ 289 4404. The huge green neon cross, visible from miles away, marks the spot of this former monastery turned 'high-end' restaurant. The waiters are dressed as monks and the view of the Central Valley is the showstopper but sadly, the very expensive international cuisine doesn't live up to the expectations and the overall ambience could be improved with better choices in interior design and lighting, as the décor does not meet the splendour of the rough-hewn stone exterior. I found the service slow and overwhelmed, as if it were their first day on the job (granted it was Valentine's Day). While the descriptions of classic high-end fare sounded good on the menu (beef Wellington, lobster thermidor, etc), the execution didn't quite hit the mark. My recommendation is to go to the bar under the restaurant, **La Cava**, for a drink, enjoy the twinkling view below and save your money for a really good meal elsewhere. *Average meal US$50. Open Mon–Sat 18.00–23.00.*

✗ Café di Bartola Plaza Hermosa, on the road to Guachipelin, north of Paco; ☎ 228 2800. Outstanding Italian food with homemade pastas, wood-fired pizzas and an extensive wine list. The chef is originally from Italy and regularly features dishes from different regions of 'the boot.' Service is attentive but not cloying, and this is where the monied-set of Escazú comes to splurge. Pricey but worth it – delicioso! *Average meal US$28. Open Tue–Sat 11.00–23.00, Sun 11.00–17.00.*

✗ Tutti Li Plaza Itkazu; ☎ 289 8768. High-end Italian with homemade pasta and wood-oven pizza. Always an excellent choice. *Average meal US$18. Open Mon–Thu 12.00–22.30, Fri–Sat 12.00–23.00, Sun 12.00–21.00.*

✗ Taj Mahal On the old road to Santa Ana; ☎ 228 0980. The only east Indian restaurant in all of Central America, Taj Mahal has a varied menu that includes tandoori and other regional delights. Thankfully, it offers up pretty good Indian fare and satisfies a curry craving. *Average meal US$20. Open Tue–Sun 18.00–23.00.*

WHAT TO SEE AND DO El Ecanto de la Piedra Blanca (☎ 228 0183; f 228 5695; e *codececr@racsa.co.cr*) offers tours of San Antonio de Escazú, with stops at sugar mills, a traditional masquerade maker, hikes into the hills and lunch, for a real taste of the local culture. Fine art pieces made out of exotic wood can be found at **Biesanz Woodworks** (☎ 289 4337; *www.biesanz.com*).

SANTA ANA

Travel a bit further west and you hit Santa Ana, a sleepy town known for its pottery and onions. But things are changing and this is quickly becoming the fashionable spot for expats to put their roots down. There are several artisans' stores on the main road selling handmade pottery.

GETTING THERE AND AWAY

By car From Escazú, follow the 'old road'. Follow the Prospero Fernandez Highway until the Santa Ana turn-off.

By bus Catch the bus at Avenida 1/3, Calle 16/18 (Coca Cola). The bus operator is Empresa Transportas de Santa Ana (☎ 203 2579).

🏠 WHERE TO STAY

All prices are based on double occupancy high-season rates (December–April) unless otherwise noted. Prices are in US dollars and do not include the 16.39% hotel tax.

🏠 **Hotel Alta** (23 rooms) On the old road between Escazú and Santa Ana; ☎ 282 4160; f 282 4162; www.thealtahotel.com. Gorgeous boutique hotel that resembles a Spanish hacienda. The circular staircases in the halls and oddly angled corridors are unlike any other hotel I've ever seen. Rooms are well appointed (although bathrooms are small) and each has a private balcony with either a view of the valley below or the pool. The 3-bedroom penthouse has an incredible amount of space, complete with large dining room and patio with fountain. There is a small gym, sauna, jacuzzi and one of the best restaurants in the Central Valley is here. Excellent service and great value for money. B/fast inc. *Rates US$155–308.*

🏠 **Apartotel Santa Lucía** (14 rooms) Main road heading towards Escazú; ☎ 282 5236; f 282 5239. Very safe and clean apts and suites within walking distance of the central area of Santa Ana. Pool, secure parking, hot water, TV, BBQ and patio. B/fast inc. *Rate US$68.*

🏠 **Paraíso Canadiense** (9 apts) Pozos de Santa Ana; ☎ 282 5870; f 282 4981. Clean, friendly complex with pool, a bit off the beaten path. Efficient apts with hot water. *Rate US$50. Weekly/monthly rates also available.*

✖ WHERE TO EAT

✖ **La Luz** Hotel Alta; ☎ 282 4160. Undoubtedly one of the best fine-dining establishments in Costa Rica. Service is first rate, the décor luxurious but not overbearing and the food is deliciously inventive and creatively presented (this is where I go for an extra-special meal). Sun brunch is simply amazing — diners can enjoy whatever they want off the menu, as much as they want, for only US$20 (includes a *mimosa*, champagne with orange juice). *Average meal US$40. Open daily 07.00–22.00.*

✖ **Rock & Roll Pollo** On the old road heading into Santa Ana, across from the petrol station; ☎ 282 9613. The name is wacky but the roasted chicken is tasty (and cheap — a quarter chicken with chips is only around US$2). Large *boca* menu and daily specials have made this the spot for west-side expats. Pool tables and sports TV. *Average meal US$8. Open daily 07.00–23.00.*

✖ **Ceviche del Rey** On the corner coming into Santa Ana on the old road; ☎ 282 8019. Excellent Peruvian food is served on a sprawling covered patio. The décor is simple but the service and cuisine more than compensate for any interior design shortfalls. Try the *chicha morada* (blue corn drink) and the *ceviche. Average meal US$20. Open daily 12.00–21.00.*

✖ **Rancho Macho** Up in the hills overlooking Santa Ana; ☎ 282 9295. Incredible views from this wooden restaurant that serves real *Tico* fare, cooked over coffee wood. The walls are adorned with photos of the owner and his horses as well as antiques, giving it a homey feel and Macho, the owner, is usually around to make sure everyone is enjoying themselves. At weekends, there's live music and dancing pleasure. Very popular with the locals and highly recommended for those seeking a real *Tico* experience. *Average meal US$6. Open 17.00–22.00; closed Mon.*

✖ **Restaurante DaMarco** Take the turnoff for Piedades from the highway to Cuidad Colon from Santa Ana; ☎ 282 4103. A real taste of Italy in Piedades. Fresh pasta with succulent sauces are served in an intimate room of rich wood tones. 3 walls of windows look out on the greenery outdoors. Fresh pastas and creative cuisine keep this place packed with locals in the know (the homemade ravioli filled with baby goat meat with a butter and fresh sage sauce is the stuff of dreams). Professional service and authentic Italian cuisine, all at more than reasonable prices make this restaurant worth the drive. I eat here weekly and have never been less than amazed by the food — and low prices. *Average meal US$12. Open Tue–Sat 12.00–15.00, 18.00–22.00, Sun 12.00–16.00; closed Mon.*

WHAT TO SEE AND DO

Santa Ana is noted for its pottery and there are a number of small stores selling handmade bowls, pots, etc dotting the main road from the Cruz Roja heading towards Escazú. The old church in the town square is quite impressive and the Sunday-morning open-air market by the church is a great way to experience *la vida Tica*. Horseriding is popular and the **Centro Equestre Valle Yos-Oy** (☎ 282 6934) has horses available to rent.

6

Alajuela and Surrounds

ALAJUELA

Home to the international airport, mangoes, football team 'La Liga' and birthplace of national hero Juan Santamaría, Alajuela is a modest cosmopolitan centre with a warmer, sunnier climate than neighbouring San José. Founded in 1782, Alajuela is known as Costa Rica's 'second city' and coffee production is king. The central square, ringed by mango trees, sees numerous old men passing the time, playing checkers and assigning witty nicknames to passers-by.

Two blocks down is Parque Juan Santamaría, named after the favoured son of Alajuela who defended Costa Rica against American invader, William Walker. A statue of the uniformed young hero with flaming torch held high is a focal point in the square – legend has it that its French sculptor accidentally mixed up Santamaría with a Haitian hero as the Costa Rican army didn't wear uniforms.

GETTING THERE AND AWAY

By car All roads lead to Rome, or to Alajuela, as following the General Cañas Highway from San José or anywhere west or north of San José will take you right to the exit by the airport.

By bus From San José, take either the red and black **TUASA** (↘ *442 6900*) buses or the tan **SWA** (↘ *222 7532*) at Avenida 2, Calle 12/14 or at the airport. To get into San José, call either bus company for times and route information.

GETTING AROUND Local bus is TUASA (↘ *442 6900*) or Coopetransasi (↘ *449 5141*) – call for routes. Taxis can be hailed or the hotel can call one for you.

WHERE TO STAY Prices are based on high-season rates (December–April) for double occupancy and do not include the 16.39% room tax unless otherwise noted.

🏠 **Hotel and Spa Xandari** (19 rooms) In Tacacori, 3km from the courthouse in Alajuela; ↘ 443 2020; f 442 4847; www.xandari.com. Set on 40 acres of a hilltop coffee plantation, Xandari is a stunner, a little piece of heaven only 15 minutes from the airport. Incredible views of the valley and mountains with 2km of trails leading to 5 waterfalls make it an ideal spot for a romantic getaway. Two lap pools, heated jacuzzi, organic gardens, spa with private *jalapas* (palm-roofed pavilions). Each spacious villa is architecturally stunning, with rounded whitewashed walls that house original pieces of art and a private

terrace from which to drink up the views. The restaurant specialises in health-conscious spa food served in elegant surroundings overlooking the valley below. Highly recommended. *Rates US$180–260.*
🏠 **Hampton Inn & Suites** (100 rooms) Behind Hampton Inn; ↘ 442 3320; f 442 2781; www.grupomarta.com. Much in the same vein as its neighbour, the focus here is on the business traveller with meeting rooms and roomy suites. Includes airport transfers, b/fast bar and pool. *Rates US$133–156.*
🏠 **Hotel Hampton Inn Aeropuerto** (100 rooms) Traffic circle across from airport; ↘ 443 0043; f 442

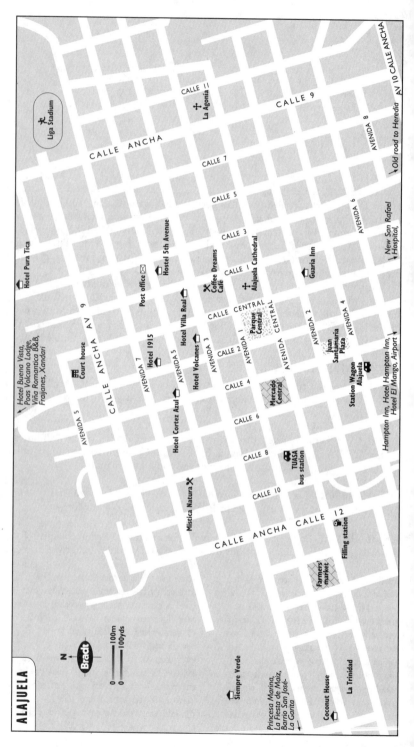

ALAJUELA

N

0   100m
0   100yds

Hotel Buena Vista,
Poas Volcano Lodge,
Viña Romantica B&B,
Fraijanes, Xandari

Hotel Pura Tica

Court house

CALLE ANCHA   AV 9

Post office

Hostel 5th Avenue

CALLE 11

La Agonía

CALLE 9

CALLE ANCHA

Liga Stadium

CALLE 7

CALLE 5

CALLE 3

Coffee Dreams
Café

CALLE 1

Alajuela Cathedral

Guaría Inn

AVENIDA 8

Old road to Heredia

AV 10 CALLE ANCHA

New San Rafael
Hospital,

AVENIDA 6

AVENIDA 5

AVENIDA 7

Hotel 1915

Hotel Villa Real

Hotel Volcanes

AVENIDA 5

AVENIDA 3

CALLE CENTRAL

Parque
Central

CALLE CENTRAL

AVENIDA 2

AVENIDA 4

Juan
Santamaría
Plaza

Station Wagon
Alajuela

Hampton Inn, Hotel Hampton Inn,
Hotel El Mango, Airport

AVENIDA 1

AVENIDA CENTRAL

CALLE 2

Hotel Cortez Azul

CALLE 4

Mercado
Central

CALLE 6

CALLE 8

TUASA
bus station

Mística Natura

CALLE 10

CALLE ANCHA   CALLE 12

Filling station

Farmers'
market

Siempre Verde

Princesa Marina,
La Fiesta de Maíz,
Barrio San José-
La Garita

Coconut House

La Trinidad

Bradt

9532; www.hamptoninn.com. If you like American-style motels, this chain hotel fits the bill. Conveniently located by the airport, it offers transfers, pool and a b/fast bar. Walls are insulated, so noise from both the airport and highway are muffled. Friends of mine stayed here and said the price was higher than the chain in the US. Reports of indifferent service coupled with relatively high rates make this a place solely for those who want to be a stone's throw from the airport. *Rates US$115–122.*

⌂ **Hotel El Mango Intercontinental** (16 rooms) 100m east of RostiPollos; \/f 443 1200; www.hotelmangoairport.com. Only 2 mins from the airport, this relatively new hotel has clean, spacious rooms with TV, hot water and decorated with a mango theme (the area is noted for its mangoes). There is a pool and restaurant. Includes airport transfers, b/fast, internet and local calls. A good option if you need to stay close to the airport. *Rate US$85, inc taxes.*

⌂ **Hotel Pura Tica! Tuetal** (formerly Hotel Pura Vida) (8 rooms) 4km from airport past courthouse; \/f 441 1157; www.puravidahotel.com. Coffee plantation home turned intimate hotel, this is one of the best spots in the Central Valley to stay. Outstanding service and food (where can you get a 3-course *prix fixe* dinner of fresh ingredients in unique Asian/Tico/California fusion for only US$16) ease guests into a relaxed state in which to enjoy the lush gardens and peaceful mountain surroundings — indeed, you don't feel like a paying guest, more a friend who is hanging out at a buddy's Secret Garden retreat. Each room and *casita* (small house) is brightly decorated with original works of art from different mediums. Free airport shuttles and b/fast inc. Highly recommended. *Rates US$75–115.*

⌂ **Hotel Buena Vista** (25 rooms) 6km north of Alajuela at Las Pilas; \ 442 8605; f 442 8701; www.hotelbuenavistacr.com. Huge, Spanish-style white house with stunning mountain views. Rooms are clean and spacious and feature carpets, 2 queen-size beds, hot water and cable TV. There is also a pool and a restaurant/bar that serves good food. Airport transfers and b/fast inc. *Rates US$70–115.*

⌂ **Hotel 1915** (18 rooms) Av 5/7, Ca 2; \ 440 7163; f 441 0495; e 1915hotel@ice.co.cr. An elegant house that was the owners' grandparents' home which has been converted into a comfortable small hotel, with large airy rooms and small apts that can house 4 to 6 people. There is a lounge and a dining area. B/fast inc. *Rates US$60–90.*

⌂ **Poas Volcano Lodge** (11 rooms) Off the road to Poas Volcano; \ 482 2194; f 482 2513; www.poasvolcanolodge.com. Situated on a working dairy farm in the former family home, this lodge is a cosy retreat, complete with fireplace and a maze of nature trails for hiking, birding and horseriding. Internet and bikes are also available to guests. B/fasts with homemade breads and milk fresh from the cows grazing but a few feet away make this a unique stop on a tropical vacation — one feels as if they've stepped into the land of 'Heidi' (aided by the distinctively European-style architecture of the lodge). Some rooms have shared baths while the master suite has a large, sunken stone tub. *Rates US$55–115.*

⌂ **B&B Viña Romántica** (3 rooms) 6km north of the courthouse across from Hotel Buena Vista in Pilas de Alajuela; \ 847 8610; f 430 3636; www.vinaromantica.com. Small hotel with great views of 3 volcanoes. DirecTV and internet. Rooms are simply decorated with rich wood walls and terracotta tiled floors. B/fast inc (with homemade bread). Small gourmet restaurant serves up delicious Mediterranean fare. *Rate US$50.*

⌂ **B&B Siempre Verde** (4 rooms) On the road to San Isidora — follow the signs; \ 449 5134; f 449 5035; www.dokaestate.com. Originally a home built in the 1940s by a British family; the house definitely looks more English than *Tico*, despite being surrounded by a massive coffee plantation. It's a charming spot with million-dollar views. Includes b/fast. *Rate US$45.*

⌂ **Hotel Volcanes** (11 rooms) Across from the museum; \ 441 0525; f 440 8006; www.montezumaexpeditions.com. One of the oldest homes in Alajuela, this 1920s house has comfortable and clean rooms, some with private bathrooms with hot water, a TV lounge, dining on the patio and internet. The owners also run the Montezuma Expeditions Tour Company (see page 219 for further details) and offer direct shuttles to the laid-back beach town, Montezuma. Free airport shuttle service. B/fast inc. *Rates US$35–55.*

⌂ **B&B Guaria Inn** (5 rooms) 100m south of the cathedral; \ 440 2948; f 441 9573; e laguariahotel@netscape.net. A long-time favourite amongst the budget crowd, thanks to the cleanliness of the nicely decorated, quiet rooms and attentiveness of the staff. There is a kitchen and TV lounge. *Rates US$30–35.*

⌂ **B&B Coconut House** (formerly Hotel La Trinidad) (7 rooms) In front of Parque de Loma; \ 441

Every 11 April, Costa Ricans pay homage to the national hero, Juan Santamaría, who was born and raised in Alajuela. Little is known about his life, other than that he was a poor farmer who joined the call to defend his country against William Walker and his filibusters who had invaded Guanacaste but had been beaten back to Rivas, Nicaragua, by the scrappy Costa Rican 'army' (composed of farmers). Legend has it that the 25-year-old Santamaría, a drummer boy with the Alajuela militia, volunteered to torch the wooden fort where Walker and company had retreated to. Without regard for his own life, the young hero ran towards the building amid a hail of bullets – with his last breath, he threw the flaming torch into the fort, igniting it which forced Walker's men to flee.

Nothing much was heard of Santamaría afterwards, until 1891 when a statue was erected honouring his brave deed. The great Nicaraguan writer, Ruben Dario, created a poem to honour him, and to this day Costa Rican children recreate the famous battle between the drummer boy and the filibusters. The memory of this simple boy was literally raised from the ashes of 40 years of obscurity – but why then and why him?

One theory is that the Liberalist government was seeking ways to galvanise the people and identity of Costa Rica, which was still a mishmash of somewhat disparate provinces. Being a peaceful country, there were few heroes or battles to use as the rallying cry of a fledgling nation. The Battle of 1856 was one of the most significant in the country's history and Santamaría was the perfect hero – young, selfless and from the lower class. Although most Costa Ricans bristle at the idea of Santamaría being a creation of the government, there is evidence that he died of cholera, not filibusters' bullets.

Like most heroes and legends, the truth is likely somewhere between the two extreme stories and matters not – what does is that which lives on in the hearts and spirits of the people.

1112; **f** 442 7158; www.coconuthouse.info. Simple, no-frills B&B with clean rooms. German owners. Rooms are large with a kitchen and patio. B/fast inc. *Rates US$24 with shared bath, US$30 with private bath and safe.*

⌂ **Hotel Cortez Azul** (6 rooms) Av Central; ☎ 443 6145; www.aventurasencostarica.com. Run by the same company as Villa Real, the Cortez offers clean, basic rooms, some with shared bathroom, hot water, kitchen available and a patio. *Rates US$12–18 pp.*

⌂ **Hostal Villa Real** Av 3, Ca 1, 200m east of the museum; ☎ 441 4022;

www.aventurasencostarica.com. Situated in an old home close to the bus station, this is a good spot for budget travellers. The rooms are simply decorated (2 with shared bathroom) with hot water, internet, a TV lounge and a shared kitchen. In addition to airport transfers, they can also arrange tours. *Rates US$10–15 pp.*

⌂ **Hostel 5th Avenue** Across from the post office; ☎ 441 1563; www.geocities.com/hostel5taavenida. Clean, basic and comfortable rooms. *Rates US$10 pp inc taxes.*

✗ WHERE TO EAT

✗ **Coffee Dreams Café** 100m north of the cathedral; ☎ 430 3970. A charming spot, patio/indoor dining, light lunches, typical fare, coffees. 'Casado' is US$3. Closed Sun.

✗ **Mistica Natura** Caña Dulce Hotel; ☎ 440 8619. Serves great pizza and grilled chicken, with *Trova* music on Fri and Sat. *Pizza averages US$5. Open Mon–Sat 11.00–23.00; closed Sun.*

✗ **Princesa Marina** Barrio San José, La Garita, at intersection by church; ☎ 433 7117. Part of the seafood speciality chain, with good fish at reasonable prices. *Main course US$4–8. Open 11.00–22.30.*

✗ **La Fiesta de Maiz** 5km past the interchange on the La Garita road; ☎ 487 5757. A popular restaurant with traditional Costa Rican corn specialities. *Meals average US$5. Open 07.00–22.00.*

WHAT TO SEE AND DO

Poas Volcano National Park (*open 08.00–15.30; entrance US$7*). Drive on the Fraijanes road for 30km, turn right at Jualares or take a TUASA bus (❭ *482 2165; leaves 09.15 and returns at 14.30*). There are few places in the world where one can stroll up to within metres of a volcano's crater and peer at the bubbling hell held within – Poas is, to say the least, an experience. One of the largest active craters in the world at 1.5km, it's famous for its brilliant-hued lake and bleak atmosphere which prompted US astronaut Neil Armstrong to remark that it reminded him of the moon. It's a beautiful yet desolate place, usually shrouded in mist that adds to its otherworldliness. Clouds usually roll in mid-morning, making viewing virtually impossible, so it's best to visit early in the day (before 10.00). Dress warmly as temperatures can plummet. There is a visitor centre with a gift shop, café and volcano exhibit. Highly recommended.

Zoo Ave (❭ *433 8989; www.zooave.org; entrance US$9, children US$1.50*) is a zoo of sorts, with a park of birds, mammals and reptiles, many of which have been rescued and are recovering (to be returned to the wild if possible). They are also involved with breeding programmes and environmental campaigns.

Doka Coffee Tour (*San Isidora de Alajuela;* ❭ *449 5152. The mill operates during the harvest months of Oct–Feb; tours US$15*). Follow the signs from downtown Alajuela. Costa Rican coffee is said to be some of the best in the world and the Java from the Doka plantation is the best of the best. This family farm produces premium coffee for Starbucks and its own brand 'Three Generations'. Peaberry beans are hands-down amazing. The tour isn't as slick as Café Britt's but the 100-year-old *beneficio* (where the beans are dried in the sun) has recently been named a national cultural treasure.

The Butterfly Farm (❭ *438 0400;* f *438 0300; www.butterflyfarm.co.cr; open daily 08.30–17.00; entrance: adults US$15, children US$7.00*). From the airport, take a right and another right for Gaucima Road; Opened in 1983 as the first commercial butterfly farm in Latin America, this operation is now the second-largest exporter of pupae in the world. The two-hour tour walks visitors through the short but fascinating lives of butterflies. Best time to visit is late morning/midday on a sunny day as this is when the mini art-canvasses on wings are warming up in the sun and are most active.

HEREDIA

A charming small town, founded in 1706, Heredia is known as 'The City of Flowers'. The Universidad Nacional is situated here and the central colonial church, built in 1796, has a very lovely façade, stained-glass windows and bells from Peru. Coffee thrives in the rich volcanic soil of the area which sits on the lower slopes of the Barva volcano.

GETTING THERE AND AWAY

By car From San José or coming from the north or west part of the country, take the General Cañas Highway and follow the signs for Heredia.

By bus From downtown San José to Heredia is a 30-minute bus ride and three companies ply the route:

🚌 **Bustetas Heredianas** Av 2, Ca 10/12; ❭ 261 7171
🚌 **Transportes Unidos La 400** Av 3/5, Ca 4; ❭ 222 8986

🚌 **Microbuses Rapidos Heredianos** Av 12/14, Ca 1; ❭ 233 8392. Runs a 24hr service.

Sitting across from the central plaza is the Il Fortin, the fortress built in 1876 by Fadrique Gutierrez, the governor of Heredia. One of the only military buildings in Costa Rica, it bears the simplistic design of other towers of the era found in the Caribbean and Puerto Rico. Originally, the architectural plans had four towers (one in each corner) but funds ran out after the first tower was completed. Built out of stone, the tower's windows widen from the inside out – making it impossible to shoot bullets out and easy for bullets to enter in. Apparently, this was deliberate (although its function remains a mystery).

GETTING AROUND Streets in downtown Heredia are gridlike and orderly (but congested with slow-moving traffic). Taxis are found along the main park, though walking is the best way to get about downtown.

WHERE TO STAY Prices are based on high-season rates (December–April) for double occupancy and do not include the 16.39% room tax unless otherwise noted.

Hotel Costa Rica Marriott (244 rooms) Belen; 298 0000; f 298 0044; www.marriott.com. As part of the Marriott chain, the service is far superior to most hotels in Costa Rica. The grounds are impeccably manicured and the buildings are reminiscent of a Spanish hacienda. Rooms are graciously appointed, although still retain a chain-hotel feel about them and they are not especially spacious while the bathrooms are downright tiny. There are 2 pools, 2 restaurants, bar, internet, par-3 golf course, driving range, spa, private chapel and gift shop. Wheelchair-accessible and b/fast is inc. *Rates US$198–640.*

Peace Lodge (17 rooms) Left at the petrol station on the way to San Miguel in the Waterfall Gardens; 482 2720; f 482 2722; www.waterfallgardens.com. In a word, gorgeous. Luxury rooms where every detail has been attended to – and how! Every room has a jacuzzi tub and manmade waterfall in the bathroom as well as a stone fireplace in the bedroom/sitting room. The large beds are 4-posters, hewn out of wood and laden with a soft down comforter (both the fireplace and quilts are put into heavy use, especially at night, as the temperature at this high altitude gets nippy). Bathrooms have colourful stained glass, dbl sinks, and an aromatherapy vaporiser with locally produced oils as well as speakers so the variety of music CDs supplied can be heard throughout the room. The large balcony has rocking chairs, hammocks and, on the deluxe levels, another jacuzzi while all rooms have a view of the forest below. Unlimited entrance to the Waterfall Gardens is inc

along with a tasty and vast b/fast buffet. Very romantic and a place where I have spent anniversary weekends with my husband. Highly recommended. *Rates US$195–345.*

Finca Rosa Blanca (9 rooms) 269 9392; f 269 9555; www.finca-rblanca.co.cr. Imagine Gaudi designed the new USS *Enterprise* and you get an idea of the architecture of this outstanding boutique hotel. Rising like a whitewashed dream out of the lush green hills, Finca Rosa Blanca has a commanding view of the valley and coffee plantations below. 3 rooms, 3 junior suites and a master suite are all furnished and decorated in a different theme. The master suite, with its circular tower housing the giant bed and surrounded by a patio, is especially romantic with its waterfall-inspired jacuzzi tub. All rooms have decks; there is a pool, horses and sumptuous gourmet food. Homey yet luxurious with truly unique artistic touches. B/fast inc. *Rates US$180–270.*

Hotel Herradura Golf Resort & Conference Centre (232 rooms) On the highway from the airport; 239 0033; f 293 2292; www.hotelherradura.com. The first large hotel in the San José area, this sprawling complex has a huge conference centre which plays home to the majority of conferences and expositions in Costa Rica. Rooms are comfortable and generous in size with AC and satellite TV, and some have private balconies with views. There are 3 pools, an orchid garden, internet, 3 restaurants, a bar, a casino, a chapel and a gift shop. Excellent service. Guests may also take advantage of the nearby Cariari Golf Course, a narrow and tricky 18-

hole course that even the most seasoned golfer will find challenging. *Rates US$140–795.*

🏠 **Hotel La Condesa** (103 rooms) In San Rafael on the road to Monte de la Cruz; ☎ 267 6000; f 267 6200; www.lacondesahotel.com. A large, luxury resort set high in the mountains, offering guests rooms or richly appointed suites. There are 3 restaurants, pool, sauna, jacuzzi, miniature golf, auditorium, bar and live music on a regular basis. While it is a nice hotel, I prefer one of the smaller, boutique hotels in the area as the rooms at La Condesa are like those found in larger chain hotels. B/fast inc. *Rate US$135.*

🏠 **Hotel Melia Cariari Conference Centre & Golf Resort** (220 rooms) On the highway from the airport; ☎ 239 0022; f 239 2252; www.meliacariari.solmelia.com. The large open-air lobby has a luxurious feel to it and the rooms are nicely appointed. Not as elegant as the Marriott, it is still a pleasant hotel (although rooms on the lower floor are a bit dark). Suites are larger and have better furnishings. Features include AC, minibar, cable TV, conference facilities, 2 pools, internet, 3 restaurants, 2 bars, casino, airport transfers, wheelchair access. B/fast inc. *Rates US$104–700.*

🏠 **Hotel Bougainvillea** (81 rooms) Santo Tomas de Heredia; ☎ 244 1414; f 244 1313; www.bougainvillea.co.cr. Although it's just 15 mins from the airport, Hotel Bougainvillea's country setting, beautiful views and colourful gardens make you feel like you've stepped into another world. The rooms are well appointed and the pricing is well below comparable hotels in San José, making it an excellent option. Although there is no AC, the fans in each room keep things comfortable as temperatures are always spring-like at this altitude. There is cable TV, a nice pool, sauna, tennis, bar and restaurant with great food. The surrounding gardens with massive bougainvillea bushes are a pleasing setting for a stroll. *Rates US$80–100.*

🏠 **Hotel Chalet Tirol** (23 rooms) On the road to Monte de la Cruz in San Rafael; ☎ 267 6222; f 267 6373; e tirolcr@racsa.co.cr. A bit of Switzerland high in the hills at 1,800m. Surrounded by a private cloudforest, it has hiking trails to explore and horses for riding. The older rooms are in chalets charmingly painted like Swiss mountain homes, while the newer rooms are in an uninspired cement block. Amenities include hot water, heating and bathtub. There is also a tennis court and the restaurant serves excellent European fare. B/fast inc. *Rates US$80–105.*

🏠 **Hotel Traveler's Inn** (34 rooms) On the highway west of the airport; ☎ 239 2633; f 293 2778; www.travelersinnhotel.com. Recently renovated, this is a good choice for those who need to stay near the airport. Rooms are comfortable and clean with AC, hot water, security box, internet, restaurant, cable TV. There is also a bar and restaurant and the facility is wheelchair accessible. B/fast inc. *Rates US$69–85.*

WHERE TO EAT

✖ **Sakura Restaurant** Herradura Hotel; ☎ 239 0033. Excellent Japanese food and sushi served in a traditional setting. Pricey. *Meals from US$12–29.*

✖ **Pan y Vino** 300m west, 100m south of the Fortín in downtown Heredia; ☎ 263 3550. Excellent Italian cuisine. *Pasta dish averages US$6. Open Mon–Thu 12.00–midnight, Fri–Sat 12.00–01.00, Sun 10.00–22.00.*

✖ **Marisqueria Santa Barbara** On the road to La Uruca; ☎ 262 9681. Delicious seafood at very reasonable prices *Main course is US$4. Open 11.30–22.00.*

✖ **Baalbek Bar & Grill** On the road to Monte de la Cruz past La Condesa; ☎ 267 6482. Mediterranean delicacies are the speciality here and the weekends feature live music and belly dancing. *Meals average US$11. Open Tue–Sun 12.00–midnight.*

✖ **La Luna de Valencia** San Pedro de Barva, 100m north of Pulpería La Maquina; ☎/f 269 6665. Excellent authentic Spanish food with the house speciality paella. *Meals average US$12. Open to the public Fri–Sun with live music. Open Thu 19.00–22.00, Fri–Sat 12.00–22.00, Sun 12.00–17.00.*

NIGHTLIFE

Oceanos Bar, downtown Heredia (*Calle 4, Avenida 2/4,* ☎ *260 7809*) has live music on weekends and is usually fairly busy.

Miraflores Disco & Tavern, downtown Heredia near the park (☎ *237 1880; open 20.00-05.00, Fri–Sun*), is the place to boogie the night away.

Around the corner from the UNA (Universidad Nacional) you'll find three bars popular with the students – **El Rancho del Fofo, La Cholo** and **El Boulevar** (the most popular), open daily 12.00–02.00 (no phone numbers).

PRACTICALITIES
Banks
$ **Banco Nacional** Ca 2, Av 2/4 and Ca 12, Av 6

$ **Credomatic** Ca 9 and Av 6

$ **Banco Popular** Av Central, Ca 3

$ **Banco de Costa Rica** Ca 1, Av 6

Post office The post office is found on the northwest corner of the plaza.

Emergencies Hospital San Vicente (↘ 237 1091) is at Calle 14, Avenida 8 while the Red Cross is at Avenida 3 and Calle Central.

The police station is at Calle Central, Avenidas 5/7.

WHAT TO SEE AND DO
INBio Parque (*Santo Domingo;* ↘ *507 8107;* f *507 8274; www.inbio.ac.cr; entrance US$12, children 3–12 years half price*). A unique science park featuring Costa Rica's ecosystems in living exhibits and videos. There are trails with many birds to observe as well as other animals. Also available are guides, a cafeteria, gift shop and nature books.

Café Britt's Coffee Tour (↘ *260 2748; www.coffeetour.com; tours US$26, children 6–12 years US$22*). The largest coffee producer in the country, Café Britt has put together a very professional tour that walks you through the various stages of coffee production on its working plantation. In addition to seeing the milling and roasting processes, visitors try tasting and watch skits performed by professional actors on the history of coffee.

Las Truchas (*San José de la Montana;* ↘ *237 0478*). Fish for trout and have it prepared by the owners. Prices depend on the weight of the fish.

Museum of Popular Culture (*Santa Lucia de Barva;* ↘ *260 1619;* e *mcp@una.ac.cr; open Mon–Fri 10.00–16.00; entrance 400 colones (less than US$1*). An adobe-style home from colonial times that has been carefully restored to demonstrate the seven stages of the traditional method of *bahareque* (reinforced adobe construction). There is an inexpensive *soda* on the grounds, rounding off this truly *Tico* tour.

La Paz Waterfall Garden (*Varablanca, just off the road to Poas;* ↘ *482 2720;* f *482 2722; www.waterfallgardens.com; entrance US$22, children under 12 years US$10*). Excellent half-day tour to a park in a cloudforest. The 3.5km trails lead you to five waterfalls – including one you can stand underneath (a truly incredible experience). There is also the largest butterfly garden in the world, an orchid garden and a hummingbird garden, where hundreds of tiny birds zip mere centimetres from you! The cafeteria offers up excellent traditional food and the surrounding gardens are full of native species. Wear comfortable walking shoes and bring a sweater and rain poncho as the weather here is erratic and cooler.

Barva Volcano (*Entrance US$6*) On the western edge of Braulio Carrillo National Park, one of the oldest volcanoes in the country. Trees over 2,000 years old dot the landscape around it, leading vulcanologists to surmise that it has lain dormant for as many years. The crater is now a brilliant emerald lake. Quetzals make their home in the cloudforests surrounding the upper areas of the volcano and hikers are likely to spot these brilliantly plumaged birds. Only the sturdiest of all-terrain vehicles can make the trek along the treacherous last 4km to the entrance of the park (most people leave their vehicle and hike in). From there, it's an hour's hike to the crater that sits 2,900m above sea level. DO NOT deviate from the trails as the vegetation here is so thick, it's unlikely anyone will be able to rescue you. If you do wander off, build a brightly coloured shelter. If no-one knows you're missing, follow a downhill stream as it will eventually bring you to civilisation.

COFFEE TOWNS

The so-called 'coffee towns' were the stops along the route for oxcarts as they lugged coffee to the port at Puntarenas. In the hills heading west out of the Central Valley, the climate is always warm and sunny. Coffee and sugarcane plantations dot the landscape and life here moves at a slower pace than in neighbouring San José. Although there isn't a Greek population here, Atenas (Athens) and Grecia (Greece) were named in honour of the Greeks fighting for independence from Turkey.

ATENAS *National Geographic* once did a study that named this tiny town as having the 'best climate in the world' and the local citizens have enthusiastically promoted their unique claim to fame. Roadside stands sell the local delicacies – *toronja rellena* (candied grapefruit stuffed with condensed milk candy) and *prestiños* (giant ear-shaped pastries), both of which are VERY sweet.

Getting there and away

By car Atenas is easily reached by following the General Cañas Highway out of San José, past the airport and take the exit across from the RECOPE oil plant. Turn left and follow the road for 40km. Or go through Alajuela to the La Garita intersection and turn left.

By bus Numerous buses run throughout the day by **Coopetransatenas** (↘ 446 5767) from San José.

Where to stay

🏠 **Hotel El Cafetal Inn** (10 rooms) On the road to Palmares; ↘ 446 5785; f 446 7028, www.cafetal.com. Situated on a coffee plantation, this family-run hotel has airy, bright rooms with incredible views of volcanoes, mountains and the valley. There are 2 easily hiked trails to a waterfall on the property as well as a pool. The round tower room has spectacular vistas. Décor is 'typical Tico', a bit busy but rooms are clean and service is friendly. There is also a *cabina* with a kitchenette. B/fast buffet inc. *Rates US$85–150.*

🏠 **B&B Vista Atenas** (6 rooms, 2 apts) ↘/f 446 4272; www.vistaatenas.com. Head through Atenas and follow the signs. The Belgian owners keep this small inn and restaurant in tip-top shape. Beautiful views and a small pool. The restaurant offers Belgian and Tico fare at reasonable rates. There are dbl rooms with hot-water showers as well as small cabins with kitchenettes. B/fast is inc. *Rates US$50 rooms, US$55 cabins.*

🏠 **B&B Ana's Place** (6 rooms) Town centre; ↘ 446 5019; www.anasplace.com. Charming setting with a small pool, indoor/outdoor lounges and simple but comfortable rooms. *Rates US$40–50.*

Where to eat

✗ **La Fiesta del Pollo** On the way from La Garita about 1km west of RECOPE; ↘ 487 5076. It's open, it's rustic and it has great coffee-roasted chicken at US$7 a main course. Open Mon–Sun 08.00–20.00.

What to see and do

Railroad Museum (↘ 446 6884; e rolando.villalobos@racsa.co.cr; *entrance free*). Take the cut-off road 4km north of Atenas and turn right at the chicken-feed factory. A community effort to commemorate the train service, the museum is still a working station (tour trains on weekends) and was originally built in 1890. Guides are available on Sunday – on other days, enquire at the store/restaurant across the street. Donations are greatly appreciated.

Agro Eco Tourism Project at the Escuela Centroamericana de Ganaderia (*on the road to Río Grande, 7km to La Balsa;* ✆ *446 7000;* f *446 8000;* e *ebarrantes@ecag.ac.cr; entrance US$20, call ahead to book*). An interesting tour demonstrating integrated farming that is a bit like a Noah's Ark – horses, cows, crocodiles and even a worm farm live side by side in harmony. There is a cheese factory, a forest and horses for rent. Lunch is available.

D'Molas & Coffee (*on the main road into Atenas from La Garita;* ✆ *446 5155; open Mon–Sat 07.30–18.00, Sun 07.30–12.00*). Huge souvenir shop with beautiful handicrafts, clothing, woodwork, ceramics, handmade *molas* from Panamá and coffee.

GRECIA The town is known for its dark red, metal-plated church that was imported from Belgium in the 1890s after earthquakes had destroyed the previous churches here. Sitting behind an impressive park with a music dome, fountains and an obelisk, the church itself is like a magical storybook castle due to its opulence, with colourful stained-glass windows, chandeliers, pumice stairs, huge marble altar and soaring cathedral ceiling.

During the sugarcane harvest (Jan–Apr), tractors loaded with cane slowly chug along the roads, so be aware.

During the colonial era, this area was noted for its sarsaparilla, the principal ingredient in root beer. Keep an eye out for the Minerva bottling plant on the road towards Alajuela, which produces a mighty fine brew of the soft drink – many local stores also stock it.

Getting there and away

By car Driving to Grecia is pretty straightforward – follow the General Cañas Highway out of San José for 36km and follow the signs – you can't miss the giant Greek columns at the town's turn-off. From Alajuela, take the road to Barrio San José and continue into Grecia.

By bus Buses are run by **TUAN** (✆ *258 2004*) from the east side of Abonos Agro, Barrio Mexico in San José.

🏠 Where to stay

🏠 **Vista del Valle Plantation Inn** (12 rooms) Off the highway between Grecia and Naranjo; ✆/f 451 1165; www.vistadelvalle.com. Poised on the edge of the Río Grande Canyon, the location is a stunner. The main building (formerly a private house) is surrounded by smaller cabins, all bearing the influence of Japanese design. Lots of gleaming hardwood, glass and stone. Cabins offer privacy and a sense that you're in your own world. The huge coffee and orange plantation has lots of trails to hike, birds to watch and beautiful botanical gardens to explore. There is a 300ft waterfall at the end of a challenging trail but the large pool and jacuzzi in the grounds will ease the overworked muscles. There is also a gym and horses for rent. B/fast inc. *Rates US$90–160.*

🏠 **Hotel Posada Mimosa Country Inn** (9 rooms) 2km from the highway exit; ✆ 494 5868; www.mimosa.co.cr. The main house has 4 rooms in a separate wing, the small guesthouse has 2 suites; efficiency cabin (very basic), family cabin and a cottage are also available. Décor is cheery with nicely painted details on cabins. Rooms have private bathrooms with hot water, cable TV and b/fast inc with organic fruit grown on the premises. There is internet access, an infinity pool, solar energy, trails to hike and lovely gardens. The multi-lingual owners have a wealth of information and have even published their own guidebook *Potholes to Paradise. Rates US$65–100.*

✗ Where to eat

✗ **Restaurant Oasis** On the corner opposite the park; ✆ 494 6303. Situated in century-old building and one of the best bets in town. Cosy with a small bar and meals averaging US$12. Open 11.00–22.00 daily.

✗ **Restaurant Casa de Miguel** 120m behind the church; ☎ 444 6767. The most 'upscale' spot to dine and the balcony is a nice spot to watch the world waltz by while enjoying a glass of wine. *Meals US$15. Open 11.00–21.00; closed Tue.*

What to see and do
World of Snakes (*on the road from Alajuela;* ☎f *494 3700; www.snakescostarica.com; open 08.00–16.00; entrance US$11, US$6 for children aged 7–15, free for children under 7*). If reptiles interest you, this is a must-see because there are over 150 snakes representing 50 species on display. Get up close and personal with reptiles from all over Costa Rica. Guided tours are available.

Cooperativo Victoria (*5km on the road to San Isidro;* ☎ *494-5219; www.coopevictoria.com*). The first agricultural co-operative in Costa Rica, it now has over 3,000 members who are small to medium-size coffee and sugarcane producers. Visitors can tour the facility (*entrance US$12*) and learn about coffee and sugarcane processing.

SARCHÍ Years ago, this was one of the main stops for the repair of oxcart caravans. Although the oxcarts no longer rumble through town, the art of creating these brightly painted wooden wagons continues. The colourful designs are proudly displayed throughout the town – on walls, benches and even bridges! An excellent spot for souvenir shopping and a popular day-trip location or stopover en route to other locations.

Getting there and away
By car Getting to Sarchí is a lot faster now than in the day of the oxcart! Take the Inter-American Highway out of San José to Grecia and then follow the signs for Sarchí.

By bus Buses are run by **TUAN** (☎ *258 2004*) from the east side of Abonos Agro, Barrio Mexico in San José.

By taxi There is a taxi stand on the west of the square or you can call Sarchí Taxi (☎ *454 4026*).

Where to eat
✗ **Restaurante Las Carretas** Next to the Fabrica Carretas Chaverri; ☎ 454 1633. In a typical rustic setting with typical food – visit the factory then have lunch here for a full-on taste of *Tico* culture. *Typical buffet US$10. Open 10.00–18.00.*
✗ **La Troja del Abuelo** At the back of Plaza de la Artesania; ☎ 454 4943. Another small eatery offering typical food. Huge menu. *Average meal US$4.*
✗ **Helechos** Plaza de la Artesania; ☎ 454 4560. Relaxed with patio dining, good food and delicious natural drinks. *Average meal US$4. Open 10.00–18.00.*

What to see and do
Fabrica de Carretas Joaquin Chaverri (☎ *454 4411; open 09.00–18.00*). Since 1903, this factory has been making oxcarts and visitors can watch artisans in the workshop behind the store, where a pleasant garden has a number of antique cartwheels on display. Its huge store offers a wide selection of souvenirs.

Plaza de Artesania Shops selling various items, including woodwork, jewellery and souvenir items. There are also small restaurants for a snack.

Sarchí Real Coffee Tour (☎ *454 1633;* f *454 1106; tours without lunch US$15, with lunch US$25*). A new coffee tour that includes a ride in an oxcart. The old factory still uses a waterwheel for power.

Mercado de Souvenirs Coope Arse (*north Sarchí;* ☎ *454 4050*). A large store that is a co-operative of artisans, with locally made souvenirs and furniture.

NARANJO Another small town on the oxcart route, Naranjo, with its attractive church, is noted as the gateway to the north and to the mountains. There isn't much here other than bungee tours and nowhere to overnight. There are a couple of *sodas*, a Musmani bakery and fried chicken booths around the main park if you're hungry.

Getting there and away
By car The drive is along the Inter-American Highway out of San José for 46km to Grecia, through to Sarchí and then along an old road for 8km until you reach Naranjo.

By bus Buses are run by **TUAN** (☎ *441 3781*) and leave from behind the TUASA bus stop in Alajuela.

What to see and do
Costa Rica Bungee (☎/f *494 5102*). From the bridge over the Río Colorado, the brave (or crazy) can take a 265ft plunge for US$50. The company also offers abseiling, canopy tours, hiking and camping. Reservations are required.

Tropical Bungee (☎ *290 5629*). The same idea but with a 250ft jump for US$50. Also offers abseiling and climbing. Call for reservations.

El Cerro del Espriritu Santo Off the highway between Naranjo and Palmares in Candalaria. If religious shrines are of interest to you, check out this popular mountaintop shrine, complete with hiking trails and a small restaurant.

Topiaries of Zarcero Pass north through Naranjo for 3km to find the magical town of Zarcero, home to the fanciful topiary park in front of the church. Here, Edward Scissorhands is alive and well and plying his trade in this sleepy little mountain town. Huge archways of carefully clipped hedges lead the way to the church while in the plaza, playful rabbits cavort with a giant green elephant, while a motorcycle riding cat 'zooms' along. Walking through these bushy masterpieces is guaranteed to recapture your childish sense of awe and wonder.

PALMARES For 51 weeks of the year, Palmares is a sleepy little agricultural town but for one week in early January, the town is besieged by revellers from all over the country for the week-long fiesta, with rodeos, music and dancing. Usually, I try to avoid driving anywhere near Palmares during this time as the traffic is unbelievable.

There is a church in the centre of town dating from 1896 with beautiful stained-glass windows that bear a strong Moorish influence.

Getting there and away
By car Palmares is very easy to get to, as once you get onto the General Cañas highway out of San José, it's 54km and the highway cuts right through the town.

By bus Two bus companies have service from Avenida 3/5, Calle 16 (Coca-Cola) in San José.

🚌 **Transportes Palmarenos** ☎ 453 3808 🚌 **Auto Transportes Palmares** ☎ 452 0518

Where to stay

⌂ **Tranquillity Hill Inn** (5 rooms) On a hill 700m from the town centre; ☏/f 453 3761; www.tranquillityhill.com. Gleaming white modern building surrounded by gardens is the setting for restoring oneself – physically, emotionally and spiritually. Hosts Sherry and Joe offer health programmes that integrate mind/body/spirit and assist in gaining self-awareness. Stays have a 3-night minimum and include 3 vegetarian meals. Relaxing and peaceful – not a hotel but a destination for those who want to make positive changes in their lives. *Programmes start at US$325.*

What to see and do

Jardines de Guaria (☏ 452 0091; open Feb–Apr; entrance US$3). Turn right at the church and left at the school, and after 200m look for the sign. Orchid gardens with a variety of orchids on display.

SAN RAMON A literary movement in the latter part of the 19th century gave San Ramon the moniker 'City of Poets' and this quiet city continues to inspire with its climate and cleanliness. The story goes that the local priest published a book in the 1870s that satirised the 'lost sheep' of his parish flock, which caught the attention of other writers and poets. There is a Gothic-style church in town built in 1928 which features photos of all its parishioners over the years.

Getting there and away

By car San Ramon is just past Palmares. Follow the Inter-American Highway out of San José (northwest) for 65km and follow the signs.

By bus **Empresarios Unidos** (☏ 222 0064) buses leave from Avenida 10/12, Calle 16 in San José.

Where to stay

⌂ **Villablanca Cloud Forest Hotel** (34 rooms) 20km from San Ramon on the road to La Fortuna; ☏ 461 0300; f 461 0302; www.villablanca-costarica.com. Owned by Si Como No and part of the Green Hotels of Costa Rica, this new hotel is on a heavenly expanse of cloudforest in the private Los Angeles Reserve. Individual cabins with fireplaces, tubs and cut-glass accents are deluxe. Guests can hike through trails, go horseriding or explore the gardens. There is also a lovely little chapel in the grounds. B/fast is inc. A top-drawer hotel in the middle of nature. *Rates US$180–200.*

What to see and do

Don Pedro's Cigars (*behind the church 75m south;* ☏ 445 5014; e cigar@costarricense.com). Cigars, cigars, cigars – including the coveted Cuban and Costa Rican (which use seeds from Cuba). You can even roll your own.

Abajo La Paz (*16km north of San Ramon;* ☏ 445 9649). A new venture in this small community where visitors are treated to living history, with *trapiches* (sugar mills), oxcarts and typical food. Home of the *Bota-cros* (boot race). Call for reservations.

CARTAGO AND THE OROSÍ VALLEY

To head from San José east towards Cartago is to follow a path of turbulent *Tico* history, past the smouldering Irazú Volcano and into fertile farming communities before dropping into the almost Shangri-La-like atmosphere of the sheltered Orosí Valley. Often missed by international tourists to Costa Rica, Cartago and Orosí's tourist infrastructure is more geared to national visitors with small family-run hotels and restaurants, so don't expect sleek mountain resorts and over-processed package tours to head this way. This really is an area to explore with a hire car, preferably a 4x4, and don't be in any hurry on the twisty narrow roads that drop into the Orosí Valley so precipitously yet decoratively.

Irazú Volcano (3,423m) last erupted in 1963, depositing inches of volcanic ash over the farmlands to the northeast. Fumaroles exude smoke from the two main craters but the whole summit area is still barren and stark as you explore the area among the numerous repeater stations and other telecommunications pylons.

A pleasant day trip can be had around the Cachí Reservoir, taking in a leisurely trout lunch and enjoying some wonderful views and the general bucolic feel of the place.

GETTING THERE AND AWAY

By car To get through San José, drive east towards San Pedro and follow the main road through San Pedro but move to the middle lane once you are in Curridibat – this will take you on an overpass which then links up to the Inter-American Highway (approx. 22km). From there, stay on the highway and you'll end up in downtown Cartago.

By bus
Cartago From San José, it is a 40-minute bus ride southeast to Cartago from Avenida 18/20, Calle 5 with **SACSA** (℄ *233 5350*).

Paraíso and Orosí Buses leave Cartago's main bus station every 30 minutes.

Lankester Gardens Catch the Cartago–Paraíso bus and ask to be dropped off at the turn-off, then walk for 0.75km south along the signed road.

Tapantí National Park An early bus from Cartago reaches Purisil via Orosí then it's a 5km walk to the park entrance. Other buses get as far as the Río Palomo turn-off, 9km from the entrance. Taxis from Orosí charge around US$10 one way.

CARTAGO Cartago, once Costa Rica's capital, is 22km southeast of its rival San José now reached on the (usually) fast Inter-American Highway. Rival because it was named the capital city in 1563 by Juan Vásquez de Coronado, then Spanish governor of the country's first city, until republican fervour occasioned by Costa Rica's independence in 1821 caused jealous bickering between the four main Central Valley cities of Alajuela, Heredia, Cartago and San José. Although they pledged neutrality, San José snatched prime spot as capital and Cartago had to back down. Earthquakes in 1841 and 1910 severely damaged much of the city and the looming Irazú Volcano has given numerous reminders of nature's destructive powers. Little architecture of value remains although the ruined main church, aptly called **Las Ruinas**, serves as a landmark and residents sit out in the little square for some people watching and some neighbourly gossip.

Still the nation's religious hub, Costa Rica's patron saint, La Negrita, is housed in the imposing grey **Basilica de Nuestra Señora de Los Angeles**. The spacious, wood-panelled interior with impressive stained-glass windows was repaired after the devastating 1926 earthquake and the tiny effigy of Our Lady of the Angels resides above the main altar attracting up to a million pilgrims during the annual 2 August *Romería* to plead for her miracle-working cures. Bottles of water from a spring under the church are collected for their health-giving powers and the fervent complete the final approach on humble knees along specially prepared pilgrim trails.

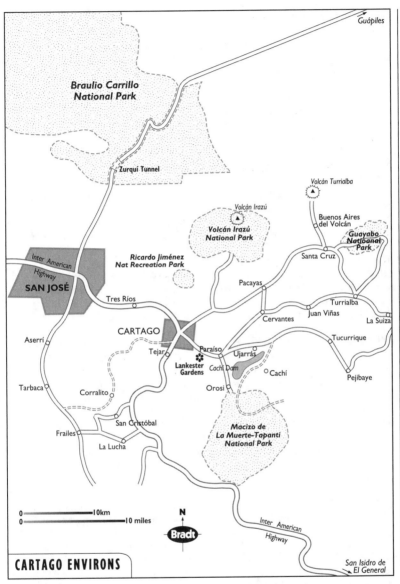

About 6km from Cartago on the Paraíso road, **Lankester Botanical Gardens** (☏ *552 3247;* f *552 3151; open 09.00–16.30; entrance: adults US$5, students US$3.50, free for children under 5*) has 10ha gardens famous for their orchids, *bromeliads*, heliconias and palms. Begun by British naturalist Charles Lankester in 1917, and now managed by the University of Costa Rica, the private gardens with some 800 species were developed by the orchid aficionado and are conveniently displayed at around eye-level for easy identification. A special flower garden attracts both butterflies and birds and provides a refuge for migrants. Visits to the gardens are sometimes incorporated into day trips with Irazú Volcano and the Orosí Valley out of San José for around US$60.

Where to stay

🏠 **Casa Mora** (6 rooms) One block north of Los Angeles Lodge; ☎/f 551 0324; e casa_mora@hotmail.com. A former family home converted into a B&B with individually decorated, comfortable rooms, telephone and TV. Internet access is available, safety deposit boxes, laundry service. Blazing fireplaces in the lounge areas and quiet b/fast room are inviting. B/fast inc. *Rate US$65.*

🏠 **B&B Los Angeles Lodge** (6 rooms) North side of Basilica; ☎ 591 4169; f 591 2218; e langeleslodge@racsa.co.cr. An older B&B with sgls, dbls and trpls, private hot-water bathrooms and cable TV. The bar/restaurant offers decent full meals and snacks. *Rate US$35.*

✗ Where to eat You do not come to Cartago for fine dining!

✗ **Restaurant Los Angeles** Just south of the Basilica; ☎ 551 4546. Popular for seafood and more. *Main dishes US$3–7. Open 10.00–02.00.*

✗ **4a Strada Pizza** 50m north of Las Ruinas; ☎ 592 2846. An inviting Italian ambience for lunch/dinner with both international and Italian dishes. *Pizzas US$5. Closed Mon.*

✗ **Restaurant 1910** On the road to Irazú Volcano; ☎/f 536 6063. Recalls the 1910 earthquake with historical artefacts and décor. A favourite weekend lunch spot specialising in Sun buffet serving *Tico* dishes. *Main dishes US$4–10. Open 11.00–16.00; closed Mon.*

✗ **Restaurant Pharo** On the road to Paraíso; ☎ 552 6223. Offers meat and seafood. *Meals average US$10. Open Mon–Wed 16.00–01.00, Thu–Sun 11.00–midnight.*

✗ **Cappuccino del Este** Just further down and on the main road; ☎ 551 9698. Friendly with excellent coffees, snacks and light lunches. *Main courses US$5–8. Open 11.00–23.00.*

✗ **Fogón de Abuelita** Near to Paraíso stadium on the main road; ☎ 574 3912. Good value for more rustic meals with daily specials. *Meals average US$8. Open 09.00–22.00.*

THE CACHÍ RESERVOIR CIRCUIT From Cartago the road leads southeast to Paraíso, the main entrance for the Orosí Valley. Once down the tortuous road you are rewarded with friendly people and a menu of options including visiting a coffee-processing plant, hot springs, catch-your-own trout lunches or some demanding hikes in the remote Tapantí National Park. If you plan to go around the Cachí Reservoir, signs will lead you to choose a clockwise route by turning left towards Ujarrás (7km) or conversely right to Orosí (8km). The Cachí hydro-electric project was completed in 1966 and the resulting lake has become a popular weekend outing for *Ticos* who peer over the retaining wall at the eastern end down onto the Reventazón River far below. Whichever way you start from, the spectacular views will have your camera clicking. Choosing the east route along the north shore via Ujarrás, the Costa Rica Tourism Institute (ICT) **Ujarrás Mirador** (*closed Mon; free entrance*) offers perhaps the best panorama of the valley below with pleasant gardens and picnic spots. There is an almost equally spectacular **Orosí Mirador** on the Orosí road which is also ICT managed.

Once thankfully on the valley floor you can visit the peaceful grounds and picturesque ruin of the **Nuestra Señora de la Limpia Concepción** church, a limestone edifice built in the 1680s in honour of the Virgén del Rescate de Ujarrás. The Virgin helped save Ujarrás from the marauding corsairs Morgan and Mansfield who were bent on pillaging the highland cities in 1666. Her miracle helped the people of Ujarrás defeat the invaders. The church was abandoned after the valley flooded in 1833 and left to fall into ruin, although the miraculous rescue of Ujarrás is still celebrated with a pilgrimage down from Paraíso on the Sunday closest to 14 April. The grounds are open and free, a popular picnic spot at weekends.

The strangely named **Paradero Lacustre Charrara** (☎ 574 7557; e charrarralfacom@racsa.co.cr. *Camping is possible, US$3 per tent. Admission is US$1.50 with car or US$0.80 if you walk in; use of picnic tables and BBQ facilities US$1*) just before the dam wall, is an ICT-run resort with spacious landscaped grounds, football pitch and basketball court, pools, trails, riding, bicycle hire, small boats for lake excursions, picnic areas and restaurant. A family-oriented complex, it is well maintained and plans for cabins are under way. After the almost obligatory stop to gaze over the dam wall, the road turns south to complete its lake circuit and the bizarre little **Casa del Soñador**, the dreamer's house, offers an amusing stopover to look at woodcarver Hermes Quesada's strange carvings created from coffee-plant roots. Life-sized figures reportedly represent the town gossips. The tiny house is completely hewn from planks covered with carvings, many dating back to Hermes's father, Macedonio, who began the 'hobby' and whose works can be seen in San José galleries. Entrance is free and some works are for sale.

Where to stay

Piedras Albas de Cachí (2 cabins) Above Cachí; 577 1462; f 577 1317; www.cabinas.co.cr. To get there, climb steeply 2.3km east after the church. Comfortably equipped for 4, light and airy, with hot water, TV and patio where you can sit and keep admiring the views or birdwatch before it gets too cold in the afternoons. There are some forest trails on the slopes of the extinct Cerro del Duan behind the cabins. With no restaurant on site, you have to do all the cooking or drive down that steep slope into Cachí for meals. *Rate US$42.*

Where to eat

Many *Ticos* like to come out to the valley at the weekend for a family lunch outing, so several larger restaurants with recreation facilities catering to children are dotted around mostly offering the speciality of locally raised trout.

Restaurant Mirador Ujarrás Next to the panoramic viewpoint. Perched over the Orosí Valley, this combines outstanding views with tasty *Tico* cooking. *Meals average US$8. Closed Mon.*

Casona del Cafetal 3km southwest of the dam; 577 1414. A coffee plantation where from November to March you can see the bean picking, sample the farm's own coffee and eat various coffee desserts at the large international/*Tico* cuisine restaurant. Riding, bicycle hire and boating on the lake costs US$3.50.

La Milpa de Cachí Opposite the Casona del Cafetal (and managed by the same family); 577 1414. Specialises in corn-based dishes. *Meals average US$6. Open 11.00–18.00.*

OROSÍ With your circuit almost done, your tour would not be complete without visiting Orosí village, the centre of the coffee-growing district and an early settlement for the Huetar indigenous people, before being forcibly removed from their lands by the Spanish. A charming colonial town, the highlight is the surviving **San José de Orosí** church, a gem of a place built by Franciscan monks in 1735 from thick adobe blocks with timber beam roof, mellow terracotta tiling and a perfectly proportioned altar. This is one of the few surviving colonial churches and the oldest still in full use. The small museum next door (Vf 533 3015; open Tue–Sun 13.00–17.00, closed Mon; entrance $0.80) was the former monastery and displays religious artefacts, woodcarvings and period furniture. If you decide to stay in the valley for a few days and many are drawn into its tranquil hospitality to emerge weeks later, there is much to choose from if you want slow-paced enjoyment.

Where to stay

Hotel Barceló Rancho Río Perlas Spa & Resort (32 rooms, 19 suites) About 7km south from Paraíso, 2.5km in from the main road; 533 3341; f 533 3085; e reservas.rioperlas@barcelo.com; www.barcelo.com. Luxury Barceló resort overlooking the Perlas River with minibar, cable TV and 5-star amenities; disabled access. If you feel the need to be pampered then go no further. Providing full spa facilities with pool, 13 jacuzzis, thermal spring water baths, massages and beauty treatments, relaxation is unavoidable! Tours around the area can be arranged and trout fishing is offered in several nearby ponds. À la carte restaurant and buffet café with *Tico* dishes. Airport pickup for here and other Barceló resorts around the country. B/fast inc. *Rates from US$140.*

Hotel Orosí Lodge (6 rooms) Near Balneario hot springs; \f 533 3578; www.orosilodge.com. A delightful German-managed hotel next door to the better of the thermal pools, spotless rooms with kitchenette, private bathrooms with hot water, coffee maker, ceiling fans and balconies for great views of Irazú and Turrialba volcanoes. Internet access. B/fast is served in the bright, colourful café along with other delicious snacks, organic coffee served along with *Tico* cigars. *Rate US$45.*

Hotel Sanchirí (10 cabins, with 12 upgraded units almost completed) From Paraíso to Orosí; \ 574 5454; f 574 8586; e sanchiri@ racsa.co.cr; www.sanchiri.com. The original, rather dark cabins are rustic and simple but with jaw-dropping vistas over the Orosí Valley, one only hopes they are well secured into the hillside. Private bathrooms with hot water, phones, and balcony. Well-recommended restaurant with *Tico* international menu, a butterfly garden (*entrance US$5*), hiking trails, children's playground. Valley safaris available. *Rate US$40.*

Monte Sky Mountain Retreat (up to 20 people) \f 228 0010; m 382 7502; e montesky@ intnet.co.cr; www.intnet.co.cr/montesky. As mentioned above, the retreat offers wonderful birding, hiking or just simply chilling out in jungle settings. Chilly is the word though for there is no electricity, only cold water, a shared bathroom in the rustic lodge or camping so bring appropriate clothing for the altitude. *Rate US$40 pp with meals, US$10 camping per tent.*

Kiri Lodge (6 rooms) Close to the national park entrance, 10km from Orosí; \ 533 2272; e kirilodge@hotmail.com. Rather Spartan rooms on a 50ha recreational area but pleasant grounds for trout fishing from the lodge's ponds (*US$5/kilo*); the restaurant will cook your catch. Hiking trails, riding in the area. B/fast inc. *Rate US$35.*

Hostel Montaña Linda (20 beds, 3 dorms, 5 rooms) and the annexe **Montaña Linda 'Dragonfly' Guesthouse** (3 rooms) Orisi; \ 533 2153; f 533 3640; e info@montanalinda.com; www.montanalinda.com. This hospitable and budget-oriented jumble of a complex is a well-established feature in Orosí. It started out as a campsite in 1994, expanding into offering economy accommodation when the first owners opened the Spanish school. The hostel offers 3 dorms with 5 bunk beds in each at US$6.50 pp or you can take a private dbl room for US$17, shared bathroom. Camping is possible for US$3; if you use their tent, US$4. Laundry service is available and a kitchen fee of US$1, book exchange, luggage storage, hammocks and board games. In 2004, current co-owner, Toine, converted her in-laws' weekend house into a more upmarket B&B with 3 bedrooms, private bathrooms with hot showers and pleasant dining and lounge areas. *Rate US$25 with b/fast.* The Spanish classes run from Mon–Fri, 3 hrs daily starting at US$99 for one-on-one teaching.

✕ Where to eat At the turn-off after crossing the Río Palomo on the narrow suspension bridge, **Hotel Río Palomo** (*open daily 08.00–18.00*), whilst having no accommodation to boast about, is a popular place with *Tico* families at weekends where the children can let rip in the spacious grounds or in the large riverside pool. The glassed-in restaurant offers several combinations of trout along with other typical dishes. Just along the road, other popular weekend eateries are **Bar & Marisqueria La Marina** and **Marisquería El Puente**, both offering seafood cuisine.

In Orosí, overlooking the football pitch, the long-time **Bar & Restaurant Coto** has been pleasing the crowds with its good typical food and tasty *bocas* over drinks. Often full at weekends especially if a match is being played.

What to see and do A centre for coffee production, a coffee farm visit is well worth it and the award-winning organic **Café Cristina Plantation** (\ 574 6426; e *organic@cafecristina.com; www.cafecristina.com*) sells coffee worldwide and offers tours of the crops and the processing mill. Best time to visit is October–February during the harvest to see the whole process. Being chemical-free it provides an excellent habitat for birds with over 270 species seen on the farm.

Of the two thermal pool complexes **Balneario De Aguas Termales** (\ 533 2156; *open 07.30–16.00; entrance US$1*) is more spacious with changing rooms, clean hot water and (very) cold pools. Restaurant and picnic areas are on site. Otherwise, also claiming to have the hottest water is the more basic **Balneario**

Wildlife

top left	**Long-tailed manakin** *Chiroxiphia linearis* (DH)
top right	**Red-lored Amazon parrot** *Amazona autumnalis* (CT) page 21
above left	**Rufous-tailed jacamar** *Galbula ruficauda* (DH)
right	**Erata butterfly** *Heliconius spp* (JG) page 26
below	**Keel-billed toucan** *Ramphastos sulfuratus* (DH) page 21

top   **White-faced Capuchin monkey** *Cebus capucinus* (VL) page 19
above left   **Baby howler monkey** *Alouatta spp* (JG) page 19
above right   **White-faced Capuchin monkey eating mango** (VL) page 19
below   **Mantled howler monkey** *Alouatta palliata* VL) page 19

above left **Jaguar footprint**
(JG) page 21

above right **Silky anteater**
Cyclopes didactylus (DH)

below left **Ocelot** *Leopardus pardalis*
(JG) page 21

below right **Jaguar** *Panthera onca*
(JG) page 21

above left   **Rainbow boa** *Epicrates cenchira* (JG)

above right   **Conehead lizard** *Laemanctus longipes* (DH)

below   **Green iguana** *Iguana iguana* (JG) page 23

top **Mexican red-kneed tarantula** *Brachypelma smithii* (VL) page 26

centre **Racoon** *Procyon spp* (VL) page 20

right **Collared peccary** *Tayassu tajacu* (VL) page 21

top   **Red-eyed leaf frog** *Agalychnis callidryas* (DH)

left   **Gladiator frog** *Hyla rosenbergi* (DH)

below left   **Strawberry poison dart frog**
                     Dendrobates pumilio (DH) page 25

below right   **Masked tree frog** *Smilisca phaeota* (JG)

top **Green turtles**, *Chelonia mydas*, **Pacific Ocean** (RD/TIPS) page 80

centre **Whitetip reef sharks**, *Triaenodon obesus*, **hunting at Cocos Island** *Triaenodon obesus* (RD/TIPS)

right **Shoal of fish, Pacific Ocean** (RR/TIPS)

above left **Heliconia** *Heliconia spp* (JG)
top right **Cacao pods** *Theobroma cacao* (VL)
above right **Coffee bush** *Coffea canephora* (VL)
left **Ginger plant** *Etlinger eliatior* (VL)
below **Spider lily detail** *Amaryllidaceae lycoris* (VL)

Los Patios (*on the road out of town to Río Palomo;* ✆ *533 3009; open Tue–Sun 08.00–16.00; closed Mon; entrance US$1*).

The town's **coffee mill**, just across from Los Patios, will let you look around and you may even find someone to give you a tour and explanation during the harvest season. They have no set tours and are grateful for your donations.

Heading south, some 9km from Orosí, take a right turn up a steep narrow lane to find, perched high in the mountains, **Lago San Ignacio** (✆ *533 3835*). They guarantee you will fish out a trout from one of the well-stocked ponds. There are three short trails, one to a 10m waterfall and possibly the best views around (which is saying something in this panorama-stuffed region), a small restaurant and picnic site. And once you have your catch, you can grill it here or in the nearby beautiful **Monte Sky Mountain Retreat** (✆/f *228 0010;* m *382 7502;* e *montesky@ intnet.co.cr; www.intnet.co.cr/montesky; entrance for the day US$8 pp*). The 536ha reserve lies at 1,680m and needs a short hike from the car park over a river to reach the centre with rustic lodge and campsite. The reserve has four trails through the forest to crystalline waterfalls – look out for the lion, man and turtle 'guardians' naturally profiled near the falls. You can cook your fish on the barbecues, take in some hikes, birdwatch and take in yet more of those stunning views. As it's chilly cloudforest up here, don't forget a warm sweater and raingear. (See *Where to stay* above for details on the lodge.)

Just about at the end of the dirt road, some 10km from Orosí, you will reach the western entrance to **Tapantí–Macizo Cerro de la Muerte National Park** (✆ *283 5970*). Source of the Reventazón River with over 58,000ha of upland rainforest, the remote, undervisited park offers superb hiking with three trails going from the ranger station, one leading to a swimming hole if you can brave the freezing waters and some picnic areas. Another leads to a dramatic waterfall viewpoint. This is known as one of the wettest regions in the country (800cm/year at the middle elevations) with an abundance of rivers and waterfalls flowing down the wild Cordillera de Talamanca mountains so come suitably dressed and booted for some challenging conditions. January to April is considered the driest time of year, but never omit the waterproofs. Many rare mammals such as the jaguar, ocelot and other cats have been recorded here but it is unlikely you'll spot these shy animals. More probably, you might see squirrels, monkeys and raccoons with some of the 200 bird species that nest in the park. Look out for the resplendent quetzal near to the ranger station. Camping can be arranged with a permit or you can stay near the ranger station on simple beds, cold showers and with cooking facilities available, but bring your own sleeping gear (*cost US$2.50 pp*). Fishing with a licence is allowed in designated spots from April–October (*open 06.00–16.00; entrance US$6*).

TURRIALBA

Dominated by the imposing Turrialba Volcano, the town offers little of note since it was sidelined by the opening of the more direct Highway 32 to Limón and the closing of the Atlantic railway in 1991. Although lacking in upmarket infrastructure, it is the main base for the kayak and rafting companies down the Reventazón (Exploding) and Pacuare rivers. The Cachí Reservoir that dammed the Reventazón lies at 1,000m with white-water stretches both above and below Turrialba town, before flattening out by Siquirres in the Caribbean lowlands. Four main sections are run on Reventazón with Class III and IV white-water conditions interspersed with lazy drifts along placid stretches. Since daily (except Sunday) dam releases ensure constant water levels during most of the year, the last section is most used because of the easy pull-out by Siquirres Bridge. Further east, Pacuare

River has some world-class white-water conditions along with spectacular canyons curtained with lush rainforest. Because access is less easy, most kayak and rafting trips last two days, either camping on the riverbank or overnighting in a nearby lodge. Safety is an issue and the serious companies have age limits, detailed safety demonstrations, helmets and life jackets. If conditions aren't suitable, they will abort a trip. Most day trips are accompanied with a delicious picnic lunch, the chance to swim or hike up to waterfalls and rapidly developed photos to take home with you.

GETTING THERE AND AWAY

By car Branch off the Inter-American Highway at Cartago for Paraíso and follow signs for Turrialba, 65km from San José.

By bus Buses from Turrialba village depart for Guayabo from Avenida 6/8, Calle 13 with **Transtusa** (✆ *556 4233*) with ever-changing schedules, or taxis can be hired for around US$30 per round trip. The main terminal covering the area including La Suiza and Tuis is at Avenida Central/2, Calle Central/2.

TOUR OPERATORS Tours can be organised from San José to Guayabo with a few agencies for about US$75 per person for a day's visit including lunch.

Green Tropical Tours ✆ 229 4192; f 292 5003. Specialise in the region.
Costa Rica Rios ✆ 556 9617; f 556 6362; www.costaricarios.com A smaller but often cheaper operator that works out of Turrialba town, ie: for white-water adventures.

Rain Forest World ✆ 556 0014; f 357 7250; www.rforestw.com
Ticos River Adventures ✆/f 556 1231; www.ticoriver.com
Explornatura ✆ 556 0853; f 556 4032; www.explornatura.com.

Many of these agencies also run horseriding, jungle safaris, mountain guides and biking trips. Otherwise, the well established and highly recommended agencies out of San José run many tour options for rafting, kayaking and canyoning.

Horizontes ✆ 222 2022; f 255 4515; e horizont@racsa.co.cr; www.horizontes.com
Rió Tropicales ✆ 233 6455; f 255 4354;

www.riostropicales.com
Aventuras Naturales ✆ 225 3939; f 253 6935; www.toenjoynature.com.

Most day trips with transport from San José, lunch, drinks, all equipment will come to around US$75–85 per person depending on the difficulty level and distance.

WHERE TO STAY

Hotel Casa Turire (12 rooms, 4 suites) 8km southeast on Tuis Road, well signed; ✆ 538 1111; f 538 1575; e info@casaturire.com; www.hotelcasaturire.com. A member of the Small Distinctive Hotels of Costa Rica, the Swiss-managed, perfectly proportioned, 3-storey hotel lies in a working coffee, sugarcane and macadamia nut plantation overlooking Lake Angostura and enjoying panoramic views of the distant Talamanca Mountains to the south. With a wide wraparound Caribbean veranda, private balconies, hot-water bathtubs, international dial telephone, cable TV, ceiling fans and room service. There are also 4 suites with refrigerators, 1 suite with 2 floors, a huge balcony and spa. Pool, tennis court, games room and small library and full international restaurant offering vegetables and fruits from the hotel gardens. As well as the usual adventure river tours, riding, hiking and birdwatching, you can also visit the nearby sugarcane mill, coffee facility and macadamia nut-processing plant when in operation. Highly recommended. *Standard room rates are US$150, junior suite US$163 to the master suite at US$243.*

⌂ **Rancho Naturalista – Albergue de Montaña**
(5 rooms, 6 cabins) 20km southeast of Turrialba,
1km beyond Tuis; ☏ 297 4134; f 297 4235;
e jkerb@racsa.co.cr; www.costaricagateway.com/
lodges/index. Not an easy place to reach up a steep
and very bumpy track, this hideaway lodge set in
pre-montane forest is a birdwatchers' paradise with
over 400 species recorded. Surprisingly elegant in
spite of its isolation, the main house has 5 spacious
rooms, 3 with private bath, 2 sharing, all with hot
water. 4 2-unit cabins, all with private bathrooms
have hammocks on the verandas but forget about
cable TV and phones although internet connection is
available. Upstairs a lounge with library and
telescopes to home in on the Tuis Valley, but some
of the bedrooms lack views so ask beforehand. The
main draw here is the birdwatching and the Rancho
has hummingbird feeders, bird-feeding tables and a
full species' list. An expert guide service is inc in the
rates. The 50ha ranch has several trails for wildlife
spotting and birding and the owners, Kathy and
John Erb recommend you stay at least 4 nights to
explore the area more fully. Riding and guided hikes
are offered and you can visit an ox-powered sugar
mill (*trapiche*) nearby. Rates include 3 meals, soft
drinks, birding guide with trips to the Tuis Valley,
riding, maid service. *Rates US$145 pp, US$943 per
pp/week (includes pickup from Juan Santamaría
International Airport).*

⌂ **Hotel Wagelia** (18 rooms) Av 4, Ca 2/4; ☏ 556
1566; f 556 1596; e hotelwagelia@racsa.co.cr. The
best hotel is an uninspiring choice, set in pleasant
gardens; the rooms are clean with TV, fans or AC
and it is often full. The hotel will arrange tours for
guests to most of the nearby areas of interest. A
good restaurant adjoins the hotel although service is
slow. Meals in the US$5–11 range. B/fast and
welcome cocktail inc. *Rate US$75.*

⌂ **Hotel Geliwa** (25 rooms) 2km northwest of
Turrialba; ☏ 556 1142; f 556 0029. Pleasant
modern rooms with fans, phones, TV, safety boxes
and hot water. Laundry service, pool and restaurant
that provides b/fast and dinner only. Co-managed by
Hotel Wagelia, overflow guests are sent here and
rates are the same as the Wagelia.

⌂ **Hotel Turrialtico** (14 rooms) About 8km on the
Siquirres road; ☏ 538 1111; f 538 1575; e info@
turrialtico.com; www.turrialtico.com. At 780m, a
comfortable friendly hilltop hotel, which was started
as a restaurant in 1968 by the local García family
with superb views. It is popular with river adventure
companies, and most of the rustic pleasant wood-
panelled rooms with huge windows to let in the

views have balconies and hot-water private baths.
One cabin is available. The open-walled restaurant
serves up flavourful *Tico* meals but can be chilly in
the evenings, and the place is decorated with
colourful Archí oxcarts and hanging baskets of
orchids. Small souvenir shop. Rates US$52 dbl, to
US$68 trpl inc b/fast. Cabins go for US$53.

⌂ **Volcán Turrialba Lodge** (22 rooms) 10km
northwest up from Santa Cruz (4x4 access only or
pre-arrange for pickup with Lodge); ☏ 273 4335;
f 273 0703; e info@volcanturriablbalodge.com;
www.volcanturrialbalodge.com. All rooms with private
bath and fireplace. The lodge commands breathtaking
views on its remote hilltop location (at 2,800m)
between Irazú and Turrialba volcanoes. Built in a
working cattle farm, converting the old milking shed,
the lodge offers cheerful wood fires in the restaurant
and lounge area and cosy cabins for a real away-
from-it-all feeling. A hike to Turrialba is about 1hr
away and guided tours on quiet horses in the hills
can be arranged and the staff will provide you with
rain ponchos, wellington boots and binoculars if you
wish. Quetzals nest on the property from February
to April. If it's too cold and wet outside, you can
play board games, watch TV or catch up on your
reading. *Tico* with some international menu options
served, buffet style inc in rates. *Rate pp with meals
US$45.*

⌂ **Hotel de Montaña Pochotel** (10 rooms) 11km
from Turrialba at Pavones on the Siquirres road;
☏ 538 1515; f 538 1212; e pochotel@
racsa.co.cr; www.pochotel.com. Forming a brother
act, this similar hilltop hotel, at 950m, is owned by
Oscar Garcia López, the brother of Hotel
Turrialtico's proprietor, Marcial. Some rooms with
balconies. Note: hot-water private bathrooms have
been criticised for being freezing cold. Set in
pleasant gardens (with helipad!), there is a pool
and children's play area. With very steep road
access, what it lacks in charm, it pays off with yet
again spectacular views of the valley, Angostura
Lake and river below, the mountains and volcanoes
in the distance. The rather strange, modernistic
restaurant reached from the old hotel by a 15m
bridge is worth the panoramic vistas alone
although the typical meals are very reasonably
priced. Reservations are recommended in high
season, as with Turrialtico since both fill up with
river-running groups. B/fast inc. Rate US$41.

⌂ **Hotel Interamericano** (23 rooms) South of the
old rail tracks; ☏ 556 0142; f 556 7790;
www.hotelinteramericano.com. Popular with budget
travellers and river adventurers, the hotel offers basic

rooms with bunks and shared bathrooms as well as dbls with private bathroom. Internet service, cable TV, book exchange, laundry facilities and café with luggage storage available, this clean and friendly

American-run establishment is good value for money and has lots of information on the region. *Rates dbl/trpl/quads with shared bath US$20–25, with private bath US$30–50.*

✖ WHERE TO EAT

Casa Turire Outstanding, for a really elegant meal; reservations required (see *Where to stay*, page 124) but well worth the effort. *Average dinner price US$25.*

Posada de La Luna In Cervantes, on the main road from Cartago to Turrialba; ☎ 534 7474. Opened in the 1960s and crammed with curios and *Tico* handicrafts, this legendary popular eatery has delicious filling b/fasts, the full gamut of meat and chicken dishes and famed cheese tortillas. Often jammed at weekends. *Meals average US$8. Open 10.00–20.00 Sun–Thu, 10.00–22.00 Fri–Sat.*

Restaurant Bocadito del Cielo (Heavenly Snacks)

Beyond Cervantes; ☎ 534 7272. Perched on a hillside with breathtaking views, this restaurant has international and *Tico* dishes, popular with *Ticos* for weekend lunches out with the family. *Meals average US$7. Open 07.00–22.00.*

Restaurant La Feria and **Restaurant La Garza** (☎ 556 1073) Turrialba is not renowned for its superb cuisine but good typical meals can be found at these long-time town favourites.

Café Gourmet For good b/fasts and excellent coffee, try this friendly café. *Open 07.00–19.00.*

Hotel Wagelia For more upmarket eating.

Otherwise, out-of-town restaurants are recommended at **hotels Turrialtico** and **Pochotel** (see *Where to stay* above).

WHAT TO SEE AND DO Good hiking, biking and birdwatching trails in the hills and the hydro-electric-producing Lake Angostura is being developed as a watersports centre.

The 3,300m Turrialba Volcano last erupted in 1866 but sulphurous steam still escapes from the crater fumaroles to warn that this is no dormant has-been. A paved road then rough trail from Santa Cruz, 12km north of Turrialba, is the main route for hikers and leads to a panoramic viewpoint and occasionally the rangers allow you to walk partly around the rim where you can look down onto the three craters. It is often wet and cold so warm raingear is recommended before heading uphill. It is possible to take a 4x4 vehicle to the top if you just want the views without the effort.

Pre-Colombian archaeological site, Guayabo National Monument, whilst not as impressive as anything in Mexico or Peru, has well-maintained paths leading to aqueducts and some cleared excavations for public viewing. The 2,000-year-old settlement was abandoned mysteriously in AD1400 and shows evidence of a town with 10,000 inhabitants at its height. The pre-montane forest covering most of the ruins is a last remnant of this kind of forest in the region, home to oropéndolas, toucans and brown jays.

The surrounding rich farmland produces sugarcane, coffee and macadamias, with dairy herds for cheese.

CATIE The Centre for Tropical Agricultural Research and Learning (*4km east of Turrialba;* ⎯ *558 2450; www.catie.ac.cr*) is a world-renowned research station into tropical crops, especially coffee. Individual visits are limited but possible with advance booking (*US$25 pp*), and tour agencies in San José arrange guided group visits around the facilities, gardens, herbarium and trails that cover the near-1,000ha site.

About 10km east, in Pavones, is **Parque Viborana** (⎯ *538 1510; open daily 08.00–17.00; entrance US$5 includes Kodak moment holding a snake*), a serpentarium with many species on display, including a boa constrictor pit where you are invited to share space with the non-venomous boas.

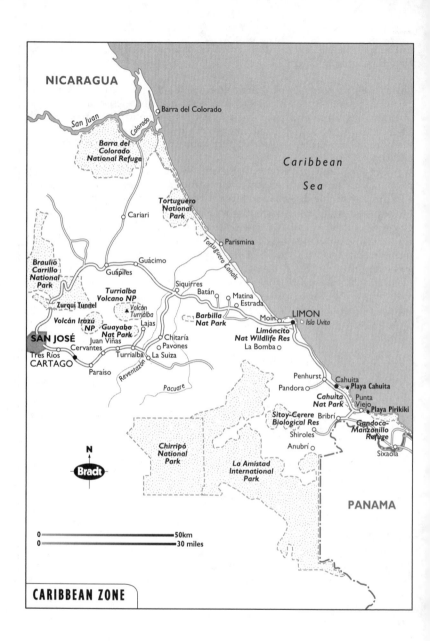

NICARAGUA

Barra del Colorado

San Juan

Colorado

Barra del
Colorado
National Refuge

Caribbean

Sea

Cariari

Tortuguero
National
Park

Parismina

Braulio
Carrillo
National
Park

Guácimo

Guápiles

Tortuguero Canals

Siquirres

Batán

Turrialba
Volcano NP

Matina
Estrada

Zurquí Tunnel

Volcán
Turriálba

LIMON

Moín

Isla Uvita

Volcán Irazú
NP

Lajas

Barbilla
Nat Park

Guayabo
Nat Park

Juan Viñas

Chitaría

Limóncito
Nat Wildlife Res

SAN JOSÉ

Cervantes

Pavones

La Bomba

Tres Ríos

CARTAGO

Turrialba

La Suiza

Paraíso

Reventazón

Penhurst

Cahuita

Playa Cahuita

Pacuare

Pandora

Cahuita
Nat Park

Punta
Viejo

Playa Pirikiki

Sitoy-Cerere
Biological Res

Bribrí

Gandoca-
Manzanillo
Refuge

Shiroles

N

Anubrí

Sixaola

Bradt

Chirripó
National
Park

La Amistad
International
Park

PANAMA

0 ⎯⎯⎯⎯⎯⎯⎯ 50km
0 ⎯⎯⎯⎯⎯⎯⎯ 30 miles

CARIBBEAN ZONE

7

The Caribbean

Lively at times, languid at others, always lush, the Caribbean is the least *Tico* of Costa Rica's regions. Until the 1940s, the black population was not allowed into the Central Valley without special permits. This beyond-the-pale isolation earned them a reputation for lawlessness, but it also helped retain a vibrant independence and individual culture that makes visiting the area so rewarding. You will hear Creole English spoken, smell and taste coconut-based cooking, snorkel among coral reefs and surf some gnarly waves. Sophisticated resort development has not reached the Caribbean but accommodation ranges from quality boutique hotels to surf camps. Province capital Puerto Limón is partially revamping its hitherto tarnished image as a tourist destination and is an increasingly busy hub for cruise ships docking for the day. A carnival in October transforms the town into a massive party attracting international bands and dance troupes.

The Tortuguero canals in the north are a magnet for sports fishing fanatics, birdwatchers and wildlife spotters. With no reliable road access, travel depends on water taxis or internal flights. The tiny village of Tortuguero offers basic services but most visitors pre-book inclusive packages out of San José with transport, hotel and trips pre-ordered and paid.

The winding highway from San José through the Braulio Carrillo National Park gives quick but often dramatic land access to Limón and the southern towns through to the Panamá border. A slower alternative road drops from Cartago via Turrialba to join the highway at Siquirres, which is used when the main road is blocked with landslides – not uncommon in the rainy season.

The region's original inhabitants, the Bribri and Cabecar ethnic groups, were pushed further back into remote settlements among the Talamanca hills to the south and are still a woefully under-represented minority ignored by central government. A few itinerant black turtle hunters had settled the coast in the 1820s but most of the region's Afro-Caribbean population stems from Jamaican workers recruited to build the Atlantic Railroad and then work the huge banana plantations. They retained their Caribbean traditions and heritage still seen today with separate cuisine, religion and language. *Ticos* finally began settling the area in the 1920s and today sees a mixture of races and nationalities with increased settlement by Europeans and North Americans.

HIGHWAY 32 – GUAPILES, GUACIMO, SIQUIRRES

The infamous twisting highway that drops dramatically to the Caribbean lowlands some 50km after leaving San José caused a stir when inaugurated in 1987 by cutting through the huge and remote Braulio Carrillo National Park. Up till then the Caribbean had been effectively cut off both from Spanish cultural influences and central government or mass tourism development that has so deeply affected provinces such as Guanacaste. The northern section around Tortuguero and Barra del Colorado with their low-lying swamps and meandering waterways has defied most efforts to build lasting roads and access still depends on small planes and boats. The Atlantic Railroad from Puerto Limón to San José, finally completed in 1890 to transport first coffee, then bananas to Limón port and the European markets brought prosperity to the flatland towns of Guápiles, Guácimo and Siquirres. Today, not much recommends them to the casual visitor as most speed through heading north to Tortuguero and Barra or south to Cahuita, Puerto Viejo and the lower beaches. That said, a few highlights along the way merit a visit.

GETTING THERE AND AWAY

By car Highway 32 leads east dropping down through dramatic Braulio Carrillo National Park with long overtaking lanes, but often hampered by fog and landslides.

By bus

Transportes Caribeños ⟍ 221 2596. Leaves from Caribbean Terminal, Av 11/13, Ca Central.

Empresarios Guapileños ⟍ 710 7780. Also departs from San José's Caribbean Terminal.

WHERE TO STAY

Hotel Country Club Suerre (55 rooms) 1.8km north of petrol station in Santa Clara just east of Guápiles; ⟍ 710 7551; f 710 6376; www.suerre.com. A pleasantly laid-out modern resort-style hotel that is useful as a stopover before heading into Tortuguero or Barra del Colorado. Also popular with *Tico* families who enjoy the Olympic pool, gym, sauna, tennis courts and other sports facilities. Rooms have cable TV, phones, private bathrooms and AC. A 'formal' restaurant and pool-side cafeteria with a couple of bars and even a casino keep body and soul together. A surprisingly well run and good find in an area otherwise starved of quality accommodation. *Rates US$87 up to US$170 for a suite.*

Casa Rio Blanco Ecolodge (2 rooms, 4 cabins) Just up the bumpy road from the Gallery At Home, along the Río Blanco, Guápiles; ⟍ 710 4124; m 382 0957; e info@casarioblanco.com; www.casarioblanco.com. Recently refurbished, this delightful B&B with its 4 prettily decorated cabins is perched over the river so you can bird from your balcony and sleep to the rush of the river. It isn't unusual to see sloths hanging from a nearby branch. The cabins and main house rooms have private bathrooms with hot water, fed from one of their 3 springs, fans and are fully screened. Attractive gardens have medicinal plants and flowers to attract hummingbirds. The owners will lead you on birding

hikes and even a night-time frog-spotting walk. Rates include b/fast and a rainforest tour for US$65 in their private reserve (wellingtons inc), but give prior notice if you want lunch and dinner. The owners also run an educational programme to help both local residents and visitors learn more about Costa Rica's unique tropical ecology. Guests get a 20% discount on the Aerial Tramway, 12km back up the main road. You can ask to be picked up at the Restaurant Ponderosa on the main road if using public transport.

Hotel Río Palmas (28 rooms) Just opposite EARTH; ⟍ 760 0305; f 760 0296; e riopalma@ hotmail.com. It's not the sort of place you would make your final destination — with the Caribbean coast so temptingly close — but it is a comfortable stopover especially for families visiting students over at EARTH. Rooms have large glass windows for ample light, fans or AC private baths with hot water and TV. It is pleasant to amble around the luxuriant gardens shaded with mature trees, visit the butterfly or frog gardens or you can fish for tilapia in the hotel pond that the chef will then prepare for you. Free-form swimming pool and trails in an adjacent reserve lead to attractive waterfalls. Riding US$6 per hr, and kayak trips can be arranged. *Rates vary if you request AC, US$30–40.*

WHERE TO EAT

Restaurant Rancho Roberto At the turn-off for Puerto Viejo de Sarapiquí (always lots of trucks parked around the several transport cafés at the junction); ⟍ 710 0050. This is about the best

roadside restaurant between San José and Limón. Recently refurbished and expanded the service is friendly and efficient with some excellent *Tico* and international dishes, with a good range of seafood and grilled meats. *Prices US$4.50–7.* You can visit the next-door **Tropical Frog Farm** to look at over 200 species of amphibians, including poison-dart frogs, to work up an appetite as you wait for your food (*entrance US$4*). *Open daily 07.00–23.00.*

✕ **Restaurant Ponderosa** 5km east of Guápiles; ☎ 710 2075. Another good stopover eatery with tasty *bocas*, snacks and a full menu; try their juicy steaks (*US$9*), for hungry travellers. *Open daily 07.00–22.00.*

✕ **Restaurant Ellis Café** Just before Siquirres, east of the filling station; ☎ 768 9517. This restaurant is useful because it has long opening hours if you are travelling at decidedly off-peak hours. They offer hot buffets for around US$4 and good seafood and meat menu. *Open 06.00–23.00.*

WHAT TO SEE AND DO Construction on the **Braulio Carrillo Rainforest Aerial Tram** (☎ 257 5961; f 257 6053; e *reservas@rainforest.co.cr*; *www.rainforestram.com*) began in 1992 by biologist Don Perry, a pioneer in rainforest canopy exploration and research. The huge pylons were airlifted in by the Nicaraguan air force; most of the other materials were manhandled in along narrow trails so habitat impact was kept to a minimum. The slow-moving 90-minute, 1.6km ride in six-person cars is preceded by an informative video and optional guided hike through the 400ha reserve. Each gondola includes a naturalist guide who explains canopy ecology as you silently glide from forest floor to 30m above the treetops. A restaurant offers international cuisine and snacks with adjoining gift shop. Ten new cabins for overnight stays include unlimited tram trips in their rates; US$80 also includes 3 meals and hot-water bathrooms. As this is a very popular tour with cruise ships from Limón and all tour operators out of Central Valley, it is advisable to pre-book a tour during the high season. At US$79, including transfer from San José, US$50 walk in, it isn't the cheapest tour around but has to be about the most accessible way to appreciate a unique perspective of primary rainforest.

Just 5km before Guápiles at the Río Blanco turn-off, **Gallery At Home** and **Muebles de Bamboo** (☎ 710 1958; f 710 2264; e *brieri99@yahoo.com*) are the two studios of Patricia and Brian Erickson. Her languid yet brightly coloured portrayals of Afro-Caribbean women showing the links to their land and culture have won international acclaim. Brian grows many rare species of bamboo and creates beautiful one-off furniture items, screens and lamp stands and can export worldwide.

Canopy Tropical Magic Forest (*3km south of Río Danta on a rough road;* ☎ 710 6541; e *canopyride@hotmail.com; open 08.00–17.00; tours US$30 per person for a half day, US$75 for full day with lunch*) is a 50ha recreational centre with canopy tour, spring-fed swimming pool, ranchos and picnic areas with palm plantation.

Beyond Guápiles and 4km south at the Servicentro Santa Clara, lies **Jardín Botánico Las Cusingas** (☎ 710 2652; e *segleau@yahoo.com*). Run by *Ticos* Jane Segleau and Ulíses Blanco, the 20ha gardens specialise in medicinal plants but also *bromeliads* and orchids. The owners offer educational guided walks for US$5 per person, discussing tropical ecology and conservation. Two trails lead to the Santa Clara River where you can bathe. A rustic cabin with hot-water shower and wood-burning stove is available for US$30.

Just north as you approach Guácimo, the huge grounds of **Costa Flores** (☎ 716 6457; f 716 6439; e *costaflo@racsa.co.cr*) provide an impressive 300ha worth of export-quality heliconias and other exotic flowers. Founded by American David Carli, the farm combines the export business with a chance to look into the fascinating tropical flower business. A lily pond with fountains and packing house for preparing palms for export are part of a tour possible with prior booking; minimum four persons. Wheelchair access is along cement pathways and restaurant. The tour costs US$15 including a tropical flower bouquet to take away.

Beyond Guácimo, 1km east, **EARTH University** or more accurately Escuela de Agricultura de la Región Tropical Húmeda (Agricultural School for Humid Tropical

Regions) (✆ *713 0000;* f *713 0001; email contact via web page; www.earth.ac.cr; guided tours US$11 for 4 hours or US$22 for a full 7hr tour*) is an internationally renowned facility providing college students from all over Latin America and Uganda with research opportunities in tropical agricultural and sustainable farming techniques, with extensive plantations of experimental banana and other crops, pig breeding and even banana paper production. Started in 1990, the university can enrol up to 100 students per year. A 400ha forest reserve has wonderful birding and hiking and the botanical garden shows off a wide variety of exotic and medicinal blooms. Visitors are welcome with prior booking. The grounds have a pool, gym, cafeteria and overnight stays are possible in rooms with private baths and fans (*rate US$55*).

Since these are the banana heartlands, the **Dole Banana Tour** (✆ *768 8683;* f *768 8137;* e *bananatour@racsa.co.cr; US$10 for tour on bagging, harvesting and packing*) is a must-do experience. Often combined with the Aerial Tramway, this is another popular shore tour for the cruise liners so it is worth calling beforehand to make sure it's not overrun with tour groups. However, you can visit only as part of a group and they are not interested in walk-in tourists except during high season. Tour operators from San José can help organise visits.

PUERTO LIMÓN

Highway 32 ends abruptly just by the cruise-ship terminal and **Parque Vargas**, the main point of reference, a rather neglected but shady park overlooking the sea wall. Puerto Limón, or more commonly simply Limón, is the only sizeable town on the Caribbean coast and its main port, along with Moín, 6km west are surrounded by container depots with queues of trucks waiting to load up. Columbus, and his young son, landed here in 1502 on his fourth and final voyage. These days, you immediately see the mix of Afro-Caribbean and Chinese, the descendants of workers brought in to construct the infamous Atlantic Railway as well as Latino races throughout the town; Spanish vying with Creole English in conversation. Still shedding its reputation as rough and dangerous, Limón is a lively place although there are few attractions laid on for the tourist. This is surprising with the rapid and voluminous increase in cruise ships coming through but apart from street vendors and the nearby market selling handicrafts, most of the shore visitors are herded into buses and away to attractions outside of town, a source of complaint among the job-poor inhabitants. Limón really turns on the heat for its October carnival week, when revellers descend from elsewhere in Costa Rica and further afield. With bands, decorated floats, carnival queen, street dances and lots of reggae and calypso this is a noisy, tumultuous melange of body-painted, costumed and rather heated humanity. The substantial Chinese community wends through the streets with a huge snapping dragon.

Boats can be hired to visit **Isla Uvita**, the only sizeable island along the whole coast, with a pleasant hike under the cliffs or even surfing when the waves are up helping to fill a day if overnighting here. The beaches at **Playa Bonita** and **Playa Portete** along the Moín road also offer good swimming, but check for the safe swim spots first.

Tourists not flying into Tortuguero or Barra will pick up their water transport from here.

GETTING THERE AND AWAY
By car Highway 32 or the Braulio Carrillo Highway takes about three hours.

By bus
🚌 **Transportes Caribeños** ✆ 221 2596. Leaves from Caribbean Terminal, Av 11/13, Ca Central.

🚌 **Empresarios Guapileños** ✆ 710 7780. Also departs from San José's Caribbean Terminal.

WHERE TO STAY

⌂ **Hotel Maribú Caribe** (52 rooms) 5km west from Limón overlooking Playa Bonita; 📞 795 4010; 📠 795 3541; 📧 maricari@racsa.co.cr. Definitely the best hotel in the area with charming bungalows arranged around swimming pools in landscaped gardens. AC, cable TV, hot-water bathrooms and laundry service. The good seafood restaurant has wonderfully dramatic views over the ocean and at night the lit-up tankers heading out to sea add to the entertainment. The friendly staff will help arrange tours to Tortuguero or fishing at Barra. *Rate US$55.*

⌂ **Hotel Park** (32 rooms) One block north of Parque Vargas next to the fire station; 📞 798 0555; 📠 758 4364; 📧 irlixie@racsa.co.cr. The only decent hotel in town. It looks rather Spartan and cold, but the light rooms have cable TV, AC and private baths with hot water. Some have sea views and balconies for a bit extra. Importantly, it has safe parking if you arrive by car (vehicle theft and break-ins being rampant) and a sunny restaurant serving *Tico* cuisine. *Rate US$45, children under 8 free.*

⌂ **Cabinas Oasys del Caribe** (15 wood cabins) Heading out west towards Playa Bonita; 📞/📠 795 0024. Basic accommodation with fan and cable TV but it's out of town with a small pool and open-air restaurant; international menu available. *Rate US$23.*

WHERE TO EAT

✘ **Restaurant Brisas del Caribe** On the north side of Parque Vargas; 📞 758 2159. A pleasant place to sit at one of the pavement tables close to the park and the sea wall and they offer a good choice of Caribbean and *Tico* dishes. *Dish of the day for US$1.80. Open Mon–Fri 09.00–22.00, Sat–Sun 11.00–22.00.*

✘ **Restaurant & Bar Placeres** Before Cabinas Oasys on the hill; 📞 795 3335. Has open-air eating with ocean views and an international Caribbean menu.

Otherwise, the restaurants in hotels **Park** and **Maribú Caribe** round off a limited choice. A few fast-food joints can be found in the centre, such as TCBY.

BARRA DEL COLORADO

Barra has become a Mecca for fishing fanatics the world over, though mostly from the US to catch and release the huge tarpon and snook that often reach world-record proportions. All-in fishing lodges working mostly out of San José give the whole package, flying/boating-in clients, and taking the work out of reaching this isolated corner of Costa Rica. But Barra has much more than simply hooking in the big ones. The 92,000ha Barra del Colorado Wildlife Refuge bordering Nicaragua offers the ultimate in remote wildlife observation. Unfortunately for the ecosystem, a dry-weather road now reaches the western extent of the refuge at Puerto Lindo and illegal loggers and hunters have taken advantage to access the area. The more swampy eastern side is too difficult for roads and is better monitored against this destruction. It's a delicate issue with area residents lobbying for an all-weather road and conservationists desperate to maintain Barra's isolation, which provides some degree of protection for the spectacular flora and fauna found here. A small ranger station works out of the Río Colorado by the village and the only settlement of note in the region. With no roads, the lodges are dotted along the river and canoes or water taxis are *de rigueur*. The airstrip on the south side is the link for most visitors from San José and beyond with scheduled daily flights.

Tarpon fishing from January to June, snook fishing from September to December mean virtual year-round angling of some kind. Barracuda and jack crevalle are other inshore catches with bluegill, rainbow bass and machaca for river fishing. It is possible to deep-sea fish for marlin and sailfish but this is not as satisfying perhaps as the Pacific. All anglers should pay US$40 for a licence, charged separately from lodging rates.

Besides the fishing, increasingly, eco-tourism is being offered to visitors really wanting off-the-main-trail exploring and wildlife spotting in these vast wetlands and steamy rainforests. Up to 600cm of rain falls here in an average year. The sea is not recommended for swimming, having some nasty currents and a daunting number of sharks.

GETTING THERE AND AWAY
By air
✈ **NatureAir** ☎ 220 3054. Daily flights. ✈ **SANSA** ☎ 222 9414. Also has daily flights.

By bus Dry-season access from Cariari to Puerto Lindo by bus to meet river taxis or hotel launches.

By boat Boats leave from Puerto Viejo de Sarapiquí, Tortuguero and Moín for Barra del Colorado.

WHERE TO STAY AND EAT The sport-fishing lodges are mostly strung along the river and around the village of Barra del Colorado. Since they all offer inclusive packages, restaurants don't exist outside other than basic *sodas* used by locals.

⌂ **Silver King Lodge** (10 units) 300m upriver from Río Colorado; ☎/f 711 0708; in the US, ☎ 888 6TARPON; www.silverkinglodge.net. Recommended as the best and most luxurious fishing lodge in the area, the huge rooms include coffee maker, large private bathrooms with hot water, fans. An indoor jacuzzi and massage will ease any aches from fighting the fish all day and a lovely pool with waterfall is surrounded by hammocks and comfortable loungers. Soft drinks, beer and rum are complimentary as is the laundry service. Internet lounge and international calling service available. Unsinkable 6m fishing skiffs for 2 anglers and guide, or larger 7m-deep V-hull boats with 150hp engines, with a wide selection of fishing gear available. For wildlife viewing, the owners provide a 5m aluminium canoe and will tow you to a nature hotspot for as long as you want. Owners, Raby and Shawn Barry go out of their way to please their guests and staff and service is excellent. Book well ahead in high season (Jan–May); the lodge is closed for Jul and Dec. *3-day, all-inc package US$4,800 with transport from San José. Non-fishing fans can stay for US$140 pp/day. Fishing guests pay around US$450.*

⌂ **Casamar Fishing Lodge** (12 cabins) 600m north up the canal on Laguna Agua Dulce; m 381 1380; f 710 8093; www.casamarlodge.com. Set in lovely gardens, the thatched cabins have screened windows, fans, and baths with hot water. Laundry inc. Excellent meals are served in the attractive restaurant decorated with *Tico* handicrafts, meals are buffet style using lots of fish and vegetables grown in the hotel gardens; *bocas* served before dinner and a dartboard in the bar. Tours are offered for non-anglers along the rivers and canals. *3-day/night fishing packages from US$1,325 from San José.*

⌂ **Archie Field's Río Colorado Lodge** (18 rooms) Just down from Tarponland and accessible by land; ☎ (in San José) 232 4063; f 231 5987; US toll free, ☎ 800 243 9777; www.riocolorolodge.com. The original lodge, built in 1971, is probably the best value and certainly the most lively with charismatic manager Dan Wise swapping fishing tales and only too ready to crank up a party. Comfortable, light and airy rooms with AC, hot-water private baths in a hotchpotch of buildings on stilts with covered walkways. 2 rooms with wheelchair access. Jacuzzi, pool table, cable TV, happy hour with free rum cocktails and all-you-can-eat meals. They advocate the use of eco-motor boats to reduce pollution along the canals and only lip gaff the catch to ensure minimal damage to the fish before releasing them. Give this lodge and any other fair warning if fishing is not your thing and you would prefer to wildlife watch instead. That way they can set up suitable guides and trips. This is about the only lodge that stays open all year. *Rates with all meals for non-anglers US$120; for a day's fishing, drinks, lodging and meals US$400 pp. Packages from San José, inc transport for 5 nights with 3 days fishing from US$2,800.*

⌂ **Tarponland Lodge** (12 cabins) In the village and one of the very few to be reached on foot from the plane; ☎ 710 2141, 710 1271. The most basic, if still not cheapest, of the lodges, next to a general store. It looks run down with a faded exterior and tatty tin roof. The rather dingy rooms are a good size with cold-water bathrooms and fans, but the beds are small. The pool is sometimes filled for swimming. *Package for 2 with meals, hotel and fishing from US$200 per night, for 3 from US$250* *per night. Will arrange boat trips for US$15. No credit cards.*

⌂ **Samay Laguna Lodge** (22 rooms) 7km south down the canals from Barra near to river mouth and almost a third of the way towards Tortuguero; ☎ 384 7074; e info@samay.com; www.samay.com. German run and more orientated towards non-fishing nature enthusiasts. The simple but comfortable rooms have mosquito nets, fans and private baths with 3-day/2-night packages from San José for US$250 inc canoe trips down to Tortuguero waterways and Barra lagoons, night guided tour, hiking, meals served

family style, accommodation and boat/land transfer from San José. A special 'budget' 3-day/2-night package is offered from Puerto Viejo de Sarapiquí for individual travellers with safe parking of your (hire) car, river transport, hotel, free use of canoes, choice of tour between hiking, canoe or boat, all meals but no drinks, for US$199 (Nicaragua US$9 visa fee not inc). Turtle-watching packages to Tortuguero Aug–Sep, US$17. Additional nights, US$75 with meals, canoe use and tours make this a very reasonable option for non-angling visitors.

TORTUGUERO

Whilst giving the impression of being as remote as Barra, Tortuguero National Park and environs are much more heavily visited thanks to closer communications with Moín, which is three hours by water taxi. The 19,000ha park comprises 11 eco-habitats from marshy wetlands to primary rainforest. Hand-hewn channels built in the 1960s connect the natural waterways between Barra, Tortuguero and Moín. A 35km narrow lagoon runs parallel to the beach and most of the lodging is dotted along the thin spit of land. Tortuguero is justly famous for its four species of turtles found here (green, leatherback, hawksbill and loggerhead), but also offers some of the most diverse wildlife in the country with 400 bird species, 57 amphibians, 111 reptiles and 60 mammals, many of which are endangered species. Tourism has boomed here, causing fears of over-exploiting the environment, but the visitors seem a lesser threat than the proposed road that the big banana and timber companies want to push through between the two protected areas to the coast. This would effectively blow apart the delicate biological corridor that exists at present and severely compromise the many endangered populations of jaguars, ocelot, peccaries and tapirs that need extensive habitat. Already the remnants of primary vegetation look alarmingly small if you choose to fly into Tortuguero and see first-hand the encroaching ranches and plantations.

GETTING THERE AND AWAY
By car Driving directly to Tortuguero is not possible; however, if you take the Gúaplies–Cariari route, you can leave your car safely in La Pavona and continue by water taxi. Leaving a rental car in Moín is less secure.

By air
✈ **NatureAir** ☎ 220 3054. Daily flights. ✈ **SANSA** ☎ 222 9414. Also has daily flights.

By bus Buses run from San José's Caribbean Terminal, Avenida 11/13, Calle Central (☎ 221 2596) to Moín then by river taxi. Take a bus no later than 06.30 to make the boat connections. The 09.00 direct bus to Cariari then local Coopetraca bus (US$2) to La Pavona hooks up with the 13.30 boat departures (US$8) This is the most popular route for independent travellers and locals (see below).

By boat River taxis and private boats run to Tortuguero from Moín. Prices one way vary from US$40 to US$75; it's worth making up a group for better rates. Alexis Soto; pager 900-296-2626 runs a reliable service. Lodges run their own launches.

WHERE TO STAY As in Barra most of the lodges spread along the lagoons offer all-inclusive but less expensive packages from San José. And there are almost endless permutations: fly in, boat and bus back; fly both ways or not, although among the various hotels they end up offering very similar deals. Fortunately for individual travellers watching their expenses, plenty of basic lodging is available in or near the village and provides an acceptable budget option if packages are not your thing. Camping is always risky with frequent downpours ready to flood you out and fer de lance snakes are not uncommon, but you can pitch a tent by the Caribbean Conservation Corporation museum or the national park headquarters. All the packages described below are at per-person rates based on double occupancy in the lodge with all meals and at least one tour with a bilingual guide.

Tortuga Lodge & Gardens (24 rooms) 257 0766; e ecotur@expeditions.co.cr; www.costaricaexpeditions.com. Costa Rica Expeditions apply their experience and expertise to create a luxury yet environmentally integrated lodge applying energy-saving measures and habitat-friendly structures. Most of the employees are from the area and low-impact, almost silent electric outboard motors work on all boats. The gorgeous wood cabins have more screened window than wall with attractive furnishings and fresh flower arrangements. The award-winning chlorine-free pool seems to fall away into the lagoon and is cleaned with small amounts of salt. Dine overlooking the lagoon surrounded by orchids, palms and heliconias. Many package options are offered and CRE will even arrange your wedding or honeymoon if you wish. *Room rate without b/fast US$99. 2-day/1-night package, fly in, boat/bus out, US$289. 3 days/ 2 nights for US$379.*

Turtle Beach Lodge (30 rooms) 8km north of village; 248 0707; f 257 4409; e info@turtlebeachlodge.com; www.turtlebeachlodge.com. Large cabins with tiled floors, picture windows to maximise on ventilation are set in spacious gardens on the spit of land between the ocean and Tortuguero lagoon. You arrive grandly through the lodge's own 'canal-drive', a narrow black-water channel that plunges into the jungle to fetch up at their private dock. A big rancho where meals are served, often with live music, is set by the small turtle-shaped pool, flippers and all. Hammocks and loungers help you get into turtle pace. Good trails through the 70ha grounds for birding and wildlife, and kayaks are available. *They offer 2-day/1-night packages with 2 tours, round trip bus/boat for US$188. Fly in, boat/bus out, US$255. Fly round trip, US$335 and so on up to 7-day/6-night package deals.*

Mawamba Lodge (54 rooms) 293 8181; f 239 7657; e mawamba@racsa.co.cr; www.grupomawamba.com. Used by many San José tour operators and part of the Grupo Mawamba that runs another lodge, this *Tico* operation offers an upmarket resort in 6ha grounds between Tortuguero lagoon and the beach. Spacious hardwood-panelled rooms have hot-water bathrooms and ceiling fans. The pleasant *rancho* with hammocks nestles in the gardens and the games area has darts, table football and pool. Nightly lectures are offered on the area's ecology. There are private trails and butterfly garden with souvenir shop and a very stylish pool with a bridge over to the bar and an island with tree frogs. *2-day/1-night package US$220; 3 days/2 nights US$280; inc bus/boat round trip from San José.*

Laguna Lodge (80 rooms) 225 3740; f 283 8031; www.lagunatortuguero.com. A larger resort whose effort at uniqueness is its 'Gaudi-style building with small conference room, reception and souvenir shop'. The pretty wood-floor rooms are housed in blocks with fans, hot-water bathrooms, reading lamps and seating outside. The open-air restaurant looks over Tortuguero lagoon and the large free-form pool boasts a small hydro-massage waterfall and palm-festooned island, 2 bars and *rancho* with hammocks. *2 days/1 night pp inc bus/boat both ways US$199; 3 days/2 nights US$249.*

Hotel Ilan-Ilan (24 rooms) 255 2031; f 255 1946; e costarica@ilan-ilanlodge.com; www.ilan-ilanlodge.com. Pool, jacuzzi and gardens set in a pleasant 8ha of grounds, opened in 1989. *2-day/ 1-night package for US$160; 3 days/2 nights US$215; inc bus/boat both ways. To fly in 1 way, add on US$57.*

Manati Ecological Lodge (10 rooms) Between the Tortuguero and Penitencia lagoons, 3km north of village; m 383 0330. A small lodge with rather charmless, plain rooms with floor fans and a couple of cabins with beds and bunks that would suit families, offering a budget alternative with an eco-lodge feel away from the village itself. An honour system operates in the screened bar with darts and pool table. You can rent kayaks for US$5 per hr. The owners live on site and are active in the Manatee Protection Project. Rooms are US$40 with b/fast but the 2-night packages out of San José from US$200 seem expensive compared with the more luxury competition.

🏠 **Pachira Lodge** On the spur between Tortuguero and Penitencia lagoons, 2km from the village; ✆ 256 7080; m 382 2239; www.pachiralodge.com. Set in 14ha of grounds. Pretty, light and airy rooms with bamboo-frame beds, fans, hot water. Very colourful Caribbean décor with large turtle pool and buffet-style meals add to the informal feel. *Packages with no minimum number from San José, 2 days/1 night inc bus/boat US$188; out by air, back by bus/boat US$259; air both ways US$359. 3 days/ 2 nights US$251, US$359 and US$455 respectively.*

🏠 **B&B Marbella** (4 rooms) ✆ 709 8011; f 709 8094; m 833 0827; e safari@racsa.co.cr;

www.casamarbella.tripod.com. Touted as the only B&B in the area, run by ebullient Canadian, Daryl Loth and his wife Luz Denia. Spotless and light-filled rooms with private hot-water bathrooms are set in flower-filled gardens with its own landing stage. The communal lounge has cable TV, library and board games. *Rate US$34.*

🏠 **Miss Junie's Restaurant & Cabins** (12 rooms) North end of the village; ✆ 711 0684. A veritable institution, Miss Junie offers simple but pretty rooms with tiled floors, fan with private bathrooms and hot water. Her daughter has taken over most of the cooking in the restaurant where you can enjoy some great Caribbean dishes but don't expect fast service. *B/fast inc. Rate US$34.*

🏠 **Cabinas Joruki** (8 cabins) ✆ 709 8068; m 839 5235. A budget alternative with screens and cold-water bathrooms. *Rate US$15.*

🍴 **WHERE TO EAT Miss Junie's** (✆ *711 0684*) is the best-known restaurant and with good reason, although several other establishments in the village will cook up good Caribbean dishes: **Miss Miriam's** (✆ *709 8107*), **Restaurant El Muellecito** (✆ *709 8104*) and nearby **Restaurant La Caribeña**. They also sell burgers, sandwiches and snacks. **La Casona Restaurant & Bakery** by the football field is a bit more upmarket and not only sells baked goods, but has a laundry service too.

PRACTICALITIES No banks or ATMs are available, though some souvenir shops will accept credit cards and travellers' cheques at a steep commission, so take enough cash to cover all costs. The excellent Tortuguero Information Center (✆ *833 0827/709-8011; www.geocities.com/tortugueroinfo/main.html*) just by the Catholic church in town will give up-to-date information on just about anything. The nearest hospital is in Guápiles, several hours away. Internet service is available in the village.

WHAT TO SEE AND DO All visitors pay the US$6 park fee at the **Cuatro Esquinas** or the more southerly ranger stations. Although you can count on rain year round, it is wettest in January, June and July. The 'driest' months are February, April and November but don't think of leaving your raingear behind. The sheltered lagoons and canals can be muggy and claustrophobic although evenings can cool down enough for a light sweater. Mosquitoes feature; bring lots of repellent. So does the sun; bring lots of sunblock and a hat.

Good hiking is possible through parts of the park and along the beach if you don't mind the stifling heat and humidity and sometimes flooded trails. It's worth the walk from Tortuga Lodge to the highest point, **Cerro Tortuga** (119m), which gives excellent views over the flatlands, coastline and swamps.

In the laid-back village of Tortuguero, you can hire canoes to explore the waterways without a guide (US$6 *first hour, US$3 for subsequent hours*). Motorised dinghies are also for hire but check them out well before paying out money and it's worth taking a guide – the lagoons and canals are deceptively easy to get lost in and strong currents are a factor. Kayaks can be rented from **Manati Ecological Lodge**. If you are travelling independently, information from the **Tortuguero Information Center** (e *tortugueroinfo@yahoo.com; www.geocities.com/tortugueroinfo/main.html*) by the church recommends guides and tours. Make sure to go out only in quiet electrically driven motorised canoes to reduce the impact on the wildlife and increase your chances of seeing more animals.

Turtle watching is a main draw and hotels arrange night tours with mandatory guide during the July–October season (green turtles), February–July (leatherbacks) and March-October (hawksbills).

Several companies arrange trips from San José. **Riverboat Francesca** (✆ 226 0986; e *fvwatson@racsa.co.cr; www.tortuguerocanals.com*) give first-class guided tours with bilingual experts in environmentally powered boats. The charming owners, Modesto and Fran Watson offer various wildlife or fishing packages with transfers and meals out of Moín.

Tortuguero Safaris (✆ 709 8011; m 833 0827; e *safari@racsa.co.cr; www.casamarbella.tripod.com*) is run by Canadian naturalist Daryl Loth who also owns B&B Marbella in town. He knows everyone around and can recommend the best local guides or arrange tours himself in his six-passenger launch. **Paraíso Tropical Store** has a good choice of handicrafts and will also sell NatureAir tickets if you want to fly back to San José. They also hire out the bizarre hydro bikes for US$10 per hour, a kind of bicycle frame on floats.

The **Caribbean Conservation Corporation** (✆ 709 8091; e *ccc@cccturtle.org; www.cccturtle.org*) is the main organisation for turtle protection with the longest-running Atlantic green turtle study, started by Archie Carr in 1962, with a small but informative visitor centre and museum showing detailed displays of egg-laying turtles; you can also watch a video on the history of turtle conservation on the area. The shops stocks natural history books. They arrange volunteer programmes out of the US during March–October to help with turtle tagging and research, or bird migrations in March–May and August–October. (*One week US$1,554, two weeks US$1,999 including first and last night hotel in San José, all lodging and food in the station, in-country transfers and guided tours.*)

The **Canadian Organisation for Tropical Education and Rainforest Conservation** (m 381 4116; *www.coterc.org*) manages the Caño Palma Research Station about 7km north of Tortuguero. Researchers, students and volunteers can stay at the station and help in various projects. Simple dorms with bunks and outdoor bathrooms accommodate the students.. Space permitting, individual visitors may stay for US$45 including three meals. There are several trails through the forest and the station can arrange boat trips.

PARISMINA

The southern limits of the Tortuguero National Park end just north of Parismina. This tiny settlement lies at the mouth of the Parismina River and is best known for its river and sea sport fishing with several world records for tarpon and snook to its name. If you are not into angling, then maybe continue through to Tortuguero.

GETTING THERE AND AWAY

By bus Buses run to Siquirres from San José's Caribbean Terminal, Avenida 11/13, Calle Central (✆ 221 2596). Then take a 45-minute taxi ride to Caño Blanco for US$30 followed by a water taxi for US$3, or the twice-daily bus from the old bus station in Siquirres run by Hermanos Caño-Aguilar (✆ 768 8172). Or head for Moín and pick up a boat there for the 45km trip.

 WHERE TO STAY AND EAT Similar to Barra del Colorado, the lodges here offer all-in packages including all meals so there is little reason to go in search of food beyond your lodgings.

🏠 **Rio Parismina Lodge** (12 rooms) US ☎ 210 824 4442; Costa Rica ☎ 236 0345; US toll free ☎ 800 338 5688; US f 210 824 0151; e fish@riop.com; www.riop.com. Set in 20ha of gardens, this comfortable lodge has wood-panelled rooms with fans and verandas, jacuzzi and pool. 21 V-hull ocean boats are used for the sometimes choppy seas. The lodge will help non-anglers with turtle-watching tours, canoe trips, riding, birdwatching or river cruises into Tortuguero National Park. *The lodge stays open all year round. Various package rates include: Sat–Sat, US$3,100 for 7 days' fishing, free local drinks and beer, round-trip flights or bus/boat*

and plane combo from San José; long weekend with 3 days' fishing, US$1,850. Non-fishing for 3 days, US$1,250.

🏠 **Jungle Tarpon Lodge** (4 rooms) US ☎ 800 544 2261; e greatalaska@greatalaska.com; www.jungletarpon.com. Large wooden rooms, tiled floors and rustic elegance in 60ha of grounds between the Parismina lagoon and the sea. Eco-fishing packages specialising in small groups; you choose your fishing schedule from lagoon to offshore or light-tackle fishing in the rivers or surf casting. 3-day/ 2-night trips from US$1,195 pp based on dbl occupancy with van/boat in and plane out to San José.

WHAT TO SEE AND DO An option for ecology-minded travellers with enough time is to volunteer at the British-managed 800ha **Pacuare Nature Reserve** (☎ 233 0451; f 221 2820; e fdezlaw@racsa.co.cr; www.rainforestconcern.org) to help with their turtle-conservation programmes. The private reserve is owned by the Endangered Wildlife Trust run in conjunction with Rainforest Concern (e rainforest@ gn.apc.org). The reserve accepts volunteers to protect nests from egg poachers, monitoring hatchlings, tagging and measuring leatherbacks from March to June, and green turtles from June to August. Volunteers should commit for at least one week and pay US$100 towards lodging and food. The reserve has a lodge with three double rooms and two cabins for groups.

THE SOUTHERN CARIBBEAN

CAHUITA Cahuita's origins began as a camp for English-speaking turtle hunters from the Caribbean Islands, who gradually settled into farming and the community grew. In 1914, then president Alfredo Flores's vessel returning from Sixaola foundered and his party sought help along the beach. The inhabitants of a small settlement provided shelter, clothing and food for which, in gratitude, Flores bought land on the bluff for the settlers to build a new township – Cahuita.

Modern travellers can follow the road from Limón past Cahuita and Puerto Viejo all the way to its end in Manzanillo. It mainly follows the coast, passing long stretches of unpopulated beaches with inland turns to cross the Bananito and Estrella rivers and at the Hone Creek junction where the road leads to the Panamanian border at Sixaola.

Now you are truly in Afro-Caribbean country and with the rise of rural community tourism, you will be able to experience both this and the ethnic Bribri cultures. Although increasing tourism has brought in more *Tico* and foreign settlers who have started up restaurants, bed and breakfasts and hotels, there is still a laid-back, do-it-our-way feel to the area where you can settle into a hammock between the palms, enjoy a coconut-based fish platter and catch some waves. Cahuita, lying as it does off the main road, has remained quieter than its boisterous neighbour, Puerto Viejo, being the better bet if you don't want loud reggae booming at night or a more commercial – in a dreadlocked sort of way – approach to souvenir sales and tour touts.

Drugs are part of the scene and single girls should take care if out alone at night. In the Cahuita area, it is recommended that they stay in town rather than along Black Beach (*Playa Negra*), which is a dark, unlit road at night.

Banks are located in Bribri: a Banco Nacional that does not accept international credit or debit cards, and a Banco de Costa Rica has been opened at the entrance

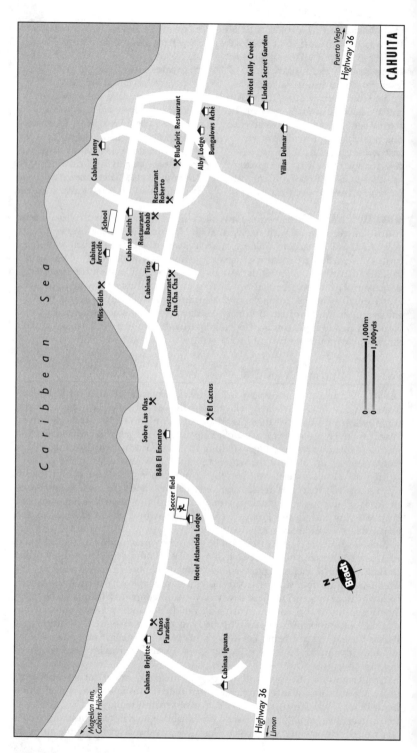

Caribbean Sea

Magellan Inn,
Cabins Hibiscus

Cabinas Brigitte
Chaos Paradise

Cabinas Iguana

Highway 36
Limon

Hotel Atlantida Lodge

Soccer field

B&B El Encanto

Sobre Las Olas

El Cactus

Miss Edith

Cabinas Arrecife

Cabinas Jenny

School

Cabinas Smith

Cabinas Tito

Restaurant
Cha Cha Cha

Restaurant
Baobab

BluSpirit Restaurant

Restaurant
Roberto

Alby Lodge
Bungalows Aché

Villas Delmar

Hotel Kelly Creek
Lindas Secret Garden

Puerto Viejo
Highway 36

0   1,000m
0   1,000yds

N

Bradt

CAHUITA

to Puerto Viejo. However, it is wise to take enough cash with you or check with your lodgings that they will accept credit cards or travellers' cheques.

Mosquitoes and sand-loving no-see-'ems are a fact of life. Most accommodation offers screened rooms or mosquito nets but take repellent for hikes and days on the beach as well as dollops of sunscreen.

Getting there and away
By *car* Follow the highway for 43km south of Limón.

By *bus*
🚌 **Transportes MEPE** ✆ 257 8129. Buses leave from San José's Caribbean Terminal, Av 11/13, Ca Central.

🚌 **Gray Line Fantasy Bus** ✆ 232 3681. Provides AC minibus service with hotel collection to Cahuita and Puerto Viejo.

Where to stay The following establishments comprise by no means an exhaustive listing. Playa Negra is a narrow lane leading into Cahuita with several hotels and restaurants; otherwise, most are in town.

🏠 **Selva Bananito Lodge** (11 cabins) 20km south of Limón and 15km inland with 4x4 access only; ✆/f 253 8118; e conselva@racsa.co.cr; www.selvabananito.com. A remote eco-lodge and farm within a private 850ha reserve that abuts the Parque Internacional La Amistad. The beautiful cabins are made with salvaged wood on stilts and have decks with hammocks to soak up the views; solar-heated water showers and oil lamps at night since there is no electricity enhances the away-from-it-all feel. Spanish courses are also offered along with hiking, riding, tree climbing and mountain biking. *Rate US$220 inc all meals.*

🏠 **Hotel Colón Caribe** (32 rooms) Just beyond the Selva Bananito Lodge turn-off; ✆ 256 5520; f 233 1090; www.coloncaribe.com. A rather characterless family resort popular with *Ticos*, over the road from the beach with pool, jacuzzi, sports amenities, hiking trails and AC cabins with DirecTV, wheelchair access and souvenir shop. *Rates inc 3 meals at US$75 pp.*

Once you reach Cahuita, there are many lodgings to suit all budgets either slung along the Black Beach road, or in Cahuita itself. Turn off left before the main Cahuita turning onto a sandy lane to reach Black Beach. The sand is indeed a dramatic black, and not all sections are suitable for swimming. Further into town and beyond are two shining white-sand beaches with better swimming but always check with locals for currents and dangerous no-swim areas.

🏠 **Magellan Inn** (6 rooms) Playa Negra, where the access lane meets the beach road, ✆/f 755 0035; e magellaninn@racsa.co.cr. An elegant part-French-run hotel with tastefully decorated, well-appointed carpeted rooms with private verandas, fans or AC, lush gardens with sunken reef pool. *Rates include b/fast for US$70 (with fan), US$90 (with AC). Children under 10, free.*

🏠 **Chalet & Cabinas Hibiscus** (5 units) Down lane from the Magellan; ✆ 755 0021; f 755 0015; e hibiscus@ice.co.cr; www.hotels.co.cr/hibiscus.html. Tucked away in pretty beachfront gardens with 2 chalets, 3 rooms all with fans, mosquito nets and terraces. A lovely hideaway place on the ocean with 2 equipped houses for 8–10 guests. Long-stay rates are quoted on request. Swimming pool and games room with pool table. Includes b/fast. *Rate: rooms* US$45, 6-person chalet US$100, 10-person chalet US$120.

🏠 **B&B El Encanto** (5 different units) Playa Negra; ✆ 755 0113; f 755 0432; www.elencantobedandb/fast.com. 3 bungalows, 1 apt, 1 3-bedroom house. Beautiful, elegant dbl bungalows and an apt with balconies, kitchen and satellite TV. The house can be booked complete but even if sharing you have private balconies. Book well ahead if you want to enjoy the peace and comfort of the French-run El Encanto (The Enchanted Place). Wonderful home-baked breads make for memorable b/fasts and if you seek peace, try out the serene meditation room or wander the Asian statue-filled gardens. Yoga and massage are available on request. *Rates: bungalows US$55; rooms US$45–55; equipped 6-person house US$140 and 3-person apt US$75.*

⌂ **Cabinas Iguana** (7 different units) Playa Negra; ↘ 755 0005; f 755 0054; www.cabinas-iguana.com. 2 houses, 3 cabins, 3 rooms. With 2 comfortable wooden houses for 2–6 people, with equipped kitchen, 3 cabins with fridge, fans, beds with mosquito nets. You can lounge in the garden by the pool, pick up a book from their bookstore, borrow a bicycle or wander along the trails. *Rates US$25–65 and rooms having shared bathroom with hot water for US$20, with laundry service.*

⌂ **Hotel Atlántida Lodge** (30 rooms, 6-person house) on beach side of Playa Negra Road; ↘ 755 0115; f 755 0213; www.crica.com/hotels/atlantida. The rooms are nicely laid out in a jungle setting and the lodge has a pool and jacuzzi with massages available. For the active there is the gym, bike rental, volleyball court and tree climbing; otherwise enjoy a drink at the poolside bar or browse the souvenir shop. *Rate US$55.*

⌂ **Hotel Kelly Creek & Restaurant** (4 rooms) Cahuita town; ↘ 755 0007; e kellycr@racsa.co.cr; www.hotelkellycreek.com. The spacious cabins, each with 2 dbl beds, private bathrooms with hot water and verandas are right by the western beach entrance to the park so providing easy access for some of the best beaches and trails. Spanish-run and popular, the rooms have verandas, fans, mosquito nets with good meals from the restaurant but order paella by 14.00 for the evening meal. Can be noisy since it is close to all the town action but good value. *Rate US$45.*

⌂ **Bungalows Aché** (2 bungalows) Along the lane from the park entrance; ↘ 755 0119; e ache_cr@yahoo.com; www.bungalowsache.com. Pleasant bungalows, one for 4 people, with fans, mosquito nets over the beds, mini-kitchens with fridge and coffee maker, hammocks. *Rate US$40, extra person US$5.*

⌂ **Alby Lodge** (4 cabins) Next door to the Aché; ↘/f 755 0031; e alby_lodge@racsa.co.cr. Set in manicured gardens, the German-run pretty thatched cabins have fans, mosquito nets and hammocks on the verandas. A communal kitchen with dining room if you wish to cook your own meals. *Rate US$40, extra person US$5, children under 12 free.*

⌂ **Hotel Sia'Tami** (10 bungalows) Off the main road southeast from Puerto Viejo; ↘ 755 0374; www.siatami.com. Rather dark bungalows with large, equipped kitchens, suitable for families, set in their own gardens within open grounds and gardens with fans and nets. *Rate US$38.*

⌂ **Cabinas Costa Azul** (8 rooms) ↘ 755 0431; f 755 0491; e cabinascostaazul@racsa.co.cr. A motel-style complex, the rooms have either fans or AC, TV, minibar, kitchen facilities and safe parking. *Rates US$30–40.*

⌂ **Cabinas & Centro Turístico Brigitte** (2 cabins) Playa Negra; ↘/f 755 0053; www.brigittecahuita.com. This is a friendly, informal place run by long-time Swiss resident Brigitte whose real love is horses. You can go out riding by the hour but she will create special tours: beach rides for US$30 for 3–4hrs, moonshine for US$35 for 2–3hrs and gentle outings for children US$20 for 1–2hrs. Bicycles also for rent at US$8 per day. Internet access and delicious b/fasts even if you're not a stayover guest. If you need information on any tours in the area or just general advice, this is your place. Also part of the business is **Anna's Laundry Service** attached to the complex (open 07.00–18.00). *Cabin rates US$25–35.*

⌂ **Linda's Secret Garden** (4 rooms) Following the side road past Kelly Creek; ↘/f 755 0327. 3 funky dbl and 1 5-person family room all brightly decorated, with hot-water bathrooms tucked away in a corner of the lane. Outside kitchen facilities available. No off-street parking. *Rates US$20–25; family room US$50.*

⌂ **Cabinas Jenny** (7 rooms) On the shorefront in town; ↘/f 755 0256. A budget option with basic rooms with hot-water showers and balconies, the upstairs rooms have nice views of the sea, popular with surfers, some with fridge, hammocks. *Rates US$23–28.*

⌂ **Villas Delmar** (6 cabins) Cahuita, further along the lane from Kelly Creek; ↘ 755 0375. There are 3 cabins with kitchenette and 3 without, all with fans and inc b/fast. 2 have cold water so ask beforehand if you like hot-water showers. Off-street parking. *Rates US$18–25.*

⌂ **Cabinas Arrecife** (12 cabins) Back in town off the main street from Playa Negra, just up from the police station; ↘/f 755 0081. A pleasant, shady jungle setting with views through the trees to the beach. The plain rooms provide all the basics with fans and porch in front with hot-water bathrooms. Small pool with hammocks nearby, safe parking and snorkelling available. The restaurant does b/fast from 07.00–10.00. *Rate US$20.*

⌂ **Cabinas Tito** (6 cabins) Playa Negra; ↘/f 755 0286. As a budget choice, these spacious cabins have kitchenettes with cold-water bathrooms set in shady gardens. *Rate US$20.*

⌂ **Cabinas Smith** (3 rooms) One block from shore; ↘ 755 0068. This establishment has big rooms with fridge, bathrooms with hot water, reading lamps, fans and porches set in a shady garden with safe off-street parking. *Rate US$18.*

Where to eat Although much of Costa Rica has an uninspiring cuisine, the southern Caribbean has an excellent choice when it comes to different flavours. From rich coconut-based Caribbean seafood dishes, Italian, Thai or a bewildering mixture of fusion you can spend many days eating your way happily through the area.

✖ **Casa Creole** ☎ 755 0104. Just by the Magellan Inn and run by the same owners, offers delicious French/Creole cuisine. *Main courses around US$14. Evenings only.*

✖ **Restaurant Cha Cha Cha** In town; ☎ 394 4153. This highly recommended restaurant has an international/fusion menu with exotic salads and a good choice of vegetarian dishes but the seafood and meat cuisine is also excellent. *Main courses for around US$7–12. Closed Mon.*

✖ **Restaurant Sobre Las Olas** ☎ 755 0109. This renowned restaurant is in a ramshackle-looking building right over the beach and shaded by tall palms but the friendly Italian owner-chef and his daughter cook up some divine dishes with an Italian-Caribbean twist for around US$6–12. A good wine list and reasonable prices. *Closed Tue.*

✖ **Restaurant Chaos Paradise** ☎ 755 0421. Near to Cabinas & Centro Turistico Brigitte, has Caribbean specialities; order *rondón* in advance for a truly typical dining experience, literally what the cook could 'run down' (not run over!) in her kitchen. *Rondón* is a hearty tasty mix of root vegetables, fish in a coconut-based broth. *Shrimp main dish US$6, lobster US$10. Also has a couple of cabins for US$20 each. Open 14.00–22.00.*

✖ **Miss Edith** Between the police station and Cabinas Arrecife. Miss Edith is an institution but becoming spoiled by its own popularity. Service can be slow and surly but she still serves up some of the best *rondón* and other typical dishes in town if you don't mind waiting. *Rondón for US$5.50 and lobster starting at $10.*

✖ **Restaurant El Cactus** ☎ 755 0276. The El Cactus will deliver pizzas and will barbecue various meats and seafood. *Pizzas average US$7.50 and main dishes US$8–12. Open 18.00–22.00.*

✖ **BluSpirit Restaurant** ☎ 755 0122. For Italian pasta and ice creams, and boasts the best piña coladas in town. *Main courses US$5–15. Evenings only, closed Wed.*

✖ **Restaurant Roberto** ☎ 758 3378. A central hangout for good juices and b/fast but Roberto will serve up a catch-of-the-day done Caribbean style that is worth trying for US$3–4. This is the place to catch up on news, gossip and any tours as he also runs Roberto Tours next door for fishing, snorkelling and national park trips. *Open 07.00–22.00.*

✖ **Restaurant Relax** ☎ 755 0322. Over Ricky's Bar on the main street, with friendly Mexican–Italian owners, has tasty mussels, grilled shark among many other dishes between US$4–8 and great cocktails. *Open Wed–Mon from 16.00; closed Tue.*

✖ **Restaurant & Marisqueria Tio Cayman** ☎ 755 0122. Just off the crossroads by the Relax, this establishment has a long name for a tiny place but they cook up *rondón* daily and make their own pasta, the salmon fettuccine is delicious and good value. *Open 12.00–midnight.*

✖ **Centro Turistico Boca Chica** ☎ 755 0415. Heading south out of town, at Puerto Vargas entrance, is a lively Italian-owned restaurant and bar for Caribbean/international dishes and barbecued food. Pool and souvenirs. *Main courses around US$6. Open 09.00–18.00.*

Practicalities The nearest bank is the Banco Nacional in Bribri, which does not accept international credit/debit cards or the Banco de Costa Rica in Puerto Viejo, which does. The fastest internet service is at Willie's Tours (☎ *755-0267; williestours@gmail.com; US$2 for an hour*). The nearest hospital is in Limón, Tony Facio Hospital (☎ *758 2222*) but the clinic (☎ *750 0220*) can give basic attention. The post office (*open Mon–Fri 08.00–12.00 and 13.30–17.00*) is just by the police station (☎ *755 0217*).

What to see and do Aviaríos del Caribe (☎ *750 0775;* f *750 0725; www.slothrescue.org*) is a private sloth rehabilitation centre started by Judy and Luis Arroyo in 1991 when some neighbours brought them a sloth orphan. Buttercup, now a grande dame of 14 is the star resident and helped the Arroyos become world experts on these little-studied animals. Now housing some 45 two- and three-toed sloths, they nurse the injured back to health (many are burned on high-tension cables) and the orphans are reared with a view to reintroducing them into the nearby rainforest. Tours with excellent explanatory video are available around the facility for US$8, so you can coo at the altogether too-adorable residents clutching their soft-toy comforters, and there is an adopt-a-sloth programme and schools' education programme. A three-hour guided canoe provides excellent birding around their property for US$30 per person.

By the Penshurt turn-off, **Orquídeas Mundo/Piedmont Restaurant** (✆ 750 0789; e *orchidpierre@yahoo.com; camping US$3 pp*) is an interesting stopover if you like orchids. French-Canadian Pierre Dubois is a dedicated orchid botanist who has built up an impressive collection over the past 25 years. Guided tours through the organic farm with birdwatching are also available and you can finish up with a delicious and healthy meal cooked 'cordon bleu Tropical' style. Night tours to observe the tree frogs and river crayfish and painting classes are also on offer. The **Cahuita National Park** starts at the southern tip of the town with coastal trails to the point, with a coral reef that offers great snorkelling. The main entrance is a further 5km south at Puerto Vargas (*entrance US$6 for foreign visitors, US$1.50 for residents*). Safe swimming and camping here for US$1.50 person but do not leave any valuables unguarded on the beach or in your tent.

The 9,950ha **Hitoy-Cerere Biological Reserve** is the most undervisited of the country's protected areas. With no facilities or guided trails, it lies to the south of the Río Estrella Valley. Very wet conditions and climbing from an altitude of 100m to 1,025m makes hiking a challenge even for the experienced. You are sure to be rewarded with some fascinating encounters with almost untouched habitat and its resident wildlife. A ranger station, often unmanned, exists at the trailhead.

Several tour operators work out of Cahuita offering snorkelling or river rafting and trips into the Bribri Indigenous Reserve and bird or wildlife-watching walks into the national park. Other operators are **Cahuita Tours** (✆ 755 0232; f 755 0082; e *cahuitat@racsa.co.cr*) which also arranges trips into Panamá; **Turística Cahuita** (✆ 75 5 0071; f 755 0069); **Willie's Tours** (✆ 755-0267; e *williestours@gmail.com*) is multilingual and recommended; **Roberto Tours** (✆ 755 0117; m 396 9864) is run by a well-known local figure with a restaurant in the town centre; charismatic **Mr Big J** (✆ 755 0328) has lots of information, riding, maps, book exchange and laundry.

There are a number of community tourism projects that would be glad of your support: check out the non-profit organisation **Red Talamanca de Ecoturismo** (✆ 224 3570; f 253 7524; *www.talamance-adventures.com*). This network, made up of 18 organisations with 60 guides, works towards sustainable tourism development and eco-tours into the Talamanca indigenous settlements. One–ten-day trips with stays in family homes are possible and provide a way to really penetrate the remote Talamanca mountain region. **Aventuras Naturales Yorkín** (✆ 200 5211; f 751 0075; e *cooprena@racsa.co.cr*) is part of the COOPRENA community tourism programme and you paddle by dugout canoe up the Yorkín River to learn about organic banana and cocoa plantations and medicinal gardens belonging to the Bribri. Offering a unique opportunity to watch migrating raptors in September–October and February–April in one of the world's birding hotspots, the **Kekőldi Wak Ka Koneke**, a Bribri reserve south of Cahuita, has trained bilingual indigenous guides to take visitors to a 10m viewing platform deep in the forest for US$30 per person that includes a typical lunch of root vegetables and corn served on leaf plates. The community is building a hostel in the reserve for overnight tourists near to the platform, to be opened in 2006.

PUERTO VIEJO

Lively and loud with dancing, restaurants and bars, Puerto Viejo also looks out to the gnarliest surf point at Salsa Brava reef. During the day and into the evenings, the main road fills with street vendors selling beach clothing, funky jewellery and Rasta crafts, especially beautiful paper lampshades decorated with natural leaves that have become fashion collectibles in San José.

The town lies 18km south of Cahuita and is much more touristy, the road lurching from crunching pot-holes to totally unpaved stretches to occasional patches of tarmac that only build up your hopes for half a kilometre to dash them in a hole just round the corner.

If arriving by bus, ignore the hotel touts that cajole and bully for trade claiming your reserved choice has closed down, or is fully booked or too ghastly for words. Puerto Viejo isn't big, you can walk anywhere in ten minutes so look around and don't be pressured.

Depending on the time of year, there is good diving and snorkelling, and surfing is a big draw. Many visitors enjoy visiting the ethnic Bribri and Cabecar communities with rural tourism trips that let you stay with indigenous families and learn first-hand about their way of life. The sand beaches and bays are perfect for sunning, swimming or sea kayaking and hikes inland will be rewarded with refreshing waterfalls, stunning forests and impressive birding.

The nearest bank so far has been in Bribri, some 10km away, but at the time of writing the Banco de Costa Rica is installing a small branch office with cash dispenser that will take most major credit and debit cards. Several internet cafés can be found and with improved telecommunications, finding somewhere to check your emails becomes easier throughout the region.

GETTING THERE AND AWAY

By car A pot-holed road heads south for 18km from Cahuita, and a further 14km to end-of-the-road town, Manzanillo.

By bus

Transportes MEPE \ 257 8129. Buses leave from San José's Caribbean Terminal, Av 11/13, Ca Central. All buses to Manzanillo (5hrs), stop at Puerto Viejo. Buses for Sixaola and the Panamanian border also stop at Puerto Viejo.

MEPE \ 758 1572. From Limón to Bribri hourly for the 2hr trip.

GETTING AROUND Taxis are based in town or call Charlie Bull (\ 750 0112) or Luis Bermúdez (\ 844 9913). Dragon Scooter Rentals (\ 750 0728) rent 50cc scooters for US$30 per day up to 135cc Kawasaki bikes for US$60 per day or US$40/50 for four/eight hours. Bicycles can be rented from Cabinas Grant (\ 750 0292) for US$28 per day, although several hotels both in Puerto Viejo and further down the road offer bicyces to their guests.

TOUR OPERATORS A number of tour agencies work out of Puerto Viejo, offering mostly the same kind of trip. The best diving operation is **Reef Runner Divers** near the main bus stop (\ 750 0480; www.reefrunnerdivers.net) with full dive equipment, boats and they will do PADI Open Water certification. **Puerto Viejo Tours & Rentals** (\/f 750 0411; e puertoviejotours@yahoo.com) offers snorkelling, rafting, kayaks, surf boards and quadricycle or motor scooter rental. **Terraventuras Tour Agency**, just off the main road coming into town (\ 750 0750) offers a canopy tour with Tarzan swing and dolphin tours. In Playa Cocles, **Xtreme Caribe** (\ 750 0507), part of the Hotel El Tesoro complex, organises riding into the forest, surf lessons with board rentals, kayaking, fishing and moped rental.

Seahorse Stables (\ 750 0468; e edwinsalem@yahoo.com) has riding tours and visits to the butterfly garden and jungle.

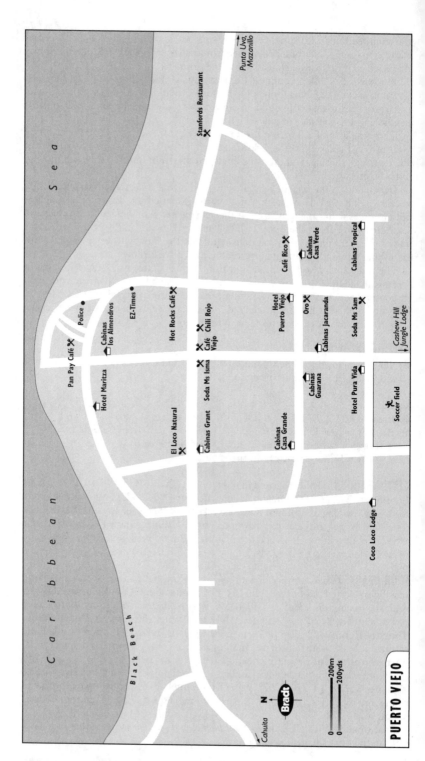

PUERTO VIEJO

Mariposario Punta Uva (↘ *750 0086;* e *junglapm@racsa.co.cr; open 08.00–16.00; entrance US$5, children free*) on the hill above Punta Uva has 75 species of butterflies, three unique to Costa Rica. It also runs guided tours. It's worth the climb just for the view. **Crazy Monkey Canopy Ride** at Playa Uva (↘ *272 2024*) is run by Almonds and Corals Tent Camp with 13 platforms for US$40 per person.

At the end of the road, in Manzanillo, you can rent snorkel gear, kayaks, boogie boards and arrange dive trips with **Aquamor**. It also does jungle tours and dolphin-watching trips.

The Talamanca Dolphin Foundation (↘ *759 0715; www.dolphinlink.org; 2–3-hour boat trips US$35 pp, min 2 people*) has protection and research programmes.

The **Gandoca-Manzanillo Wildlife Refuge** is largely undeveloped offering dramatic beaches, coral reefs with good snorkelling from just off the beach, mangroves and rainforest. You can watch turtles during the season. Local guides will take you hiking, birding and wildlife spotting.

WHERE TO STAY Puerto Viejo also has its Black Beach, not to be confused with Cahuita's, before reaching the town proper. A dirt road leads off to access the northern part away from town.

🏠 **Viewpoint Resort Hotel** (4 bungalows) Some 7km north on the main road; ↘/f 750 0238; e mademar@racsa.co.cr; www.viewpoint-resorthotel.com. This hotel commands an imposing position high above the road with ocean views. The affable Swiss owner maintains spotless bungalows with kitchens, fridges, private hot-water bathrooms, ceiling fans, balconies for between 2 and 6 people. They are set in 12ha of grounds with trails, pool with a magical view over Cahuita National Park, an open-air gym with all the machines for a good workout, giant chessboard, darts and a good restaurant that bakes its own bread and has a good choice of vegetarian dishes. You are a little out on a limb if you don't have your own vehicle, and the steep drive almost needs a 4x4 just to get up but it is away from the bustle of town and a good base for families. *Rates US$55 for 2, children aged 4–12 pay US$6 each.*

🏠 **Samasati Nature Retreat** (17 different units) By the Black Beach turn-off; ↘ 750 0315; www.samasati.com. 9 bungalows, 5 rooms, 3 houses. Comfortable polished-wood bungalows with lofts and balconies and the dbl rooms are in a sgl guesthouse with shared bathrooms at either end; the houses are located in a secluded part of the grounds with between 2 and 4 bedrooms. Vegetarian meals are inc and all-in packages with yoga sessions are also available. *Rates US$107 pp in the bungalows, US$69 pp for the rooms.*

🏠 **Hotel Perla Negra** (24 rooms) At the end of Black Beach Road; ↘ 750 0111; f 750 0114; www.perlanegra-beachresort.com. Large well-ventilated rooms with sea views and balconies in attractive wooden buildings around the pool. It lies right by the beach and sea kayaks with life vests are on offer. Restaurant and bar with satellite TV, basketball and tennis for the more athletic. B/fast inc. *Rate US$51.*

🏠 **Cabinas Los Almendros** (14 rooms, 3 apts) One block north of the main street; ↘ 750 0235; f 750 0246; e flchwg@racsa.co.cr; www.c-rica/al.html. Offers rather stark motel-style rooms, some with fans or with AC. The apts are self-contained with DirecTV and sleep up to 6 people. *Rates US$35–50; apts US$70; children under 5 free.*

🏠 **Coco Loco Lodge** (5 bungalows, 1 house) Set back one block from the football pitch; ↘/f 750 0281; e atecmail@racsa.co.cr; www.cocolocolodge.de/coco2e.htm. The charming thatched bungalows built on stilts lie in lovely, spacious landscaped gardens in a quiet backwater with hammocks on the balconies. Laundry service, book exchange, safety deposit and board games round off this recommended lodging. *Rates US$30–45.*

🏠 **Hotel Hawa** (8 rooms, 1 house) 1km before town; ↘ 750 0594; f 750 0564; www.hotelhawa.com. The light and airy carpeted rooms have DirecTV and ceiling fans, the house can sleep 2 to 4 people and comes with kitchen and fridge. A jungle trail leads to the beach and the screened restaurant serves African/Caribbean dishes. A pool is set in the gardens with bar. Karaoke is also served up over the weekends. *Rates: room US$40; house US$200 per week; children under 10 free.*

🏠 **Cabinas Casa Verde** (21 units) Quietly set 2 blocks in from the main street in Puerto Viejo;

↘ 750 0015; **f** 750 0047; www.cabinascasaverde.com. With 4 cabins and 17 rooms, Swiss-owned Casa Verde keeps on growing and my last visit revealed a free-form pool being finished in the gardens. Recommended as excellent value for its spacious cabins with fridges and choice of rooms, some with shared bathrooms. There is also a laundry service, safe guarded parking, jacuzzi, tropical frog garden, gift shop and tours. B/fast only is served 07.30–10.30 but coffee is free all day. Safety boxes are available but the reception closes at 20.00. *Rates: rooms from US$45 with private bathroom, US$26 without; cabins US$45.*

🏠 **Cabinas Tropical** (10 rooms) Opposite Casa Verde; ↘/**f** 750 0283; **e** rblancke@racsa.co.cr; www.cabinastropical.com/english_index.htm. Run by German biologist and nature writer, Rolf Blancke and his wife, Juana, these immaculate rooms nestle in lush gardens and provide a haven of peace although just minutes from the town centre. Some of the rooms have fridges and one has DirecTV, all have mosquito nets and fans. Wildlife and birding tours with Rolf can be arranged and there is a resident tame toucan that has the run of the grounds. No meals provided unless b/fast is pre-ordered for group bookings. *Rates US$30–40.*

🏠 **Cashew Hill Jungle Lodge** (8 units) High on a hill reached by the path from the football pitch; ↘/**f** 750 0256; www.cashewhilllodge.co.cr. 6 rooms and 2 colourful cabins perch on the hilltop above town, all with fans; one shares a bathroom and kitchen between the 2 rooms. The main house has 2 further rooms with shared bath. The cabins have been recently refurbished and owners, Eric and Wendy Strebe are planning more, but if you don't mind the trek up the hill, it is a great place to relax close to the forest and enjoy the spectacular view from the viewing tower. *Rates US$21–44. No credit cards.*

🏠 **Kaya's Place** (29 different units) Just before the narrow bridge into town; ↘ 750 0690; www.tinkoff.com/kayasplace/. With 26 rooms, 1 cabin and 2 apts. An attractive jumble of rooms creatively decorated with recycled driftwood and lumber cast-offs so no two are the same. In flower-filled gardens, some have shared bathrooms and the cabin sleeps up to 5 people in 2 bedrooms. The apts have kitchen facilities for self-catering. An open-air restaurant and bar overlook the sea. Laundry service is available. You can rent bikes, snorkels and boogie boards and there is off-road parking. Continental b/fast inc. *Rates: US$35 for rooms with private bathrooms, US$40 with ocean view, US$27 with shared bathroom; cabin US$85; apts US$70; children under 4 free. No credit cards.*

🏠 **Cabinas Guaraná** (12 rooms) One block south of main street; ↘/**f** 750 0244; **e** vistago@racsa.co.cr; www.greencoast.com/cabinasguarana.htm. Everything is hand painted creating a colourful charming setting in pretty gardens. The bright rooms are good value with fans, hammocks on the front patio with screened windows, ceiling fans, reading lamps with desks, communal kitchen, internet service, safety deposit, laundry and safe parking. *Rate US$33.*

🏠 **Cabinas Jacaranda** (12 rooms) Close to the football pitch; ↘ 750 0069. Attractively decorated tiled-floor rooms with colourful Guatemalan bedspreads with nets, with some private, some shared bathrooms and small bungalows with a communal kitchen and off-road parking making this an excellent-value economy choice in a quiet part of town. *Rates US$15–30.*

🏠 **Cabinas Grant** (11 rooms) On the main street; ↘ 750 0292. A budget option with basic rooms for 2 to 5 people but it has safe parking with night guard and garden with restaurant attached. The owner has the biggest bike rental operation in town and will arrange tours. Includes a filling *Tico* b/fast served upstairs on the balcony above the courtyard. *Rate US$28.*

🏠 **Chimuri Beach Cottages** (3 cottages) A 20-min walk from Puerto Viejo on Black Beach Road; ↘ 750 0119; **e** chimuri@racsa.co.cr. The colourful pretty all-wood cottages in typical Caribbean gingerbread style with hammocks on the balconies to lounge in, kitchen and pleasant garden can take 2 to 4 people. Owner Mauricio Salazar is highly knowledgeable about the area and will guide birding or hiking tours into the nearby Keköldi Reserve for US$25 pp. *Rates US$35–50, weekly rates available, 2-night minimum stay.*

🏠 **Hotel Pura Vida** (10 rooms) Round the corner from Cabinas Jacaranda; ↘ 750 0002; **f** 750 0296; **e** hotelpuravida@msn.com; www.hotelpuravida.com. This hotel has charming, good-sized rooms, some with shared bath with fans and hammocks. Set in pleasant gardens with terrace, it offers kitchen facilities for self-catering with a breezy, tiled community room for hanging out. *Rates from US$19 with shared bath, US$25 private.*

🏠 **Hotel Puerto Viejo** (50 rooms) Half a block off the main street; ↘ 750 0620. This long-time sprawling warren is backpacker and surfer friendly with its basic, dark rooms and just-about-anything-goes attitude. Bring the kids, bring the dog, camp in the back if you want – owner Dan García doesn't mind. Rooms have fans, screened windows with some shared bathrooms. Safety deposit is available and kitchen facilities, storage and off-road parking. A good place to get the gossip, it's close to the notorious Salsa Brava break and much of the nightlife. *Rates US$10–20.*

🏠 **Hotel Maritza** (14 rooms/cabins) By the bus stop is a famous establishment although mostly for its jumping nightlife and weekend dances so don't come here for a quiet time. Popular with surfers. *Rate for room with shared bathroom US$15.*

✎ **WHERE TO EAT** People come and go and so do restaurants. Every time I visit Puerto Viejo, new eateries have sprung up, others have changed their names, and some have disappeared into oblivion. Between here and Manzanillo there are some fine dining spots, both high budget and simple *sodas*.

✗ **Café Viejo Ristorante** ☎ 750 0817; e cafeviejo@racsa.co.cr. A runaway success story of 4 Italian friends who have created the buzz hotspot in town. They are perfectly placed smack in the middle with a corner location but the quickfire service, huge portions of superbly cooked pasta or pizzas and a well-stocked bar guarantee return visits. It's becoming a bit pricey but worth the splurge to enjoy the food and the atmosphere. *Main courses US$6–11. Open 18.00–midnight, closed Tue.*

✗ **EZ-Times Restaurant** ☎ 750 0663. Close to the police station by the beach, open air, relaxed with delicious wood-baked pizzas and great focaccia, also grills and the bar mixes a mean cocktail. Live music some nights. *Pizzas from US$6. Open 11.30–02.30, closed Mon.*

✗ **Restaurant Oro** ☎ 750 0469. The Oro has a large blackboard on the street with a huge array of Mediterranean seafood plus good catch-of-the-day dishes cooked to your choice. *Spanish specialities, paellas US$4.50–9. Open 13.00–22.00.*

✗ **El Loco Natural** ☎ 750 0263. Upstairs and overlooking the main street, El Loco has a dinner-club atmosphere with a mixture of Asian-fusion food, curries, with artwork on show and live music most nights. It's worth booking if a popular band will be playing. *Main dishes around US$6. Open Thu–Mon 18.00–late.*

✗ **Chili Rojo** Just next door to Café Viejo, tiny hole-in-the-wall English-run Chili Rojo more than stands up to its ebullient neighbour. Andrew Bacon cooks up delicious Thai curries and Middle Eastern specials gleaned from his years of travel to places afar. He also offers cookery classes and is now running the local deli so grateful residents can buy hard-to-locate gourmet items normally only found in San José. *Curries from US$4.*

✗ **Hot Rocks Café** ☎ 750 0525; www.hotrockscafe.com. On the large corner lot heading out east from Puerto Viejo, this casual, open-air eatery come bar cooks up no-oil barbecued dishes on a special volcanic-rock grill with large salads. They also sell the tasty locally brewed beer on draught. In the evenings, big-screen 2-per-night movies attract customers. *Meals US$4–8, with pizza delivery service. Open 10.00–late, depending on movies.*

✗ **Pan Pay Café & Panaderia** ☎ 750 0081. Be prepared to wait for table space at this popular b/fast place. It serves all day but people head for the delicious freshly baked pastries and breaks with mugs of coffee. They have book rental and lots of information boards. *Full b/fast from US$5.00. Open Thu–Tue 08.00–18.00; closed Wed.*

✗ **Stanford's Restaurant** ☎ 750 0608. Heading east out of town on the beachfront. Over the disco, the restaurant can be noisy to say the least but it's also a b/fast place. Main dishes include lobster and Caribbean seafood specialities. *Lobster for around US$12. Open 08.00–22.00; closed Tue.*

✗ **Café Rico** ☎ 750 0325. The Rico hides behind pretty hedges but serves up filling b/fasts and lunch. Also offering gourmet sandwiches (try the smoked salmon) and speciality coffees. *B/fast around US$4, free regular coffee with meals. It also offers a laundry service. Open from 07.30.*

✗ **Soda Ms Sam** Popular with anyone on a budget for the great value, good b/fasts and tasty rice 'n' beans. *Meals from US$3. Open 08.00–18.00.*

✗ **Soda Ms Isma** Another well-known local resident who cooks up cheap, filling b/fasts and a few other Caribbean dishes. It's worth asking what she has on offer since the menu board looks limited to 'omelette' but that's just to deceive the uninitiated! *Meals from US$3. Open 08.00–18.00.*

PRACTICALITIES The medical clinic is open Mon–Fri 10.00–19.00 or at weekends for emergencies (☎ *750 0758*). In Puerto Viejo town, the post office (☎ *750 0404*) opens Mon–Fri 07.30–17.00. The police station (☎ *750 0230*) is two blocks east of the bus stop near Pan Pay. Internet access is readily available now in Puerto Viejo and many hotels along the beach although Ipromer in town has low rates at US$1.25 per hour. Laundry service is available at US$3 per load from Flash (☎ *750 0467*).

WHAT TO SEE AND DO If you are around in March–April, take advantage of the **South Caribbean Music Festival** (☎ *750 0062*). Indefatigable promoter of culture, Wanda Patterson organises a whole array of cultural events from local and international musicians, artists, dancers with concerts, workshops, film shows and just about anything arty. In September–October, the **Caribbean Summer Festival** shows films on regional culture, with craft fairs, food stands and more music.

Some 500m before reaching town, the **Finca La Isla Botanical Gardens** (☎/f *750 0046*; e *jardbot@racsa.co.cr; www.greencoast.com/garden.htm; open Fri–Mon 10.00–16.00*) is a converted cocoa farm begun in 1987. Using permaculture techniques, the gardens have an impressive collection of tropical plants with 60 varieties of tropical fruits so something is always ripe and you get to taste. There are trails throughout the 4ha of grounds that are good for birding and the *bromeliad* gardens are home to four species of poison-dart frogs. With the tours, you can learn about the many exotic, medicinal and just plain bizarre plants that flourish in the region. The entrance fee of US$5 includes a fruit juice and self-guided books are available in several languages. For US$10 you can have a two-hour tour, minimum three per group. The **Samasati Nature Retreat** (☎ *750 0315; f 224 5032; www.samasati.com*) by the Black Beach turn-off is set in 100ha of forest and at an altitude of almost 200m. It offers a refreshing climate and luxuriant setting for yoga (*US$12*), meditation (*US$5*) and massages (*US$60*). Eco-sensitive tours are arranged. (For accommodation, see *Where to stay* above.)

Energy Balancing (*Magic Moon Beach Bungalow;* ☎ *750 0115; www.magicmooncr.com*) offers therapeutic massages for US$30 per hour, Bach flower therapy sessions and will arrange visits to the nearby Bribri communities. They also have a pretty four-person house for rent at US$420 per week.

ATEC (Talamanca Ecotourism & Conservation Association) (☎ *750 0398; f 750 0191; www.greencoast.com/atec.hntm*) in the centre of Puerto Viejo promotes culturally and ecologically sensitive tourism, involving local families in conservation projects and small-scale tourism so the profits stay with the community. Visits to the Bribri indigenous reserves at Yorkin and Keköldi, hikes into the Gandoca-Manzanillo Wildlife Refuge and turtle-watching tours can be arranged from their office. They sell books about the area.

Heading down towards Manzanillo, the **Chocolate Tour** (*Playa Chiquita;* ☎ *750 0075; entrance US$15 pp, min four to a group*) is a Swiss-run, 2½-hour visit of an organic cacao plantation. You see the whole process and can sample fresh hot chocolate and buy chocolate goodies from their shop.

FROM PUERTO VIEJO TO MANZANILLO

GETTING THERE AND AWAY MEPE buses (☎ *758 1572*) run up and down the single highway from Limón every hour to Puerto Viejo and every four hours through to Manzanillo. MEPE also goes hourly to Bribri from Limón. Taxis based in town or call Charlie Bull (☎ *750 0112*) or Luis Bermúdez (m *844 9913*).

WHERE TO STAY Strung along the only road southeast to its abrupt end in Manzanillo you can find many hotels and lodging of all categories. From Puerto Viejo you pass by Playa Cocles, a Blue Flag beach denoting particular cleanliness, with lifeguards funded by the local hotels; Playa Chiquita and Punta Uva, also Blue Flag beaches. The deep, forest-lined bay of Punta Uva with its fine white sands is arguably the prettiest in the area.

Almonds & Corals Lodge (24 tent rooms) 12km from Puerto Viejo; ☎ 272 2024 in San José; f 272 2220; www.geoexpediciones.com. If you want to get a feel of being immersed in the jungle but with creature comforts (yours) intact, then try out this unusual concept of sleeping under canvas on wood platforms, also roofed but open to the trees full of howler monkeys, sloths and birdlife. I found the place rather dark and oppressive but it's popular with tour groups and heavily promoted by its company Geoexpeditions. The tents are furnished and have fans with an adjoining hot-water shower and bathroom. The site also offers a jacuzzi, full restaurant, bike rentals and tour information and runs the Crazy Monkey Canopy Tour (US$40 pp). B/fast inc. *Rate US$130 – rather steep since you can observe the wildlife at many of the other lodgings along the road in equal comfort.*

Tree House Lodge (3 units) Punta Uva; ☎ 750 0706; www.costaricatreehouse.com. The tree house is wrapped around a native *sangrillo* (bloodwood) tree; the loo separated from the shower by tree buttresses in the bathroom! The 5-person house or 6-person suite combine hi-tech luxury with eco-friendly construction. The UFO-style bathroom in the suite has coloured roof glass tiles that glow in the afternoon sun. Definitely a one-off experience. *Rates US$120–245, dbl occupancy, US$45 per extra person.*

Casa Viva (4 cabins) Punta Uva; ☎/f 750 0089; e puntauva@racsa.co.cr; www.puntauva.net. Each beautiful cabin has 2 bedrooms with hot-water bathroom, a very complete kitchen, living room and wraparound veranda decked with hammocks. Beach access is just a few metres away and there is safe onsite parking. *Rates for a minimum 2-night stay US$150, weekly and monthly rentals for US$450 and US$1,200 respectively.*

Jordan's Jacuzzi Suites (2 rooms) Heading east out of town; ☎ 750 0232. Ignore the strange name; these 2 Asian-themed rooms are beautiful with huge hydro baths, AC and oriental décor. A 3-day stay earns free sushi at the adjoining Lotus Garden Restaurant. *Rates (not cheap) US$90–100.*

Bungalows Cariblue (17 units) Cocles; ☎ 750 0025; f 750 0057; e cariblue@racsa.co.cr; www.cariblue.com. The fabulous, Ultimate Service award-winning hotel has placed its beautiful hardwood cabins and house among secluded gardens along lit paths. The porches have hammocks and the huge bathrooms are imaginatively decorated with hand-laid mosaic tiles. The house comes with full kitchen facilities and 2 bedrooms for 2 to 7 people. All have safety deposit boxes. Also on site is a pool,

jacuzzi, spa, gift shop, gourmet Italian restaurant with live music on some nights. There is a snack-bar service all day for sandwiches, salads and fruit drinks. Cable TV, games, books and magazines for the lazy; gorgeous split-level free-form swimming pool and bicycle rental for the more active. Come here and be spoiled rotten! Buffet b/fast inc. *Rates US$75–100, extra person US$15; complimentary coffee all day.*

Shawandha Lodge (12 cabins) Playa Chiquita; ☎ 750 0018; f 750 0037; e info@shawandhalodge.com; www.shawandhalodge.com. It's worth staying here just to marvel at the wonderful mosaic bathrooms, and the large thatched high-ceiling cabins reflect the romantic elegance of their French owners, Maho Diaz and Nicolas Bufille. The pastel walls glow with subtle lighting and 4-poster beds are perfect for an intimate getaway. Gourmet French/Caribbean meals are served in the open-sided rancho. American-style b/fast inc. *Rate US$90.*

Hotel Punta Cocles (55 rooms, 5 cabins) Playa Chiquita; ☎ 750 0338; f 750 0336; e reservations@puntacocles.com; www.hotelpuntacocles.com. A resort-style hotel on the landside of the road, set in landscaped gardens. Comfortable rooms have AC and the bungalows sleep 6 with kitchenette. There is a pool, jacuzzi, open-air restaurant and *rancho* with bar. *Rates US$80–110.*

Hotel Suerre (40 rooms) Punta Uva; ☎ 759 9091; f 759 9076; www.suerre.com. This is about the only resort of size in the whole southern Caribbean apart from the barely functioning, sinister Las Palmas next door where we were virtually seen off the premises whilst researching the hotel (which has since been closed by the Ministry of Environment for its blatant violation of environmental regulations). Most foreign visitors avoid this standard, characterless facility although it is clean and comfortable with AC, minibar and satellite TV because there are just so many lovely boutique hotels and cabins that exude character and charm to head for instead. It has a large pool, tennis court, conference facilities and a bare-looking international restaurant. *Rates are an expensive US$95.*

Villas del Caribe (12 villas) Playa Chiquita, on the beachfront; 5km from Puerto Viejo; ☎ 750 0202; f 750 0203; e info@villasdelcaribe.com; www.villasdecaribe.com. Set in a coconut grove, the spacious 2-storey cabins have sky-lit bathrooms filled with plants, ceiling fans, big wardrobes, private terraces, balcony and outside beach showers. Downstairs the living area seating can be converted into extra beds to sleep up to 6 people, a modern well-equipped kitchen with b/fast bar; upstairs some units have 2 bedrooms. The hotel also has 40ha of forest reserve with hiking trails. Includes continental b/fast. The ocean-facing restaurant serves international/Caribbean dishes. *Rate US$89; children under 10 free.*

🏠 **Casa Camarona Lodge** (20 rooms) Cocles; ☎ 750 0151; f 750 0210; www.casacamarona.co.cr. Just past the village football pitch on the beachside. The rooms come with either fan or AC but include b/fast at the adjoining Restaurant La Palapa (see *Where to eat* below). You can enjoy a drink at the beach bar then lounge in deckchairs on the sands or under the shady trees. Wheelchair access and off-road parking. A private bus shuttle leaves San José (Hotel Irazú) at 07.30 arriving at Camarona around 13.00 and departs at 14.20 arriving into San José at 18.20 approximately for US$36 round trip. For more than 2 guests on a multi-day stay, the hotel will arrange free taxi pickup from San José. *Rates US$72 (with AC); US$59 (with fan).*

🏠 **Resort Hotel Kashá** (10 bungalows) Playa Chiquita; ☎/f 750 0205; www.costarica-hotelkasha.com. The bungalows can sleep either 2 or up to 4 people and are set in the forest with pool, jacuzzi and souvenir shop. Kashá won the 2004 Ultimate Service award. Direct-dial phones are in each bungalow, with AC, hairdryers, safety deposit boxes and hammocks on each veranda. Internet access and email are available in the reception area. You can order up a massage and honeymoon specials are possible. In fact, you can even be married from Kashá and they offer package deals. French cuisine is served at the adjoining recommended Magic Ginger Restaurant. B/fast inc. *Rates per night US$81 and if you choose to include dinner, US$115.*

🏠 **Cabinas Escape Caribeño** (18 units) Down the road from Puerto Viejo; ☎/f 750 0103; e escapec@racsa.co.cr; www.escapecaribeno.com. Comprising 14 bungalows and 4 houses, the neatly laid-out units face the beach or the gardens, with private bathrooms, hot water and mosquito nets, a minibar and verandas with hammocks. Most have fans, 2 have AC. Safe parking, and no children. The wooden houses are located down the road in Playa Chiquita and are available for weekly or longer rentals. *Rates US$50–70.*

🏠 **Cabinas & Restaurant Totem** (5 cabins) Playa Cocles; ☎ 750 0758; f 750 0825; www.totemsite.com. Once you get by the large bare-breasted stone lady sculptures in the front, the huge 4-person cabins are attractively tiled with original beds made from thick bamboo lengths, private bathrooms, living room and balcony in the bamboo gardens. The attractive blue and yellow reception area and restaurant offers internet service, cable TV, safety deposit boxes, hammocks and off-road parking. The 2-storey restaurant run by Italian Nicolo Bareti makes its own pasta, bread and *romagnola piadina* – regional flat bread that he stuffs with delicious fillings. Board rental and instruction for beginners. *Rate US$70.*

🏠 **Bungalows Azania** (12 bungalows) Cocles; ☎ 750 0540; f 750 0371; e info@azania-costarica.com; www.azania-costarica.com. High-ceilinged thatched wooden bungalows with large screened windows in lush gardens with beds for 4, fans, reading lamps, bamboo furniture and extra bed up in the loft, minibar and security boxes. Laundry service and safety deposit boxes are available. The secluded verandas have hammocks and the free-form pool has a waterfall with jacuzzi nearby. The restaurant and bar offers Argentinian/Caribbean dishes and the hotel will arrange car rental. B/fast inc. *Rate US$65.*

🏠 **Cabinas La Costa de Papito** (8 cabins) Cocles; ☎/f 750 0080; e costapapito@yahoo.com; www.greencoast.com/papito.htm. Just adding to the string of comfortable, attractive cabins along this Puerto Viejo–Manzanillo road, the individually decorated *cabinas* are well separated for privacy in jungle gardens full of heliconias, gingers and palms with large porches and yet more hammocks. Friendly American owner, Eddie Ryan has created an original place of calm and total relaxation. Internet service is available as is laundry, bicycle rental, massages on the beach and you can even get your hair braided in your cabin. B/fast for US$4 pp can be served on your own porch. *Rates US$40–56; young children go free.*

🏠 **Cabinas Rio Cocles** (5 different units) Cocles; ☎ 750 0142; e information@riocolcles.com; www.riococles.com. 4 rooms (inc 1–2-room suite) and 1 bungalow. Friendly German-run cabins to which more are being currently added, the large landscaped gardens fall right to the beach. The rooms are spacious with absolutely enormous bathrooms while the suite has a balcony that could comfortably cater for a party of 50! The owner Horst bakes delicious breads for b/fast (inc). *Rates: rooms US$35; suite US$70; bungalow US$60.*

🏠 **Playa Chiquita Lodge** (16 units) Playa Chiquita, 7km from Puerto Viejo; ☎ 750 0062; f 750 0408; www.playachiquitalodge.com. The 12 cabins and 4 houses are owned and run by Wanda Patterson who organises most of the cultural events in the area. The rustic cabins are located in thick forest grounds with screened window, private bathrooms with hot water with a trail leading to the beach. B/fast inc. The 2 large houses with 4 dbls are rented out for US$1,200 per month; the smaller 2-room houses rent for US$800 per month. Concerts, seminars and workshops are held here during the Spring/Summer Music Festival. *Rate US$55.*

🏠 **Itaitá Villas** (7 cabins) Playa Chiquita; ☎ 750 0414; e manager@costaricaitaitavillas.com; www.costaricaitaitavillas.com. The 2-bedroom wood cabins are attractively decorated if rather dark with ceiling fans, private hot-water bathrooms and kitchen. Typical *gallo pinto* b/fast inc. *Rate US$55.*

🏠 **Cabinas Pachamama** (2 bungalows) Punta Uva; ☎ 759 9196; e pachamamacaribe@yahoo.com; www.greencoast.com/pachamama.htm. Close by the river, the Italian-run wooden bungalows have 2 rooms each and reflect the Pachamama (Mother Earth) philosophy for down-to-earth comfort and a relaxing place to enjoy one of the best beaches around. Set in lush gardens, b/fast is served on each bungalow's private veranda. The owners also have a 2-bedroom house in the grounds to sleep up to 6 for rent. You can rent kayaks to explore the river and Stefano cooks up great pizzas at the weekend, though he might just oblige midweek if you ask nicely and there are enough of you. *Rates US$50–70.*

🏠 **Cabinas & Marisquería Arrecife** (8 cabins) Punta Uva; ☎ 759 9200. Right on the beach, these cabins make the most of the sea breezes with high ceilings and balconies. They aren't much to look at, but offer the basics and have hot-water private bathrooms. At the weekend, you can eat delicious seafood from their restaurant, which is popular with tourists or have a beach barbecue. Camping is possible and kayaks can be rented for US$3.50 per hr. *Rate (a reasonable) US$39.*

🏠 **Cabinas El Tesoro** (16 cabins/rooms) Playa Cocles, 1km southeast of Puerto Viejo; ☎ 750 0128; f 750 0507; www.puertoviejo.net. This multi-service centre is quite an institution offering accommodation, all-day b/fasts, tour office (**Xtreme Caribe**), evening movies, free coffee, free local calls and email to guests, internet and happy hour, baggage storage and Wed-night jam sessions. You can't criticise American owner and musician Charlie Wanger for not covering all his bases (see next listing).

🏠 **Beach Break Jungle Lodge** (dorm rooms with up to 30 beds) Also run by Charlie Wanger. A variety of screened rather dark cabins with fans behind the restaurant with porches, some have large dorm-style sleeping with bunks or just plenty of beds crammed into huge rooms; a couple of AC rooms with private

bathrooms, TV and fridges. *Rates US$55; cabins US$20–35; bunks US$9 pp. Group rates are available.*

🏠 **La Isla Inn** (13 rooms) Playa Cocles; ☎/f 750 0109; e islainn@racsa.co.cr. These attractive rooms have ocean-facing balconies, some with AC and b/fast. The restaurant opens from 07.00–17.00 and serves up good b/fasts. *Rates US$45–100.*

🏠 **Hotel Yaré** (21 units) Cocles; ☎ 750 0420; f 750 0106; e hotelyare@tutopia.com; www.hotelyare.com. The brightly painted rooms and cabins have private bathrooms and come with b/fast. The spacious wooden cabins can sleep up to 4 people and have kitchens with fridges. The restaurant has a large international/Caribbean menu. *Rates US$42–92.*

🏠 **Punta Uva Beach Cabinas** (5 rooms) Bahía Uva; ☎ 750 0431; e crchichi@yahoo.com; www.puntauva.com. The beachfront all-wood rooms are distributed between the main house and a separate guesthouse, some with shared bathroom and fridge. There is a communal kitchen with laundry service. In the densely planted gardens, a fountain plays near the 2 gazebos. *Rates: rooms US$46; the 8-person guesthouse can be rented in its entirety for US$150.*

🏠 **Bungalows Calalú** (5 units) On a side road off to the right after leaving Puerto Viejo; ☎ 750 0042. 3 cabins, 2 bungalows. The attractive thatched cabins and bungalows with kitchenette are in a jungle setting by the free-form pool. All have porches with hammocks and the French owners will help organise tours. B/fast is served in the next-door Butterfly Garden among all the butterflies. *Rates: cabins US$34; bungalows with kitchen US$40.*

🏠 **Cabinas Yucca** (5 units) Just on leaving Puerto Viejo; ☎ 750 0285; e cabinas_yucca@yahoo.de. 4 cabins, 1 bungalow. The shoreside cabins enjoy an ocean view with balconies and nets; the bungalow has a kitchen. *Rates US$25–40.*

🏠 **Cabinas Pangea** (4 rooms) Manzanillo village up from Aquamor; ☎ 759 9204; e pageacr@racsa.co.cr. These delightful cabins have fans, mosquito nets and bright bedspreads to add colour, set in pretty gardens off the main street. The American owner is keen to make your stay pleasant and offers good value. He also has a 4-person house for rent, min 3 days for US$60, weekly/monthly rates on request. The only drawback if you have a car is no off-road parking. *Rate US$35.*

🏠 **Miraflores Lodge** (10 units) Playa Chiquita; ☎/f 750 0038; e mirapam@racsa.co.cr; www.mirafloreslodge.com. 4 rooms, 6 cabins. The pretty thatched wood and bamboo cabins are set in beautiful *heliconia* and exotic flower gardens and based on traditional Bribri designs. Owned by American Pamela Carpenter, who started out with a flower nursery, the lodge is committed to sustainable tourism and helping the indigenous communities. The ceilings are lined with narrow bamboo stems and flowers adorn every cabin in huge vases. The 4 lodge rooms have king-size beds that can be split into 2 wide sgls with mosquito nets. The balconies have wooden rocking chairs and hammocks. Some have shared bathrooms. The garden rooms and suites have private entrances and bathrooms, sleeping up to 4. B/fast inc. The Rainforest Café offers Caribbean cuisine. Shuttle service to San José can be arranged. *Rates: rooms US$30; cabins US$50. Children aged 12–16 get a 50% discount, under 12s go free.*

☖ **Cabinas Something Different** (14 rooms) Behind Maxi's; ☎ 759 9014. A modern, rather featureless place with motel-style rooms all in a row, but spotlessly clean and good value being able to sleep 4 on 2 dbl beds, with fans, private bathrooms, fridge, cable TV, little front porches. *Rate US$30.*

☖ **Cabinas David** (8 rooms) Just on leaving Puerto Viejo; ☎ 750 0542. A budget place, the large rooms with fans and private bathrooms are in gardens with off-road parking. *Rate US$25.*

☖ **Cabinas Monte Sol** (5 units) On leaving Puerto Viejo; ☎/f 750 0098; e info@montesol.net; www.montesol.net. Next to Cabinas David. 4 cabins, 1 jungle house. German managed, these economy cabins are set in pretty gardens with fans, nets and hammocks. There is a fully equipped wood jungle house built in the trees that is rented out on a weekly basis. Buffet-style b/fast is US$5 in the roofed open-air dining area, and they also sell snacks and keep a bar. Internet hook-up available and Birgit will cut your hair in her small salon. *Rate US$25.*

✖ WHERE TO EAT

✖ **Pecora Nera** Beyond Casa Camarona towards Playa Chiquita; ☎ 750 0490. This is probably the classiest restaurant around attracting a wide clientele from the area. It isn't cheap but worth splurging to enjoy excellent Italian dishes with an extensive wine list prepared by the exuberant chef-owner who cruises the tables afterwards to get your reaction to his food. It gets busy so worth reserving if you are a group. *Prices for a main course US$12–20. Closed Mon.*

✖ **Restaurant Magic Ginger** ☎ 750 0205. Adjoining Hotel Kashá, this pretty restaurant serves up Mediterranean food for dinner *from US$18–22. Closed Mon.*

☖ **Cabinas Lunatica** (4 cabins) Towards Playa Cocles; ☎ 750 0635. These cute candy-coloured cabins have fridges, fans and screened windows with a communal kitchen. *Rate US$20.*

☖ **Casa Wal-Aba** (13 beds) Punta Uva; ☎ 750 0147; e recahji@racsa.co.cr. This friendly budget hostel has a ramshackle wooden house sleeping 12 in dormitories and a 6-person house for rent. Affiliated to Hostelling International. You should call ahead for reservations and groups can be accepted. There are bathrooms with hot water and the rooms have fans. You can sling a hammock; use the laundry service, kitchen, telephone and fax. Off-street parking and baggage storage is available. *Rate US$14 pp.*

☖ **Rocking J's** (20 beds in dorms/rooms/cabins, plus camping and hammock hotel) ½km from Puerto Viejo; ☎ 750 0657; www.rockinjs.com. Dormitory, rooms, hammocks, cabins. You can't miss the place — it has huge cement snakes and dragons adorning the entrance! Backpacker heaven, this funky friendly muddle of sleeping options also offers covered camping with lockers, solar showers, barbecue with a communal *rancho* for hanging out, and kitchen. You can sling your hammock in the covered hammock hut and there is a precarious tree house that requires some faith in its construction to rent. They have video rental, internet and international phone-calling service, bike hire for US$13 per day, kayaks plus many activities suited to the young or economy traveller. As they say on their website, 'It's simple, come in, store your stuff, find your spot (tent, hammock, room or tree house), enjoy your stay'. *Rates: cabins with loft US$14–24; dorm US$7 pp, hammock with locker US$5, hang-your-own-hammock US$4, camping US$4, tent rental US$6; tree house US$60.*

✖ **Restaurant Ranchito Beach** Back in from the beach at Punta Uva; ☎ 759 9048. The attractive thatched-covered tables dot spacious grounds and we were knocked out by the sublime, imaginative Italian/fusion dishes for around US$7.50. Try the various ravioli options and don't miss out on the wonderful cocktails. You can also work off the meal by renting sea kayaks and hit the waves or, more sedately, paddle upriver until you grind to a halt but look in the trees for all sorts of wildlife. *Closed Mon.*

✖ **Restaurant La Palapa** ☎ 750 0151. Part of Casa Camarona, offering elegant al fresco dining with a Caribbean/Asian twist. *Meals around US$7–10. Open for lunch/dinner, closed Tue.*

✘ **El Duende Felíz** Playa Chiquita on the land side; ☎ 750 0356. The Feliz has a reputation for fine Italian cuisine eaten in a wooden 2-storey house set off the main road. *Open evenings and with prior booking only. Meals around US$7–10.*

✘ **Restaurant Maxi's** At the road's end in Manzanillo; ☎ 759 9073. Another Caribbean institution and deserving its reputation for the best seafood, especially whole fried fish and lobster around with prices varying according to the size of the catch, US$6–12. The noisy, busy wood restaurant sits right on the beach with downstairs bar and upstairs for meals with a view. Good value. *Whole fried fish US$5–8, lobster US$12. Open 12.00–22.00.*

✘ **Big Breakfast Bar & Café** (see *Cabinas El Tesoro*, page 153) In Playa Cocles and part of the El Tesoro emporium, the kitchen will serve up all-day b/fasts and other hearty snacks, but don't be in a hurry as service is decidedly casual. Read all the information boards or browse a book while you wait. *All-day b/fast US$5–6. Open 07.30–22.00, happy hour 17.00–19.00.*

✘ **Elena's Bar & Restaurant** ☎ 750 0265. This place has a reputation for good traditional Caribbean dishes but we found the service so slow and 'laid back' (with an almost 2hr wait) that it just about killed off what appetite we'd had. *Main dishes around US$7. Open 12.00–21.00.*

✘ **Selwin's Bar** At the entrance to Punta Uva, this is a fun and funky place run by charismatic owner Selwin, who may or may not be around. He cooks up good Caribbean food Wed–Sun served with lots of stories and information of the area. He also has a few basic cabins for rent. *Caribbean dishes US$5–8. Open Wed–Sun 08.00–20.00.*

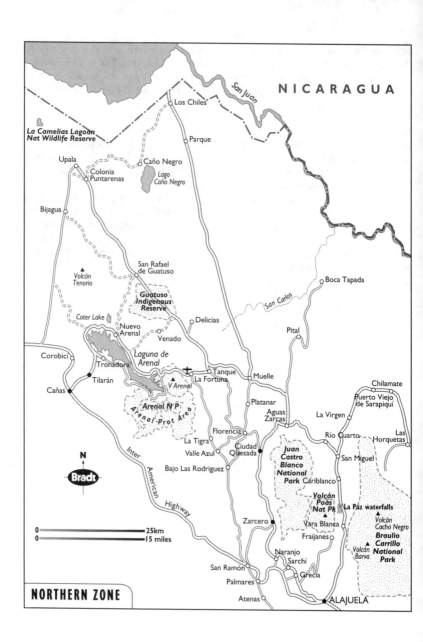

NICARAGUA

San Juan

Los Chiles

Parque

La Camelias Lagoon
Nat Wildlife Reserve

Upala

Caño Negro

Colonia
Puntarenas

Lago
Caño Negro

Bijagua

Boca Tapada

San Rafael
de Guatuso

Volcán
Tenorio

San Carlos

Guatuso
Indigenous
Reserve

Coter Lake

Delicias

Pital

Nuevo
Arenal

Venado

Corobici

Laguna de
Arenal

Tronadora

Tanque

Tilarán

V Arenal

La Fortuna

Muelle

Chilamate

Cañas

Platanar

Puerto Viejo
de Sarapiquí

Arenal N P

Aguas
Zarcas

La Virgen

Arenal Prot Area

Florencia

Río Cuarto

Las
Horquetas

La Tigra

San Miguel

N

Valle Azul

Ciudad
Quesada

Juan
Castro
Blanco
National
Park

Cariblanco

Bradt

Bajo Las Rodriguez

Inter

Volcán
Poás
Nat Pk

La Paz waterfalls

American

Volcán
Cacho Negro

Zarcero

Vara Blanca

Braulio
Carrillo
National
Park

0   25km
0   15 miles

Highway

Fraijanes

Volcán
Barva

Naranjo
Sarchí

San Ramón

Grecia

Palmares

NORTHERN ZONE

Atenas

ALAJUELA

156

8

Northern Zone

Despite the name Costa Rica (meaning 'Rich Coast'), there is a lot more to this country than beaches and the Northern Zone offers an abundance of discoveries for both intrepid and relaxed travellers. Here one will find jungle rivers, a fiery volcano and cool cloudforests. Rough and tough in parts with luxurious hot springs and spas to relax overtaxed muscles, the Northern Zone has something for hikers and hedonists alike. And for those into windsurfing, Lake Arenal is a definite 'must-see' as it's regarded as one of the top four spots in the world for this fast and challenging sport. The border region, around Los Chiles, offers little other than small villages as independent border crossings are prohibited, although the Caño Negro Wildlife Refuge is an excellent spot for birding and the Río San Juan (technically Nicaraguan territory) offers up some excellent sport fishing.

SARAPIQUI

This fertile plain northwest of Guápiles was mostly jungle until the area was deforested for cattle ranches a few decades ago. Add banana, pineapple and palm plantations and it's no surprise trees were being felled faster than you could crank up a chainsaw – not the picture that comes to mind when one thinks of 'eco-minded Costa Rica'. Thanks to the efforts of dedicated environmentalists, national parks and privately owned eco-tourism projects are conserving the area and, in turn, tourism is quickly becoming the main industry in the area.

Puerto Viejo de Sarapiqui (82km north of San José) is named after the river running through this area and is the major town in a region that is otherwise jungle or farms. The town has several hotels and there are lodges within the rainforest reserves in the area.

GETTING THERE AND AWAY

By car From San José, head northeast out of the city and follow the signs along the Guápiles Highway (Highway 32) through Braulio Carrillo National Park (note: avoid driving this road at night and always be aware of fog and mudslides). Or, the 'scenic route' is from Heredia, through Barva and Vara Blanca.

By bus **Empresarios Guapilenos** (↘ 222 2727) buses leave from the Gran Terminal del Caribe (*Av 11, Ca Central*) in San José.

WHERE TO STAY AND EAT All the lodges listed include meals with their stays, owing to their remote location.

🏠 **Hotel Selva Verde Lodge** (45 units) ↘ 766 6800; f 766 6011. One of the first eco-lodges in Costa Rica, the location keeps packing them in. Set just off the main road on the banks of the Río Sarapiqui, few places can compete with the flora and fauna surrounding the lodge. Rooms are built out of gleaming hardwood on elevated and covered platforms, ensuring the creepies and crawlies don't collide with *Homo sapiens*. Rooms are large but Spartan affairs with fan, telephone, verandas and private bathrooms with hot water. There are also cabins further in the reserve geared towards school groups. Meals are typically *Tico*, nothing inspiring cuisine-wise, and are served in an open communal dining room and bar, which clears out early in the evening (everyone here is an early riser). Birders and hikers delight in the 500-acre private reserve across the river and the suspension bridge is quite spectacular. There is also a butterfly garden, boat ride, rafting and guided hikes. A popular day trip has lunch and a boat trip here so there is a bit of a busy, 'Nature Disney' feel to the place but still a good spot to explore nature. *Rates US$62–81 pp, meals and taxes inc.*

🏠 **Gavilan Lodge** (13 rooms) 2km south of Puerto Viejo; 🔌 234 9507; f 253 6556; www.gavilanlodge.com. Situated on a private 60ha reserve along the Sarapiqui River, this lodge was one of the first in the area. Rooms are simple but clean and open onto a large breezeway. Private baths with hot water, fans. There are hiking trails, a jacuzzi and open-air dining room. *Rates US$50, no meals inc.*

🏠 **Rara Avis** (12 rooms) 17km south of Puerto Viejo; 🔌 764 3131; f 764 4187. A unique private reserve, Rara Avis is dedicated to demonstrating that the rainforest can be more profitable standing than being clear cut. A team of scientists continues various studies and farming the reserve's biodiversity and there is a research station where rainforest crops, such as orchids and palms, are being developed for commercial activity. Home to a number of unique (and some thought extinct) palm species, most of the forest here is either primary or 30-year-old secondary. Getting there is half the adventure – from the town of Horquetas, you take a 3hr tractor ride (leaving Horquetas at 09.30). The Waterfall Lodge is the most comfortable accommodation option. Rustic and wooden, it has 8 rooms with wraparound veranda, private bath and is only 600m from the spectacular waterfall. The river-edge cabin is deep in the jungle and has private baths with hot water, shared balcony with

hammocks and solar-powered electricity (romantic for honeymooners). Those on a budget can stay in the simple *casitas* with bunk beds and shared cold-water showers. Note: this is the real deal for true eco-tourism and should be considered only by those in good physical shape as it is a slog to get here. But the experience of being right in the heart of untouched rainforest is remarkable. *Rates US$45–80 pp, meals, guide and taxes inc.*

🏠 **Hacienda Pozo Azul Resort** (10 rooms, 25 tents) 🔌 7161 1360; www.haciendapozoazul.com. A 2,000-acre working eco-farm. Visitors can horseback ride (the owners are breeders), raft, zip along a canopy, rappel, hike or mountain bike. They also offer tours of their dairy production, black pepper farm and butterfly farm. It's a little bit of everything but makes for an interesting slice of Costa Rican life – agriculture meets adventure. Lodging is in a transformed hacienda in which 10 rooms have bunk beds and shared baths with solar-heated hot water or in 25 luxury tents built on a platform with electricity and shared baths with hot water. Amenities include a pool, jacuzzi, restaurant and lush gardens. *Rates US$40 pp, meals and taxes inc.*

Sueño Azul Resort (55 rooms) 🔌 253 2020; f 224 3552; www.suenoazulresort.com. This large complex, 2km out of town, offers a variety of tours including birdwatching, horseback riding and river tubing, as well as gorgeous waterfalls. The restaurant is housed in a former stable, while the bar is in a 100-year-old building. Rooms have a fan, AC, private bathroom with hot water and a terrace. Amenities include a jacuzzi, hot tub, spa and yoga classes. *Rates US$92–130.*

Hotel Claribel (12 rooms) In La Virgen on north side of town; 🔌/f 761 1190. Budget rooms with TV and cold water private baths. *Rates US$12.*

Rancho Leona (5 rooms) 🔌 761 1019; www.rancholeona.com. 400m south of Hotel Claribel. Rustic yet charming, accommodations are in wooden surroundings with colourful stained-glass windows in an 80-acre forest. There is a spa, plunge pool, sweat lodge and camping. Atmosphere is relaxed and communal. Great meals for US$4–8. Excellent budget option. Shared bathrooms. *Rates US$9 pp.*

WHAT TO SEE AND DO

Boat trips Most hotels can arrange boat trips down the Río Sarapiqui to Barra de Colorado National Wildlife Refuge and Tortuguero National Park. It is easy to arrange a short boat trip (one–two hours) by talking to the boat operators at the town dock. Check out **Aventuras Sarapiqui** (🔌 766 6768; *www.sarapiqui.com*).

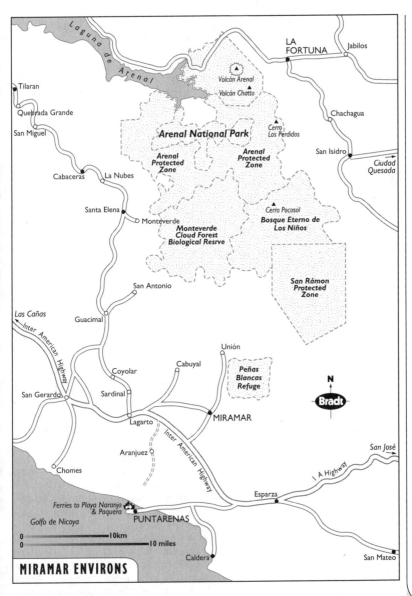

MIRAMAR ENVIRONS

White River Rafting Aguas Bravas (↘ *292 2072*) runs trips down the Sarapiqui ranging from Class III to Class V. They also provide kayak trips. Other operators include Aventuras Sarapiqui (see above) and **Costa Sol Rafting** (↘ *293 2150; www.costasolrafting.com*).

Nature Reserves La Selva Biological Station (↘ *766 6565; entrance US$40 full day, US$25 half day, children US$12*). This 1,560ha research station and biological reserve is part of the Organisation for Tropical Studies. It borders Braulio Carrillo National Park. There is a variety of tropical plants and animals, including more than 450 species of trees, 113 species of mammals, 81 species of reptiles, 48 species

159

of amphibians, and more than 400 species of birds have been identified. The Audubon Society has an annual Christmas bird count.

Centro Neotropico Sarapiquis 2km north of La Virgen (☎ 761 1004; f 761 1415; *www.sarapiquis.com; entrance varies vary according to activity but range from US$7 (archaeological park) to US$24 (all inclusive)*) is a unique, non-profit education centre that encompasses a wide scope of interests and, thankfully, it's being done in a first-rate fashion. A pre-Columbian tomb has been excavated on the premises and guests can take a fascinating night tour of the premises. Other offerings include a museum, biological park, organic farm, botanical gardens, medicinal plants and a canopy walk.

Wildlife El Jardin de Serpientes (*300m west of Centro Neotropico;* ☎ 761 1059; f 761 1060; *entrance US$6, children US$3*). Snakes, snakes and more snakes with 40 of the slithering reptiles on display.

Hacienda Pozo Azul (☎ 438 2616; f 438 2619) offers a canopy tour with 12 zip lines, horses, bikes, dairy farm and butterfly farm.

ARENAL VOLCANO, LA FORTUNA, LAKE ARENAL

After the beaches and rainforests, Arenal Volcano is one of the biggest tourist attractions in Costa Rica and no wonder – perfectly conical in shape, it's one of the ten most active volcanoes in the world. Constantly rumbling and tumbling massive boulders from its depths, Arenal is a reminder of mother earth's power and that she's not to be trifled with. For hundreds of years, the volcano slept until 29 July 1968 when it woke up with a vengeance, destroying the nearby town of Tabacon, killing 80 people and shooting rocks as far away as Turrialba (my mother-in-law still remembers her roof being covered with ash). Since then, it's been under constant surveillance and vulcanologists keep constant vigil, evacuating the area if any possible danger is detected. Note: you cannot hike up the volcano on account of the constant showers of boulders and toxic gasses Arenal emits. People have died hiking up the volcano's side so don't disobey the rangers and safety gates.

Night-time is when Arenal pulls out all the stops – red lava streams down the western slope or shoots high into the air like natural fireworks. Unfortunately, the volcano is often shrouded in mist and fog so many a tourist has come away hearing the volcano but never seeing it. Regardless of what the weather does, there is enough to do in the area to keep anyone busy and happy.

Further down the road is Lake Arenal, the largest lake in Costa Rica, set against rolling hills and the majestic volcano on one end. It's actually a manmade lake, created when the Arenal dam was built in 1973. Fortuna is on the east side and the town of Tilaran on the west while Nuevo Arenal (so named as the original Arenal town lies under the lake) is between the two. Besides its bucolic setting, Lake Arenal is popular for fishing, particularly for *guapote* (rainbow bass), and is one of the top five windsurfing spots in the world.

GETTING THERE AND AWAY

By car There are a few routes you can take. The most popular is taking the Inter-American Highway west of San José, turn north at Naranjo through Zarcero (home of the cute church and funky topiaries) to Ciudad Quesada. From there, take either the Jabillos or Muelle road. The faster route is to take the Inter-American Highway through to San Ramon then north through La Tigra. Either will take 3½–4 hours.

By air NatureAir (☎ 299 6000) has a daily flight from San José to Arenal.

By bus Buses leave three times a day from Avenida 7/9, Calle 12. **Auto Transportes** (☎ 255 4318) from San José to San Carlos takes approx 4½ hours.

GETTING AROUND Downtown La Fortuna is easily accessed by foot and taxis are found around the football field. If you're staying up the road from or outside of La Fortuna, you'll need to rely on taxis, the local bus or have a rental vehicle to get around easily.

WHERE TO STAY If you're on a budget and don't have a vehicle, staying in the town of La Fortuna is recommended. There are numerous lodges outside of town but some are fairly remote and require a vehicle – be aware that tour companies will charge an additional pickup fee for out-of-the-way hotels so double check first. Despite the prolific amount of *cabinas* and hotels in the La Fortuna/Arenal areas, space here books up extremely quickly so it is highly recommended that you secure reservations many months in advance of your trip.

🏠 **Hotel La Mansion Inn Arenal** (21 cottages) On the road between La Fortuna and Nueva Fortuna; ☎ 692 8018; f 692 8019; www.lamansionarenal.com. Intimate, exclusive and luxurious, this is the most upmarket small hotel in the entire Northern Zone. Roughly a 45-min drive to La Fortuna. The volcano is not visible from the grounds but sitting on the banks of Lake Arenal, it's still a gorgeous view. Cottages are all private and have split-level design, with original artwork, private hot-water bath, satellite TV and private garden — more luxurious cottages have antiques, private pools and full living rooms and dining rooms. Amenities include an excellent restaurant, horses, free use of canoes, colourful gardens, pool and outstanding service. In 4 years, I've yet to hear a single complaint or slight about this outstanding retreat. B/fast inc. *Rates US$175–1,150.*

🏠 **Arenal Kiori** (52 rooms) ☎ 461 1700; f 461 1701; www.hotelarenalkioro.com. Newly opened in December 2005, this resort is poised to give Tabacon a run for its money as it is the closest to a Marriott-style full-service hotel in the area (yet still intimate). Truly luxurious, each room is tastefully decorated and has a breathtaking view of the volcano. Rooms have 2 queen beds, sofa bed, balcony with view, hot tub in room with view, private baths with hot water, phone, minibar, AC and satellite TV. Services include a restaurant/bar, trails through 11ha of private reserve, private hot springs, pool, spa, beauty salon, games room, laundry service, gym, room service and tennis court. B/fast and entrance to Kioro Hot Springs inc. *Rate US$250.*

🏠 **Tabacon Resort** (109 rooms) ☎ 256 1500; f 221 3075; www.tabacon.com. For a long time, Tabacon was the most luxurious hotel in the Northern Zone.

Offering free entrance to the hot springs for its guests (note that the springs are not on the same grounds so guests are shuttled), the hotel quickly became the most popular lodging in all of Costa Rica, requiring reservations many months in advance. Thanks to heavy marketing, everyone wants to stay at Tabacon. My advice is to look elsewhere. Tabacon seems to be resting on its laurels and I've heard so many complaints about very poor service, smelly rooms, broken windows and ripped linens, that I've come to think happy guests are the exception, not the norm. The reservations department is notorious amongst agents as being the most unresponsive and difficult to work with and messing up reservations. Rooms are average in size and amenities (pool and gardens are very nice), and standard rooms do not have views to the volcano. Food at the restaurant is pricey as are the rooms. I think a better bet is to stay elsewhere and use the hot springs on a day pass. B/fast buffet inc. *Rates US$175–290.*

🏠 **Iguana Perdida Hotel** (20 rooms) First right after Hanging Bridges; ☎ 461 0122; www.lostiguanaresort.com. One of the newest resorts in the area and one of the best. Beautifully constructed and appointed, rooms are an oasis, with Egyptian cotton sheets, local artwork, AC, minibar, satellite TV, fans, private baths with hot water and private balcony with volcano view. The luxury suites have a dining area, sitting area, outside garden shower (first-floor units) and jacuzzi baths on the deck with views (super romantic). There is a restaurant and bar with very good food, split-level pool with waterfall and 100 acres of grounds and a river to explore. Future plans include a spa and 20 more rooms. Gorgeous! *Rates US$135–185.*

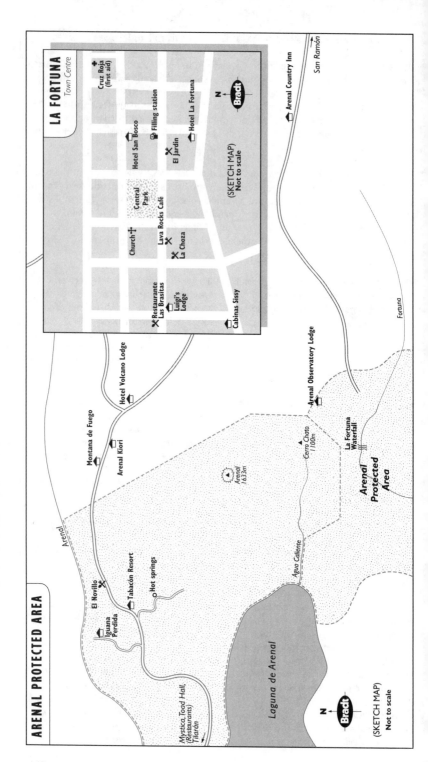

ARENAL PROTECTED AREA

LA FORTUNA
Town Centre

Cruz Roja (first aid)

Hotel San Bosco

Filling station

El Jardin

Hotel La Fortuna

Church

Central Park

Lava Rocks Café

La Choza

Restaurante Las Brasitas

Luigi's Lodge

Cabinas Sissy

N

Bradt

(SKETCH MAP)
Not to scale

Arenal Country Inn

San Ramón

Hotel Volcano Lodge

Montaña de Fuego

Arenal Kiori

Arenal

Arenal 1633m

Cerro Chato 1100m

Arenal Observatory Lodge

La Fortuna Waterfall

Fortuna

El Novillo

Iguana Perdida

Tabacón Resort

Hot springs

Agua Caliente

Arenal Protected Area

Mystica, Toad Hall (Restaurants) Tilarán

Laguna de Arenal

N

Bradt

(SKETCH MAP)
Not to scale

Montaña de Fuego Resort & Spa (50 cabins) On the road from La Fortuna to Tabacon; ☎ 460 1220; f 460 1455; www.montanadefuego.com. Spectacular views of the volcano are had from the cabins' private, glassed-in porches (almost all, as some standard cabins have obstructed views). Cabins, constructed out of dark wood are simply appointed (Spartan, really) with private hot-water baths and cable TV. Deluxe cabins and suites have AC and refrigerators. The grounds are beautifully landscaped and there is a very good spa, pool and jacuzzi. The restaurant is horribly overpriced. The staff are not overly helpful and older rooms are getting a bit threadbare. Good b/fast buffet inc. *Rates US$112–170.*

Hotel Volcano Lodge (40 rooms) On the road to Arena Lake; ☎ 460 6080; f 460 6020; www.volcanolodge.com. Each room is simply but nicely appointed, bright and has private bath with hot water, cable TV and a patio with rocking chairs (rooms 1 through 12 have the best volcano views). Amenities pool and jacuzzi with views, laundry service, gardens and a restaurant. A free shuttle service to Tabacon Hot Springs and La Fortuna is also available. B/fast inc. *Rate US$100, taxes inc.*

Rock River Lodge (14 rooms) On the shores of Lake Arenal; ☎ 293 2121; www.rockriverlodge.com. Geared to windsurfers and mountain bikers, this lodge is built of gleaming hardwood and sits upon stilts. Rooms have private baths with hot water and the small cabins offer more privacy and have hand-shaped tubs. In the main building, there is a huge open fireplace and restaurant. Sitting upon a hill overlooking the lake, it's a long jaunt to actually get to the shores so a vehicle is strongly recommended. B/fast inc. *Rates US$76–94.*

Hotel Arenal Country Inn (20 cabins) On the road south to San Ramon; ☎ 479 9670; f 479 9433; www.arenalcountryinn.com. Cheerful and airy cabins are set amidst beautiful gardens with good views of the volcano. Each has AC, minibar, telephone, TV, private baths with hot water and a patio. Amenities include a pool, billiards table and an open-air restaurant in the former stable. B/fast inc. *Rate US$86.*

Arenal Observatory Lodge (37 units) ☎ 692 2070; f 692 2074; www.arenalobservatorylodge.com. The only lodge in the Arenal National Park, this was originally built as the observatory for the Smithsonian Institute's vulcanologists. Only 4km from the volcano and high upon a ridge, the view of the cone is spectacular. Despite the close proximity, the lodge is not in a danger area, as the deep gorge of the Agua Caliente River provides a buffer zone. Basic rooms with shared baths and sitting rooms are in the *casona*, the original farmhouse. Standard rooms have private baths and were originally built for the scientists. The nicest rooms are the Smithsonians, which have glass walls allowing perfect views of the volcano, private baths and king-size beds – 5 of these rooms are fully wheelchair accessible. A large villa is also available for larger groups. Amenities include an infinity pool, jacuzzi with a view and a restaurant/bar. The surrounding park offers excellent hiking and birdwatching. If you really want an intense volcano experience, this is the place – however, because of its distance from La Fortuna, tour pickups have an additional cost and there aren't other facilities nearby. If you want to explore La Fortuna and area at all, I highly recommend you rent a 4x4. B/fast and daily guided hike inc. Full meal plan available for US$35 per day. *Rates US$66–375.*

Luigi's Lodge (20 rooms) Downtown La Fortuna; ☎ 479 9909; f 479 9898; www.luigislodge.com. A good option, this 2-storey wooden lodge has basic carpeted rooms with AC, fan, coffee maker, veranda with view of volcano, and private baths with hot water and tubs – some have cable TV and minibar. Amenities include pool, jacuzzi, gym, spa, garden and a pizzeria/restaurant with good food. B/fast inc. *Rate US$60.*

Hotel San Bosco (34 rooms) Downtown La Fortuna; ☎ 479 9050; f 479 9109; www.arenal-volcano.com. One of the best budget bets, if you can spring for the larger, newer rooms with stone walls and TVs – cheaper rooms are very basic. All have private bathrooms with hot water, fan and AC. Amenities include a small pool, jacuzzi, gym, laundry service, observation deck. *Rates US$38–46, taxes inc.*

Hotel La Fortuna (13 rooms) Downtown La Fortuna; ☎/f 479 9197. Basic and clean with private bathrooms with hot water, this is a relatively new building replacing the original that was destroyed by fire in 1997. Nothing fancy but one of the best deals in town. There is a small restaurant at the front of the hotel. B/fast inc. *Rate US$26.*

Cabinas Sissy (12 rooms) Downtown La Fortuna; ☎ 479 9256. Very basic but clean and bright, some rooms with shared bathrooms and hot-water showers. *Rate US$9 pp.*

✦ **WHERE TO EAT** Arenal isn't the spot for fine dining and most restaurants offer simple fare.

✘ **El Jardin** In downtown La Fortuna; ✆ 479 9360. A simple *soda* popular with budget travellers. Delicious fresh fruit *batidos* and filling *casados*. *Meals average US$6. Open daily 05.00–12.00.*

✘ **El Novillo** On the road to Tabacon; ✆ 460 6433. Nothing fancy décor-wise in this open-air *rancho* with plastic furniture but the food is tasty and cheap. In my opinion, this is the best restaurant to sit at night and watch the volcano. *Main course runs about US$6–8. Open daily 10.00–02.00.*

✘ **Lava Rocks Café** ✆ 479 8039; e lavarocks@racsa.co.cr; www.arenaltour.com. Offers basic *Tico* food in an open-air bar/restaurant. Cheap, good and filling with a funky atmosphere. *Main course averages US$10. Open daily 07.00–21.30.*

✘ **La Choza de Laurel** In downtown La Fortuna; ✆ 479 9231. A rustic, thatched-roof spot with typical and international fare (try the coffee-roasted chicken). At weekends, marimbas entertain. *Meals average US$7. Open daily 06.30–22.00.*

✘ **Restaurante Las Brasitas** In downtown La Fortuna; ✆ 479 9819. This is the spot to head to if you're tired of the typical *Tico* fare offered in town. Decent Mexican food, nice view and good service. *Main course US$7. Open Sun–Thu 10.00–22.00, Sat 10.00–23.00.*

✘ **Mystica** On the road from Arenal to Tilaran; ✆ 692 1001; e mystica@racsa.co.cr; www.mysticalodge.com. Delightful and cosy spot on a hill overlooking the lake with excellent thin-crust pizza and pastas. *Pizzas average US$6, pasta US$5. Open daily 07.30–21.00.*

✘ **Toad Hall** On the road from Tabacon and Nuevo Arenal; ✆ 692 8020; www.toadhall-gallery.com. Tucked behind a delightful gift shop, you'll find this quaint coffee shop with delicious fresh bread, juices, sandwiches and an ever-changing menu of main courses. Lovely view of the lake. *Salad is US$7. Open daily 08.00–17.00.*

PRACTICALITIES
Banks
$ **Banco Nacional** On the northeast side of the football field.

$ **Banco Popular** 100m southeast of Banco Nacional.

Emergencies
Police station 100m east of the football field; ✆ 479 9689.

✚ **Hospital San Carlos** Ca Central in the nearby town of San Carlos; ✆ 460 1173.

WHAT TO SEE AND DO Almost as popular as the volcano are the hot springs, whose spring waters are fired deep underground by the heat of the volcano.

Tabacon Hot Springs (✆ *256 1500; open 10.00–22.00*) is the oldest and largest spa in the area. Numerous thermal pools and waterfalls of various temperatures (up to 38°C) are located amid a luxurious garden, a natural stream providing the hot water (be careful entering and walking in the water as stones and rocks make it tricky). There is also a manmade pool with a waterslide and swim-up bar by the restaurant. A soothing spa offers massage and mud treatments. It has become the most touristy spot in Arenal, and if you are coming during the high season, you should pre-book your spot as only a limited number of people are allowed in daily. The restaurant is pricey (as are the drinks at the bar – check out the little outdoor bar at the far end of the river, as they have two for one drinks during happy hour in the early evening).

Safety note: the springs are located in a high-risk zone, vulnerable to pyroclastic flows (avalanches of rocks, lava and gases that can travel at 80km/h). Twice this spot has been in the direct path of eruptions (1968 and 1975) and was almost hit again in 1993, which has led some tour operators to no longer book reservations at Tabacon Hot Springs on account of the risk (the hotel is on a ridge and not in the danger zone).

A cheaper option is to head down the driveway across the street from Tabacon and enjoy basic facilities but the same spring water. There isn't a view but there are showers and changing rooms (*entrance US$8*).

There is also a popular spot that is free – along the road between Tabacon and the park, keep your eyes open for a number of cars parked by the side of the road as you head past Tabacon, away from La Fortuna. You'll see a dense forest and then a path (there is a small sign). If you get lost, ask any local and they'll steer you the right way.

Baldi Termae (↘ 479 9651; *entrance US$10*) on the main road in La Fortuna, has seven thermal pools and a large swim-up bar. It's much smaller than Tabacon and not as nice. If staying for a couple of days, I suggest hitting the waters here for a night and at Tabacon for another. Make sure to bring your own towel.

Eco-Termales (↘ 479 8484) is the smallest private hot spring with only four pools.

Arenal Hanging Bridges (↘ 253 5080; *www.hangingbridges.com; rates US$20–35*) is a new addition to the area and located in a private forest reserve just outside of La Fortuna. With eight fixed and six hanging bridges, it's an interesting way to view the forests below and easy enough for anyone to walk. They offer an intriguing night tour, which is recommended. **Venado Caverns** (↘ 479 9415) are limestone caves located 35km north of La Fortuna and contain eight chambers with an assortment of stalactites, stalagmites, and underground streams. Interesting but not for those who are claustrophobic or afraid of bats. Although you can spelunk alone, guided tours provide transportation, torches, rubber boots (it's wet) and bilingual guide. **BoBo Adventures** (↘ 479 9390) are the specialists in Venado Caverns.

Pure Trek Canyoning (↘ 479 9940; *www.puretrekcostarica.com; rate US$80*) is the most professional abseiling operation in the country. After a short hike, you make four abseils, three of which are through waterfalls. Recommended.

The **Río Fortuna Waterfall** is located 5.5km outside of La Fortuna and it's a gorgeous cascade of water, tumbling in a thin stream from 75m above. There are two ways to reach the falls – one is a strenuous 20-minute hike down a steep, rocky hill (good walking shoes are a must). The other is on horseback. You can swim at the waterfall's basin but be wary, as the currents are extremely strong.

White-water rafting enthusiasts have two options in the Arenal area. For Class III–IV rapids, the Río Toro offers a two-hour thrill-athon with 45 rapids. Those seeking a gentler trip can check out the Class II–III Río Arenal, perfect for beginner rafters or individual inflatable kayaks (called 'Duckies'). **Desafio Adventure Company** (↘ 479 9464; f 479 9463; *www.desafiocostarica.com*) is the long-established operator in the area for rafting as well as horseriding.

There are a couple of options for **Canopy Tours** in the area – **Arenal Paraiso** (↘ 460 5333; *www.arenalparaiso.com*) at the hotel of the same name and **SkyTrek Arenal** (↘ 479 9944; *www.skytrek.com*).

Sky Tram Arenal (↘ 479 9944; f 479 8014; *www.skytram.net*) is an Austrian-built sky tram near Lake Arenal and offers stunning views of the volcano, surrounding forests and the lake from the tram and from the observation platform at the top of the mountain. To get down from the top, you can either take the tram again or zip down the canopy ride on site, the Sky Trek. The full tram ride is highly recommended for those with limited mobility.

Cultural tours are offered through **Casona Río Fortuna** (\f 469 1279; *www.casonariofortuna.com*), a former plantation estate. Visitors board a tractor-pulled wagon and travel through the countryside, visiting farmers, *pulpería*, even a local school. Activities offered include a tour via oxcart, horseback rides and a cooking class.

Volcan Arenal National Park 12km west of Fortuna (*open daily 08.00–16.00; entrance US$6*) is the protected area housing the volcano. Owing to the safety issues, it's not permitted to hike on the volcano. You can view the cone clearly from the surrounding areas. There is some limited rugged hiking in the park but pay heed to the rangers' warnings and do not step off the paths – a volcano and its lava are not to be trifled with.

Arenal Botanical Gardens 4km east of Nuevo Arenal (℡ *694 4273; open May–Oct, Mon–Sat 09.00–17.00*) has 2,500 plant species, butterfly garden, serpentarium and guided one-hour tours. **Windsurfing** on Lake Arenal is good all year but excellent from December to April when trade winds reach speeds of up to 80km/h. **Ticowind** (℡ *694 4445; www.ticowind.com*) arranges lessons and rents gear while **River Rock Lodge** (see above) is a hotel catering to the windsurfing crowd.

From the Arenal area, it's easy to take a day trip to **Caño Negro National Wildlife Refuge** (*open 06.00–16.00; entrance US$6*), which is 100km north of La Fortuna, near the Nicaraguan border town of Los Chiles. It is considered one of the best spots for birdwatching in the western hemisphere. Every rainy season, the Río Frio floods the vast majority of the park's 10,000 acres so, depending on when you visit, you will either see a lake or dry, mud-caked riverbeds – both seasons offer interesting mammals, reptiles and birds. The best time for birding is between January and March when the largest population of migratory birds is present. In the rainy season, you may spot a garfish, a 'living fossil' as it is a fish with lungs, gills and a nose. The refuge is best viewed with a trained guide and I recommend an organised tour for a one-day viewing. Most hotels in the Arenal area can arrange for a tour.

Heading north to the border, **San Carlos Sport Fishing** (℡ *395 5053; www.nicaraguafishing.com*) arranges fishing trips on Río San Juan along the Nicaraguan border.

MONTEVERDE

Cool mountain forests, shrouded in misty clouds, with layer upon layer of plantlife – this is Monteverde, one of the most internationally recognised tourist spots in Costa Rica and the most difficult to get to. Sitting high on the Tilaran mountain ridge at 1,220m, the cloudforest is a unique natural phenomenon, created by the northeasterly trade winds of the Caribbean drifting across the continental divide where they cool and become dense clouds. Humidity is usually at 100%, so be sure to bring your wellingtons and a raincoat.

Monteverde is an intriguing and beguiling place for a number of reasons. Settled by American Quakers in 1951, there is an aura of gentleness and congeniality about the place. Unlike the logo from the oatmeal box, Quakers are not identifiable by dress or appearance. A movement founded by George Fox (1624–91), Quakerism is an optimistic, altruistic belief system in which followers are encouraged to 'see the God in everyone'. It also values pacifism and this belief is what prompted a group of American Quaker families to make the arduous journey south to Costa Rica, a land with no army. When they arrived in Monteverde, the only means of transportation up the horrible roads was via oxcart. The verdant mountainsides were perfect for dairy farming and the Monteverde Cheese Factory has become legendary for its 'cultured' products.

Birdwatching is one of the main activities for tourists here and spotting a quetzal is practically a Monteverde rite of passage (March and June are prime months, when the 100 pairs of quetzals in the area are mating). Big cats make their home in the cloudforests but rarely are they ever seen (which is probably a good thing). Hiking and canopy tours are the other attractions here – there is really no nightlife to speak of (it is a sleepy Quaker town, after all). This is an area to commune with nature, unplug from the hustle and bustle and to marvel at the wonder that is the cloudforest. It's an arduous journey but well worth it to do no more than marvel at how many different shades of green can be found in one magical, misty mountain range.

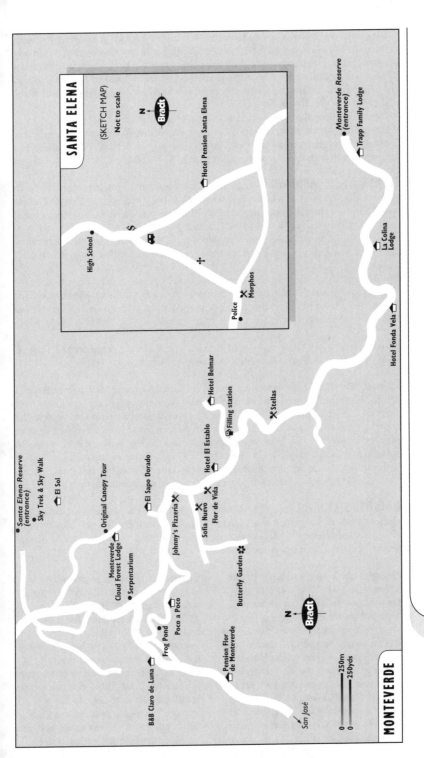

MONTEVERDE

San José

0 ___ 250m
0 ___ 250yds

B&B Claro de Luna

Frog Pond

Poco a Poco

Serpentarium

Monteverde
Cloud Forest Lodge

Original Canopy Tour

Santa Elena Reserve
(entrance)

Sky Trek & Sky Walk

El Sol

El Sapo Dorado

Johnny's Pizzeria

Pension Flor
de Monteverde

Butterfly Garden

Sofia Nuevo
Flor de Vida

Hotel El Establo

Filling station

Hotel Belmar

Stellas

Hotel Fonda Vela

La Colina
Lodge

Monteverde Reserve
(entrance)

Trapp Family Lodge

SANTA ELENA

(SKETCH MAP)
Not to scale

High School

Police

Morphos

Hotel Pension Santa Elena

Northern Zone **MONTEVERDE**

8

167

Despite the popularity of Monteverde, the roads are rocky, steep and pot-holed, making driving slow and tortuous. Area residents are happy to keep things this way as more tourists would drastically alter the landscape and their lifestyle (in the past 25 years, the number of visitors has mushroomed from 3,100 to 100,000). If you are going to undertake the journey here, you should stay for at least two or three nights.

There are actually two areas that comprise what is commonly referred to as 'Monteverde' – one is the town of Santa Elena, which has all the amenities and cheaper lodgings, and the other is Monteverde proper, which isn't a village but farms and hotels spread out along a dirt road.

GETTING THERE AND AWAY The roads are incredibly rough, especially from Tilaran, riddled with pot-holes and boulders. Note: pregnant women and those with bad backs should reconsider trekking to Monteverde as it's a long, bumpy and uncomfortable ride (2½ hours from Tilaran).

Although you can make it in a regular car in the dry season, most car-rental shops will not rent you a two-wheel drive for Monteverde. Best to go in a 4x4.

By car From San José, take the Inter-American Highway heading north (towards Liberia) and about 31km past the Puntarenas turn-off, you'll see the turn-off for Monteverde (roughly 2½ hours to this turn-off) at Lagarto. From here, it's a slow and bumpy 38km (another 2 hours) to Monteverde.

By bus Buses leave twice daily from Avenida 7/9, Calle 12. **Transportes Tilaran** (\ 222 3854) from San José to Monteverde, takes five hours.

By boat or horse There is a transfer between Arenal/Monteverde that crosses Lake Arenal, cutting the travel time to three hours. You are picked up in a Jeep, then cross the lake in a small boat and then in a Jeep to Monteverde (or vice versa). The other option is a full day's ride on horseback, which should be undertaken only in the dry season, as it's strenuous and dangerous in the rainy season. **Desafio Adventure Company** (\ 479 9464; f 479 9463; www.desafiocostacrica.com) offers both options and looks after its horses (various companies offer this horse option but some do not look after their animals so stick with a reputable operator).

WHERE TO STAY Budget travellers should head to one of the *pensiones* in Santa Elena while those seeking higher-end nature lodges should look to Monteverde. Regardless of where you decide to stay, accommodation is limited and books up quickly so make your reservations months in advance.

Hotel El Sapo Dorado (30 cabins) On the road to Monteverde; \ 645 5010; f 645 5180; www.sapodorado.com. Named after the famous golden toad (see the box in Chapter 2, *The mystery of the missing Sapo Dorado*, page 25) that has since vanished from the area (scientists believe it is now extinct), this hotel has long been viewed as the most upmarket in the area. Each private wooden cabin has a private porch, baths with hot water and 2 queen-size beds. All have lovely views and the mountain suites have the addition of a fireplace (it gets chilly up here). Nothing luxurious, however, as it is a bit basic. It's a steep climb to the rooms and not advised for those with mobility issues. There are trails for self-guided hikes and a restaurant. *Rates US$89–99.*

Hotel Fonda Vela (40 rooms) Next to Monteverde Reserve; \ 645 5125; f 645 5119; www.fondavela.com. My favourite hotel in Monteverde, it is one of the most luxurious. All rooms have private baths with hot water and are spacious and airy. Some have 3 beds, making them ideal for families as are the junior suites that have a separate loft (although some do not have a view). There is a huge restaurant with stunning views, a bar, hiking trails, horseriding and laundry service.

Paul Smith, one of the original Quakers, is the owner and his artwork is displayed around the hotel. A great option as it's walking distance to the reserve. *Rates US$94–112.*

⌂ **Hotel El Establo** (40 rooms) On the road to the reserve; ↘ 645 5110; f 645 5041; www.hotelelestablo.com. Owned and operated by one of the original Quaker families, this mountain resort has just completed a large addition and the suites in this building have stunning views, large and airy rooms with huge windows, modern baths with hot water and balconies. The honeymoon suites have jacuzzis and the suites, with loft bedrooms, are a great option for families. Standard rooms are in the original building and are clean but a bit Spartan and dark. There is a large restaurant and a pool (although I've never seen anyone use it as it's too cold up here). The management is to be applauded for its conservation efforts that have made this one of the most eco-friendly hotels in the country. Service is very personal and you truly feel like a special guest. B/fast inc. *Rates US$84–250, taxes inc.*

⌂ **Trapp Family Lodge** (20 rooms) Next to reserve; ↘ 645 5858; f 645 5990; www.trappfam.com. Neat, clean, cute mountain chalet whisks your imagination away to a hill with a lonely goatherd. Situated only 1km from the reserve, it is the closest hotel to the park. Rooms are spacious and have lovely views of the forest, phones, private baths with hot water. There is a common lounge with big, comfy couches, dining room with tasty food. Wheelchair accessible. *Rate US$87.*

⌂ **Hotel Belmar** (29 rooms) Northeast of the petrol station; ↘ 645 5201; f 645 5135: www.hotelbelmar.net. Two gleaming, wooden Swiss-chalets on a hill, each of the spacious rooms has a balcony with a gorgeous view, private baths with hot water and phones. Amenities include a jaccuzzi, duck pond, playground, billiard table, lounge, bar, restaurant and an art gallery. Wheelchair accessible. *Rates US$85–95.*

⌂ **Monteverde Cloud Forest Lodge** (20 cabins) Northeast of Santa Elena; ↘ 645 5058; f 645 5168; www.cloudforestlodge.com. Set on 70 acres with primary forest, the lodge is comprised of individual wood and stone *cabinas*, 2 of which are wheelchair accessible. Bathrooms are spacious and have hot water. Hikers can enjoy 5km of trails through the property and is home to the Original Canopy Tour. Great views of the Nicoya Gulf from the deck. There is a restaurant, bar and reading area. *Rate US$82.*

⌂ **El Sol** (3 rooms) Only 10 mins outside of Santa Elena; ↘ 645 5838; f 645 5042; www.elsolnuestro.com. 2 hand-built and beautifully decorated cabins are a place to really get away from it all. The larger cabin can hold up to 4 guests while the smaller is perfect for a romantic honeymoon. A spring-fed pool is the sidekick to a Finnish sauna, a perfect way to finish a healing massage session with Elisabeth, the owner while Ignacio, her husband, cooks up a mouthwatering meal. Great food, great views and great hosts. *Rates US$75–95, taxes inc.*

⌂ **Poco a Poco** (11 rooms) East of the Frog Pond and Santa Elena; ↘ 645 6000; f 645 6264; www.costaricahotelsguide.com/pocoapoco. Cute family-run hotel that is cosy and has a friendly atmosphere. Rooms are spacious and nicely decorated, with private hot-water baths with tubs, phone and cable TV. *Rate US$65.*

⌂ **B&B Claro de Luna** (8 rooms) Santa Elena; ↘/f 645 5269; www.claro-de-luna.com. Very cute, 3-storey Swiss B&B beautifully constructed out of cedar wood. Rooms are very bright, spacious and nicely decorated, the private bathrooms are huge, with hot water, and the balconies afford lovely views. B/fast inc. *Rates US$59–62.*

⌂ **La Colina Lodge** (11 rooms) West of the reserve; ↘ 645 5009; f 645 5580; www.lacolinalodge.com. Formerly FlorMar, this lodge is under new management and is a charmer. Rooms are brightly decorated with furniture and fabrics from Guatemala. Standard rooms all have queen beds, hot water and some have shared baths. Rooms in the main house have balconies. There are also bunk rooms with shared baths. There is a restaurant and a lounge with satellite TV. Camping is also offered at US$5 with hot shower (the only campsite in the area). *Rates US$38–45, inc b/fast.*

⌂ **Pension Flor de Monteverde** (7 rooms) On the road to Monteverde; ↘ 645 5236; f 645 6105. A long-standing favourite for a quiet stay. Basic rooms, some with shared baths. *Rates US$15–20.*

⌂ **Hotel Pension Santa Elena** (25 rooms) ↘ 645 5051; f 645 6060; www.pensionsantaelena.com. With new owners, this is a great budget option. Wide range of accommodation, from dorms (male and female) to private rooms, to private cabins, some with shared baths, hot water, community kitchen, recycling system. *Rates US$5–35.*

✦ WHERE TO EAT Most visitors eat at their hotel's restaurant but there are some good options in the area.

✕ **Sofia Nuevo Latino Restaurant** South of Sapo Dorado; ✆/f 645 7017. A new Latino restaurant, serving up delicious and creative dishes, such as chicken in *guayaba* sauce. Great ambience. *Meals average US$16. Open 11.30–21.30.*

✕ **Poco a Poco** By the Frog Pond; ✆ 645 6000; f 645 6264; www.hotelpocoapoco.com. A nice mix of international cuisine, including sushi. Good food, good service at a good price. *Main course US$8–21. Open daily 06.00–21.00.*

✕ **Stellas Bakery** On the road to the reserve; ✆ 645 5560. This place bakes lovely pastries and has great options for lunch that change daily. *Sandwich US$1.50–5. Open daily 07.00–17.00.*

✕ **Flor de Vida** On the road to the reserve; ✆ 645 6081. Funky spot with bagels, vegetarian specials, pasta and delicious home-baked pastries. There's the occasional jam session and live performances. *Meals average US$8. Open 07.00–22.00.*

✕ **Johnny's Pizzeria** On the road to the reserve; ✆ 645 5066; www.johnnysrestaurant.com. This is practically an institution, thanks to its excellent wood-oven pizza and Italian food. Everyone seems to hang out here and the atmosphere is jovial and inviting. *Pasta US$8–10, pizza around US$5–21. Open 11.30–22.00.*

✕ **Morphos** Santa Elena; ✆ 645 5607; e morphoscorporations@hotmail.com. This place is popular with the backpack crowd on account of its affordable food and vegetarian menu. *Main course US$3–11. Open daily 11.00–21.30.*

✕ **El Sapo Dorado** At the hotel of the same name on the road to Monteverde; ✆ 645 5010, www.sapodorado.com. This is the only fine-dining establishment in the area. Great food with an emphasis on worldly cuisine and vegetarian dishes, served in a cosy ambience. *Main course US$7–16. Open daily 06.30–10.00, 12.00–15.00 and 18.00–21.00.*

PRACTICALITIES Supermarkets, stores, internet cafés and services are found in the town of Santa Elena. The town also has a Banco Nacional branch, a police station (across from the Super La Esperanza) and a Red Cross (on the north side of town).

WHAT TO SEE AND DO Flora and fauna are the reason people make the arduous trek up to Monteverde. **Monteverde Cloud Forest Reserve** (✆ 645 5122; f 645 5034; *open daily 07.00–16.30*) is one of the best-maintained parks in the country. Sitting on 26,000 acres with six ecological zones, the trails are well marked and gentle enough for almost anyone. Lush, damp and dark, it's an ocean of green upon green. Orchids and *bromeliads*, creating unbelievable textures and colours, cover trees – it can be a bit boggling to the untrained eye. Take a guided tour and discover the hidden world living in this magical place, which includes 2,500 species of plants, 100 species of mammals (including ocelots, tapirs and jaguars), 490 species of butterflies, over 400 species of birds and 120 of amphibians. There is a restaurant and a very good information centre. Good hiking shoes and a rain poncho are recommended and if the trails are very muddy, you can rent a pair of rubber boots at the information centre for US$2. Temperatures are cooler here, reaching 15°C, so dress accordingly. Owing to the delicate nature of the reserve, only 120 people a day are allowed on the trails at any one time. Serious birders should avoid the peak tour group times of 08.00–10.00. Reservations can be made 24 hours in advance through your hotel.

Santa Elena Cloud Forest Reserve (✆/f 645 5390; *open daily 07.00–16.00*) is smaller than the Monteverde Reserve, with 765 acres but offers excellent birding and hiking as it's not so visited as its more famous neighbour. At an altitude of 1,650m, it's the highest cloudforest in the area and has scenic views of Arenal Volcano. Located next to the Monteverde Reserve, the plant and animal life is similar, although quetzals are not as numerous. There is a souvenir/coffee shop, managed by Santa Elena High School and a percentage of the profits support educational environmental programmes and local schools.

Sky Walk & Sky Trek (✆ 645 5238; f 645 5796) offers seven suspension bridges through the forest canopy connected by easy jungle trails. For those who want something more adrenalin-charged, Sky Trek (on the same property) has the longest zip line in the country (make sure you get a good run as it's a loooong one and most people run out of speed and get stuck). There is also an eight-storey observation tower and a restaurant. **The Original Canopy Tour** (↘ 645 5243; *www.canopytour.com*) was the first commercial canopy tour operation in Costa Rica and the most safety conscious.

Horseriding tours can be had at **Sabine's Smiling Horses** (↘ 645 5051), home of well-trained and cared-for horses. **Meg's Stables** (↘ 645 5052) prides itself on being an organic stable.

OTHER PLACES OF INTEREST A couple of small galleries allow you to get closer to mother nature than normal. **Monteverde Butterfly Garden** (↘f 645 5512) has hundreds of butterflies, an all-weather greenhouse and leaf-cutting ant house. **Orquideas de Monteverde** (↘ 645 5510; *open daily 08.00–17.00*) has over 430 species of orchids, including the smallest orchid in the world. **Serpentario de Monteverde** (↘ 645 5238; *open daily 08.00–17.00*) houses over 40 species of snakes. The **Frog Pond** (↘ 645 6320; *open daily 09.00–20.30*) houses 20 species of live frogs and toads.

Monteverde is home to a highly organised arts community and every year, during March and April, international performers take to the stage during the **Monteverde Music Festival** at the Monteverde Institute (↘ 645 5053). **Community Arts Centre** (↘ 645 6121), near the cheese factory, is an ecologically friendly art studio/gallery. **Art House** (↘ 645 5275; e *bertalva@hotmail.com*) is a community-based art gallery and school working with the community and schools to educate through art. They also run a drug-rehab programme using art. All proceeds from the gallery sales benefit the community.

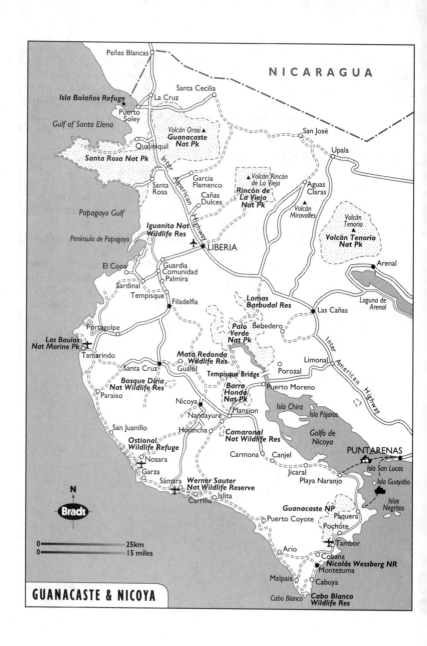

GUANACASTE & NICOYA

9

Guanacaste

Although it was the last province to join the Republic of Costa Rica in 1824, Guanacaste has had an incredible cultural influence over all the land. The vast, dry plains with their herds of long-eared Brahma cows and attending *sabaneros* (cowboys) are more reminiscent of the Wild West than of the lush, tropical paradise that is Costa Rica. Nevertheless, those things that have become quintessentially *Tico* – rodeos, *bombas* (rhymes), *marimba* (type of xylophone) and even the national dish of *gallo pinto* – are, in fact, *Guanacasteco* in origin.

The driest area of the country, Guanacaste is also home to some of the most celebrated beaches. Factor in the recently expanded international airport in Liberia and a shorter rainy season than the rest of the country and, *voila*, you have the perfect environment for tourism. Historically one of the poorest provinces in the land, the new boom in tourism projects, especially in the Gulf of Papagayo area, has given a much-needed boost to the local economy. Now the largest tourist area in Costa Rica, the province's infrastructure is trying to catch up to the recent explosion of tourists. Slowly, roads are improving but water availability is an ongoing concern, especially as larger resorts and golf courses appear on the dusty landscape.

CAÑAS

A typical cattle town, Cañas is a central hub for the nearby towns but not much of a 'stopping-off' point for tourists.

GETTING THERE AND AWAY

By car It's difficult to get lost driving to Cañas from San José – take the Inter-American Highway west of Esparza, then north to Cañas for 180km.

By bus Buses run by **Transportes Deldu** (✆ *256 9072*) leave daily from Avenida 1, Calle 20.

WHERE TO STAY

⌂ **Palo Verde Biological Station** (dorms) ✆ 240 6696; f 240 6783; www.ots.ac.cr. The station is run by the Organisation for Tropical Studies and offers visitors dormitory rooms, meals and a guide at US$50 a person. A great option for those who want to explore this fascinating park more in-depth.

⌂ **Hotel Capazuri** (16 rooms) 2km north of Cañas; ✆ 669 6280; f 669 6080; e capazuri@racsa.co.cr. Clean, basic rooms with b/fast, some with AC, TV, pool, bar/restaurant. *Rate US$50.* Camping is available on the grounds for US$4 or US$6 if you want b/fast inc.

⌂ **Hotel Nuevo Cañas** (26 rooms) One block east of the bullring in town; ✆/f 669 1294; e hotelcanas@racsa.co.cr. Nothing fancy, just a place to lay one's head. Cold water, cable TV, some rooms with AC plus a pool and jacuzzi. *Rate US$45.*

⌂ **Hotel Viejo Cañas** (45 rooms) Near to Hotel Nuevo Cañas; ✆ 669 0039; f 669 1319; e hotelcanas@racsa,co.cr. Same owners, same amenities as Hotel Viejo Cañas. *Rates US$20–30.*

✖ WHERE TO EAT

✖ **Restaurante Mi Finca** South of Cañas at the turn-off for the Tempisque Bridge; ✆ 662 8686. Popular stop for its classic Tico fare. 'Casados' average around US$4–8. Open daily 06.00–21.00.

✖ **Restaurante Rincón Corobici** A few kilometres north of Cañas; ✆ 669 6006; e Rincón@racsa.co.cr. Has a lovely view of the river and typical Tico food. Meals average US$10. Open daily 08.00–18.30.

WHAT TO SEE AND DO Las Pumas (*off the Inter-American Highway just north of Cañas;* ✆ *669 6044;* f *669 6096; www.laspumas.com; open 08.00–17.00; entrance by donation*) is a shelter for injured wild cats and allows visitors a chance to see ocelots, pumas and, the most elusive cats of all, jaguars, up close. **Palo Verde National Park** (✆ *671 1062; park entrance US$6 pp*) is south of Cañas, near Las Juntas and this 19,804ha park is one of the most important sanctuaries for migrating waterfowl in all of Central America and is home to 280 resident species of birds as well. Roughly 15 different habitats, ranging from deciduous dry forests to both salt and freshwater wetlands, can be found here. From November to January, look for the rare, endangered jabiru, the largest stork in the world. Camping is allowed (*US$2 pp*) and the Tempisque Conservation Area staff can arrange for a local guide to accompany you. If travelling by bus, get off at Bagaces and take a taxi from there.

Safaris Corobici (*2km north of Cañas;* ✆f *669 6091; www.safariscorobici.com*) offers gentle float trips down the Corobici River. Birdwatching trips are scheduled every day (*07.00–15.00*). The trip lasts approximately three hours.

LIBERIA

One of the few Costa Rican cities with colonial buildings, Liberia is often referred to as 'The White City' because early adobe homes were whitewashed with lime from the area. It is the provincial capital and has a lot more going for it than just the Daniel Oduber International Airport (✆ *668 1010;* ✆f *669 1032; open 06.00–12.00*) used by airlines such as Continental, American Airlines and Air Canada. The historic Calle Real has an impressive number of beautiful buildings, including the **Sala del Sabanero Museum** (Cowboy Museum) (*opening hours are irregular*) on the corner across from the church, which pays homage to the area's unique cowboy culture. It's one of the many houses with *puertas del sol*, a unique architectural detail with two doors on the northeast corner of the house, offering views of both the rising sun and twilight, thus maximising the natural light in the house. **The Tourist Information Centre** (✆ *665 0135; open Mon–Sat 09.00–17.00; closed Sun*), 300m south of Central Park, then east, also has a small folk museum. The **Religious Art Museum** is found in Our Lord of Agony Convent, 400m east, 75m south of the main church. The town council is discussing plans to make Liberia into a tourist spot in its own right but concrete plans are still years away. For now, it remains the central hub of the northwest.

GETTING THERE AND AWAY

By air **Daniel Oduber International Airport** (✆ *668 1010*) is the other international airport in Costa Rica. Most flights are charters and many of the larger airlines (American Airlines, Delta, Continental) have various flights throughout the week. Local airlines **Sansa** (✆ *221 9414*) and **NatureAir** (✆ *220 3054*) also have daily flights from/to San José.

By car Thanks to recent repavement, the drive to Liberia is one of the smoothest in the country. Get onto the Inter-American Highway and it will take you right through the city. Drive time is approximately four hours from San José.

By bus Buses run by **Pulmitan** (✆ 222 1650) leave from Avenida 5/7, Calle 24, and take approx 4½ hours.

GETTING AROUND Taxis are found at the bus station and at the northwest corner of the plaza.

WHERE TO STAY Calle Real offers a number of backpacker-type hotels in historic buildings. Liberia has two Best Western hotels to choose from, both of which are just on the outskirts of town.

🏠 **Best Western Las Espuelas** (44 rooms, 2 suites) 2km south of town on the main highway; ✆ 666 0144; f 666 2441; www.bestwestern.com. Comfortable, clean rooms with AC, TV and phones face a pool and hot tub shaded by palm trees. In addition, there is a restaurant and bar as well as a conference centre for up to 120 people. B/fast inc. *Rate US$75.*

🏠 **Hotel Best Western El Sitio** (55 rooms) ✆ 666 1211; f 666 2059; www.bestwestern.com. Heading west towards the airport, this is a larger hotel than its sister Las Espuelas and has a new gym, spa and conference centre as well as 2 pools. Rooms are airy and large, with hot water, safe, phone, TV. B/fast inc. *Rate US$76.*

Other places to stay are as follows:

🏠 **Hotel Boyeros** (70 rooms) On the main highway as you approach town; ✆ 666 0722; f 666 2529; www.hotelboyeros.com. This 2-storey hotel and conference centre is one of the largest hotels in the area and reminiscent of many North American motels. Rooms have 2 dbl beds, TV, hot water, AC, safe, phone and a balcony overlooking the 2 pools in the centre of the court (1 for adults, 1 for children). The restaurant is open 24hrs and offers up typical *Tico* fare. Nothing fancy but clean, comfortable accommodation. *Rate US$46.*

🏠 **Hostal Ciudad Blanca** (12 rooms) 25m east of Ca Real, 25m south; ✆ 666 3962; f 666 4382. An elegant small hotel set in an old stone mansion. Rooms are small but very comfortable with AC and cable TV. There is also a restaurant/bar in the hotel. An excellent choice for a short stay. *Rate US$45.*

🏠 **Hotel Primavera** (30 rooms) Facing the park on the south side; ✆ 666 0464; e cammi@ costarricense.cr. In a newer building, this hotel is a definite step up with its clean, modern rooms that have been recently upgraded. Its rooms have TV, cold water, some with AC, parking. *Rates US$37 (with fan), US$50 (with AC).*

🏠 **Hotel La Guaria** (55 rooms) 200m east of Hotel Primavera and run by the same owners; ✆ 666 0000. Not surprisingly, Hotel La Guaria is very much in the same vein of Hotel Primavera but with additional amenities. Rooms are bright, clean and fresh with TV, some with hot water and AC, safes,

pool. *Rates US$40–51 (with AC).*

🏠 **Hotel Guanacaste** (27 rooms) 200m north of the main entrance road to Liberia, near the beer distribution centre; ✆ 666 0085; f 666 2287; www.hicr.org. Affiliated with Hostelling International, an excellent bet for backpackers as various cheap food options are nearby and the hotel is a stopping point for buses heading to other points in northern Central America. Dormitory rooms with fans and shared, cold-water bathrooms. *Rates US$7 pp, private rooms US$30.*

🏠 **Hotel Casa Real** Across the street from La Posada; ✆ 666 3876; www.posadadeltope.com. Managed by the same people and offers more of the same basic accommodation for those on a budget, but this place also has a small garden to liven up the surroundings. Rooms with shared cold-water bathrooms, fans. *Rates US$10–12.*

🏠 **Hotel La Casona** ✆ 666 2971; e josealbertochavarria@hotmail.com. Next block. Small, basic rooms with TV, some with private bathrooms and AC. *A good bet at US$10–15.*

🏠 **Hotel Liberia** 50m south of Liberia's Central Park; ✆ 666 0161; f 666 4091; e hotelliberia@ hotmail.com; www.hotelliberia.com. This hotel has very basic, small rooms with water, fans and some private bathrooms. *Rates US$5–10.*

🏠 **Hotel La Posada del Tope** (17 rooms) ✆/f 666 3876; www.posadadeltope.com. Has basic rooms with shared cold-water bathrooms and TV. *Rates US$5–17*

WHERE TO EAT Liberia is the one city outside of the Central Valley to offer American-chain fast-food restaurants such as **Pizza Hut**, **Subway**, **TCBY** (east on main street) and **Burger King/ Papa Johns** (food court on highway). Another affordable option is **Panaderia Pan & Miel** (two locations – centre of town and west of town, next to Pali) with cheap, yummy b/fast and lunch offerings.

For a more upmarket meal, head to **Restaurant El Café** (*Ca 8;* ✆*f 665 1660; open Mon–Fri 10.00–18.00*), 75m south of Bancredito. Comfortable, air-conditioned surroundings inspire images of sipping Chardonnay along the Champs-Elysées while the French-accented menu whisks taste buds to the other side of the Atlantic. Patés, cheeses and pastries make for a delectable afternoon. Meals average US$15.

PRACTICALITIES
Banks Most banks are found along Avenida Central.

$ **Banco Popular** Av Central at Ca 12
$ **Banco San José** Next to Banco Popular
$ **Banco de Costa Rica** Ca Central and Av 1
$ **Banco Nacional** Calles 6/8

Shopping There is a large shopping mall before you hit the airport. For groceries, there is a **Pali** at Avenida 3, Calle Central, where you can stock up.

Emergencies
Hospital Emiliano Baltodano ✆ 666 0011
Police station is on Avenida 1, one block west of the plaza.

RINCÓN DE LA VIEJA

One of the active volcanoes in Costa Rica, Rincón de la Vieja may not be as spectacular as Arenal (few volcanoes are) but it has some wonderfully relaxing mud pools and hot springs to enjoy in a more rustic setting than its more famous cousin. The 14,000ha national park has beautiful waterfalls and excellent hiking. Rincón de la Vieja means 'place of the old woman'. During the dry season, the trees here occasionally shed their leaves – an unusual occurrence in the tropics.

GETTING THERE AND AWAY
By car Travel 5km north of Liberia on the Inter-American Highway and look for a rough dirt road on the right-hand side that leads to the eastern slope of the volcano via Curubande or travel 7km north on the Inter-American Highway and look for the paved road to Cañas Dulces, which becomes a dirt road after the first 5km.

 ## WHERE TO STAY AND EAT

⌂ **Hotel Borinquen Mountain Resort & Thermal Spa** (33 rooms) 2km uphill from Buena Vista; ✆ 690 1900; f 690 1903; www.borinqueresort.com. Opened in 2000, this resort is the most luxurious in the mountain area and is centred on providing a relaxing spa experience in deluxe surroundings. Facilities are all top-notch, with rooms in large, Spanish-styled villas with balconies overlooking the incredible mountain views. The spa has various temperature plunge pools, hot springs, jacuzzis, mud huts and large steam room. Massages are also available. The swimming pools are large and lovely and there are lush hiking trails to waterfalls on the property for exploring. A canopy tour, horses and ATVs (all-terrain vehicles) are available for adrenaline junkies. There are also 2 restaurants on site, offering up delicious meals. B/fast and spa inc. *Rate US$182.*

⌂ **Hotel Hacienda Guachipelin Adventure Centre** (40 rooms) 14km down a dirt road to Curubande, 1km past town; ✆ 666 8075; f 442 1910; www.guachipelin.com. For over 100 years, the Hacienda was a working cattle ranch, as it remains today. When the Batalla family bought the property in 1975, they began to create the unique visitor centre/nature reserve that now exists. The 1,600ha parcel of land has 700ha for conservation of the dry tropical forest, 575ha for pasture land and 325ha for reforestation of endangered trees. 4 of the hotel's 40 rooms are in the old *casona* (little house) while the remainder are in long buildings, reminiscent of old Costa Rican farmhouses. The wide, long verandas, with their rough-hewn pillars and folksy paintings on the whitewashed walls give visitors a feeling of stepping back in time to the hacienda's cattle-ranching heyday. Rooms are clean and neat (although in serious need of a good decorator) with hot water, private bathrooms and fans. The restaurant and reception are housed in part of the original hacienda building, surrounded by pleasant gardens. The hotel is working hard to be self-sufficient, using solar panels for hot water, their own waterwheel for hydro-electric power and planning a methane gas biodigestor for the kitchen waste (if only all hotels could be this eco-friendly!). 3 waterfalls and various natural pools are all within hiking distance of the hotel. A natural spa (mud pools, hot springs) is a 3km hike. Those seeking something more adventurous can try the inner-tube ride down the Río Negro (helmet definitely required) or the canopy tour on the grounds. *Rates US$67 b/fast and taxes inc, US$127 3 meals and tax inc.*

⌂ **Buena Vista Mountain Lodge & Adventure Centre** (90 rooms) On the second partially paved road to the southwest slope, 18km north of highway; ☎ 661 8156; f 661 8158; www.buenavistacr.com. Part private nature reserve, part working farm, part adventure centre, this family-owned operation is a going concern with one of the most popular day tours in the northwest. 6 beautiful waterfalls are on the property (one has a natural waterslide) and the natural spa, hidden deep in the woods, is a must. The lodge offers simple but comfortable accommodation in rooms situated in the main house around the tropical patio, while the cabins are near the woods. There is no hot water in the cabins. Amenities for lodge guests include a pool, internet and cable TV. The restaurant/bar offers hearty, tasty local fare, cooked up over a wood stove. Some weekends will see the cowboys presenting *sabenero* customs to guests and *marimba* performances at dinner are always a possibility. *Rates US$35–70.*

⌂ **Rincón de la Vieja Lodge** (60 rooms) 60km via rough road northeast of Liberia on the eastern slope; ☎ 361 9803; www.turismoruralcr.com. Simple, wooden cabins are tucked in amongst the forest and offer visitors a rustic but authentic experience. Owned and operated by the Rincón de la Vieja agro-ecological association, the lodge is part of the rural tourism co-operative. Guests can choose rooms, cabins or camping. Hot water comes from the natural springs and bathrooms are shared. Food is local and prepared over a wood stove. Tours to the waterfalls, mud pools and hot springs as well as horseriding and fishing in the Río Negro are all offered at very reasonable prices. *Rate US$30 pp, 3 meals inc.*

WHAT TO SEE AND DO Hiking the park is one of the most popular activities as well as birdwatching, as over 300 species call the park home. The park's headquarters are found in an old adobe hacienda about 27km northeast of Liberia (a sign on Highway 1 'Sector Santamaría' points the way) and guides can be arranged through the rangers at Santa Rosa Park (☎ 665 5051). This area is notorious for ticks so be sure to wear long trousers. Do be careful when walking around the *Las Pailas* (Caldrons) area, as the earth's crust can sometimes give way, exposing the hot mineral waters or geysers below.

An excellent day trip is to **Buena Vista Lodge & Adventure Centre** (☎ 661 8156; www.buenavistacr.com; entrance US$47). This 1,600ha private reserve has six waterfalls, great hiking trails, canopy tours, horseriding, hanging bridges (a night tour is also available) and a natural spa set in the woods. A simple wooden house has been built over a natural mud pot, creating a sauna while a concrete and stone hot tub has both hot mineral waters and a cold mountain stream feeding into it. Slather yourself up with the nutrient-rich mud and then relax in the hot springs and emerge with baby-soft skin. Various tour operators offer the 'Buena Vista Combination Tour' with a hike, horseback ride, canopy tour, spa, lunch, snacks, guide and transportation from major north Pacific beach towns – check with your local hotel or call Buena Vista directly.

LA CRUZ AND SANTA ROSA

One of the last towns in this area before the Nicaraguan border, La Cruz sits on a hill overlooking the scenic Salinas Bay, the second-biggest windsurfing spot after

Lake Arenal. La Cruz is en route to Penas Blancas, the border post for Nicaragua. If crossing the border, make sure to have all of your documents as well as a lot of patience, as the queue can take several hours.

GETTING THERE AND AWAY

By car Get onto the Inter-American Highway and head 65km north from Liberia. There are two Costa Rican immigration checkpoints along the way so make sure to have your documents handy.

By bus Buses run by **Transportes Deldu** (↘ *256 9072*) leave from San José, Avenida 1, Calle 20, and take 6½ hours.

WHERE TO STAY AND EAT

Hotel EcoPlaya Beach Resort (36 rooms) On the beach at Salinas Bay; ↘ 228 7146; f 289 4536; www.ecoplaya.com. Clean, modern and spacious, the resort's rooms are either villas or suites with fans, AC, TV and hot water. Grounds are well manicured and the restaurant, a huge *palenque*, sits next to a large, crescent-shaped pool. Alas, the beach itself is no stunner, as it is skinny and bland. Windsurfing is the main draw here and the EcoWind Windsurfing Centre, set on the resort's grounds, caters to the sport. Other activities include horseriding, diving, kayaking and boat tours. *Guests can choose an all-inc package for US$75 pp (food, drinks, taxes inc) or just rent the studios US$88 or villas US$121–208.*

Los Inocentes Lodge (69 rooms) 15km east of the second border check; ↘ 679 9190; f 679 9224; www.losinocenteslodge.com. A sprawling former ranch that was owned by the grandfather of Violeta de Chamorro, an ex-president of Nicaragua. The original hacienda was built in 1890 of beautiful hardwood indigenous to the area and was remodelled in 1989 when the lodge was converted to an eco-tourism lodge. The 11 rooms in the lodge and 12 private cabins all have solar-powered hot water. Some rooms in the lodge have shared baths. Meals are filling and tasty and there is a bar to keep things lively into the evening. A huge kidney-shaped pool is the focal point of the property, complete with jacuzzi and swim-up bar. Guests can hike through primary forest, horseback ride, take a tractor tour, mountain bike or play football. A lovely spot to really get away from it all. B/fast inc. *Rate US$69.*

Pura Vida Residence (7 villas, 6 rooms) 13km west of La Cruz in Playa Copal; ↘ 676 1055; m 389 6794; e germanandrea@racsa.co.cr. The Pura Vida has simple, clean rooms with kitchenettes, fans and a pool. Guests can enjoy horseriding, mountain biking or kite surfing. *Rates US$50–100.*

Hotel Cañas Casitilla (6 rooms) 1km north and 2km east of La Cruz; ↘ 381 4030; f 679 9329; www.canas-castilla.com. Nestled against the Sapoa River, this 68ha farm offers visitors 4 airy, simple *cabanas* to choose from. Meals feature fruit grown on the property and milk products from their cows. It's a relaxing, lazy spot deep in the heart of nature. Horses are available for a reasonable US$8 per hr and mountain bikes and windsurfers are also available. A small serpentarium hosts various scaled creatures. Trips to Nicaragua's Granada, Masaya and Ometepe can be arranged through the staff. *Rate US$38; camping is offered in the grounds for US$5.*

Amalia's Inn (9 rooms) La Cruz town centre; ↘ 679 9618; f 679 9181. Perched on the hill, this grand white house has huge, airy rooms with tile floors and private bathrooms (some with bathtubs). Walls are decorated with modern art, painted by the owner's late husband, Lester Bounds. The veranda is a perfect spot to enjoy the majestic vista of the ocean and neighbouring Nicaragua while the pool is the perfect spot for a cooling dip. *Rates US$25–35.*

Hotel Bella Vista (30 rooms) On the main road at the top of the hill in La Cruz; ↘ 679 8060; e hotelbellavista@yahoo.de. Its clean cabins are fresh and up to date with fans and hot water in some. There is a pleasant pool, a small restaurant and bar and secure parking. *Rate US$20.*

Cabinas Santa Rita (38 rooms) On the road into La Cruz; ↘ 679 9062; f 679 9305. This place brings the word 'Spartan' to mind. Shared baths with cold water, some private baths, fans, TV, AC. *Rates US$12–22.*

Camping

Playa Murcielago Santa Rosa Park. *Cost US$2.*

Junquillal Bay National Wildlife Refuge ↘ 679 9692. *Cost US$4.*

WHAT TO SEE AND DO Guanacaste National Park (📞 *666 5051;* 📠 *666 5020;* *www.acguanacaste.ac.cr*), north of Liberia, next to Santa Rosa is a massive 32,512ha, encompassing mountains, lowlands, an extinct volcano, rainforest and one of the last stands of tropical dry forest in the western hemisphere. Primarily for research and preservation, the general public may have access to the park's trails only if they stay overnight as there are no day visits allowed. Cacao Biological Station, at an altitude of 1,100m, is in a cloudforest and has dormitory-style accommodation for up to 30 people. There is no electricity and you must bring your own food. From here, you can hike to the summit of Cacao Volcano (1,659m) and to the Maritza Biological Station (a three-hour hike up a very bad road with the last 18km passable only by foot or horseback; a local guide is recommended). Maritza lies on the fringes of the Orosí Volcano and the temperature tends to be cooler and it's windier. The facilities at this station are a bit more modern but you must still bring your own food. Jaguars are in the area, making their presence known by killing local cattle. From the station you can hike two hours to view petroglyphs over 1,500 years old carved into volcanic stone. Pitilla Biological Station is situated in the Atlantic watershed in primary forest. Basic accommodation; bring your own food. Excellent birding and hiking here with views of Lake Nicaragua and the Orosí Volcano.

Santa Rosa National Park (📞 *661 8150;* 📠 *661 8151; open 08.00–16.00*) is not only a 10,700ha dry tropical forest park but also the location of one of the most triumphant battles in Costa Rica's history. It was here in 1856 that a ragtag army of Costa Rican farmers rallied against William Walker and his filibusters chasing them into a large house that was set ablaze in a suicide mission by Juan Santamaría. The historic building, La Casona, 7km from the park entrance, has been rebuilt after suffering another fire and now houses the museum dedicated to the Costa Ricans' triumph over Walker. There is a variety of hiking trails that the park rangers can point out to you. The trail at Quebrada Duende features rocks with petroglyphs carved by indigenous peoples. The Murcielago (Bat) section of the park at one time belonged to Anastasio Somoza when he was president of Nicaragua. The 7km drive west of Cuajiniquil requires fording of some rivers so enquire at the ranger station before heading out.

Turtle watching Two of the beaches in Santa Rosa Park, Naranjo (12km) and Nanacite (17km), are nesting sites for Olive Ridley, green and leatherback turtles from August to December. During the rainy season, these beaches can be reached only by foot and there aren't any facilities so bring drinking water with you (and remember to take everything out with you when you leave). There are camping sites for US$2. Beach visits must be co-ordinated with the park headquarters (📞 *666 5051;* 📠 *666 5020*).

Kite-Surfing Center 2000 (38 rooms) (📞/📠 *676 1042;* m *826 5221;* *www.suntoursandfun.com*), 3km west from La Cruz at Playa Copal, offers lessons and rentals for kite surfing from November to May, when the winds are in top form. They also offer rooms with shared bath and kitchen (no children) for US$15.

SANTA CRUZ

'National Folklore City', Santa Cruz is the hub for the roads leading to the beaches around Tamarindo. The town itself is largely unremarkable, although civic leaders have tried to spruce it up a bit with some nice light fixtures. Most people continue on their way to the beach, stopping in town to buy groceries or fill up the petrol tank.

GETTING THERE AND AWAY

By car Driving on the Inter-American Highway from San José, you'll see a large petrol station on the left (about 48km north of Puntarenas). Turn left and take the Tempisque Bridge (or 'Taiwan Friendship Bridge' as it's also known) then go 30km west and continue following the signs. The road passes right through Santa Cruz.

By bus Alfaro-Tracopa (\ *222 2666*) buses leave from San José, Avenida 5, Calle 14 or **Tralapa** (\ *223 5859*) buses from Avenida 3/4, Calle 20; both take approx 5 hours.

WHERE TO STAY

⌂ **Hotel Diria** (50 rooms) Main street diagonal to BNCR (National Bank); \ 680 0080; e hoteldiria@ hotmail.com. The Diria has basic rooms with AC, TV, phones, pool and a restaurant/bar. *Rate US$45.*

⌂ **Calle de Alcala** (29 rooms, 2 suites) East of Plaza Lopez; \ 680 0000; f 680 1633; e hotelalcala@hotmail.com. Rooms with AC, TV, pool and a restaurant. *Rate US$40.*

⌂ **Hotel La Pampa** (29 rooms) In town; \ 680 0586. Dingy rooms, fans, cold water, TV. *Rates US$25–30.*

WHERE TO EAT

✕ **Restaurant El Milenio** In town; \/f 680 3237. This is a fairly good Chinese restaurant. *Main courses are around US$6–12. Open daily 10:00–midnight.*

✕ **Coopetortillas** In the centre of town, this must-visit place offers up hot, fresh tortillas made by the women's co-op. Yum! *Open daily 10.30–midnight.*

WHAT TO SEE AND DO

Guaitil Pottery Only 12km east of Santa Cruz is this small town renowned for its pottery, Most of the town's folk are descendants of the Chorotegas and the clay artisans use the same techniques their ancestors did – turning the pots by hand, painting artistic renderings of monkeys, birds and fish in black and ochre paint. Vases, plates and decorative bowls are all for sale by the artists'and throughout the entire Guanacaste region, you'll find roadside stands displaying these works of art. One of the few true Costa Rican handicrafts, they make lovely, and very affordable, souvenirs. I bought a beautiful plate for only 3,000 colones (US$8). Please note that bartering is not a common practice, especially amongst these artists.

10

North Pacific

Ridging the dry forest and plains of Guanacaste, the beaches of the north Pacific offer cool relief from the dust and heat. Soft sand in a variety of colours, world-class sport fishing, calm coves for snorkelling, curling waves for surfers and heart-stoppingly beautiful sunsets have made this the fastest-growing area for tourism in Costa Rica. Add some jumping beach towns and there is truly something for everyone here.

Accommodation prices are based on double occupancy during high season (December to April) unless otherwise noted. Mandatory hotel tax of 16.39% must be added to prices unless otherwise noted. All Blue Flag designated beaches, winners of the coveted award for their cleanliness and water quality, are noted with an asterisk.

PENÍNSULA DE PAPAGAYO

Poised to become the largest resort area in Costa Rica, the 'Papagayo Project' has been in the pipeline for years and only recently have resorts started to open here, with grand plans for more developments over the years. Other than the resorts, there is no community or restaurants and beach access is somewhat limited for those who are not resort guests. There is a variety of tours that can be done from the resorts – tour operators in Playas del Coco and Tamarindo also cater to the resort crowds and the tour desks at each resort can set you up with anything from sport fishing to canopy tours.

GETTING THERE AND AWAY

By air The international airport at Liberia is only 20 minutes away and taxis can be hired there. Both **Sansa** (⚲ *221 9419*) and **NatureAir** (⚲ *220 3054*) run daily flights from San José.

By car From San José on the Inter-American Highway, take the Sardinal turn-off from Liberia for 35km. Turn right at the 'Do It' Centre and follow the signs.

⌂ WHERE TO STAY

⌂ **Four Seasons Resort Costa Rica at Península Papagayo** (153 rooms) Several kilometres past the Allegro entrance on Playa Blanca; ⚲ 696 0000; f 696 0010; www.fourseasons.com/costarica. Opened in 2004, this is the new *crème de la crème* of resorts in Costa Rica and not just exclusive, but very exclusive (so exclusive it's impossible for lowly travel guide writers to wangle a site inspection). From what I've heard from those who work at the resort, it is grand and first class in every respect. Being a Four Seasons establishment, it could be any Four Seasons on the planet and if a guest never set foot outside of the resort, they'd never know they were in Costa Rica — as one worker said, 'It's like entering another world.' Apparently the food is divine (and very expensive), there are private villas owned by sports stars and the golf course is supposed to be world class (but not open to the public).

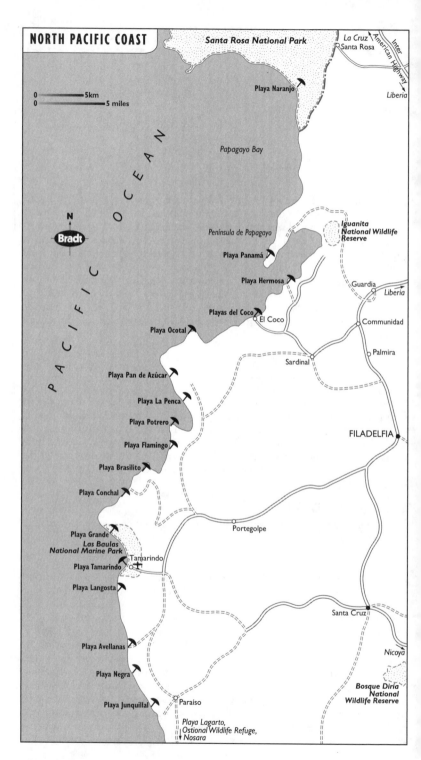

NORTH PACIFIC COAST

Santa Rosa National Park

La Cruz
Santa Rosa

Inter American Highway

Playa Naranjo

Liberia

PACIFIC OCEAN

N
Bradt

0 ━━━ 5km
0 ━━━ 5 miles

Papagayo Bay

Península de Papagayo

Iguanita
National Wildlife
Reserve

Playa Panamá

Playa Hermosa

Guardia
Liberia

Playas del Coco

El Coco

Communidad

Playa Ocotal

Sardinal

Palmira

Playa Pan de Azúcar

Playa La Penca

Playa Potrero

Playa Flamingo

FILADELFIA

Playa Brasilito

Playa Conchal

Portegolpe

Playa Grande
*Las Baulas
National Marine Park*

Tamarindo

Playa Tamarindo

Playa Langosta

Santa Cruz

Nicoya

Playa Avellanas

Playa Negra

**Bosque Diría
National
Wildlife Reserve**

Playa Junquillal

Paraíso

Playa Lagarto,
Ostional Wildlife Refuge,
Nosara

Everything sounds incredible and for those who can afford to park their Pradas here, the experience would be deluxe (so I've been told). *Rates US$395–1,050.*

⌂ **Occidental Allegro Papagayo Resort** (300 rooms) 20km north from the Guardia turn-off; ✆ 690 9900; f 690 9910; www.occidental-hotels.com. All-inc resort on the black-sand beach of Playa Manzanillo is one of the most stylish of the all-incs, with architecture that conjures up images of Spanish villas. The beach isn't attractive but most guests while away their days at the humungous pool, eating at one of the 3 restaurants or 2 bars or sunning at the beach club. There are live shows in the evening; activities throughout the day, a gym, kids' pool, kids' play area and a small disco. *Rates US$190 pp, all-inc.*

PLAYA PANAMÁ

This is part of the Papagayo region, and resorts are the main focus of this area and as all the resorts are all-inclusive, there isn't much in the way of restaurants around. There is a small hamlet, Panamá, down a turn-off from the main road where locals lead a simple and traditional lifestyle.

GETTING THERE AND AWAY

By air The international airport at Liberia is only 20 minutes away and taxis can be hired there. Both **Sansa** (✆ *221 9419*) and **NatureAir** (✆ *220 3054*) run daily flights from San José.

By car From the Inter-American Highway, take the Sardinal turn-off from Liberia for 35km. Turn right at the 'Do It' Centre and follow the signs.

By bus Tralapa (✆ *221 7202*) has a daily service from San José to Playa Panamá.

WHERE TO STAY

⌂ **Fiesta Premier Resort & Spa Papagayo** (160 rooms) North end of the road; ✆ 672 0000; f 672 0200; www.fiestapremier.com. Formerly the Blue Bay Resort, the Fiesta chain has completely remodelled the property and transformed it into a 4-star resort where service is foremost. The rooms are spread out along the massive, hilly property, all with AC, coffee maker, cable TV, minibar and a balcony overlooking the tranquil, golden-sand Culebra Bay. Oversized golf carts zip about, transferring guests to and fro. There is a large main pool and a smaller lap pool in front of the spa/gym that is supposed to be for adults only but apparently, a lot of parents can't read. The AC gym (one of the few in the country) is surprisingly well equipped with a number of machines and free weights and there is also a jacuzzi, steam room, sauna and Serenity Spa has a franchise here. Food is quite good and the variety at the buffet restaurant is excellent while the Mediterranean, à la carte restaurant 'El Dorado' is tastefully decorated, with large pillar candles dancing against the brick wall. A healthy snack/juice bar is set up by the spa, offering alternatives to the nachos, burgers and hot dogs of the main snack bar. There is a casino, small disco and nightly entertainment (in a word, cheesy) — overall, though, one of the better all-incs. There have been problems in the first year of operation, however, of overbooking during high season, forcing groups of guests to be moved to other hotels. Hopefully, they will have fixed their reservations system by the time this book is published. *Rate US$190 pp all-inc.*

⌂ **Hotel Costa Blanca del Pacífico** (28 rooms) On the beach, at the end of the road; ✆ 672 0096; f 672 0239; www.costablancadelpadifico.com. 4 large white low-rises, in a pseudo-colonial style, house rooms that each have a breathtaking vista of Culebra Bay from their balconies. All have a private terrace, full kitchen, living and dining rooms, AC, cable TV, loads of closet space and hot water. The *rancho* restaurant, on a terrace just below the rooms, has wood-oven pizzas. There is a free-form pool with a swim-up bar and guests can walk to 2 beaches adjacent to the resort (which, despite the hotel's advertising, are not really private). *Guests can choose either an all-inc plan for US$90 pp or just the room at US$120.*

⌂ **Nakuti Papagayo Resort** (97 rooms) On the beach; ✆ 672 0121; f 672 0120; e monfeugo@ racsa.co.cr. Another all-inc offering with a large pool. Rooms have all the basic amenities ie: AC, but it's a small resort, with little to offer guests other than one restaurant and bar. The beach directly in front has lava rock so moving to either side of the resort's beach will find better swimming spots. Not the best offering in the area. *Rate US$75 all-inc, pp.*

🏠 **Hotel Giardini di Papagayo** (20 rooms) On the beach; ✆ 672 0067; f 672 0223; www.grupopapagayo.com. Red-tiled villas with 4 rooms in each are spread throughout the gardens and hills. Standard rooms have AC, minibar, cable TV,

phone, safe and hot water while superior rooms have a view and a terrace. There are also suites with chaise longues, sofa bed, living room, covered terrace and a private plunge pool. There is a pool with a jacuzzi, restaurant and everything is a short walk to the beach. It's a smaller resort for those who want an all-inc experience with a bit more intimacy. *Rates are pp and all-inc: US$64 room, US$100 suite with private pool.*

PLAYA HERMOSA

A pleasant, curving beach of grey sand, the name 'Beautiful Beach' is well earned. There are tide pools at the northern end of the beach, perfect for snorkelling or wading in.

GETTING THERE AND AWAY

By air The international airport at Liberia is only 20 minutes away and taxis can be hired there. Both **Sansa** (✆ 221 9419) and **NatureAir** (✆ 220 3054) run daily flights from San José.

By car From the Inter-American Highway, take the Sardinal turn-off from Liberia and follow the road west for 9.5km.

🏠 WHERE TO STAY

🏠 **Hotel Condovac La Costa** (101 rooms) On the beach by Hotel Villas Sol; ✆ 672 0150; f 672 0166; www.condovac.com. Set on a steep hill, red-tiled villas have a nice view of the ocean from their small verandas; each has a sitting area, kitchen, cable TV, separate bedroom and AC. The restaurant has a pleasant view and there is a pool, tennis court, gym, small disco, spa and basketball court and vans shuttle guests around the large grounds. Although it is part of the RCI timeshare group, on my last visit I saw mostly *Tico* families and the North Americans I spoke with were happy with their stay. The staff were nice and helpful – overall, it's an OK resort and I'd strongly recommend renting a car as more than a few days on the property might make you squirrely. B/fast inc. *Rates US$118–192.*

🏠 **Hotel Villas Sol** (160 rooms) On the beach; ✆ 672 0001; f 672 0212; www.villassol.com. Formerly Sol Playa Hermosa and part of the Meliá chain, Villas Sol has been renovated and is now all-inc. It's a large resort with villas and a hotel, 2 restaurants, 2 pools, tennis court, disco and gym. Rooms are comfortable, with AC, phone, safe while the villas have 1-, 2- and 3-bedroom options, some with private pools. Transportation whizzes guests around the monstrous property from 06.00–22.00. *Rates are all-inc, pp: room US$107; villa US$146.*

🏠 **Hotel Villa Huetares** (31 rooms) The second entrance road to the beach; ✆ 672 0052; f 672 0051; www.villaheutares.com. Simple accommodation for up to 6 people with kitchen, TV, AC, hot water and 2 bedrooms in each cabin. The property has 2 pools, garden area and secure parking area. *Rate US$90.*

🏠 **Hotel El Velero** (22 rooms) On the beach; ✆ 672 1017; f 672 0016; www.costaricahotel.net. The whitewashed Mediterranean-style hotel has spacious rooms, all with AC, hot water, TV, safe and phone and everything is kept neat as a pin. The restaurant overlooking the pool hosts BBQs with live music and is the place to be on Wed and Sat nights. A 38ft Beneteau sloop owned by the hotel (hence the hotel's name, which means 'sailboat') gives a 5hr tour each day as well as a sunset cruise with an open bar. Nicely maintained hotel just steps from the beach, it's one of the best deals anywhere. *Rate US$72.*

🏠 **Hotel La Finisterra** (9 rooms) On the beach; ✆ 672 0293; f 672 0227; www.finisterra.net. Beautifully conceived with incredible views, this airy, breezy hotel offers 10 standard or deluxe rooms with contemporary décor and original pieces of art. A cooling pool beckons, with a tastefully tiled patio offering hammocks and bamboo furniture for curling up with a good book. Recommended. B/fast inc. *Rates US$70–80.*

🏠 **Hotel/Restaurant Villa del Sueño** (41 rooms) The first entrance road to the beach; \/f 672 0026; www.villadelsueno.com. A tropical treasure, Villa del Sueño has beautifully decorated rooms at bargain prices. Rooms are breezy, tiled and tastefully put together with batik art, soft colours and gleaming hardwood accents. The entire atmosphere is one of calm relaxation and the

elegant restaurant offers outstanding cuisine. Pool, short walk to the beach, choice of standard or superior rooms, efficiency unit or 1-bedroom apt. *Rates US$59–169.*

🏠 **Cabinas La Casona** (7 rooms) On the beach; \ 672 0025; f 672 0049. This establishment has basic rooms in an old wooden house, with kitchenette and fan. *Rate US$35.*

☚ WHERE TO EAT

✗ **The Monkey Bar** On the main road into Hermosa; \ 672 0267. A tree-house bar and restaurant, it's a great spot for having a cold beer, catching Monday night football, throwing darts or enjoying live music. *Italian, Mexican, American (fast food) runs US$4–10. Open 12.00–22.00; closed Sun.*

✗ **Restaurant/Bar Pescado Loco** Second entrance road to the beach; \ 672 0017. This place offers great seafood in al fresco dining.

✗ **Aquasport** Second entrance road to the beach; \ 672 0050; www.costarica-beach-hotel.com. Aquasport has excellent seafood and is worth a visit.

Main course US$5–55. Open Mon–Sat 11.00–21.00.

✗ **Ginger** On the main road towards the north end of the beach; \ 672 0041. This place has a unique menu featuring all appetisers (my kind of place) with Asian and Mediterranean flavours. Their wonderful wine selection is second only to their dessert offerings. *Appetisers US$4–8. Open Tue–Sun 17.00–22.00.*

✗ **Hotel La Finisterra Bistro** The restaurant's speciality is seafood, artfully prepared by the cordon bleu-trained chef and is open to the general public. *Open 07.00–22.00; closed Tue dinner.*

PLAYAS DEL COCO

Grey-coloured sand ensures that this is not the prettiest beach around, but nevertheless, Playas del Coco is popular with *Ticos* who crowd the town on holiday weeks (and leave mounds of rubbish on the beaches – best to avoid the area at Christmas and Easter). Popular with the college crowd, there is no shortage of discos and bars to keep things jumping and folks from the nearby towns will find the happening nightlife they seek here. Playas del C oco is technically two beaches (hence, the plural name), with the more touristy area to the north and the sleepy fishing town to the south (which is a bit sketchy and best avoided). Truth be told, the entire town has a run-down look and feel to it, like a former film star clutching at the last vestiges of past glory. Expats are doing their best to clean things up and revitalise the area and it's happening, although in baby steps. But if you want a lively town where you can rub elbows with the locals, this is the place.

GETTING THERE AND AWAY

By air The international airport at Liberia is only 20 minutes away and taxis can be hired there. Both **Sansa** (\ 221 9419) and **NatureAir** (\ 220 3054) run daily flights from San José.

By car From the Inter-American Highway, 7km west of Sardinal (follow the signs).

By bus **Pulmitan** (\ 222 1650) has a daily bus service from San José, taking five hours. There are also daily buses from Liberia with **Arata** (\ 666 0138).

☛ WHERE TO STAY

🏠 **Rancho Armadillo** (6 rooms) Off the road approaching town; \ 670 0108; f 670 0441;

www.randoarmadillo.com. Easily the most unique property in the Coco area, this is a true respite

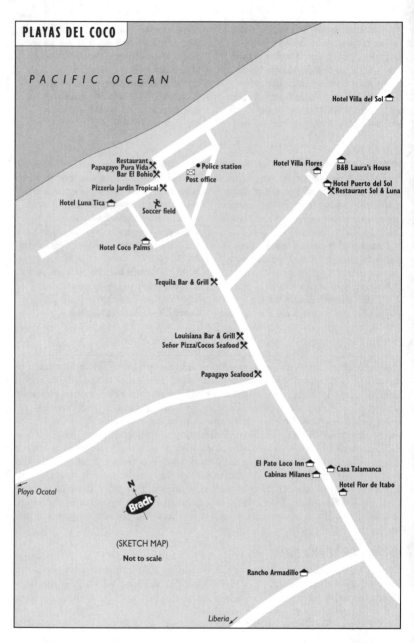

PLAYAS DEL COCO

PACIFIC OCEAN

Hotel Villa del Sol

Restaurant
Papagayo Pura Vida
Bar El Bohio
Police station
Post office
Pizzeria Jardin Tropical

Hotel Villa Flores
B&B Laura's House
Hotel Puerto del Sol
Restaurant Sol & Luna

Hotel Luna Tica
Soccer field

Hotel Coco Palms

Tequila Bar & Grill

Louisiana Bar & Grill
Señor Pizza/Cocos Seafood

Papagayo Seafood

Playa Ocotal

N

Bradt

(SKETCH MAP)
Not to scale

El Pato Loco Inn
Cabinas Milanes
Casa Talamanca
Hotel Flor de Itabo

Rancho Armadillo

Liberia

from daily life. Set on 25 acres, yet a short drive to the town and beach, it's the best of both worlds — tranquillity and ease of access. Each room is thoughtfully decorated with handmade wooden furniture, colourful bedspreads and hangings from Guatemala and all have AC and large outdoor 'rainforest' showers. There is a huge pool and a commercial kitchen that is at the guests' disposal (they'll even do the dishes). If you prefer not to cook, their experienced chef will do it for you. True luxury! The entire ranch (and the chef if you want) can be rented weekly for US$5,250. B/fast inc. Recommended. *Rates US$104–146.*

⌂ **Hotel Puerta del Sol** (10 rooms) North of town on inland road; ☎ 670 0195; f 670 0650; www.lapuertadelsol.com. Undoubtedly the most elegant hotel in town; the 10 rooms are beautifully decorated and appointed with soothing pastels and very comfy beds — AC, cable TV, phone and a safe and 2 suites, with more living space and refrigerators, are also available. There is a pool, lovely gardens, a small gym and a great Italian restaurant. If in Coco, this is the place. *Rates US$80–110.*

⌂ **Hotel Villa Flores B&B** (9 rooms) North of town on inland road; ☎ 670 0269; f 670 0787; www.hotel-vill-fores.com. A short walk to the beach, this hotel offers comfortable, although small accommodation, with some real wood panelling in some rooms (which makes them a tad dark). All rooms have AC and private bathrooms with hot water. Deluxe rooms have cable TV. There is a fair-sized pool with a swim-up bar and jacuzzi, lush gardens and an open-air restaurant where a gigantic b/fast is served every morning. The common areas are light, airy and breezy. *Rates US$64–74.*

⌂ **Hotel/B&B Villa del Sol** (10 rooms) North side of town on inland road; ☎/f 670 0085; e hotelsol@racsa.co.cr. A lovely setting with bright, airy rooms with either fan or AC, some with private baths and ocean view. A small pool and garden create a tranquil environment. *Rates US$45–75.*

⌂ **Hotel Flor de Itabo** (35 rooms) On the boulevard into town; ☎ 670 0292; f 670 0003; www.flordeitabo.com. One of the original hotels in town, for over 20 years this Italian-owned property has been keeping guests happy. The focus is on sport fishing and the hotel owns a number of sport fishing boats. Guests have a choice of bungalows, rooms, suites or apts (for up to 6). All are nicely decorated with gleaming hardwood and huge bathrooms and all have hot water, private bathroom, cable TV, phone and AC (except for bungalows). There is a pool with a jacuzzi, casino and Italian restaurant bar. Gardens are colourful, overflowing with bougainvillea and birds. *Rates US$45–170.*

⌂ **El Pato Loco Inn** (4 rooms) On the boulevard into town; ☎/f 670 0145; www.costa-rica-beach-hotels-patoloco.com. The 'Crazy Duck Inn' is actually a nicely run small hotel with spacious rooms decorated with handmade hardwood furniture. There are 2 apts for long-stay guests. Rooms have hot water and either fans or AC. *Rates US$40–50.*

⌂ **Hotel Coco Palms** (24 rooms) Facing the football field; ☎ 670 0367; f 670 0117; e hotelcocopalms@hotmail.com. Simple but clean, spacious and comfortable rooms, with safe, fans or AC and a pool. *Rate US$36.*

Casa Talamanca (5 rooms) Along the boulevard into town; ☎ 670 0717; e guwi@racsa.co.cr. Offers basic rooms with fan as well as an apt for up to 7 with kitchenette and cable TV. *Rates: rooms US$30; apt US$30–65.apt*

⌂ **Cabinas Milanes** (8 rooms) Across the boulevard; ☎ 670 0364. Milanes has bright rooms with cold water, fan and cable TV. *Rate US$28.*

B&B Laura's House (8 rooms) North of town on inland road; ☎ 819 3552; e casalauracr@yahoo.com. Clean, simple rooms with either fans or AC, cold water and a small pool. *Rates US$25–35.*

⌂ **Hotel Luna Tica** (15 rooms) Centre of town near the beach; ☎ 670 0127; f 670 0459. The hotel has Spartan rooms with cold water and fan. *Rate US$20.*

✖ WHERE TO EAT

✖ **Papagayo Seafood** Main street on the south side; ☎ 670 0298. Offers clean, al fresco dining with Cajun-style seafood. *Main course US$8. Open daily 10.00–22.00.*

✖ **Señor Pizza/Cocos Seafood** Main street on south side; ☎ 670 0532. This place offers pizza and seafood served in a garden setting with friendly service. *Pizza averages US$10. Open daily 11.00–23.00.*

✖ **Louisiana Bar & Grill** Next door; ☎ 670 0882. The closest thing to New Orleans in Costa Rica, featuring spicy gumbo, fish, jambalaya and 10 different sauces. *Meals average US$25. Open daily 11.00–22.00.*

✖ **Tequila Bar & Grill** One block over from the Louisiana; ☎ 670 0741. Good Mexican food with jazz music in the background. *Average meal US$10. Open 13.00–21.00; closed Wed.*

✖ **Pizzeria Jardin Tropical** In the centre of town; ☎ 670 0428. Offers up pizza and pasta. *Main course US$4–8. Open daily 07.00–22.00.*

✖ **Bar El Bohio** Across the street from Pizzeria Jardín Tropical; ☎ 670 0447. Features roast chicken. *Casado US$4–6. Open daily 11.00–12.00.*

✖ **Restaurant Porto Belo** Facing the football field; ☎ 670 0153. This new addition serves sushi and *Tico* food. *Meals average US$15. Open 06.00–22.00.*

✖ **Restaurant Papagayo Pura Vida** On the beach; ☎ 670 0272. Has fresh seafood. *Main course US$5–22. Open daily 11.00–22.00.*

✕ Restaurant Sol & Luna At Hotel La Puerta del Sol, has authentic Italian food in a lovely al fresco setting. *Meals average US$15. Open Wed–Mon 18.00–21.00.*

OTHER PRACTICALITIES

Internet **Leslie Internet** on the main street, also offers photocopying. **E-Juice Bar Internet** (☎ *670 0563*), also on the main street, is the place for international phone calls and bike rentals.

Medical The closest services are in Sardinal, 7km away, including the **Red Cross** (☎ *670 0190*) and the **clinic** (☎ *670 0192*).

Police The police station is facing the plaza (☎ *670 0258*).

Shopping There are a number of souvenir shops and stands on the road heading towards the plaza. **Souvenirs Sussy** (☎ *670 0569*) has a nice assortment.

Spa **Coco Verde Spa** (☎ *670 0354*) next to the Hotel & Casino Best Western Coco Verde, has massages and beauty services.

WHAT TO SEE AND DO There are several **discos** offering lots of options for dancing the night away: **Banana Surf Disco/Bar** (☎ *670 0708*) on the second floor on the main street above La Rana Restaurant; **Lizard Lounge Bar** on the main street next to E Juice Bar Internet; and **Disco Coco Mar** on the beach.

Sailing *Spanish Dancer* (☎ *670 0448*) is a 36ft catamaran that has daily fun cruises. **Ecantador** (☎ *670 0473*) has sunset cruises.

Sport fishing Coco is one of the best spots for sport fishing and there are a number of boats to choose from. **Hotel Flor de Itabo** (☎ *670 0292*) has a number of boats available. **TranquilaMar** (☎ *670 0833*) has sport fishing as well as tours to Witch's Rock for surfing.

OCOTAL

Not a town or village per se, but more of a gated community with private villas, rental villas and a smattering of small hotels scattered throughout the steep hills. The beach has dark, soft sand and is an excellent jumping-off spot for diving and sport fishing.

GETTING THERE AND AWAY Once you're in Playas del Coco, turn left at the sign, follow the road and watch for the signs.

🏠 WHERE TO STAY

🏠 **Bahia Pez Vela** (40 units) At beach level; ☎ 670 0129; f 670 0726; www.bahiapezvela.com. Recently completed 2-storey condos, this is a beautiful complex offering both beach-level and hillside accommodation. Each of the condos has 3 bedrooms with 2 full bathrooms and a powder room, AC in the bedrooms, fully equipped kitchen, washer, dryer, living room, dining room, cable TV and VCR and some even have private outdoor jacuzzis. All are nicely decorated and the overall feeling is definitely one of luxury.

The infinity pool is beautifully designed and the black-sand beach is the nicest in the area – being in a cove, it offers complete privacy. A rental car is highly recommended for stays of any length as this is an out-of-the-way spot. The perfect spot for a quiet beach getaway. *Rate US$360.*

🏠 **Hotel Los Almendros de Ocotal** (17 condos) Near the beach; ☎ 670 0442 ext 100; f 670 0526; www.losalmendros.com. A great option for groups or families, fully equipped villas with 3 bedrooms and

2 bathrooms each, with AC in the bedrooms, fans, cable TV, a pool with jacuzzi and a beach club, all within a short walking distance to the beach. *Rate US$139.*

🏠 **Hotel El Ocotal Beach Resort** (59 units) Up the hill on the left; ☎ 670 0321; f 670 0083; www.elocotalresort.com. The first resort in the area, El Ocotal has recently changed ownership, with the new management planning to remodel the entire hotel over the next 2 years. Its main buildings have a commanding view from their cliffside location and sunsets are usually nothing less than stunning. The rooms are either at the top of the cliff in new buildings or at beach level and all have hot water, safe, AC, balcony, cable TV, coffee maker and hairdryer. Beachfront rooms could use a remodelling but the new cliffside rooms are nicely appointed. Built down the side of the steep hill are bungalows with 2 suites and a plunge pool each. There are also newly built suites in the new buildings that are spacious, each with a living room, huge bathroom with a jacuzzi, refrigerator and impressive ocean view. There are pools at the top of the cliff, at the main building and at beach level, which also has a swim-up bar. Other facilities include tennis courts, 2 bars, a restaurant with very good cuisine and a small gym. The beach club is a perfect spot for hanging out by the pool and is literally steps from the beach. A good option now – after the remodelling, sure to be stellar. B/fast buffet inc in all accommodation. *Rates: rooms US$130; bungalows US$200; suites US$245*

🏠 **Hotel Villa Casa Blanca** Up the hill on the left; ☎ 670 0518; f 670 0448; www.hotelvillacasablanca.com. Resembling a Spanish villa on the outside and decorated in a Victorian theme on the inside, this small, luxury American-owned hotel is unique. Rooms are each distinctively decorated and all have a canopy bed, AC and a private bathroom with hot water. While they aren't large, they are comfortable. The 2 suites have a small kitchenette and a living area. There is a small pool with a jacuzzi and a *rancho* set amongst lovely gardens. A gem! B/fast inc. *Rate US$80.*

🏠 **B&B Ocotal Inn** (5 units) ☎ 670 0835; f 670 0526; www.ocotalinn.com. The Ocotal has private bathrooms, hot water, fan, AC and a small pool. There is a Peruvian restaurant that has good food and the hotel is only a 5-min walk to the beach. With taxes and b/fast inc, the most affordable option in Ocotal. *Rate US$55.*

WHERE TO EAT

✗ **Father Rooster Bar & Grill** On the beach; ☎ 670 1246. The strange name comes from a play on words – 'Papagayo' sounds like 'papa gallo' or 'Father Rooster' in Spanish. Playing on this theme, the placemats and menu have many such witticisms in Spanish – although beginner Spanish speakers will be left scratching their heads. Built to resemble an old barn, the restaurant's atmosphere is lively and relaxed – think 'roadhouse meets beach' and you get the gist. Menu offerings are typical bar food – burgers and such with chicken taking centre stage. Servings are huge and the steak was one of the best I've ever tasted. Excellent selection of mixed drinks as well. *Meals average US$20. Open 11.00–22.00 daily.*

Picante ☎ 670 0901 At Bahia Pez Vela; ☎ 670 0129. Open-air setting overlooking the pool and beach at the Bahia Pez Vela resort, this restaurant has quickly established itself as being the place to eat in the area. Serving an interesting fusion of flavours and inspirations, the menu is inventive and satisfying. Anything with fresh fish is outstanding here. Highly recommended. *Main course US$8–25. Open Mon–Sat 10.00–22.00, Sun 10.00–14.00.*

WHAT TO SEE AND DO Ocotal is one of the best areas for diving, with seahorses, jacks, rays, giant mantas, sharks, whales and even the odd black marlin being spotted by divers. **El Ocotal Resort** (☎ 670 0321 ext 261; e info@ocotaldiving.com) has the only PADI Gold Palm Beach Resort in the Pacific and is right at beach level. They offer daily area dives, dives to the nearby Catalina and Bat Islands as well as certification courses.

Sport fishing is also excellent here and the resort has a number of large fishing boats available.

PLAYA POTRERO* AND PLAYA PENCA

The grey-sand beach isn't as pretty as its neighbour to the south, Flamingo, but Potrero is a quiet spot, perfect for lazing and swimming in the sheltered waters. A number of expats have made their homes here – mostly Italians and French-Canadians – so the small village has an international flair about it.

Playa Penca is 2km north of Playa Potrero and has been awarded the Blue Flag for its pristine beach.

GETTING THERE AND AWAY

By car The fastest route from Playa Coco is via the bumpy, 16km Monkey Trail, passable only during the dry season and only in a 4x4. From Coco, turn right at the Congo Trail Canopy Tour sign on top of the bus stop, just past the turn-off for Playa Hermosa.

Driving from San José, take the Inter-American Highway until you see signs for Puente de Amistad (approx 2 hours). Turn left at these signs (there is a huge petrol station on the left) and continue across the Puente de Amistad (Friendship Bridge) and on until the road ends, turn right and follow signs for Santa Cruz and continue until you see the Belen exit on the left. Then follow the signs from the Belen exit.

🏠 WHERE TO STAY

🏠 **Bahia del Sol** (25 rooms) On the beach; ✆ 654 4671; f 654 5182; www.potrerobay.com. Set on manicured lawns in front of the beach, this resort was recently remodelled and is now a comfortable boutique hotel. The attention to detail and design is evident, giving an overall feeling of luxury. All rooms have AC, cable TV, phone, hot water with the addition of kitchen, living room and dining room to the suite. Furnishings are handcrafted out of rattan and exotic hardwoods and the interior design is well planned. The pool, just metres from the beach, is large, with a jacuzzi and wet bar. There is also a restaurant with local fare. Wheelchair accessible. *Rates US$96–156.*

🏠 **Villagio Flor de Pacifico** (100 rooms) The first hotel at end of the Monkey Trail; ✆ 654 4664; f 654 4663; www.hotelflordepacifico.com. Italian-owned resort with Mediterranean villas set amongst shady trees. Villas are spacious, spotless with AC and kitchenette. It's a quiet, relaxing setting with well-manicured gardens, tennis court and 2 pools. The management has thoughtfully included a shuttle service to the beach for guests, as walking would take a while. Service is excellent. *Rates US$77–95.*

🏠 **Cabinas Isolina** (11 rooms) Near the beach in Playa Penca; ✆ 654 4333; f 654 4313; www.isolinabeach.com. Recently remodelled, the terracotta stucco walls contrast with the dense green garden surrounding this small hotel. Rooms and villas are sparsely furnished but have lovely tiled bathrooms with hot water – the villas have kitchens. There is a small pool and the grounds have nicely detailed wrought iron, giving the feeling of being inside a villa near the Aegean. *Rates US$70 and up.*

🏠 **Monte Carlo Beach Resort** (5 rooms) On the beach; ✆ 654 4674; f 654 5048; www.montecarlobeachresort.com. Calling this hotel a resort is stretching it a bit but it is a charming and intimate spot on a pristine stretch of beach. Villas are nicely designed and fully equipped with cable TV, AC, dining room, kitchen and large bathroom, all with a veranda with ocean view. Furnishings are hand carved from Nicaragua and the overall look is Santa Fe, with brightly painted adobe walls. The restaurant features well-executed French cuisine and nicely appointed furnishings (not the typical white plastic lawn furniture). *Rate US$60.*

🏠 **Hotel Bahia Esmeralda** (14 rooms) At the end of the Monkey Trail; ✆/f 654 4480; www.hotelbahdiaesmeralda.com. Set amongst lush gardens, this charming Italian-run hotel has simply furnished rooms, apts and villas to choose from The rooms have hot water, AC and cable TV. In the apts, which can hold up to 4 people, there is a fully equipped kitchen and an outdoor shower while the villas have 2 separate bedrooms. There is a kidney-shaped pool and a restaurant serving Italian and Tico cuisine. B/fast inc. *Rates US$56–66.*

🏠 **Cabinas Cristina** (7 rooms) Near the beach; ✆ 654 4006; f 654 4128; www.cabiascristina.com. Simple rooms and apts have some interesting details inside such as hardwood ceilings. Buildings resemble typical Tico farmhouses, all whitewashed with pillars of Guanacaste wood. Kitchenettes are available in all rooms and apts but the stove and utensils must be booked. All have hot water, private bathroom and a fan. Apts have either 1 or 2 rooms with fan or AC as well as a small dining area. A small pool is on site. *Rates US$30–60.*

🛖 **Mayra's Camping & Cabinas** (4 rooms) Heading to Flamingo just past the bridge; ☎/f 654 4213. With basic, rustic rooms and camping. There is also a small restaurant with *Tico* food. *Rates: rooms US$25; camping US$4.*

🍴 WHERE TO EAT

✗ **Bar/Restaurant Las Brisas** On the beach; ☎ 654 4047. Offers up seafood, Tex-Mex food and great Caesar salads. *Main course US$4–12. Open daily 12.00–23.00.*

✗ **Bar La Perla** Just after the bridge. A laid-back place with burgers and BBQ. *Average meal US$4.*

✗ **Ristorante Marco Polo** Villagio Flor de Pacifico; ☎ 654 4664. Serving wonderful Italian food. The wood-oven thin-crust pizza is delicious. *Pizzas US$6. Open 06.00–22.00.*

✗ **Harden's Gardens** On the road to Flamingo; ☎ 654 4271. This is a little shop renowned for its gourmet cinnamon buns and cookies. Bakery, coffee, bar & restaurant. *B/fast US$6, lunch US$7 and dinner around US$9.50. Open daily 06.00–22.00*

✗ **Matapalo Tex-Mex Food** Adjoining Harden's. A lovely al fresco café with, unsurprisingly, Tex-Mex fare. *Meals average US$7. Open 07.30–18.00.*

✗ **Maxwell** On road to Flamingo; ☎ 654 4319. This is a lively pub, offering up burgers and other pub grub, with live music throughout the week. *Burgers US$6. Open daily 01.00–22.00.*

PLAYA PAN DE AZUCAR (SUGAR BEACH)

Called the most beautiful beach in Costa Rica, this idyllic spot is not the easiest place to get to. From Potrero and La Penca, it's a bone-jarring 4km ride along rough, steep roads (a 4x4 is recommended). When you arrive, there is but one hotel on the beach, **Hotel Sugar Beach** (32 rooms) (☎ 654 4242; f 654 4239; www.sugar-beach.com) and it is a gem, with large cabins tucked amongst the trees and along the small stream that runs through the 24-acre property. Deserted white-sand beach, lovely rooms in a lush forest setting and an overall relaxed atmosphere in tune with mother nature – paradise found!

The beachfront suites are just steps from the water and the sound of the waves can lull you to sleep if you leave the windows open – the honeymoon suite on the second floor of the airy beach house has one of the best locations of anywhere in the country to watch a romantic sunset (if only there was a jacuzzi). Both the three-bedroom beach house and the five-bedroom grand villa have full amenities and an incredible amount of living space. The entire hotel received an overhaul in 2004, adding master suites, the coati suite and deluxe rooms. The open-air restaurant has a commanding view of the ocean below and the food is highly recommended. Set in a crescent-shaped bay, the beach is protected from strong winds, making it an ideal spot for swimming and snorkelling, Amenities include AC, hot water, refrigerator, balconies, pool, kayaks and outrigger canoes. Breakfast is included. (*Rates: rooms and suites US$110–190; villas US$450–600.*)

FLAMINGO BEACH

Noted for its pinkish white-sand beach (there aren't any actual flamingoes in the area), Flamingo is the most Americanised beach in Costa Rica. Huge million-dollar villas sit perched on cliffs overlooking the bay, which was the largest marina on the Pacific side between Acapulco and Panamá until the government closed it in 2004, citing numerous violations against the management. At the time of writing, the government had yet to resolve the issues surrounding the marina's closure, despite pressure from sport fishing boat operators and boat owners who kept the docks humming with activity. Those seeking cheap accommodation won't find what they're looking for here, as hotels are geared to gringos with money.

GETTING THERE AND AWAY

By air Both **Sansa** (☎ *221 9419*) and **NatureAir** (☎ *220 3054*) run daily flights from San José to Tamarindo, which is about 30 minutes away by car.

By car Driving from San José, take the Inter-American Highway until you see signs for Puente de Amistad (approx 2 hours). Turn left at these signs (there is a huge petrol station on the left) and continue across the Puente de Amistad (Friendship Bridge) and on until the road ends, turn right and follow signs for Santa Cruz and continue until you see the Belen exit on the left. Then follow the signs 35km from the Belen exit.

By bus Tralapa (☎ *221 7202*) has a daily service from San José.

WHERE TO STAY

Flamingo Beach Resort (91 rooms) Along the curve at beach level; ☎ 654 4444; f 654 4060; wwww.resortflamingobeach.com. A large, uninspired hotel that reminds me of a giant concrete box with shades of set décor from the TV series *Falcon Crest* while the rooms are desperate for a makeover. The beach across the road is lovely and the pool is nice but the food is nothing to write home about. The honeymoon suite is huge but the décor — think really bad Vegas and you'll get the picture. Rooms have cable TV, phone, AC, coffee maker, safes, hairdryer and minibar. The hotel has a restaurant, bars, large pool, kids' pool, gym and a playground. Personally, I find the prices high for the overall quality of the hotel. B/fast inc. *Rates: rooms US$103–173; apts US$208–324.*

Flamingo Marina Resort (90 rooms) On a steep hill; ☎ 654 4141; f 654 4035; www.flamingomarina.com. The largest resort in Flamingo, it underwent renovations recently and has rooms, suites and apts in condos and bungalows, decorated in the style I've come to christen 'Basic Beach' — rattan or wooden furniture, tropical print curtains/bedspreads, a few token pieces of artwork.

Nothing outstanding but very functional. The views of the bay from the hillside location are stunning. In the main building, the 22 deluxe rooms have 2 dbl beds, AC, safe, hot water, phone, minibar and balcony with ocean view and the 8 sportsman's suites have a jacuzzi and kitchenette/bar in the sitting area. Condos with 1 or 2 bedrooms are set closer to the beach level, offering large living space. The resort has 4 pools, jacuzzi, kids' pool, lit tennis court, dive shop, new conference centre, restaurant, snack bar and the famous Monkey Bar (they know how to mix some mean drinks). A shuttle service to airports at Liberia, Tamarindo and San José is available for a fee. Friendly staff, great views, lovely grounds and proximity to the beach make this a good option. *Rates US$110–245.*

Mariner Inn (8 rooms) By the docks; ☎ 654 4081; f 654 4024; e marinerinn@racsa.co.cr. The only 'bargain' spot in town. The rooms are small and basic with AC, cable TV and nice dark wood while the suites have microwave, refrigerator and a balcony. There is a small pool and the famous Spreader Bar, where the salty-dog crowd hangs out. *Rates US$34–69.*

WHERE TO EAT

Marie's Restaurant On the curve around the corner from Mariner Inn; ☎ 654 4136. Marie's is famous for its seafood, shish kebab, rotisserie chicken and delicious banana chocolate bread pudding. The open-air restaurant is brightly painted with scenes of underwater life and the food is generous and delicious. Highly recommended. *Main course US$10–15. Open daily 06.30–21.30.*

Hillside Bistro On the hill above Maries; ☎ 654 4226. This place was in transition at the time of writing and was moving towards offering only homemade (and delicious) ice cream.

Restaurant Pleamar At the bridge; ☎ 654 4521. This place opened in 2005 and the seafood has received good reviews. *Meals average US$17. Open 08.00–21.30; closed Mon.*

WHAT TO SEE AND DO

Shopping Que Pasa Gifts & Art (☎ *654 5159*), on the steep hill, has two floors of gifts and souvenirs. **Bobatik** (☎ *654 4839*) also on the steep hill, offers décor and clothing from the Far East, Bali and India.

PLAYA BRASILITO

Just 4km south of Playa Flamingo, Brasilito is a small, bustling beach town that is still very *Tico*. The beach is home to local fishers and the odd surfer. Laid back and low key, it has some interesting restaurants and the beach is usually fairly deserted.

GETTING THERE

By car If coming from Playa Flamingo, continue south on the dirt road 4km. If coming from Tamarindo, turn left at the intersection out of town and follow the signs for Flamingo.

WHERE TO STAY

🏠 **Hotel Guanacaste Lodge** (10 rooms) 200m south of Potrero/Flamingo crossroads; ☎ 654 4494; e portolsa@racsa.co.cr. Basic rooms with AC, TV and pool. *Rate US$50.*

🏠 **Hotel Brasilito** (17 rooms) Beachside; ☎ 654 4237; f 654 4247; www.brasilito.com. This is a tidy little spot that's been well run for 12 years by its German owners. Rooms are simple with fans, cold water and private bathrooms. There is a lovely little garden and restaurant. Great deal for bright, cheery and safe accommodation on the beach. *Rate US$30 (taxes inc).*

🏠 **Cabinas Ojos Azules** (13 rooms) On the main road heading south; ☎ 654 4346; f 654 4802. Clean, simple rooms with cold water, shared kitchen and some rooms have AC. *Rates US$20–35.*

WHERE TO EAT

✗ **Restaurante Les Arcades** Just before Brasilito; ☎ 654 4385. This is an elegant bistro set in a garden patio in the middle of nowhere. The food, however, with a Belgian-French flavour, is worth the drive. Stylish and delicious. *Main dishes US$13. Open 07.00–22.00.*

✗ **Camaron Dorado** Beachside, at the end of the main road in town; ☎ 654 4028. Simple and unassuming with plastic tables and chairs set up on the beach, the food is good and plentiful. Seafood is the thing here as is presentation – a huge sundae dish with coloured ice water is brought out to freshen your hands with and all the ladies are presented with a bright hibiscus to wear in their hair. Popular with tourists, the small restaurant has a free shuttle service to nearby hotels. *Main dishes US$10. Open 11.00–22.00.*

✗ **The Happy Snapper** Beachside; ☎ 654 4413. This place has been a happenin' spot in the area for years, with its fun-loving atmosphere, live music and dancing (and good seafood). *Main courses US$10. Open 11.00–22.00.*

✗ **Restaurant/Pizzeria Il Forno** On the main road heading south; ☎ 654 4125. Satisfies cravings for pizza, pasta and *calzone*. *Meals US$9. Open 12.00–21.30.*

PLAYA CONCHAL

Right next to Brasilito is Playa Conchal. Conchal means shell in Spanish and this beach is made up of bits and pieces of shells, washed smooth. Huge seashells covered the beach, now but a memory after years of souvenir hunters combing the shores. The white sands make this one of the prettiest beaches in Costa Rica, but it's not the easiest to get to, unless you're a guest at the resort. Otherwise, travel down the beach from Brasilito at low tide, as once the tide comes in, passage is virtually impossible.

WHERE TO STAY

Paradisus Playa Conchal (302 rooms) On the beach; ☎ 654 4123; f 654 4181; www.paradisusplayaconchal.com. The resort is the only thing on the beach and is the priciest all-inc resort in the country. Each room is a suite, featuring a small sitting and dining area with a minibar, bedroom area (open) and large bathroom as well as a balcony. Suites are arranged with 8 units per building on 2 storeys. Some have views overlooking the small lakes or golf course but only a handful of units actually have an ocean view and these are reserved for the Royal Service suite (for an extra US$50 pp, per day you receive a private check-in area, a butler, private pool area, unlimited top-shelf alcohol in the minibar, special trolley carts just for Royal Service members, first options at dinner reservations as well as a pillow menu). There are also Bali suites, which have been decorated with furniture from Indonesia and 2 presidential suites with 2 bedrooms. The resort has 7 restaurants, both buffet and sit down, with the Italian restaurant being the overall favourite from guests' comments. There is 24hr room service and everything is included, even the minibar (at last a minibar you're not afraid to raid). Personally, I've found the food a bit inconsistent (such as a tuna steak requested rare that arrived charred), drinks watered down and service, while friendly, ineffective – being part of the huge Sol Melia chain from Spain, the resort is weighed down by layer upon layer of bureaucracy leaving employees without the ability to make any decisions. For amenities, the resort has the largest free-form pool in Central America, a small disco, an even smaller casino, a large conference centre, spa, numerous shops and an internet café. For a small fee, you can try out the mini-canopy tour that zips you across the pool. The Garre de Leon golf course is a stunning 18-hole course designed by Trent Jones III and is open to non-guests. Live song and dance shows are featured every evening at the open-air theatre – while the quality of the performances is the best amongst the country's resorts, it's a long way from cruise ship shows. If you want an all-inc holiday in a better-quality resort, this would be it. But if you want to get even the smallest taste of the country, culture and people you are visiting, get off the resort and head into one of the local towns, as the resort is a resort and won't give you any true local flavour. *Rates US$329–499 pp, all-inc.*

PLAYA REAL

If you want a beautiful beach virtually to yourself, this is worth the 8km trek from the Tamarindo/Conchal crossroads down really rough roads (don't try this without a 4x4 in the rainy season). There is nothing here (and I mean nothing) other than two large hotels – no other services, not even a *pulpería*. If you come to stay at either of these resorts and want to eat off site at any point, a rental car is highly recommended as taxis are not available.

WHERE TO STAY AND EAT

⌂ **Condor Lodge & Beach Resort** (22 rooms) The first hotel on the road; ☎ 653 8950; f 653 8844; www.condorlodge.com. A large resort set across from the beach, with the perfunctory accoutrements – pool, jacuzzi, AC, in-room fridge, small disco – but, other than the empty beach it's near, nothing outstanding. B/fast inc. *Rate US$90.*

⌂ **Hotel Bahia de Los Piratas** (8 rooms) 2km further up the road; ☎ 653 8951; f 653 8956; www.bahiadelospiratas.com. Set on a steep hill, this large resort project has Spanish colonial-style villas with 2 bedrooms, kitchenette and balcony as well as beach suite. The entire resort is a bit tired and could do with some sprucing up. Service is slow. There is 1 small restaurant/bar on site, Restaurante El Galeon, with uninspired fare (a wedding reception featured store-bought white bread toasted). Other than the beautiful secluded beach, there is no reason to stay here. Pool, AC, b/fast inc. *Rates US$87–115.*

PLAYA GRANDE

One of the most important nesting spots for leatherback turtles, Playa Grande is a protected area so buildings on the beach must adhere to strict guidelines designed to keep the turtles as unaffected by humans as possible. During the laying season (October–March), access is restricted to scientists and selected tour groups after sunset, so as to not disturb the turtles. Surfing is great here and hotels are generally aimed at either turtle watchers or surfers.

GETTING THERE Driving from San José, take the Inter-American Highway until you see signs for Puente de Amistad (approx 2 hours). Turn left at these signs (there is a huge petrol station on the left) and continue across the Puente de

Amistad (Friendship Bridge) and on until the road ends, turn right and follow signs for Santa Cruz and continue until you see the Belen exit on the left. Then follow the signs 36km from the Belen exit and then follow the signs down 15km of very rough roads from Playa Real.

WHERE TO STAY

🏠 **Hotel Las Tortugas** (11 rooms) Main road to the beach, next to the ranger station; ☎ 653 0423; ℱ 653 0458; ℯ surfer@racsa.co.cris. A lovely, eco-friendly hotel where guests feel instantly at home. The rooms are comfy, the suites are nicely appointed and the turtle-shaped pool with jacuzzi is a sweet homage to the magical creatures nesting nearby. AC, restaurant, bar, pool, tour desk. Rates US$80–125.

🏠 **Playa Grande Inn** (8 cabinas) South side of the beach, left at the first fork; ☎ 653 0719; ℱ 653 0672; www.playagrandeinn.com. A popular surfer hangout, with its sports bar, restaurant and surf shop. Wooden cabins are simply appointed, offering either fans or AC. Rates US$50–90.

🏠 **Hotel Parque de Agua** (4 rooms) Next to Playa Grande Inn; ☎ 653 0594. Basic rooms with AC and a pool. Rate US$45.

🏠 **Rip Jack Inn** (8 rooms) On the beach; ☎ 653 0480; ℱ 653 0575; www.ripjackinn.com. Formerly El Bucanero, new management has given this place an extreme makeover. Each room is uniquely decorated and has AC, private bath with hot water and orthopaedic mattress. Bar/restaurant upstairs with lovely view and excellent food and yoga classes are offered in the mornings. Rate US$75.

🏠 **Playa Grande Surf Camp** (5 cabins) 2km south of Playa Grande; ☎/ℱ 653 0469; www.playagrandesurfcamp.com. Another surfer spot, offering basic accommodations in thatched or elevated *cabanas* (cabins). Fans, AC in some rooms, shared bathrooms, b/fast inc. Rates US$15 pp (fans), US$25 pp (with AC).

🏠 **Kike's Place** (13 rooms) Main road; ☎/ℱ 653 0834. Kike's is pretty much as basic as you can get for accommodation but it's a friendly place and popular with surfers and students. The sundeck, pool and billiard tables are great spots to meet other travellers whiling away the hours. Shared bath, cold water, fans, pool, camping. Restaurant/bar features cheap and tasty *Tico* fare as well as pizza. For those on a budget, you can't go wrong here. Rates US$14 pp; apt US$35; camping US$2.

TAMARINDO*

A once sleepy surfing town, Tamarindo has become one of the major beach destinations in the country. Golden sandy beaches and a variety of beachside hotels offer something for surfers and non-surfers alike. Although there are great surf breaks up and down the beach for novices and pros, the beach in front of the main area of town is perfect for swimming. For those who want to learn how to surf, Tamarindo is the ideal spot and there are a number of excellent surf schools to choose from.

In addition to hotels to suit every budget, Tamarindo boasts some of the best restaurants in Costa Rica as well as many interesting boutiques. Area activities include sailing, snorkelling, sport fishing, estuary tours, horseriding, ATV tours and estuary tours.

Tamarindo is suffering from its own success, however, as it is currently experiencing an explosion of new projects which its archaic infrastructure is struggling to keep pace with. Electricity blackouts are an almost daily occurrence (although thankfully short) so don't rely on electric alarm clocks. Water has always been an issue during the dry season when rationing is *de rigueur* by all the town's inhabitants so please, no lingering showers. New strip malls and condos are sprouting up seemingly every week and the endless parade of dump trucks has turned the dirt roads into pot-hole paradise – in the rainy season, parts of the road are reduced to lake-sized puddles which make walking a tricky endeavour. All the construction and its ensuing dirt and puddles of standing water has created ripe conditions for dengue, so do slather on the bug spray if visiting during the rainy season (while there are no statistics on tourists contracting the disease, I know of a few locals infected during the last two rainy seasons).

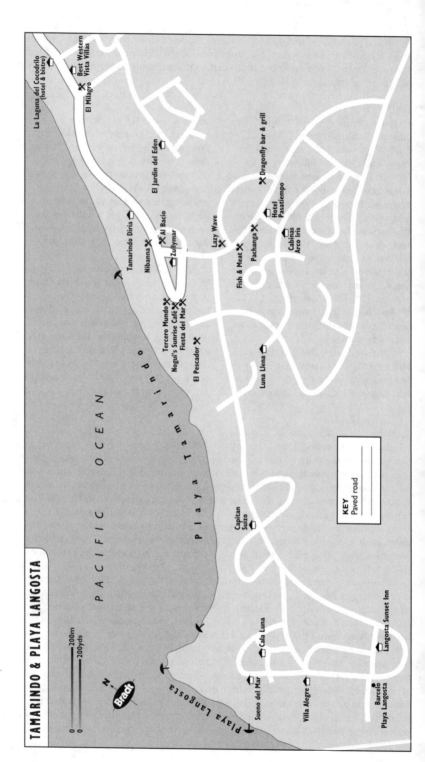

TAMARINDO & PLAYA LANGOSTA

PACIFIC OCEAN

La Laguna del Cocodrilo (hotel & bistro)

Best Western Vista Villas
El Milagro

El Jardin del Eden

Dragonfly bar & grill

Tamarindo Diria
Al Bacio
Nibanna
Zullymar

Hotel Pasatiempo

Lazy Wave
Fish & Meat
Pachanga
Cabinas Arco Iris

Tercero Mundo
Nogui's Sunrise Café
Fiesta del Mar

El Pescador

Luna Llena

P l a y a   T a m a r i n d o

Capitan Suizo

KEY
Paved road

Cala Luna

Langosta Sunset Inn

Sueno del Mar

Villa Alegre

Barceló Playa Langosta

P l a y a   L a n g o s t a

N
Bradt

0 — 200m
0 — 200yds

196

With the boom has also come an increase in theft. Don't leave anything in your vehicle and make sure to roll up your car windows tightly, as crafty thieves will open the door to pop open the petrol-tank cover and siphon out the petrol. The town council and the local businesses are being proactive, however, and one hopes the charm that enchanted so many to come to Tamarindo is not lost.

GETTING THERE AND AWAY

By air Both **Sansa** (↘ *221 9419*) and **NatureAir** (↘ *220 3054*) run daily flights from San José.

By car Driving from San José, take the Inter-American Highway until you see signs for Puente de Amistad (approx 2 hours). Turn left at these signs (there is a huge petrol station on the left) and continue across the Puente de Amistad (Friendship Bridge) and on until the road ends, turn right and follow signs for Santa Cruz and continue until you see the Belen exit on the left. Then follow the signs 36km from the Belen exit.

By bus Buses leave twice a day from Avenida 4, Calle 14 in San José: **Tracopa** (↘ *221 4214*); **Alfaro** (↘ *222 2666*) – takes six hours.

WHERE TO STAY

🏠 **Tamarindo Diria** (113 rooms) Beachside at the beginning of the bd; ↘ 653 0031; f 653 0208; e www.eldiria.com. The grande dame of Tamarindo, the Diria was the first luxury hotel in the area. Having undergone recent renovations, it retains its crown and has added the honour of being the largest non-all-inc hotel in the Tamarindo area as well as occupying the most cherished location in town — right on the beach and on the main street so everything from restaurants to stores is within walking distance. Rooms are large and simply but elegantly appointed. A few Hollywood stars have been spotted at the Diria, no doubt enjoying the ambience and helpful service. Premium and sunset categories have ocean views while the tropical rooms on the street side should be avoided by light sleepers as the noise from bars emptying and cars gunning late at night can be easily heard. There are 2 pools, large garden area, ocean-view bar and open-air restaurant. Food is pricey but good. A handful of stores and a pharmacy are located on the main level. Across the street is parking, more hotel rooms, privately owned condominiums, a large free-form pool with swim-up bar and an amphitheatre where the hotel hosts musical performances from time to time. Pool, AC, hot water, large buffet b/fast inc. *Rates US$144–189 (tax inc)*.
🏠 **Tamarindo Vista Villas** (33 rooms) On the hillside across from La Laguna de Crocodilo as you enter Tamarindo; ↘ 653 0114; f 653 0115; tamarindovisavillas.com. The sign outside proclaims Vista Villas as 'host of Wild On!', having played home

to the international party show on 2 occasions. The owner is an avid surfing buff and hosts the annual Robert August Surf and Turf competition — there are even surf lockers for guests' boards. Built into the side of a hill, the views of the ocean are incredible, although the climb up and down the stairs makes it difficult for anyone not in at least average physical shape. Standard rooms are very small. Villas and suites are a good size and offer small kitchens and living areas. Overall, rooms could use a décor update. The hotel's Monkey Bar has a swim-up bar, live music throughout the week and is *the* place to be for ladies night every Fri. The restaurant offers generous portions and food is fairly tasty, though a bit pricey. As the hotel is aiming for the party crowd and often has loud dance bands performing, not recommended for those with young families or seeking a quiet holiday. Pool, AC, hot water, hairdryers, safety box, b/fast inc. *Rates US$89–204*.
🏠 **El Jardin del Eden** (21 rooms) Up the hill, entrance from the main road before the bd starts; ↘ 653 0137 f 653 0111; e frontdesk@ jardindeleden.com. Charming, French-run hotel with wonderfully attentive staff. Spacious rooms all have a stunning view of the ocean, bright colours and handcrafted furniture. There are smaller rooms for solo travellers as well as 2 apts available for those needing more space. Large pool area is transformed into a veritable 'Garden of Eden' by vibrant flowers and plants, making it an idyllic spot for a lazy afternoon. A private path from the hilltop hotel to the street level is a nice touch that allows for easy

access to the beach and surrounds. Restaurant features excellent fare with a French flair (and Gallic-style prices). Surprisingly, the menu is one of the priciest in town, despite the hotel being one of the most reasonably priced. Pool, AC, hot water, hairdryer, cable, safety box, b/fast inc. *Rates US$85–135.*

⌂ **Luna Llena** (13 rooms) From the road to Langosta, left at road to Wayra School; ☎ 653 0082; f 653 0120; www.hotellunallena.com. Run by a congenial Italian couple, Pino and Simone, this small, laid-back hotel features colourful painted walls and various artistic touches throughout each room and bungalow. A recognised artist in her homeland, Simone has transformed the hotel's walls into a larger-than-life canvas for her whimsical figures and paint combinations. The 2-storey bungalows, situated around the pool, have a small kitchen which opens onto a bedroom with 1 queen bed with a TV and a loft with 2 dbl beds. The small hotel just behind the bungalows has spacious rooms as well as an internet café. B/fast is served at the poolside *rancho*. B/fast, AC, solar-powered hot water, TV, kitchenettes in bungalows. *Rate US$85.*

⌂ **Hotel Pasatiempo** (18 rooms) ☎ 653 0096; f 653 0275; www.hotelpasatiempo.com. An integral part of the Tamarindo 'scene', Hotel Pasatiempo has a laid-back, welcoming attitude, much like its American owners. Rooms face the large pool that is flanked by the restaurant and bar, home to 'Open Mike' nights, a local tradition where locals and tourists alike are encouraged to jam. Food is plentiful, tasty and reasonably priced. Rooms are clean and recently renovated. Good value for money. Note: the car park in front of the hotel is not secure so do not leave anything in your vehicle. Pool, AC, hot water, b/fast. *Rates US$80–99.*

⌂ **El Milagro** (32 rooms) Next to Vista Villas; ☎ 653 0042; f 653 0050; e flokiro@racsa.co.cr; www.elmilagro.com. Simply furnished bungalows set back from the road, El Milagro is walking distance to everything in town and a short jaunt to the beach. Nothing fancy here but it does have a medium-sized pool as you enter from the street. Also has a small restaurant (nothing miraculous about the food, though). Recent renovations have spruced the place up a bit, as it was getting a bit ragged. A good option for those seeking a moderately priced hotel easily accessed. Pool, AC, hot water, b/fast inc. *Rates US$72 sgl, US$77 dbl with fan; US$10 more per night for rooms with AC.*

⌂ **La Laguna de Cocodrilo** (10 rooms) Beachside as you enter Tamarindo; ☎ 653 0255; f 653 1029;

www.lalagunadelcocodrilo.com. Billed as the 'quietest hotel in Tamarindo', no-one could fault them for false advertising. French-owned, the hotel is a clean, 2-storied building with all rooms facing the small lagoon that plays home to a family of crocodiles. A wooden boardwalk allows access to the beach. Rooms are spacious with a number of artistic touches and private patios on the ground level. Only complaint is the bathroom's 'saloon' doors, as they are not only noisy when they swing back and forth upon opening but offer little privacy from bathroom activity – best suited for couples or very close friends who aren't shy. B/fast is not inc but there is a lovely French bakery on the premises, open early for croissants and coffee, as well as a small bar/bistro for dinner. AC, hot water. *Rate US$70.*

⌂ **Hotel Zullymar** (35 rooms) On the corner of the main road and the road to Langosta; ☎ 653 0140; f 653 0028. On the busiest corner of Tamarindo, Zullymar is a favourite with those on a budget. Two storeys overlooking the secured car park and the main road, its rooms are Spartan but do feature balconies. Walking distance to everything. *Rate US$64.*

⌂ **Cabinas Arco Iris** (5 cabinas) Near Pasatiempo; ☎/f 653 0330. Funky and artistic cabins have fans, private baths and shared kitchen. Daily yoga, meditation and exercise classes are held here and it's a great spot to get a massage as it's the 'holistic' health spot in town. *Rate US$46.*

⌂ **Kandices Place** (4 rooms) Next to the Hotel Kalifornia; ☎ 653 0869; e sulexchange@racsa.co.cr. Run by long-time resident, Kandice Sul, these multi-hued rooms are a funky place to chill out and just steps away from Tamarindo's hotspots. Some with private baths and communal kitchen. *Rates US$20–50.*

⌂ **La Botella de Leche** (11 rooms) Next to the mini-mall and Hotel Pasatiempo; ☎ 653 0189; www.labotelladeleche.com. One of the most creatively named hostels around, it's one of the hotspots amongst the young and penniless. Choice of large dorm rooms or private rooms, all have AC, there are lockers and a big-screen TV. Guests can cook in the communal kitchen and help themselves to complimentary coffee, tea and bicycles for riding around town. Clean and comfortable, it's a fun spot. *Rates US$10–12 pp.*

⌂ **Tsunami Backpackers** On the main road coming into town; ☎ 653 0956. A popular surfer hangout with a choice of dorm or Spartan private rooms. Guests can use the communal kitchen, watch TV and use the hostel's bicycles. *Rates: rooms US$9–23; camping US$5.*

WHERE TO EAT

✗ **La Laguna del Cocodrilo Bistro** Hotel Cocodrilo; ☎ 653 0469. A new addition to the fusion cuisine world in Tamarindo, the dinner-only bistro offers up interesting dishes with a decidedly French flavour. Dining under sprawling palm trees festooned with white twinkle lights while enjoying a martini makes everything all right with the world. Credit cards accepted. *Meals average US$15. Open 18.00–22.00.*

✗ **Mama's Deli** On the main street in El Peubolo Centro Comercial; ☎ 653 0178. A taste of Italy on the beach, this small deli/restaurant presents a delicious array of *pannini* sandwiches, fresh pasta dishes, soups and homemade pizza for take-away. Or just linger over an espresso on the small patio. *Main courses US$5–10. Open Mon–Sat 11.30–23.30.*

✗ **Nibanna** On the main road in town, beachside, across from SuperTamarindo supermarket; ☎ 653 0447. Lovely location on the beach, with palm trees waving overhead as Moroccan lanterns cast intricate shadows across the sand. Unfortunately, the food doesn't match the atmosphere while the prices are somewhere flying about with the bright stars winking down at diners. Service is extremely slow, portions are incredibly small. Steamed fish fillet with vegetables in parchment paper sounded enticing on the page but the meal on the plate was the size of a goldfish with some slivers of soggy onions — definitely not worth US$19. Szechuan mussels were very tasty but arrived lukewarm with soggy, cold French fries on the side while the trio of *ceviche* was disappointing and largely inedible. Discussions with the locals confirmed our findings — this is a tourist trap. There are a number of excellent (and more reasonably priced) restaurants within walking distance to choose from and this one should be given a miss. *Meals average US$25. Open daily 09.00–22.00.*

✗ **Fiesta del Mar** On the main street, left side of the traffic circle; ☎ 653 0914. Don't let the humble appearance of Fiesta del Mar fool you — the *Tico* fare and seafood are generous, delicious and affordable. Proudly *Guanasteco*, a number of menu items are cooked in the traditional wood-burning oven. The seafood soup is truly divine and the full fish dinner for US$5 is a bargain. The only late-night option in town, it's the perfect spot to beat the munchies. A visit to this Tamarindo institution is a must. Credit cards accepted. *Meals average US$6. Open 24hrs.*

✗ **Nogui's Sunrise Café** At the end of the traffic circle, on the beach; ☎ 653 0029. Excellent food at a beachside patio with legendary shrimp *tacos* and affordable prices — heaven! Try the fresh-fruit slices on banana bread spread with cinnamon cream cheese for a filling b/fast alternative. Upstairs is the Sunset Café, featuring fairly sophisticated nibbles (open only after 17.00 Fri–Sun). Credit cards accepted. *Meals average US$8. Open Thu–Tue 06.00–21.30.*

✗ **Tercero Mundo/Zullymar** At the traffic circle, on the beach; ☎ 653 0023. Popular spot for enjoying a cold beer while beach watching but the food is overpriced for the fare offered, eg: a plate of fries is US$4. *Open daily 06.00–22.00.*

✗ **El Pescador** On the beach, 100m south of the circle; ☎ 653 0109. It doesn't get any fresher than this — the fish are practically jumping off the plates. Simple, *Tico* fare in a simple open-air setting at simple prices. A whole fish dinner will set you back less than US$4. *Open daily 06.00–22.00.*

✗ **Lazy Wave** In the small strip shopping mall at the crossroads; ☎ 653 0737; www.lazywave.com. Lazy Wave has garnered numerous accolades over the years and was one of the best restaurants in Costa Rica — sadly, a recent change in ownership has not been able to retain the level of excellence this eatery was so known for. Portions are very generous and the wine list is impressive but the kitchen's success has been largely hit-and-miss, to the disappointment of all (especially the locals). Reservations are not accepted. Cash payment only. *Meals average US$20. Open Tue–Sun 18.00–22.00; closed Mon.*

✗ **Fish & Meat Sushi Bar & Grill** Uphill from the crossroads, on the right across from Hotel Pasatiempo. If you're needing a sushi fix, Fish & Meat is a good option. The menu isn't huge but offers up a pleasing assortment of Japanese fare in a relaxing atmosphere. *Meals average US$16. Open for dinner only 17.00–22.00.*

✗ **Restaurant Pachanga** Uphill from the crossroads, on the right across from Hotel Pasatiempo; ☎ 653 7983. One of the true culinary gems in the country, Pachanga's menu is a unique blending of local ingredients with a Mediterranean twist, reflecting the chef's training at the cordon bleu cooking school and his globetrotting experiences. Fish and seafood take centre stage but the barbecue ribs are the star performers, with the slow-braised meat falling from the bones like butter. The wine list is a small but carefully chosen mixture of Italian labels. Cash payment only. *Meals average US$20. Open 17.00–22.00; closed Sun.*

✘ **Dragonfly Bar & Grill** On the dirt road between the hostel and Pasatiempo; ☎ 653 1508; www.dragonflybarandgrill.com. Beautiful wooden, open-aired *rancho* with funky white lamps serves up some of the most incredible food you're likely to ever put into your mouth. With emphasis on fresh and local ingredients, offerings are creative and delicious (the chilli-rubbed pork with chipotle mashed potatoes is dreamy and the chocolate brownie is a must-eat!). *Meals average US$15. Open 17.00–22.00; closed Sun.*

PRACTICALITIES

Banks Banco Nacional is in Plaza Colonial, while Banco San José is in the strip mall on the road heading towards Pasatiempo.

Information To keep up to date with what's going on, check out www.tamarindobeach.net. Once in town, look for the cheeky free magazine *Flyswatter* for a biting and irreverent slice of life in 'Tama'. *The Howler* is the monthly free magazine loaded with info on local events.

WHAT TO SEE AND DO

Surf Tamarindo boasts some of the best surf spots in the area, as the numerous surf shops and schools attest to the popularity of the sport. The best waves are found in Langosta, Avellanas, Negra and further north at the legendary Ollie's Point and Witch's Rock, which are only for 'big dogs', and can be accessed via boat (as they are located in a national park, there is a regulated number of surfers allowed each day and operators must be licensed). In town, there is a decent break just past Tamarindo Vista Villas, perfect for beginner surfers.

If you want to learn to surf, take a lesson, as it's not an easy sport and one lesson with a good teacher will have you hanging ten in no time. One of the best schools is **Tamarindo Surf School** (☎ 653 0923; *www.tamarindosurfschool.com*) located beachside right before the circle. Class sizes are small and they guarantee you will accomplish your immediate goal in your class or the next lesson is free. Group lessons cost US$30. Other surf schools include **Chicasurf** (☎ 653 1045; *www.chicasurf.com*), the only all-female surf school in town. Anyone who saw the *Endless Summer* films will want to check out the star's self-named school and shop, the **Robert August Surf Shop** (☎ 653 0114) at the Vista Villas Hotel. Every year, this legend of the waves hosts a surf/golf competition at the hotel, raising funds for local projects (contact the shop for more information). As you enter town on the beachside, you'll find **Witch's Rock Surf Camp** (12 rooms) (☎ 653 1262; *www.witchsrocksurfcamp.com*).

Turtle watching From October to March, massive leatherback turtles make the arduous journey to lay their eggs on the beach at **Las Baulas National Marine Park** (☎ 653 0470) in Playa Grande. A limited number of tourists are allowed to watch the night-time spectacle, accompanied by trained guides and scientists (reservations can be made through hotels). As it is mother nature and the turtles are endangered, not every tour is guaranteed to find a turtle nesting so patience is required – if you are lucky, it is a once-in-a-lifetime experience. If you're in the area, it's worth the three or so hours and the cost of US$25.

Diving Not the best spot in the country for diving but there are a lot of fish in these waters. **Agua Rica Diving Centre** (☎ 653 0094; *www.aguarica.net*) is the largest and longest-running dive centre in the area.

Sport fishing Great inshore and offshore fishing, although the Papagayo winds in January usually cause the fish to move further south down the coast. Sailfish are pretty much guaranteed year round, however. **Tamarindo Sportfishing** (☎ 653 0090; *www.tamarindosportfishing.com*) is one of the most professional operations around and always has happy clients.

Sailing What better way to enjoy a spectacular Pacific sunset than from the deck of a boat? **Mandingo Sailing** (☎ 653 0623) offers sunset cruises aboard a replica of a 19th-century New England schooner while **Blue Dolphin Sailing**'s (☎ 653 0867) catamaran is perfect for a sunset cruise.

Golf A relatively new sport to Costa Rica, the best courses in the country are found around Tamarindo. Just up the road is **Hacienda Pinilla** (☎ 680 7000), an 18-hole, par-72 course with wide fairways. The **Paradisus Playa Conchal** (☎ 654 4123) is a challenging par-72, 18-hole championship course designed by Trent Jones III.

PLAYA LANGOSTA

Just south of Tamarindo is Playa Langosta, although it's often considered part of the larger town on account of its proximity. There are three large hotels here, a few charming bed and breakfasts, a couple of small restaurants and large, private beach homes (mansions might be a better word). The numerous rocks just off the beach make swimming treacherous, although there are some lovely tidal pools at low tide. Surfing offers strong left and right waves which tend to close quickly. There are far fewer people on these beaches than in Tamarindo, so those seeking more privacy will find it here.

GETTING THERE Walking or driving, just continue on the dirt road at the first right after turning off Tamarindo's main street. There is also a bus stop at the corner of the main street at the intersection by Hotel Zullymar.

WHERE TO STAY

Cala Luna (41 rooms) On the road to Langosta; ☎ 653 0214; f 653 0213; www.calaluna.com. One of the most elegant (in a minimal way) beach hotels in the country, Cala Luna is one of my favourite spots and the villas are quite spectacular. The 2-bedroom villas (maximum 4 guests) are super, offering up 150m² of living space while 3-bedroom villas (maximum 6 guests) are up to 200m². Each villa has a fully serviceable kitchen (including a cappuccino machine), large living/dining area, equal number of bathrooms for bedrooms, private parking, CD player, patio and private pool. The 20 deluxe rooms feature massive bathrooms with tubs but very small patios. If travelling with a small family or group, you're better off to go the villa route, as the pricing for a 2-bedroom villa is equal to 2 deluxe rooms while a 3-bedroom villa is a virtual bargain when compared with the pricing of 3 deluxe rooms. The restaurant and bar bookend the large, free-form pool, which is the hotel's focal point. Although the hotel grounds are not on the beach, it's only a short walk down a set of stairs to the water's edge. Pool, AC, hot water, safety boxes, internet, b/fast inc (only with deluxe rooms). Rates US$167–418.

Sueño del Mar (6 rooms) On the beach in front of Cala Luna; ☎/f 653 0284; www.sueno-del-mar.com. Stepping through the whitewashed wall, one is enveloped in a magical place, where an artist's imagination has created whimsical flashes of fancy throughout. Tiny but impeccably designed, the space feels cosy but never cloistered. Welcoming you to the property, there are 2 small *casitas* (one named after Osita, the shaggy pooch of the house) on either side. Each features a loft and small kitchen, although the steep ladder-like stairs of Casita Misha should be avoided by those with vertigo or bad knees. Down the corridor are 3 more rooms, each with 1 queen bed. Upstairs is the spacious and romantic honeymoon suite with one of the best beach views to be found. All bathrooms feature a Bali-style shower where there is no roof but the sky above – private but incredibly exhilarating. Handicrafts from Guatemala, Nicaragua and Bali are scattered throughout and the imported mattresses guarantee the most comfortable night's sleep ever. Huge gourmet b/fasts are served on the patio overlooking the small plunge pool and the hammocks peppering the property provide a perfect spot for a post-meal nap. Innkeepers Nancy and Paul are extremely hospitable and helpful. AC, hot water, use of boogie boards, snorkelling equipment and mountain bikes. B/fast inc. No children under 12 years. *Rates US$170–235.*

Villa Alegre (7 rooms) On the beach, on the corner across from Cala Luna; ☎ 653 0270; f 652 0287; e vialegre@racssa.co.cr; www.villaalegrecostarica.com. Occupying a large property bordered by the beach and a nature reserve, Villa Alegre offers a quiet respite. Globetrotting owners Barry and Suzye Lawson have named and decorated each room and villa after a country they've travelled to, creating a miniature United Nations under one roof. The main house is bright and airy, with guest rooms off the large living/dining room area. All rooms have private bathrooms and most can be configured for either 1 king bed or 2 sgls. The Japan and Russia villas are just steps from the main house and feature a private bedroom, bathroom, patio, living/dining area with a futon and kitchenette. A tasty, homemade b/fast is served on the large patio overlooking the infinity pool and palm-thatched *rancho*. There are a number of board games available to while away the hours (be sure to challenge Barry to a game of Scrabble) and even a shuffleboard area. The Lawsons are one of the town's 'power couples', involved in a myriad area projects, and are an excellent resource to find out what's going on in Tamarindo. AC, hot water. B/fast inc. Wheelchair accessible (Mexico room). *Rates US$145–195.*

Capitan Suizo (30 rooms) Beachside, on the road to Langosta; ☎ 653 0075; f 653 0292; www.hotelcapitansuizo.com. A member of the 'Small Distinctive Hotels of Costa Rica', Capitan Suizo has earned a reputation for excellence and rightly so. Its beachfront location is prime, the service friendly and the rooms large and well appointed. Standard rooms are on 2 levels, with AC on the ground floor while those on the second storey rely on ceiling fans and the ocean breezes to keep occupants cool and comfortable, as do the bungalows. There is an apt available for up to 8 guests. Everything has an understated elegance, which complements its stunning oceanfront location perfectly. The huge free-form pool has a rope swing for 'Tarzan' pool entrances, which is as

energetic as it gets here. The restaurant is comfortable with excellent food and extremely reasonable prices for a hotel of this quality. The original owner of the hotel (who has sadly passed on) was Swiss and the menu bears many influences of his native land but the food has been modified for the tropical climate. Word has spread about this small hotel and subsequently, rooms are hard to come by unless booked well in advance. Pool, AC in some rooms, hot water, b/fast inc (except with the apt). *Rates US$140–440.*

Barcelo Playa Langosta (135 rooms) End of the Langosta road, on the beach; ☎ 653 0363; f 653 0415; www.barcelo.com. The only all-inc property in the Tamarindo/Langosta area, the Barcelo Playa Langosta is a 3-star offering from the Spanish hotelier, Barcelo. Set on a lovely stretch of golden beach, the hotel itself, unfortunately, doesn't live up to its spectacular location. The rooms are pleasant and spacious but unimaginative. Housed in 2-storey buildings with 4 units each, the rooms feature 2 queen beds, TV, large bathroom with a tub and a garden patio or balcony, depending on which floor the room is on. I've heard numerous complaints about the food coming out of the resort's 2 à la carte restaurants, driving some guests to seek culinary refuge in the many excellent restaurants in Tamarindo. Offerings from the all-inc bar are limited to draught beer and 'house' liquors (cheap, vile stuff) so prepare to pay extra for name-brand liquors. Other features are a large pool, children's pool, disco, casino, child's park, convention room (max 60 people), pool bar, cafeteria, boogie boards, kayaks, beach volleyball and a variety of daily activities (such as dance lessons, aerobics). Poolside theatre features nightly lip-synched song and dance but don't expect West End-performance quality, as the aerobics instructors/social directors double-duty it as hoofers and don't know a plie from a triple time-step. Pool, AC, hot water, all food and house liquor inc. *Rates US$137 pp, all food and drink inc.*

Langosta Sunset Inn Just up the road from Barcelo, next to Maria Bonita Restaurant; ☎ 653 1045; e langostasunset/inn@hotmail.com. A recent addition to the growing beach community, Langosta Sunset Inn offers clean, fresh rooms, a lounge, pool, view of the ocean and a communal kitchen. A good bet for those on a mid-range budget. *Rate US$70.*

✖ WHERE TO EAT

Restaurante Maria Bonita Next to Langosta Sunset Inn and Supermarket Langosta; ☎ 653 0933. The fresh-food menu features Latin and Caribbean dishes

offered up in an appealing atmosphere. *Meals average US$12. Open 19.00–21.00, closed Sun.*

GETTING THERE

By car If driving from Santa Cruz, take the first left after the bridge and follow the rough dirt road for 20km and watch for the signs. If driving from Tamarindo, turn right at the T-intersection out of town and follow the dirt road.

WHERE TO STAY

🏠 **Hacienda Pinilla** 10km south of Tamarindo; ☎ 680 7060; f 680 7063; www.haciendapinilla.com. A new resort set on 4,500 acres of beachfront property, formerly a working cattle ranch for over 100 years. In addition to its impressive golf course is the Casa de Golf luxury villas. *Rate US$250.*

🏠 **Posada del Sol Hotel** (22 rooms) Formerly the houses of the architects and builders of Hacienda Pinilla, they have been converted to nice suites, with sitting room, TV, AC, fridge, private baths with hot water and phones. Some have wheelchair access. There is a lovely pool and a restaurant. *Rates US$100–145 per night.*

Three rental houses on the beach echo Costa Rican architecture of the 1900s and offer an excellent alternative for group lodgings. They are all part of Hacienda Pinilla.

🏠 **Casona Matapalo** This establishment can accommodate up to 20 people in its 4 bedrooms and 3 bathrooms. *Rate US$450.*

🏠 **Estancia El Ensueno** Features 3 bedrooms/private bathrooms. *Rate US$400.*

🏠 **Faro Lindo** Has 2 bedrooms/bathrooms and a sofa bed in the living room.. All rooms/houses feature hot water, AC, satellite TV, safe box and balconies. There is a restaurant as well as a stable on the property. *Rate US$300.*

PLAYA AVELLANAS

Down a very rough road, you'll find this idyllic surfers' paradise with stretches of white sand and nothing else. Beachside is **Lola's on the Beach** (☎ *658 8097; e lola@playaavellana.com; open daily 06.00–15.00 with special dinner menus Fri and Sat nights*), a funky open-air restaurant famous for its wood-oven pizzas, having won rave reviews in such magazines as *W* and *Gourmet Magazine*. Grab a fruit smoothie and say hello to Lola, the 700lb pig and restaurant's namesake. Sitting under a towering palm tree in a handcrafted wooden chair while watching the surf crash against an impossibly white-sand beach and munching on a gourmet thin-crust pizza is nirvana. Definitely worth the drive. Cash payment only. Meals average US$15.

GETTING THERE

By car From the dirt road to Hacienda Pinilla, continue past San José de Pinilla for 3km.

WHERE TO STAY AND EAT

Cabinas Las Olas (10 cabinas) ☎ 658 8315; e olassa@racsa.co.cr. This is one of the few places to overnight and its large glass and stone bungalows are good value. Nothing fancy but there is a restaurant and bar to quell those post-surfing munchies. *Rate US$65.*

Cabinas Rancho Iguana Verde (5 rooms) ☎ 653 8310. This place also offers up basic rooms with cold water, TV and a dining room. *Rate US$10 pp.*

Surf Camp Eureka Has simple cabins on the beach with cold water. *Rate US$6 pp; camping US$3.*

Cabinas & Bar/Restaurant Gregorio's (3 rooms) ☎ 658 8319. South of Avellanas and passable only in the dry season, and featuring simple, clean rooms with cold water and fans. *Rate US$6 pp.*

PLAYA NEGRA

Another surfer hotspot, this black-sand beach is accessible via the beach road (sometimes) or the 6km dirt road from Paraiso (best bet). Lodgings (all along the main road) are generally basic and geared towards the surfing crowd.

WHERE TO STAY AND EAT

Hotel Playa Negra (10 rooms) 658 8034; f 658 8035; www.playanegra.com. Answers the dream of staying in a funky, thatched-roof hut on the beach. Each of the brightly coloured villas is completely round and has a queen bed, 2 sgl beds and bathroom with hot water. The high roof and many windows create a cross-breeze, so nothing more than the ceiling-mounted fan is required to keep things comfy. The large pool is perfect for whiling away the hours while the adjacent kiddie pool keeps the little tykes at bay. Hot water, fan, safe, restaurant, bar, 2 pools. *Rate US$66.*

B&B Mono Congo Lodge (5 rooms) 658 8261; f 658 8260; www.monocongolodge.com. A Swiss Family Robinson-style tree house in an 8-acre wooded glade, with touches of Balinese décor and luxurious Indian cotton sheets on the comfy orthopaedic mattresses. There is a master suite, junior suite and 3 rooms (with shared bathrooms). Delicious b/fasts are inc with all rooms. AC, hot water, TV with a pool. *Rates US$65–85.*

Pasta Mike's Cabinas (3 cabinas) 658 8270; e pastamikes@yahoo.com. Cabins with cold water, shared bathrooms, fan, some with AC and vegetarian dinners. *Rates US$25–40.*

Diwo's Place (5 rooms) 658 8140; e leforaneo@hotmail.com. Offers basic rooms with cold water. *Rate US$15.*

Piko Negro At the crossroads; 658 8369. For pizza. Cash payment only. *Closed Tue.*

PLAYA JUNQUILLAL

Located 3km south of Paraiso, Playa Junquillal is a beautiful beach that has been discovered by the surfing set but not yet by the general public. Lodging here is simple for the most part but there are some interesting spots, owned and run by Swiss, Germans and Canadians. It's a spot where you can be walking and have the entire beach to yourself. Heaven! Owing to its small size, getting lost is impossible and everything is located either on the beach or the one main road.

WHERE TO STAY AND EAT

Hotel Land Ho! at Villa Serena (10 rooms) 658 8430; f 658 8091; www.land-ho.com/villa. On the beach. This hotel is a lovely spot with an unusual name. Congenial owners, O J and John Murphy, decided to escape the bracing winters of their native Cape Cod (where they own the Land Ho! restaurant) and opened this charming villa on the beach. The rooms are large, with high ceilings and a relaxed elegance. The food is excellent and the view from the balcony overlooking the ocean is picture perfect. There is a lovely spa as well as a small art gallery, a large pool surrounded by shady trees and beckoning hammocks as well as a tennis court. For the romantics, there is a honeymoon suite tower room. Fans, AC. *Rate US$80.*

Hotel Iguanazul (24 rooms) 658 8123; f 658 8124; www.iguanazul.com. North end of beach. The hilltop setting is dramatic, with the pristine beach and excellent surfing spots just steps below. The large pool makes it a perfect place for families while the open-air restaurant is a favoured spot for sunset watching amongst locals and tourists alike. Hot water, AC, b/fast inc. *Rates US$60–80.*

La Guacamaya Lodge (6 bungalows, 1 villa) 658 8431; f 658 8164; www.guacamayalodge.com. On main road to beach. This place is neat as a pin, and is a warm oasis on the beach, with 6 bungalows and 1 2-bedroom villa surrounding a large pool. The on-site restaurant serves up a variety of flavours with a Swiss twist. An excellent option. Hot water, AC, some wheelchair access; the villa's main features are a living room and full kitchen. *Rates US$55–120.*

Hotel Hibiscus (4 rooms) /f 658 8437. On the main road and a short walk to the beach. Rooms are simple but clean with a fan. A lovely garden surrounds the grounds and there is a decent seafood restaurant on site. *Rate US$40.*

Hotel El Castillo Divertido (6 rooms) /f 658 8428; e castillodivertido@hotmail.com. On main road to beach. An unusual spot which literally means

'Fun Castle' and that's exactly what it is — a small castle in a Costa Rican beach town. Rooms have a fan and there is a rooftop star deck as well as a German restaurant. *Rates US$32–39.*

⌂ **Los Malinches Camping** ↘ 658 8429. Only 1km off the main road and offers shaded spots. *Rate US$3 pp.*

✕ **Restaurant Lak Ampu** ↘ 658 8339. Ampu means heaven in Inca and this is an appropriately named eatery. Serves up Peruvian food in a relaxed setting overlooking the ocean. *Meals average US$8. Opening depends on tide. Closes around 23.00 (approximately).*

WHAT TO SEE AND DO While surfing is the big draw to the beach, the tranquillity is perfect for those seeking to be far from the madding crowds. Horseriding can be arranged through **Casa QuErica Riding** (↘ *658 8162; www.paradiseriding.com*).

Arenal Volcano

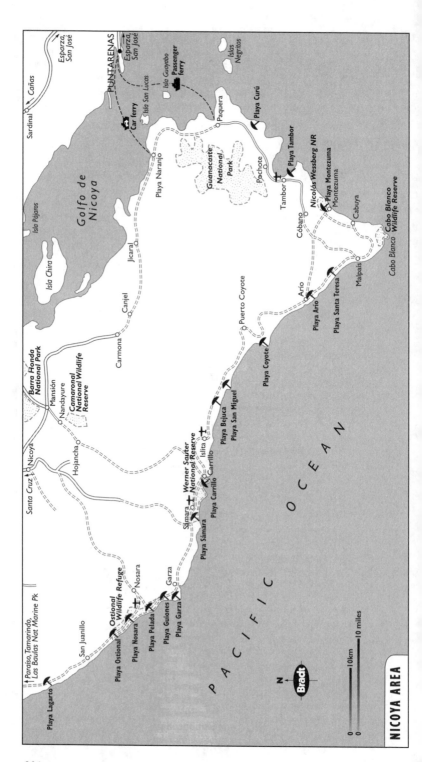

NICOYA AREA

11

Nicoya Peninsula

Although these areas are all part of the same land mass, the lack of a unifying roadway typically has the west shore (south of Playa Avellanas) considered a separate area from the east shore, accessible from the Puntarenas ferry. Attempting the journey between Samara (west) and Santa Teresa (south tip) is not advisable on account of extremely poor roads and necessary river crossings.

Regardless of the hazardous road conditions, this is an area to be explored as development has been slow to make its presence known in these parts. Long stretches of white-sand beaches fringed by lush green palms burnished by blazing sunsets are like postcards come to life. Generally, hotels are smaller and simpler than in other areas of the country (with a few noteworthy exceptions) and food is pricey, because of the area's remoteness. Flying is the recommended method of transport but if you are going to drive, splurge on renting a full-size 4x4 (and fill up an extra jerry can as petrol stations are limited) – when you see an unfortunate Terios stuck in mud up to its axles, you'll be thanking yourself for spending the extra cash on your Pathfinder or ForeRunner.

WEST SHORE

It's a given that most roads in Costa Rica are bad, but the roads in this area are exceptionally bad and thus, development has not sullied the pristine beaches dotting the coast. If you want a quiet spot, this is probably a good bet but be ready for slow driving in a serious 4x4, especially if travelling during the green season. Despite the horrendous roads, the overwhelming beauty of green trees against lonely white beaches makes the arduous trek worthwhile.

GETTING THERE AND AWAY
By air Both **Sansa** (✆ 221 9414) and **NatureAir** (✆ 220 3054) fly daily from San José to Nosara.

By car The roads are quite rough in parts and the coastal road south of Junquillal is often flooded, especially during the green season. The road from Nicoya is now paved as far as Playa Carrillo but the drive to Nosara is bone rattling. A 4x4 vehicle with good clearance is a necessity.

Driving from San José, take the Inter-American Highway until you see signs for Puente de Amistad (approx 2 hours). Turn left at these signs (there is a huge petrol station on the left) and continue across the Puente de Amistad (Friendship Bridge) until you see the Nicoya intersection on the left.

From Nicoya, there are signs to direct you to Nosara and then on to Samara.

By bus Empresa **Alfaro-Tracopa** (✆ 222 2666) run buses from Avenida 3/5, Calle 14 in San José, to Nosara and twice a day to Samara.

Empresa Rojas (☎ *685 5352*) run buses from the main bus station in Nicoya three-times daily to Nosara, Garza and Guiones, and several more buses run to Samara and Carrillo.

OSTIONAL

A sleepy little beach, the main attractions here are the upwards of 120,000 Olive Ridley turtles that lumber ashore to nest from October to April. The best place for turtle watching is via an organised tour at the **Ostional Wildlife Refuge** (☎/f *680 0241; open 24 hours; entrance US$1*) which also offers trails and birdwatching at the park's estuary where 190 species have been identified.

⌂ WHERE TO STAY AND EAT

⌂ **The Sanctuary Resort & Spa** (32 rooms, 14 houses) Playa Azul; ☎ 682 8111; www.thesanctuaryresort.com. High-end resort in a remote area, guests can stay in rooms, cottages or even a luxury villa. All the amenities are inc – AC, hot water, microwave, satellite TV and fully equipped kitchens in all the cottages and villa. All rooms have ocean views and are mere steps from the white-sand beach. Facilities include an infinity pool with swim-up bar, full-service spa, 2 restaurants, diving centre and horseriding. While the resort is nicely appointed and in a picture-perfect setting, reports have been inconsistent. Food and drink is extremely expensive and the goods in the resort grocery store are overpriced. It seems staff have been instructed not to give information on outside activities or restaurants under fear of death, prompting complaints from a number of guests. It's the swankiest hotel in the vicinity and in order not to pay through the nose, savvy travellers are advised to have a rental vehicle and explore the nearby towns for affordable dining options. *Rates US$175–6,000.*

⌂ **Hotel Rancho Brovilla** (16 rooms) 3km from Ostional on a hilltop; ☎/f 280 4913; www.brovill.com. Simple rooms with gleaming hardwood walls, AC, private baths with hot water and a balcony. Small villas and apts, fully furnished, are also available. There is a pool, Turkish baths and a restaurant where Hungarian delights are the focus. B/fast inc. *Rates US$45–150.*

⌂ **B&B Tree Tops** (1 room) Just north of San Juanillo; ☎/f 682 8298; e jphunter@racsa.co.cr. Play Tarzan and Jane in this unique and romantic honeymoon suite – in a tree house. Beautiful view and the amiable owners offer candlelight dinners. No kids. B/fast inc. Recommended. *Rate US$75.*

⌂ **El Sueno de Juanillo** (10 rooms) In San Juanillo, 14km north of Nosara; ☎ 682 8074; www.sanjuanillo.com. A sleepy little fishing village with gorgeous beaches, San Juanillo is off the beaten path but these funky cabins are a bit of civilisation found. Simply decorated with touches from Bali, rooms offer fans and some have AC. There is a calming fountain in the courtyard and the restaurant offers up tasty vegetarian and seafood. There is also a 'Buddha Bar' with trance, reggae, world and house music. *Rate US$40 (taxes inc).*

⌂ **Cabinas Restaurant Casa Mango** (6 rooms) 3km south of Marbella; ☎ 682 8032; e donjim@racsa.co.cr. These new, simple rooms have shared bathrooms with cold-water showers, fans, a pool table to while away the hours and an organic garden for produce. *Rate US$25.*

⌂ **Cabinas Ostional** (6 rooms) In Ostional; ☎ 682 0428. Very basic rooms with cold water and fans. *Rate US$20.*

⌂ **Cabinas Guacamaya** (4 rooms) In Ostional; ☎ 682 0430. More very basic rooms with cold water and fans. *Rate US$16.*

NOSARA

Nosara is actually several beaches, most of which are deserted. The village of Nosara – which is nothing more than a football field, a *pulpería* and a petrol station – is set up in the hills while houses and hotels are tucked in around the surrounding hills and beaches. Upon arriving in town, you'd never guess that Hollywood's jet set regularly visit to decompress. The international community here have been intrinsic in keeping the area as natural as possible – over half of the Nosara district has been set aside as a nature reserve so this area is one of the greenest you'll find in

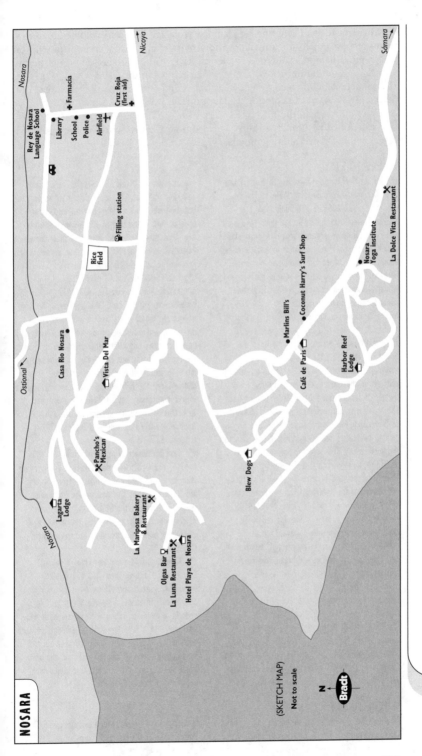

NOSARA

(SKETCH MAP)
Not to scale

the Guanacaste area. Hunting was banned years ago here and wildlife abounds – keep your eyes open for armadillos, howler monkeys and jaguarundi (a wild cat whose grey, diamond-patterned fur looks black from a distance). During the dry season, grey and humpback whales are often spotted in the waters.

A vehicle is highly recommended as hotels and restaurants are very spread out. Check out www.nosara.com for the latest on the area.

GETTING AROUND Nosara is fairly spead out so it's advisable to have your own vehicle or you'll need to rely on taxis.

WHERE TO STAY

Harbor Reef Lodge (15 rooms, 10 houses) Left at a fork in the road heading south in Playa Guiones; ↘ 682 0059; f 682 0060; www.harborreef.com. Surfing is the thing here, with surf racks for those precious boards. Accommodation includes a choice of rooms, suites or fully furnished houses. All have AC, private baths and hot water. Gorgeous pool with swim-up bar, lush gardens and upmarket restaurant, serving excellent steak and seafood, make this a higher-end surf hotel. The management runs a surf school, board rental shop, mini-mart and sport fishing. *Rates US$74–250.*

Hotel Playa de Nosara (16 rooms) On a hill in Nosara; ↘ 682 0121; f 682 0123; www.nosarabeachhotel.com. One of the more bizarre buildings in the country, this hotel seemingly holds the record for constantly being under construction. The architecture can best be described as 'Gaudi Goes to Disneyland', with round, white curves and brightly painted bubble-like towers. Surprisingly, the rooms are extremely simply decorated (boring almost). Views can't be beaten, however, from the 6-storey-high dome. There is a pool and b/fast is inc. *Rate US$70.*

Lagarta Lodge Biological Lodge (7 rooms) On a hill 2km from town; ↘ 682 0385; f 682 0135; www.lagarta.com. A large, white-stuccoed lodge amidst a 125-acre private reserve. Each of the comfortable rooms has a fan, private bathroom with hot water and a view of the ocean, river and gardens. There is a pool and international restaurant. Great spot for birdwatching – 270 species – and hiking down botanical trails. *Rate US$68; includes transport from Nosara to the lodge.*

Hotel Café de Paris (20 rooms) On the main road in Playa Guiones; ↘ 682 0087; f 682 0089; www.cafeparis.net. This popular French bakery has grown over the years to include a cute hotel and villas. White stucco and wood offer an almost Zen-

like atmosphere. All rooms and villas have private bath, hot water and AC. Super deluxe rooms and the bungalow also have a fully equipped kitchen, an open-air and palm-thatched *rancho* with hammocks. Two villas have the added advantage of ocean views. Amenities include a pool, internet and a pool table. Recommended. *Rates US$40–120.*

Hotel Vista del Mar (7 rooms) On a hill overlooking Playa Guiones; ↘ 682 0633; www.lodgevistadelmar.com. Look up, way up — from its vantage point, guests have a panoramic view of the ocean and mountains. Rooms in this 3-storey hotel are basic and offer either an ocean or jungle view, private baths with hot water and optional AC for US$5 extra (although the breezes make it unnecessary). The fully equipped penthouse (complete with 2 bathrooms) has an incredible panoramic view. Lower-level rooms are smaller. There is a communal kitchen as well as a lap pool. B/fast inc. *Rates US$39–180.*

Casa Rio Nosara (7 rooms) In town; ↘ 682 0117; f 682 0182; www.rionosara.com. Cute *rancho*-style hardwood cabins with thatched roofs. Rooms are clean and have fans and private hot-water showers. There is a shared kitchen and a giant *rancho* where BBQs are held on the weekends. A number of horses are available for riding. *Rate US$25.*

Blew Dogs Cabins and Surf Club (8 rooms) Entrance of Playa Giuones; ↘/f 682 0080; www.blewdogs.com. Focused on the surf crowd, accommodation ranges from the 'flop house' (4 sgl beds in a room) to cabins with private bath and kitchenette to a fully furnished 1-bedroom apt. Cute pool has a waterfall detail and the open-air restaurant/bar is the happening spot in the area (those seeking quiet accommodation should look elsewhere). *Rates US$10–80.*

WHERE TO EAT

Olga's Bar On the beach in Nosara (no phone). Olga's is legendary for its traditional *Tico* food and

incredible sunset views. *Meals average US$6. Open daily 06.30–22.00. No credit cards.*

✗ Pancho's Mexican Market & Taqueira On the road to Playa Pelada; ☎ 682 0591; e panchosnosara@racsa.co.cr. Serves up Mexican favourites as well as seafood and steak. *Average price per meal US$8. Open 12.00–20.00; closed Mon.*

✗ Marlins Bill's Restaurant ☎ 682 0249. Offers seafood and a variety of international dishes with a great view. *Meals average US$14. Open Mon–Sat 11.00–14.30, 18.00–21.00.*

✗ La Dolce Vita Restaurant and Pizzeria In Guiones, on the main road up the hill, south of town; ☎ 682 0107. Serves excellent and authentic Italian food. *Average price per meal US$15. Open 07.00–20.00.*

✗ Hotel Café de Paris On the main road in Playa Guiones; ☎ 682 0087; f 682 0089; www.cafedeparis.net. Excellent French bakery and restaurant with wide range of options – from fondue to paella. Recommended. *Meals average US$12. Open 07.00–23.00.*

✗ La Luna Bar & Grill Beachside in Nosara; ☎ 682 0122. This ocean-view restaurant offers the most sophisticated dining in the area, with a good international menu featuring Thai and Mexican. *Meals average US$15. Open for lunch and dinner daily.*

PRACTICALITIES There is only one bank, Banco Popular, by Café de Paris. The Red Cross (☎ 685 5458) is on the northeast side of the football field as is the police station. Taxis are available around the football field or by calling 682 0142.

WHAT TO SEE AND DO Learn Spanish at **Rey de Nosara Language School** (☎/f 682 0215; www.nosara.com) across from the town's football field.

If yoga's your thing, the **Nosara Yoga Institute** (☎ 682 0071; www.nosarayoga.com) offers retreats as well as high-quality teacher training. Its stunning location and well-respected staff make it a popular spot with a number of movie stars.

Further down the road, about 4km north of Samara, is the **Alegria Retreat Centre** (☎ 390 9026; www.alegria-cr.de), offering various workshops in meditation, yoga, dance and t'ai chi. Its hilltop location offers stunning views and simple accommodation. For sport fishing you can contact **Harbor Reef Lodge** (☎ 682 0059; www.harboreef.com); **Abusadora Charters** (☎ 682 0396); **Reel Deal Charters** (☎ 396 9894); or **Grand Slam Charters** (☎ 682 0012).

Playa Guiones has garnered a reputation as a world-class surf spot thanks to its long, rideable break. Surfers can check out **Coconut Harry's Surf Shop** (☎ 682 0574) or **Nosara Surf Shop** (☎ 682 0186). For lessons, **Corky Carroll's Surf School** (☎ 682 0385) offers top-quality instruction.

Iguana Expeditions (☎ 682 0450) in Guiones, offers canopy tours, kayaking and hiking tours.

PLAYA SAMARA*

Whereas Nosara is a sleepy spot with superb surfing, Samara is the party-loving sibling with the best swimming beach in Costa Rica. The horseshoe-shaped bay offers up a long, pretty white-sand beach. Thanks to the well-paved road, cheap *cabinas*, plentiful *sodas* and wide, safe swimming beach, Samara is the preferred getaway spot for *Tico* families so weekends and holidays are busy and noisy. Midweek is a good time to visit and enjoy the quiet waters.

The main road goes directly through the town of Samara, located at the bottom of a large hill, and continues past the ubiquitous football field, juts to the left and up the hill (to the majority of hotels) and ends at the beach.

Beaching and partying are the two activities here, with the town's small disco pumping up the volume until the wee hours of the morning (if you don't plan on joining in the fun, best to stay up the hill). If hanging with the masses isn't your cup of tea, head further south to beautiful but deserted Carrillo (but only if you have a high-clearance 4x4).

Check out www.samarabeach.com for up-to-date information.

GETTING THERE AND AWAY

By air Both **Sansa** (✎ *221 9414*) and **NatureAir** (✎ *220 3054*) fly daily from San José to Samara. There are also daily flights with both airlines to Punta Islita.

By car Driving from San José, take the Inter-American Highway until you see signs for Puente de Amistad (approx 2 hours). Turn left at these signs (there is a huge petrol station on the left) and continue across the Puente de Amistad (Friendship Bridge) and on until the Nicoya turn-off on the left. From Nicoya, there are signs to direct you to Nosara and then on to Samara.

By bus **Empresa Alfaro-Tracopa** (✎ *222 2666*) run buses from Avenida 3/5, Calle 14 in San José twice a day to Samara.

Empresa Rojas (✎ *685 5352*) run several buses from the main bus station in Nicoya to Samara and Carrillo.

WHERE TO STAY

Around the football field there are several cheap places to flop but these are recommended only for the extremely budget conscious. A better bet is to camp over at Camping Coco's (for details, see page 213).

Prices are based on double occupancy during the high season (December–April) unless otherwise noted. Mandatory hotel tax of 16.39% must be added to prices unless noted.

Resort and Spa Hotel Punta Islita (40 rooms) Playa Islita; ✎ 661 3332; f 661 4043; www.hotelpuntaislita.com. Romance redefined, this is a world unto itself. Two majestic mountains kiss the sea and in between you find this first-class hotel with a local flavour. Accommodation ranges from rooms to suites with private pools or jacuzzis to villas. All have an ocean view, private patio with hammock, AC, private bathrooms with hot water and handcrafted furnishings. Red-tiled floors, thatched roofs and Santa Fe styling blend in perfectly with the surroundings in a blend I call 'upscale tropical'. Two restaurants and 2 bars offer a good variety of food and drink – thankfully, the quality is top notch as there aren't any other options for dinner. The more formal 1492 Restaurant sports memorabilia from the film of the same name that was shot in Costa Rica. The beach is a light, greyish-white and is fairly sheltered – it's a 10-min walk or a quick shuttle ride. The beach club includes a large, free-form pool, swim-up bar and light meals amidst beautifully manicured gardens. Other facilities include a gym, a spa and various tours. Punta Islita is a leader in environmental and community stewardship, setting up various programmes ranging from assisting with turtle nesting on the nearby beaches to creating foundations to assist local schools. Its community art programme has paired noted artists from San José with painters from the surrounding villages to create unique works of art throughout the village of Playa Islita, resulting in the first Latin American Open Air Contemporary Museum. Eye-popping murals adorn the plaza's buildings while whimsical 'lollysigns' brighten nooks and crannies. Although it's only 10km from Samara, it's not advisable to attempt the drive – both Sansa and NatureAir offer daily flights to the hotel's airstrip. If you must drive, take the Puntarenas ferry and head through Jiccaral through to Coyote. B/fast inc. *Rates US$218–600.*

Hotel Villas Playa Samara (57 rooms) Only 5 mins from south of town on the beach; ✎ 256 8228; f 221 7222; www.villasplayasamara.com. The largest hotel in the area and trying hard to be a full-on beach resort. Pleasant Mediterranean-style white-stuccoed, red-tiled villas have 1, 2 or 3 bedrooms and a limited number of rooms (marketed for 'honeymoons' as they accommodate only 2 people) are also available. Villas are fully equipped, with kitchens, living and dining rooms and terraces with hammocks. There is a pool with a swim-up bar, jacuzzi, bar, disco and restaurant and a wide range of tours are available. Part of the Interval International exchange programme, the service, nonetheless, leaves something to be desired. *Rate US$146.*

Hotel Marbella (14 rooms) On the inland road heading south; ✎/f 656 0362. Don't judge this book by the neighbourhood – rooms are large, cool and airy with either fans or AC and private baths with hot water and a small balcony (but no view). There is a small pool as well as a restaurant and small bar. *Rates US$25–30.*

🏠 **Hotel Mirador Samara** (12 rooms) Up the hill from Marbella; ☎ 656 0044; f 656 0046; www.miradordesamara.com. Wonderful ocean view apts are fully furnished and can sleep up to 6 people. A second building was finished at the end of 2005, a twin to the original apartotel. The north/south positioning ensures cooling breezes so the lack of AC is not an issue. Lush gardens, pool, restaurant, bar and impressive towers with a 360° view round off this gem. *Rate US$90.*

🏠 **Hotel Giada** (24 rooms) On the main road at the entrance to town; ☎ 656 0132; f 656 0131; www.hotelgiada.net. Very clean and airy rooms have fan, AC, cable TV, private baths and a balcony. There is a pool, jacuzzi and restaurant with excellent pizza. Pleasant owners are eager to assist with tours. Proximity to beach and walking distance to all services. B/fast inc. Recommended. *Rate US$50.*

🏠 **Bar & Cabinas Las Olas** (4 cabinas, 4 bungalows) On the beach; ☎ 656 0187; e olas@virtualsamra.com. A new addition, these funky grass huts on stilts are fittingly tropical for this beach setting. Bathrooms are shared and have cold-water showers. There are small bungalows for those who seek a bit more privacy. A *rancho* restaurant with international food menu and a bar make this a happening beach spot. *Rates US$19–25. Camping is also available for US$4 pp.*

🏠 **Cabins Arena** (12 rooms) On the main road about 150m from the beach; ☎ 656 0320. Clean and basic rooms have private baths with cold water and fan. *Rate US$15.*

🏠 **Cabins Playa Samara** (58 rooms) By the football field; ☎ 656 0190. This run-down, 2-storey wooden hotel has private baths with cold water. The noise from the disco is guaranteed to keep you awake during the weekends. *Rates US$12.*

🏠 **Camping Coco's** 400m north of the town centre; ☎ 656 0496. Simple campsites with showers, coffee maker and electrical hookups. *Rate US$3 pp.*

🍴 **WHERE TO EAT** Numerous *sodas* dot the centre of town and most hotels have their own restaurants.

✕ **Anana's Heladeria y Reposteria** On the main road approaching town; ☎ 656 0491. Anana's has delicious homemade ice cream and freshly squeezed juices. Meals average US$3. Open for b/fast and lunch.

✕ **Restaurant Las Brasas** Next to the football field; ☎ 656 0546. A Spanish restaurant dishing up excellent paella. *Average price per meal US$12. Open 12.00–22.00.*

PRACTICALITIES The police station is near the beach, close to the football field. Super Samara, by the football field, sells groceries.

WHAT TO SEE AND DO **Pura Vida Dive** (☎ 843 2075) offers boat tours for snorkelling, diving, dophin tours and fishing. They also offer PADI ceritification.

Knead to work it out? Head to **Marisel Massage** (☎ 656 0341) for massages in a quiet garden.

Wing Nut's Canopy Tour (☎ 656 0153; e *wingnutscanopytour@hotmail.com; www.samarabeach.com*) will have you flying through the trees.

Learn Spanish at the **Samara Language School** (☎ 656 0127; *www.samaralanguageschool.com*).

Interested in flying an ultralite? **Flying Crocodile** (☎ 656 8048; f 656 8049; *www.flying-crocodile.com*) offers flying lessons as well as flying tours.

Tio Tigre (☎ 656 0098) offers a variety of tours, such as snorkel trips, sport fishing aboard a *panga*, dolphin tour, horseriding and kayaking.

Barra Honda National Park (☎/f 685 5667; *tours begin at 07.00 and the last one leaves at 13.00*). Spelunking is the main draw here, as there are 42 caves here that were once a coral reef beneath the sea. Only 19 caves have been explored by scientists thus far and only one, the Terciopelo (fleur de lance) Cave, is open to the public (the strange name originates from a squished snake found on the floor by speleologists). The stalactites and stalagmites here are stunning and there is a large column that resounds with different tones when gently tapped – not surprisingly, it's called the Organ. As shafts are mostly vertical and the only way in or out is via a 27m-long ladder, only the stout of body and heart should attempt this tour. The total tour time, including the walk to and from the entrance, is about three hours. Cave tours are permitted only when accompanied by a trained guide.

For those who prefer to stay above ground, the park offers up some interesting vistas, hiking trails and wildlife. The Los Laureles Trail is 5.5km long and on it, you can expect to see howler and white-faced monkeys, coyotes and parakeets. If you hike on your own, buy a map and stay on the trail – two tourists became lost and died here in 1992.

EAST NICOYA

Bad roads have kept this area a bit of a secret, although surfers have long cherished the long breaks and deserted white-sand beaches. Improved roads and word of mouth have seen a steady increase of tourists make the sometimes arduous trek to this still undeveloped area, which is poised to potentially become another Tamarindo in a decade. Cattle farming is the staple industry here so once-lush forests have been clear cut for cud chewers but a number of nature reserves allow visitors to explore the flora and fauna. To me, it's one of the most beautiful spots to get away from it all in that picturesque 'Margaritaville' way.

During the dry season, the countryside is awash with yellow when the corteza amarilla (*Tabebuia ochracea*) tree explodes with blooms. The flowers of a single tree last only a few days but one tree may bloom up to three times during the dry season. Its durable hardwood is favoured by farmers for fence posts and the bark holds medicinal qualities, helpful in combating anaemia and malaria.

Prices are based on double occupancy during high season (December–April) unless otherwise noted. Mandatory hotel tax of 16.39% must be added to prices unless noted. All Blue Flag designated beaches, winners of the coveted award for their cleanliness and water quality, are noted with an asterisk.

GETTING THERE AND AWAY

By air Sansa (☏ *221 9414*) and **NatureAir** (☏ *220 3054*) make regular 20-minute flights to Tambor.

By bus Empresa Alfaro-Tracopa (☏ *222 2666*) runs buses from Avenida 3/5, Calle 14 in San José to Nicoya. **Asociacion de Desarrollo Integral Paquera** (☏ *641 0515*) runs buses from Puntarenas to Montezuma every two hours.

By ferry Leaving from Puntarenas, there are three ferries that run daily, sailing to Naranjo or Paquera. Strictly first come, first served, prepare for a wait, especially during the high season. When you arrive at the dock, you must get out of your vehicle and purchase a ticket at the wicket, get back into your vehicle and wait. Passengers on foot must also purchase tickets. Schedules vary according to season so call first.

⛴ Playa Naranjo ☏ 661 1069. 1hr transfer.   ⛴ Ferry Peninsula ☏ 641 0118. 1hr 30min transfer.
⛴ Tambor Ferry ☏ 661 2084. 1hr 30min transfer.

PLAYA TAMBOR

Home to the first all-inclusive resort in Costa Rica, the Barcelo Tambor, the sleepy village of the same name has not seen the mega-growth projected in the early 1990s. There is not much in the way of restaurants and hotels outside of the resort and while the beach here is sheltered and good for swimming, the beaches are a drab, brown colour with a great deal of flotsam and jetsam washing up on the shores (obviously, not my favourite beach). The 'reality' TV show *Temptation Island* however, loves this area as, at the time of writing, they were filming a new season at the Barcelo Tambor, having tempted couples at the nearby Tango Mar in earlier seasons.

WHERE TO STAY

🏠 **Hotel Barceló Playa Tambor** (402 rooms) 📞 683 0303; **e** 683 0304; www.barcelo.com. The first all-inc in the country is still the biggest (and the most controversial, having taken apparent liberties with zoning and environmental laws when being constructed — it's been said Barcelo was caught carting in white sand to dump on the lacklustre beach because the promotional brochures showed a picturesque white-sand beach). Rooms are scattered about the huge grounds in quaint, 2-storey structures resembling pastel Caribbean homes. The interiors, however, are standard issue, with AC, cable TV, phone, mini-fridge and safe. Every room is the same, with 2 dbl beds and the same uninspired décor. (Note: despite having 2 beds, no more than 3 adults can share 1 room.) There is a massive buffet restaurant, snack bar and an à la carte restaurant that is actually a decent spot for dinner, both in food and atmosphere — guests, however, may eat at the restaurant only twice in a week with prior reservations and groups are not eligible. The hotel's centrepiece is the enormous pool (the largest in Central America until the Conchal was constructed) with its swim-up bar. There is a minuscule casino, a few shops, tennis courts, a beauty salon, children's area, watersports and, to all intents and purposes, a private beach. There is a huge bar with a stage area where they present excruciatingly bad shows nightly (on one visit, the highlight was 2 men in a horse outfit 'peeing' water onto unsuspecting audience members — now that's entertainment). I admit that I'm not an all-inc fan but you'd have to be a hard-core resort fanatic to enjoy this place — weekends during low season, the hotel is packed with *Josefinos* taking advantage of low-priced specials, resulting in the pools being filled to the brim with screaming children, floating plastic cups and drunk young *Ticos*. The alcohol offered free is vile and, during my visits, the draught beer so skunky that it was undrinkable — with the numerous all-incs offered in Papagayo, I think one could find a smaller resort with better offerings on a much nicer beach. *Rate US$110 pp in a dbl room, inc meals and local drinks.*

🏠 **Hotel Tambor Tropical** (10 suites) On the beach just down the road from town; 📞 683 0011; **f** 683 0013; www.tambortropical.com. This adults-only hotel (no-one under 16 years old is allowed) is a wood lover's dream come true, as every villa is constructed of gleaming exotic hardwoods — every surface is some kind of wood, every piece milled at the hotel's own workshop. While their craftsmanship is outstanding, that much wood can be a bit overwhelming for some (such as yours truly). The walls are actually shutters — slatted blinds that you can open or close. Fridge, kitchenette, pool, jacuzzi, horses, bar, snorkelling, restaurant, tours to Tortuga Island, children not allowed. B/fast inc. *Rate US$174.*

🏠 **Hotel Tango Mar Beach and Golf Resort** (18 rooms, 17 suites, 3 villas) On the beach just outside of Tambor; 📞 683 0010; **f** 683 00 03; www.tangomar.com. A setting for the 'reality' TV show *Temptation Island*, this hotel, with its secluded, idyllic beach and air of romance was the perfect backdrop to lure couples to stray. The 3-storey beachfront building houses rooms that are quite spacious, with 2 beds, AC, fans, TV, telephones, minibar, hot water and balconies so close to the sea you can practically feel the ocean spray at high tide. On the hill are the tropical suites that, in addition to all the amenities of the rooms, have beautifully carved 4-poster beds and a jacuzzi tub. Below the suites and near the beach are the octagonal tiki suites, which are set up on stilts and very romantic (a king-size bed is the focal point of the suite). 3 private villas, each unique and nicely decorated, are spread out amongst the large grounds. The villas and some suites are a distance from the beach and restaurant so a private vehicle or a golf-cart is recommended. There is an open-air, beachfront restaurant serving up international fare, 2 pools (the main pool is quite stunning, especially when lit at night), 2 tennis courts, horseriding, hiking trails, a mini-spa and yoga dojo, restaurant, golf with carts, trails and spring-fed pools. *Rates start at US$92.*

🏠 **Hotel Costa Coral** (10 villas) On the main road heading into town; 📞 683 0001; **f** 683 0003; www.costacoral.com. A cute, Santa Fe-style hotel with lovely bathrooms, spacious villas with a dining area, kitchenette, sofa, phone, AC and private patio.

There is a decent little restaurant and a small pool and jacuzzi and the only real drawback is the fact that it's situated 200m from the beach. If that's not a concern, this is a wonderful spot to call home for a few days. B/fast inc. A great deal. *Rate only US$60.*

🏠 **Cabinas Cristina** (9 rooms) Very close to the beach; ☎ 683 0028; e cabinascristina@racsa.co.cr. Basic rooms, some with private bathrooms and all with cold water, some shared bathrooms. There is a small, basic restaurant as well. *Rates US$17–25 (up to 4 people).*

WHAT TO SEE AND DO

Curu National Wildlife Refuge (*16km south of Paquera;* ☎ *710 8236;* e *refugiocuru@yahoo.com; entrance US$6, tours to Tortuga Island US$20*). Three gorgeous beaches, 223 species of birds, 78 mammal species, 23 species of amphibians and over 500 species of plants make for outstanding hiking and birdwatching. This private reserve started out as Hacienda Curu in 1933 and when squatters took over part of the land, owners Federico and Julieta Schutt turned 84ha of their land into a wildlife refuge. In addition to 17 walking trails that range from easy to challenging, the snorkelling here is very good, with lobster, oysters and giant conches found offshore. Olive Ridley and hawksbill turtles nest here as well. A number of conservation projects are under way, including reforestation, reintroduction of the white-faced monkey and natural pest predators for use on farms in an effort to reduce pesticide use. Visitors can ride horses and take kayak trips to Tortuga Island. Camping is allowed and there are some very simple, rustic cabins available for overnight stays for US$25, although most tourists opt for day visits.

Cabo Blanco Absolute Wildlife Reserve (☎/f *642 0093; limited facilities*). Occupying the entire southwest tip of the Nicoya Peninsula for 12km, this is the oldest protected area in the country. Karen Morgensen, a Dane, and her Swedish husband, Olaf, set aside this piece of property as a haven for nature in 1963 and until 1989 visitors were forbidden (hence the 'absolute wildlife' aspect). Famous for pelicans and seabirds, visitors will experience a mix of flora and fauna in this Pacific lowland tropical forest, unique to this particular area. A 5km hiking trail leads from the ranger's station, through a deciduous forest to Playa Cabo Blanco and Playa Balsitas, neither of which is a good swimming beach, but both are excellent spots to sit and watch the ocean without another soul around. Be aware of high tide, however, as the trail becomes impassable so check with the ranger before heading out to ensure you can get back out.

Golf Respectable nine-hole golf courses are found at the Los Delfines Country Club at Tambor and Tango Mar (☎ *683 0001*).

Diving Not one of the better spots for diving but you can contact Hotel Bahia Luminosa (☎ *641 0386*) or Cabo Blanco Diver (☎ *642 0467*). There is also a dive shop on the Barcelo Tambor resort for guests.

MONTEZUMA

Nicknamed 'Montefuma' (Mount Smoke) by the locals, this is a laid-back beach town where peace, love and the pursuit of happiness is king. It's got a 'hippy' feel to it, with vegetarian restaurants, yoga, bonfires and coal-walking rituals on the beach. Personally, I find this to be the most 'Caribbean' beach on the Pacific, where development has been abated and everything's groovy. A few years ago, a plethora of beach campers were creating a mess on the pristine beaches and sullying the town's reputation with drugs, garbage and late-night noise. Thanks to concerted efforts by local businesses, beach camping is no longer allowed, hotels in a variety of pricing have sprung up and peace, quiet and cleanliness have descended where chaos once ruled. White-sand beaches with crystal-blue waters make this one of the prettiest areas in the country and those seeking some downtime in a dreamy little beach town should find happiness in Montezuma.

GETTING THERE AND AWAY
By air Sansa (✆ 221 9414) and **NatureAir** (✆ 220 3054) make regular 20-minute flights to Tambor and from there, you can hire a taxi.

By car The main road from Tambor was recently repaved and it's now a great stretch to drive. Montezuma is about 18km south of Tambor and then down a very steep hill. At the bottom of the hill, the road becomes dirt and then you're driving down the main road. Hotels, restaurants, shops and bars are scattered within an easy walking radius.

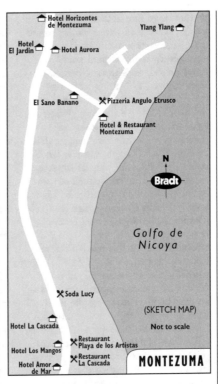

By bus Take a bus to Puntarenas, then take the Paquera ferry with **Asociacion de Desarrollo Integral Paquera** (✆ 641 0515). Once on the other side, take the bus from Paquera to Cobano with **Transportes Rodriguez** (✆ 642 0219). **Asociacion de Desarrollo Integral Paquera** (✆ 641 0515) run buses from Puntarenas to Montezuma every two hours.

GETTING AROUND The town is small enough to get around by walking or by bus. The local network is **Transportes Rodriguez** (✆ 642 0219).

WHERE TO STAY
🏠 **Ylang Ylang Beach Resort** (8 bungalows, 6 suites) North of town (reception in Sano Banano Restaurant); ✆ 642 0638; www.ylanylanresort.com. It's a 15-min walk down the beach (no road) but once you arrive, you won't want to leave. The beachfront bungalows are small but literally steps from the surf and have romantic outdoor showers (they were set for a makeover and balcony enlargements at the time of writing). Coconut Joe's is the quaint honeymoon suite with a romantic loft – don't be surprised if a monkey pokes its head into the window over the bed while you're sleeping! The hotel features spacious rooms and beautiful beach views. All rooms have a fridge, coffee maker, ceiling fan, hot water and a balcony. Although none of the windows has screens, insects aren't an issue and many guests don't bother with the mosquito netting over the beds. A lovely pool, spa, restaurant, gift shop and lush gardens complete this beachfront paradise. B/fast inc. *Rate* US$105.

🏠 **EL Sano Banano Village B&B** (11 rooms) In town; ✆ 642 0636; www.elbanano.com. Situated right above the restaurant, these small, clean and artistically appointed rooms have AC, satellite TV, private bathrooms with hot water and b/fast inc. Some rooms don't have windows but it is the most 'upmarket' hotel in downtown Montezuma. *Rate* US$75.

🏠 **Nature Lodge, Finca Los Caballos** (8 rooms, 1 bungalow) 3km before entering town, on the road to Cobano above Montezuma; ☎ 642 0124; www.naturelodge.net. This charming, peaceful Santa Fe-style ranch has simply appointed rooms with private bathrooms, fans, hot water and a small patio. Rooms at either end offer good cross-ventilation. The hotel grounds feature a number of hammocks for lazing about, a pool, bar and restaurant serving wholesome and creative food. As the hotel's name indicates, the main draw here is the well-kept horses, which guests can ride through the property's 40 acres. The Canadian owner is a championship rider and takes great pride in her horses and is more than eager to take guests on moonlit rides and riding trips to the beach. Recommended. *Rate US$62.*

🏠 **Hotel Horizontes de Montezuma** (7 rooms) About 2km above Montezuma; ☎ 642 0534; f 642 0625; www.horizontes-montezuma.com. This neat-as-a-pin B&B resembles a Victorian mansion in the Caribbean, with large balconies running around the second storey, offering ocean and forest views. Rooms are very white, clean and bright, with private bathrooms, hot water and fans. There is a small restaurant, a good-size pool and well-tended grounds. Spanish courses are offered and this is a great, quiet spot for those who want to learn. *Rate US$59.*

🏠 **Hotel Amor de Mar** (11 rooms, 2 houses) 600m southwest of town; ☎/f 642 0262; www.amordemar.com. Sitting on beautifully manicured lawns that slope down to the ocean, this is a tranquil setting for those who prefer not to stay in town. Hexagonal, 2-storey cabins are built out of local hardwood and the rustic rooms have fans, a porch, hammocks overlooking the ocean and private or shared baths. Ask for a top-floor room with an ocean view. There are also 2 houses for rent, suitable for up to 6 guests. There is a dining room for guests, a good spot to relax after exploring the tidal pools at the front of the property. *Rates US$55–95.*

🏠 **Hotel Los Mangos** (10 rooms, 9 cabins) On the road to Cabuya; ☎ 642 0076; f 642 0259; www.hotellosmangos.com. Right across from the beach,

this lovely spot has a bohemian feel to it that fits perfectly with the Montezuma 'vibe'. The orange and blue 2-storey hotel has 4 large rooms with 3 beds and private bathrooms on the main floor, 4 dbl rooms upstairs with a shared bath and 2 more large rooms with private baths. All are brightly painted with wooden ceilings, fax, interesting art on the walls and a lovely patio or balcony to enjoy the ocean view from. Funky cabins out of Nazareno wood are found behind the hotel. Inspired by Balinese architecture, each *cabina* features a cathedral ceiling and a wide, covered veranda. As these are all wood, they are a bit dark. Each one has a dbl and a sgl bed, a bathroom with hot water, a fan and wall hangings from South America. The pool and jacuzzi are very inviting. There is an open-air yoga pavilion beautifully constructed out of wood and bamboo cane that overlooks the expanse of gardens and the ocean. Recommended. *Rates US$35–82.*

🏠 **Hotel La Cascada** (19 rooms) On the road to Cabo Blanco; ☎ 642 0057. Nothing fancy but a very relaxing spot to rest one's head. The Spartan rooms are clean with fans, a balcony and hammocks and the nearby stream is guaranteed to lull you to sleep. *Rate US$35.*

🏠 **Hotel Aurora** (16 rooms) In town; ☎/f 642 0051. Run by environmentally friendly owners, rooms are nice and have screens or mosquito netting, fans, some have AC, some hot water and there is a communal kitchen. Upstairs rooms are a bit more expensive but feature hammocks and cooling cross-breezes. *Rate US$30.*

🏠 **Hotel Montezuma** (18 rooms) Centre of town; ☎/f 642 0058. Very basic rooms with fans. The rooms in the old hotel are above the bar and restaurant so they can be noisy but the view overlooking the bay from your balcony makes up for it. Across the street is the newer building and rooms are much quieter. *Rates US$20 in old hotel, US$25 in new building.*

🏠 **Hotel El Jardin** (14 rooms) In town; ☎ 642 0548; e 642 0104. Spacious, basic rooms feature wooden ceilings, tiled baths and verandas or patios, fans and TV. *Rate US$20.*

✕ WHERE TO EAT

✕ **Soda Lucy** South beach side of town; ☎ 642 0273. Simple *soda* at the beach with big portions, typical *Tico* fare and fish so fresh it's almost swimming. Good, homemade food at affordable prices. Recommended. *Meals average US$6. Open daily 07.30–21.00.*

✕ **Bar/Restaurant Montezuma** Downtown Montezuma

in Hotel Montezuma; ☎ 642 0657. New owners have given this long-standing fixture a new lease of life and the menu has greatly benefited, thanks to an emphasis on Spanish favourites. Opt for the paella, *gazpacho* (perfect for a hot afternoon) or fresh *calamari. Meals average US$11. Open daily 07.30–22.00.*

✕ Pizzeria Angulo Etrusco Downtown Montezuma at the crossroads; ☏ 642 0489. Nothing fancy but good Italian fare such as pasta, *calzones* and pizzas. Very laid back with equally laissez-faire service but who's in a hurry in Montezuma? *Meals average US$12. Open 17.00–22.00.*

✕ El Sano Banano Natural Foods Restaurant and Coffee Shop On the main road in town; ☏ 642 0638; ☏ 642 0631; www.elbanano.com. One of the best places in town, featuring creative and tasty vegetarian meals that would delight even the most hardcore of carnivores. Menu offerings also include excellent pizzas as well as some chicken and seafood. The blackboard outside announces the daily specials and the smoothies are divine. Movies are shown at night throughout the week for those needing a film fix. Highly recommended. *Meals average US$7. Open daily 07.00–22.00.*

✕ Restaurant Playa de los Artistas On the road to Cabuya; ☏ 642 0920. Craving amazing food on the sand under the trees, the sea lapping at your toes? This small, beachside eatery is *the* spot in the area for sophisticated Mediterranean cuisine. On account of its popularity and limited seating, it's best to arrive early. The menu changes daily, depending on what's available, but there is always some kind of tantalising seafood dish. Cash payment only. Highly recommended. *Meals average US$15. Open for lunch and dinner 10.00–22.00; closed Sun.*

✕ Ylang Ylang Restaurant On the beach at Ylang Ylang Hotel; ☏ 642 0638; ☏ 642 0631; www.elbanano.com. Run by the folks at Sano Banano, this open-air beachside restaurant is undoubtedly the most 'upmarket' option in Montezuma, with an emphasis on fresh, fusion vegetarian/Asian cooking with seafood and chicken options. Excellent sushi, excellent *gazpacho*, killer cocktails and unmatched surroundings make this worth the stroll down the beach. Highly recommended. *Meals average US$20. Open daily 07.00–22.00.*

WHAT TO SEE AND DO The beaches here are gorgeous and being a 'beach bum' is one of the more popular activities. Do be careful when swimming, though, as the water can get rough and stay aware of stray rocks. Yoga is another popular pursuit as is horseriding. The horses from **Finca Los Caballos** (☏ *642 0124*) are by far the best cared for. A popular tour is a guided ride to the waterfall.

Hiking to the **waterfalls** is another 'must-do' while in the area and there are two to choose from. One is just south of town, on your right as you pass Las Cascadas Restaurant. It's a bit of a challenging hike through a stream and along rocks so make sure you're wearing a good pair of sport sandals or tennis/running shoes (not flip-flops as I once did on a trip where I forgot my own advice on what to pack). The 20-minute hike following the river is definitely worth it as the waterfall spilling into a deep tidal pool is spectacular (be sure to have your bathing suit on underneath as there aren't any facilities here – you're in the middle of mother nature). Note: do NOT jump off the top of the waterfall into the pool below. A number of thrill-seekers have chosen to ignore the signs posted and ended up dead after hitting one of the boulders beneath the water's surface. Don't make the same mistake.

You can also hike or ride a horse to **El Chorro Waterfall** on the beach, a stunning setting 8km north of town. Here, the water plunges off a cliff into a pool at the foot of the ocean, resulting in a mix of fresh and salt water to swim in. During low tide, it's like a storybook come to life but at high tide, the pool disappears so try to time it right.

Waterfall Canopy Tour (☏ *642 0911*) offers a canopy tour with 11 platforms, taking you high above the Montezuma River.

Montezuma Expeditions (☏ *642 0919; www.montezumaexpeditions.com*) offers a variety of tours and transfers to other parts of Costa Rica.

PLAYA SANTA TERESA* – MALPAIS*

The name Malpais literally means 'bad land' but nothing could be further from the truth as this area is the picture-postcard setting most people imagine – white-sand beach stretching for ever, ringed by lazy palm trees with hardly a soul around.

11

Surfers were the first to discover the area, noted for its consistent waves, and the main focus is still surfing, although the secret is out – more restaurants and small hotels are popping up, giving travellers a wider assortment of options. Malpais and Santa Teresa are lumped together as they are essentially one long patch of pseudo-civilisation along the beach.

GETTING THERE AND AWAY

By air Fly to Tambor and from there, private transport, such as the taxis always waiting at the airstrip, can make the one-hour trip.

By car In the dry season Malpais is accessible by coastal road south of Playa Manzanillo but the roads are rough and unpaved – during the rainy season, the rivers swell, making it impossible to drive. The easiest access is via ferry from the port of Puntarenas, across the Gulf of Nicoya to Playa Naranjo or Paquera. Make sure you have a very good 4x4, as the dirt roads and steep hills are treacherous and almost impassable during the rainy season. Follow the road 12km south of Cobano. At the intersection, turn left for Malpais and right for Santa Teresa.

By bus Take the bus to Puntarenas and cross on the ferry. Take the Paquera–Cobano bus with **Transportes Rodriguez** (*642 0219*) and catch a minibus or taxi to either beach.

WHERE TO STAY

Hotel Flor Blanca Resort (10 villas) On the beach at end of Santa Teresa; 640 0232; f 640 0226; www.florblanca.com. Quite simply, my favourite hotel in the country. Hotelier Susan Money, the creator of Tamarindo's Sueno del Mar B&B, has excelled herself with this ultra-luxurious boutique resort that surrounds guests in a womb of sumptuousness in the middle of the jungle. Massive villas are an oasis of calm and Zen styling, with Balinese furnishings and high-quality finishings. Each villa has a large sitting and dining room with a small kitchenette, either 1 or 2 bedrooms (with the most comfortable mattress I've ever slept on) and an open-air bathroom surrounded by gardens (soaking in the sunken tub with only the stars over your head is something everyone should experience at least once in their lives). Although the key word here is luxury, the emphasis is on the ecology, with grey water being recycled and all cleaning products being environmentally friendly. The pool is gorgeous and great for families. There is a yoga dojo of gleaming teak wood that overlooks the ocean, where daily yoga and Pilates classes are held. Additionally, there is a small spa on the grounds, an art studio and a music room. Although there aren't TVs in the villas (and frankly, who wants to watch TV when you're in paradise?), there is a large-screen TV in the music room/lounge for those who need a fix. A gigantic gourmet b/fast is inc and guaranteed to keep you full until lunchtime. Recommended. *Rates US$338–570.*

Bungalows Vista de Olas (6 bungalows) \/f 640 0183; www.bungalows-vistadeolas.com. Sitting high on a hill with a commanding view of the ocean, these luxury stucco and hardwood bungalows are nicely decorated with a nod to Bali, open and airy, each with a king bed, a sofa bed, ceiling fan, AC, fridge, coffee maker, safe and an open-air bathroom complete with garden. The infinity pool is gorgeous and there is a jacuzzi as well. An open-air restaurant and bar next to the pool offer tasty meals throughout the day (and a great view). Recommended. *Rate US$128.*

Cabinas Milarepa (4 cabinas) On the beach; 640 0023; f 640 0168; www.milarepahotel.com. Small, Indonesian-style bamboo cabins have a fan, patio and open-air bathrooms and showers. There is a small but nice pool and a small restaurant with French food. Given the simplicity and small size of the cabins, I feel the price is a bit high. The restaurant, I think, is trying to compete with the neighbours next door, Flor Blanca, in pricing (the food is very expensive) but without the quality, service or atmosphere – on my last visit, there was bright lighting and no music yet entrées were hovering in the US$20 range. *Rate US$120.*

The Place (5 bungalows, 2 rooms, 1 villa) Just south of the crossroads; \/f 640 0001; www.theplacemalpais.com. Cool, stylish and with a touch of Euro-sophistication, this is one of the places to stay in the area for those seeking a boutique hotel experience. Bungalows, artistically decorated in various themes such as African, Mexican and a beach house, are airy and comfortable. A *rancho*, named the 'Nido de Amor' (Love Nest), is the perfect setting for a tropical honeymoon. 3 rooms in the main building offer AC. All rooms have private bathrooms with hot water. A pool, restaurant and yoga classes round off the experience. *Rate US$80.*

🏠 **Star Mountain Eco-Resort** (11 rooms) Between Cabuya and Malpais in the mountains; ✆ 640 0101; www.starmountaineco.com. Set on a 3,000-acre nature reserve, this small resort is a diamond in the rough – in the midst of wild jungle springs this Santa Fe-style hacienda, with a handsomely tiled pool and jacuzzi. The 4 upmarket rooms are tastefully decorated and quite spacious, each with fan and a private bathroom with hot water. There is also a small *casita* for up to 7 people. A lush fruit garden will delight those with green fingers while nature lovers will find a variety of animals (small wildcats, monkeys) and birds in the surrounding green hills. B/fast inc. *Rates US$85–95 (taxes inc).*

🏠 **Tropico Latino Lodge** (10 rooms, 1 villa) ✆ 640 0062; f 640 0117; www.hoteltropicolatino.com. One of my favourite spots in the area, this Italian-run small hotel has huge thatched-roofed bungalows, each with an incredible amount of space, a full-size and modern bathroom, hot water, fan and some have AC. Although some have garden views and others partial ocean views, it's just a few metres to the beach. All the furniture is made from bamboo and native wood, matching perfectly with the lush gardens and numerous trees on the property. There is a lovely pool with a jacuzzi and an open-air restaurant with very good Italian food. Highly recommended. *Rates US$75–95.*

🏠 **Sunset Reef Marina Lodge** (14 rooms) At the end of the road on the beach; ✆ 640 0012; f 640 0036; www.sunsetreefhotel.com. The largest hotel in Malpais, each spacious room is finished in hardwood and sports handmade furniture, a full bathroom and AC. Owned by the same group as the first-rate Hotel Alta in San José, the service at the Sunset is top-notch. The gardens and grounds are well tended and there are hammocks and a pool to enjoy. Good food is served up at the restaurant and bar. *Rate US$85.*

🏠 **Hotel Casa Cecilia** (4 rooms) On the beach in Malpais; ✆ 654 0115; www.casacecilia.com. This small beachfront hotel is a good option for a quiet stay.

Rooms are pleasant, with fan and private bathrooms. There are hammocks on the beach to relax in and the affable American owners will assist you in setting up tours. B/fast inc. *Rate US$85.*

🏠 **Blue Jay Lodge** (10 rooms) On the main road in Malpais; ✆ 640 0089; f 640 0141; www.bluejaylodgecostarica.com. Simple, hardwood cabins set on stilts with only screens for windows allow for an up close and personal experience with nature. Cabins have private bathrooms and fans. There is a new pool and cute little restaurant. B/fast is inc. Recommended. *Rate US$85.*

🏠 **Malpais Surf Camp** (40 rooms) On the beach in Malpais; ✆ 640 0031; f 640 0061; www.malpaissurfcamp.com. Set in 10 acres of tropical gardens, this is a place run by surfers for surfers with accommodation to meet any budget. There are poolside houses, crafted out of local hardwood and featuring hot water and kitchen, that can sleep up to 5 while the villas with kitchen can sleep 4. There are also thatched-roofed, simple *ranchos* for up to 4, rooms with shared bathrooms and camping facilities for US$7. There is a kidney-shaped pool, restaurant and bar, and lots of surfers to get 'stoked' with. *Rates US$30–105.*

🏠 **Frank's Place** (21 rooms) At the crossroads; ✆ 640 0096; f 640 0071. Simple rooms, some with AC and private baths, cold-water showers, fridge, fan, small pool and restaurant. *Rate US$28.*

🏠 **Cabinas Iguana** (8 rooms) On the beach in Malpais; ✆ 640 0050. Basic cabins with fans and cold water with a small restaurant. *Rates: cabins US$25; camping US$3 pp.*

🏠 **Point Break Cabins** (8 rooms) Located a few metres from the point break (purportedly the best surf spot in Santa Teresa), this newly opened hotel is a gem. Simple yet well-crafted cabins of wood, netting and thatched palms feature 2 sgl beds, bar fridge, fan and kitchen utensils as well as a well-shaded patio with chairs. Bathrooms are shared and have cold-water showers. Two second-storey rooms can accommodate up to 4 people and have a full kitchen and private bath. Clean, secure and cute – I think it's one of the best budget options in the area. *Rate US$30.*

🏠 **Cabinas Playa El Carmen** (8 rooms) ✆ 640 0179. For the budget traveller; you'll find very basic rooms with fans and shared cold-water showers. There is a communal kitchen and washing machine. *Rate US$15.*

🏠 **Camping Santa Teresa** On the road to Santa Teresa just past the supermarket. Very basic facilities. *Rate US$5 pp.*

✗ WHERE TO EAT

✗ **Nectar** At the Florblanca Hotel in Santa Teresa; ☎ 640 0232. One of the best eateries in the country, the food is simply divine, with imaginative fusions of Eastern flavours with fresh Costa Rican ingredients — if you're going to splurge on a meal during your trip, this is the place and it's worth the drive if you're anywhere in the peninsula. Service is efficient but relaxed and friendly. Reservations strongly suggested. Highly recommended. *Meals average US$30. Open daily 07.00–21.00.*

✗ **Frank's Place** In Frank's Place Hotel at the crossroads of Malpais/Santa Teresa; ☎ 640 0096; f 640 0071; www.franksplace.com. A simple setting for so-so *Tico* and international food, Frank's is an institution favoured by surfers and backpackers. *Meals average US$7. Open daily 08.00–22.00.*

✗ **Bliss** Near the Hotel Point Break in Santa Teresa (no phone). From this small, unassuming shack comes delicious and filling fish *tacos*, breakfast *burritos* and blissful burgers. Fresh smoothies and baking has the locals flocking here for good reason. Cash payment only. *Meals average US$6. Open daily 07.30–15.00.*

✗ **Mary's Pizza** At the north end of Malpais; ☎ 640 0153. The saying 'do one thing and do it well' could very well be the motto of this tiny eatery, as your menu choices are almost exclusively pizza. Nonetheless, Mary's has served up the best wood-oven thin-crust pizza you'll find in these parts and has built up a loyal clientele in the process. *Meals average US$6. Open daily 17.00–22.00.*

✗ **Soda Piedra Mar** On the beach in Malpais; ☎ 640 0069. A budget *soda* with a million-dollar location, you'll enjoy simply prepared fresh fish and seafood as you listen to the waves crashing below you. Cash payment only. *Meals average US$5. Open daily 07.00–20.00.*

WHAT TO SEE AND DO The gnarly talk in the restaurants, laid-back groove and proliferation of surf shops are the first signals that you've reached surf central. Excellent surf and point breaks are found throughout the region and any local will be able to steer you to the best spot. It's a tough place to learn to surf but the folks at **Mal Pais Surf Camp** (☎ *640 0031; www.malpaissurfcamp.com*) will teach you how to hang ten.

A number of small bars and discos appear and disappear with regularity so best ask around for where the action is. Occasionally, there are 'happenings' on the beach, with fire dancers and DJs spinning trance or house beats.

Because of the strong surf, swimming isn't recommended but non-surfers will enjoy beachcombing or working on a tan.

12

Central Pacific

The first beach area popular with tourists, the Central Pacific region seemingly has it all – beautiful beaches, gorgeous sunsets, lush rainforests, world-class hotels and restaurants, adventure sports, jungles and loads of wildlife. From the party-on atmosphere in Jacó to the tranquillity of the beaches at Palo Seco to the national park teeming with monkeys in Manuel Antonio, this stretch of sandy beaches tinged by rainforest is the ideal tropical setting for many travellers.

TURRUBARES

If you decide to take 'the back route' through Puriscal to Orotina and onwards to Jacó or Manuel Antonio, you'll be rewarded with a leisurely and picturesque drive through curvy mountains .

WHERE TO STAY AND EAT

⌂ **Ama Tierra** (10 units) Near Turrubares, 2km east of San Pablo; ☏ 419 0110; www.amatierra.com. Tucked away in the middle of nowhere is one of my favourite little spots for a romantic getaway. Newly opened, these 5 *casitas* with 2 junior suites each offer the utmost in privacy, nestled on a lush hillside. Each is uniquely decorated and quite spacious and features a queen bed in the sleeping area, a jacuzzi, a private patio and garden with seating, satellite TV, DVD player, mini-fridge, coffee maker, telephone and complimentary snacks, mineral water, coffee and tea. There is a beautiful pool and patio (with an honour bar). The all-wood restaurant overlooks the mountains and valleys surrounding the area and is the perfect spot to enjoy gourmet cooking with Middle Eastern, Italian and French touches. In addition to delicious combinations of flavours and textures, the food is beautifully presented. B/fast, dinner, internet access and DVD films are inc. Highly recommended. *Rate US$149 pp.*

WHAT TO SEE AND DO

Turu Ba Ri Tropical Park (*in Turrubares between Puriscal and Orotina;* ☏ *428 6070;* f *428 6069; www.turubari.com; entrance US$45 with additional costs for adventure tours; day trips from San José US$75*). Spanning 495 acres, this former cattle ranch has been dramatically transformed into an 'Eco-Adventure Theme Park' that offers a wide variety of gardens, including orchids, *bromeliads*, butterflies, cacti, bamboo and palms. For the more adventurous, there is horseriding, canopy tours and a 'sensational cable' where one flies like a bird on a zip line, heading along headfirst (the only one in Central America offering this method). There are also two restaurants and a European tram that takes visitors to the main areas. It's a big, ambitious project with heart, totally *Tico*-owned, that is striving to offer opportunities for area residents who have otherwise limited prospects. It's an interesting tour but bring a lot of water and a good sunhat, as this is a very hot area, without the benefit of cooling sea breezes.

12

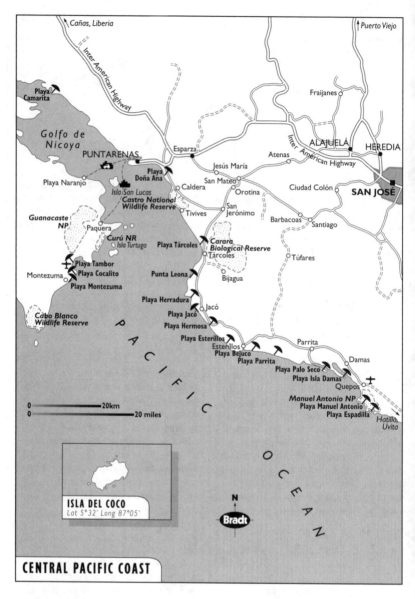

Central Pacific Coast

PUNTARENAS

Once the most important seaport on the Pacific, Puntarenas wears the ravages of time like a former film star long past her prime, bedecked in faded, moth-eaten finery. When the first tourists disembarked on the Rich Coast's shores in the 1850s, it was here in Puntarenas – today, a quick glance around this port town would have all but the hardiest of travellers looking to beat a quick exit. Currently, Puntarenas (which translates to 'Point of Sand' which is exactly what this town is – a long, skinny spit of sand) is a port for fishing and ferries to the Nicoya Peninsula, as most commercial activity has shifted to Caldera Port further south.

The Paseo de los Turistas has a number of handicrafts for sale and some of the architecture in the area makes for an interesting stroll. The beaches are usually packed on the weekends with *Ticos*, but the water and beaches aren't as clean as other areas – I recommend driving a bit further to Playa Herradura or even Jacó.

GETTING THERE AND AWAY

By car Take the General Cañas Highway heading west out of San José for approx 90 minutes and follow the signs.

By bus Express buses (✆ *222 0064*) leave from Avenida 12, Calle 6 in San José.

WHERE TO STAY
Given that there is little here to attract tourists, most people overnight in Puntarenas simply to ensure a good spot in the ferry line-up the next morning. There are many low-budget options around (many downtown rent rooms by the hour so beware the seedy quotient) but most of the better hotels and restaurants/bars are found on the Paseo de los Turistas. This is one of the muggiest towns in Costa Rica – if you can get a room with air conditioning, go for it, as you'll be glad you did.

Prices are based on double occupancy during the high season (December–April) unless otherwise noted. Mandatory hotel tax of 16.39% must be added to prices unless noted.

🏠 **Hotel Yadran** (42 rooms) At the tip of the point of Paseo de los Turistas; ✆ 661 2662. Overlooking the point of the spit, each room features cable TV, AC, private bathrooms, hot water and a balcony or patio. There are 2 small pools, a casino, 2 restaurants and an underground disco (a thoughtful measure so others can sleep peacefully). This is as 'top drawer' as Puntarenas gets, but don't expect the Marriott. The general consensus is that it's a nice hotel but overpriced. B/fast inc. *Rates US$76–100.*

🏠 **Hotel Tioga** (52 rooms) On Paseo de los Turistas; ✆ 661 0271; www.hoteltioga.com. Built in 1959, this hotel has the look of a classic 1950s beachside hotel – the bright-blue pool even has its own teeny-tiny island with a little palm tree. There is a casino, small gymnasium, restaurant and bar. All rooms have AC, cable TV and telephone but not all have hot water. Generally, rooms are clean and tidy but vary in size and view – the larger rooms have balconies overlooking the ocean while the smaller rooms, facing the garden, have cold water. B/fast inc. *Rates US$63–99.*

🏠 **Gran Hotel Imperial** (36 rooms) Next to the bus terminal on Paseo de los Turistas; ✆ 661 0579. Very basic rooms with hot water in a rickety wooden building with a funky balcony. Take an upstairs room with a shared bathroom for the balcony and light, as the downstairs rooms are quite dingy. *Rate US$22.*

🏠 **Hotel Rio** (91 rooms) Av 3, Ca Central; ✆ 661 0331. Super basic rooms with fans and cold water downtown but well managed. *Rates US$8 pp with shared bath; US$12 with private bath.*

WHERE TO EAT
Home to the largest fish-processing plants in Costa Rica and being a port town, it's no surprise that seafood is a speciality.

✗ **Restaurant Aloha** Paseo de los Turistas; ✆ 661 2375. A great spot for delicious seafood dishes at a reasonable price. *Casado is US$4. Open daily 09.00–12.00.*

✗ **Casa de Los Mariscos** Across from the police station; ✆ 661 1666. Serves up great ceviche. *Ceviche is US$3. Open 11.30–22.00; closed Tue.*

✗ **Restaurant Kimbos** Next door to Clínica San Rafael; ✆ 661 2923. Specialises in Creole and seafood. *Main course US$4–11. Open daily 10.00–03.00.*

✗ **Restaurant La Yunta** Paseo de los Turistas; ✆ 661 3216. Serves up heaping platters of seafood and steak. The 2-storey building has nice views of the ocean from its balconies and is a pleasant spot to tuck into succulent meats expertly prepared. Recommended. *Main course US$10. Open 10.00–midnight daily.*

PRACTICALITIES
There are two banks: **Banco Nacional** (✆ *661 0233*) on Avenida Central and Calle Central and **Banco de Costa Rica** (✆ *661 0444*) on Callet Central, Avenida 3

12

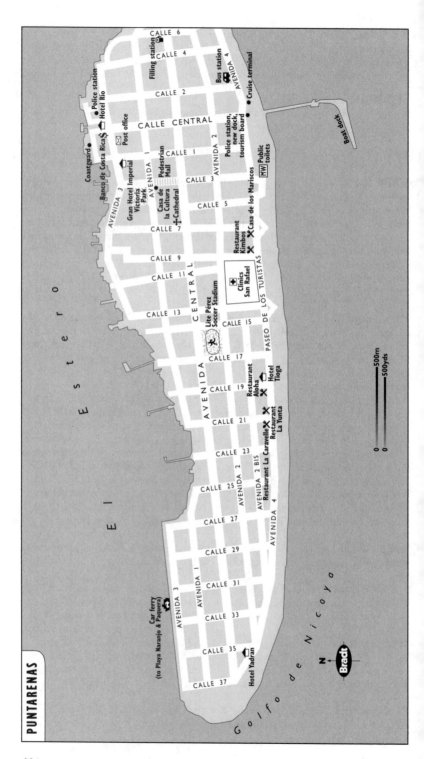

PUNTARENAS

CALLE 6
CALLE 4
Filling station
Bus station
AVENIDA 4
Cruise terminal
CALLE 2
CALLE CENTRAL
Police station
Hotel Rio
Post office
Police station,
new dock,
tourism board
AVENIDA 2
Coastguard
Banco de Costa Rica
CALLE 1
Pedestrian
Mall
CALLE 3
Public
toilets
AVENIDA 3
Gran Hotel Imperial
Victoria
Park
AVENIDA 1
Casa de
la Cultura
Cathedral
CALLE 5
Restaurant
Kimbes
Casa de los Mariscos
CALLE 7
CALLE 9
CALLE 11
Clinics
San Rafael
CENTRAL
Lic Pérez
Soccer Stadium
CALLE 13
CALLE 15
PASEO DE LOS TURISTAS
CALLE 17
AVENIDA
CALLE 19
Restaurant
Aloha
Hotel
Tioga
CALLE 21
Restaurant
La Yunta
Restaurant La Caravelle
CALLE 23
CALLE 25
AVENIDA 2
AVENIDA 2 BIS
AVENIDA 4
CALLE 27
CALLE 29
CALLE 31
AVENIDA 1
AVENIDA 3
CALLE 33
Car ferry
(to Playa Naranjo & Paquera)
CALLE 35
Hotel Yadran
CALLE 37

El Estero

Golfo de Nicoya

N
Bradt

0   500m
0   500yds

The local hospital is **Monseñor Sanabria Hospital** (✆ *630 8000*).

WHAT TO SEE AND DO Most people come to Puntarenas to catch the ferry to the Nicoya Peninsula. It's strictly first come, first served, so prepare for a wait, especially during high season. When you arrive at the dock, you must park your car after the last vehicle in line, get out of your vehicle and purchase a ticket at the wicket, get back into your vehicle and wait. Passengers on foot must also purchase tickets. Schedules vary according to season so call first.

🛥 **Playa Naranjo** ✆ 661 1069. 1hr.   🛥 **Ferry Peninsula** ✆ 641 0118. 1hr 30min.
🛥 **Tambor Ferry** ✆ 661 2084. 1hr 30min.

Another favoured activity here is day trips to the islands in the peninsula. The following companies offer return trips to the uninhabited Tortuga Island, a picture-perfect tropical spot with white sand and crystal waters.

🛥 **Bay Island Cruises** ✆ 258 1189;
www.bayislandcruises.com
🛥 **Calypso Tours** ✆ 256 2727;
www.calypsotours.com. This company also offers tours to Punta Coral Private Reserve, which is less crowded than Tortuga. Trips run in the neighbourhood for US$100 pp.
🛥 **Coonatramar** ✆ 661 9011; e coonatra@ racsa.co.cr. Offers tours to the mangroves as well as to San Lucas Island, the *Tico* equivalent of Alcatraz.

This former penal colony, with its horrific conditions, inspired former inmate José Leon Sanchez to write the book *The Island of Lonely Men* which was made into a movie. The jail was closed in 1991 and the island is strictly off-limits but the crumbling walls are still visible from the ocean.
🛥 **La Casa de la Cultura** Downtown; ✆ 661 1394. Speaking of former jails, landlubbers can check out this place which now houses drama, dance, music, sculpture and paintings.

PUNTARENAS TO JACÓ

Between Puntarenas and Jacó there are some lovely spots to stop and enjoy for a bit of time or to explore over a number of days.

GETTING THERE AND AWAY Continue driving along the Coastal Highway southeast toward Orotina. Follow the signs for Herradura and Jacó.

↱ WHERE TO STAY
🏠 **Marriott Los Sueños Beach & Golf Resort** (211 rooms) In Playa Herradura; ✆ 630 9000; www.marriotthotels.com. This is a very large resort, complete with an 18-hole, Ted Robinson-designed golf course and a marina. The complex is also home to numerous condominiums that are privately owned. This being a Marriott hotel, guests know what to expect — excellent service. The architecture and décor are very much in the same vein as the Marriott in San José, drawing heavily on Spanish colonialism with decorative tiles, dark woods and ornate carvings. Rooms are spacious and have either 1 king- or 2 queen-size beds. Each room has a balcony but those not facing the ocean have very small, *Juliet*-style balconies while the rooms with ocean views have some balconies large enough to fit a chaise longue — be sure to enquire as to what type of room you're receiving. The pool is beautifully designed to recreate the canals of Venice, there is a Serenity Spa, a gym, tennis courts, 5 restaurants and a casino — everything to pamper the discerning traveller who wants to stay in a luxury chain hotel. The beach, however, is one of the least attractive in Costa Rica, with hard dark-brown sand and rocks (although it's sheltered so the swimming is very safe). Rates US$200–400.
🏠 **Villa Caletas** (36 rooms) In Playa Herradura; ✆ 637 0606; www.hotelvillacaletas.com. One of the most remarkable hotels in Costa Rica, the location alone is enough to take your breath away (unfortunately, the multitude of stairs to the rooms will do the same as the hotel is aptly named — *caletas* means 'stairs' in Spanish). High atop a steep mountainside, the 180° view of the ocean

and rainforest is incredible. Featuring architecture influenced by French colonialism with a dash of Greek revivalist, the buildings have an easy grace about them that is luxurious but never stuffy. Each room is built into the side of the hill and offers great privacy and includes AC, cable TV, telephone, minibar and bathrooms with hot water. Junior suites and upwards all have ocean views as well as jacuzzis and a living room. The master suites are truly spectacular, with a separate sitting/minibar room, a separate jacuzzi room, king-size bed, sofa bed, private pool and gardens all behind a high wall ensuring absolute privacy (perfect for honeymoons). The infinity pool is beautiful and there is a Serenity Spa on the premises. A Greek amphitheatre plays host to an annual music festival during Jul and Aug and is the perfect spot to watch a sunset any time of year while enjoying a beverage at the terrace bar. The hotel staff are very accommodating and make guests feel like VIPs. There is a beach at the bottom of the mountain (a 10-min drive down a very steep dirt road that requires a 4x4 — the hotel has hourly shuttles) complete with a small beach bar and lounge chairs. Alas, the beach is white pebbles. During high tide, it's possible to swim (there are stairs built into the sea wall) but sunbathing is the preferred activity at this beach. Highly recommended. *Rates US$150–380.*

🏠 **Punta Leona*** (108 units, 72 apts) Just outside of Jacó; ☎ 231 3131; www.hotelpuntaleona.com. This sprawling resort has access to 4 beaches, 3 being Blue Flag winners of which 2 have beautiful white sand. The setting, with majestic rock outcrops and lush rainforest, is gorgeous — unfortunately, the resort isn't. One of the first large-scale resorts in Costa Rica, this was *the* place for monied *Ticos* to have a beach house. Over time, however, the resort has become run down and the weekends see it crowded with *Josefinos*, complete with jet skis, noisy boom boxes and loud disco music. There is the hotel as well as privately owned homes and apts but there is no sense of urban planning to the resort so the overall feeling is of development gone wild. Some of the rental homes are in varying states, with some in desperate need of repair. Despite the beaches being public by law, the resort has made it virtually impossible for outsiders to enjoy them and anyone 'caught' on the sand who isn't a guest will be quickly escorted off the beach by security. There are 2 restaurants, 2 bars (one which is a disco at night), 2 swimming pools, a tennis court, miniature golf and a supermarket. There is a lovely little beach church on the premises. My recommendation is to give this place a miss, as there are far nicer hotels/rental properties to choose from in the area. *Rates US$87–240.*

🏠 **Villa Lapas Lodge** (58 rooms) Next to Carara Biological Reserve ☎ 637 0202; f 637 0227 www.villalapas.com. Simple, almost Spartan rooms, in long buildings resembling traditional *casas*, are surrounded by trees, birds and with a picturesque river running through. Rooms have 2 dbl beds, ample bathroom with hot water and AC. This is the place for the birding crowd and everyone seems to have a set of binoculars around their neck. There is a lovely recreation of a typical town across the river, 'Santa Lucia Town', complete with a church and antique posts and beams. Quaint, cute and a good spot for nature lovers. There is a pool, restaurant, hiking trails, waterfalls and canopy trails. *Rates US$100.*

✗ WHERE TO EAT

✗ **La Fiesta Mariscos** On the main road heading towards Jacó; ☎ 637 0172. This place offers outstanding value for money. As it's located right on the beach, you can watch the fishing boats as they bring in the catch of the day, moments before it arrives on your plate. The setting is basic, with cement round patio tables and benches under a giant tent and the odd beach dog coming by for a snack but the service is very attentive. Each order includes a complimentary *boca* of either bean dip or seafood soup — both are incredible (the best bean dip I've ever had). Portions are huge and the seafood sampler for 2 people can easily fill up 4 people. It's a place where the locals hang out and by far some of the best food in the country. Highly recommended. *Meals average US$8. Open daily 08.00–22.00.*

WHAT TO SEE AND DO En route, you'll cross the **Tarcoles Bridge**, which is worth a stop on account of the multitude of crocodiles on the banks and in the river below. There is a new **Three Generations** coffee shop on the north end of the bridge where you can park and walk along the bridge to take photos. Note: theft from cars is a problem here (despite the police station being on the south end of the bridge) so make sure to lock your doors. Also, do not walk on the road of the bridge – this is still one of the main thoroughfares in the country and cars/trucks rule the road. Stick to the narrow pavements.

Carara Biological Reserve (✆ *383 9953; open Nov–Apr 07.00–17.00, May–Oct 08.00–16.00; entrance US$6*) is located a short drive 11km north of Jacó. This biological reserve, with ranger station, water, bathrooms and cafeteria is famous worldwide for its more than 300 scarlet macaws, which visitors can usually see flying overhead in the early morning and late afternoon. Their loud squawking is heard long before spotting them so keep an ear and eye open for these mystical birds. Most of the park's 12,953 acres is primary forest, home to a cornucopia of plants, animals, reptiles and birds. Day hikes on well-marked trails include the Las Araceas Trail at only 1.2km long, the Laguna Meandrica Trail which can take up to four hours to complete and the Quebrada Bonito Trail, clocking in at 1½ hours. If you trek this trail, do not deviate from the path or go near the lagoon or river as large crocodiles live in both. Hiring a guide is recommended, as there is so much to see that an untrained eye will miss the many treasures here.

JACÓ

Being the closest beach town to San José and home to some of the best surfing spots in the country, Jacó (pronounced 'Ha-ko') has garnered the reputation as being *the* party beach, if not the party place, of Costa Rica. At weekends, the town often resembles a 'Spring Break' teen movie, with partiers spilling out into the roads in the wee morning hours. Bars, casinos and discos line the streets, offering various enticements for pleasure seekers.

Despite Jacó's popularity, the beach itself is not the cleanest and there is a problem with water contamination that has plagued the area for a number of years. Swimmers should take extra precautions near the estuary and river mouths on account of the dirty water and be aware of strong currents, making these dangerous spots for swimming. Head to the southern part of the beach, which is the cleanest and safest swimming area.

GETTING THERE AND AWAY
By car Jacó is about a two-hour drive from San José on a fairly good, but very curvy road. Travelling through the mountains is not advised at night, as there are several hairpin turns and mudslides during the rainy season. Take the Inter-American Highway west then follow the Coastal Highway (follow the signs).

By bus Transportes Jacó (✆ *223 1109*) departs from San José's Coca Cola Bus Terminal, Avenida 1/3, Calle 16.

GETTING AROUND
Downtown Jacó is easily accessed by walking. Buses Transportes Jacó (✆ *223 1109*) run regularly and there are numerous taxis always on the main roads. Try Taxis Jacó (✆ *643 3009*).

WHERE TO STAY
Jacó has an abundance of simple cabins and rooms, catering to the young surfing crowd. Those seeking higher-end hotels should look to the areas on the fringe of town.

⌂ **Club del Mar** (22 condos, 10 rooms) On the road to Playa Hermosa; ✆ 643 3194; f 643 3550; www.clubdelmarcostarica.com. After Los Sueños, the nicest hotel in the Jacó area. Situated on a lovely stretch of beach and nestled in well-tended gardens,

it's easy to forget you're only a 2-min drive to Jacó. Remodelled in 2002, the entire hotel feels almost new and the attentive staff ensure clients are well cared for. There are deluxe rooms, 2 penthouse suites and 1- and 2-bedroom condos, which are

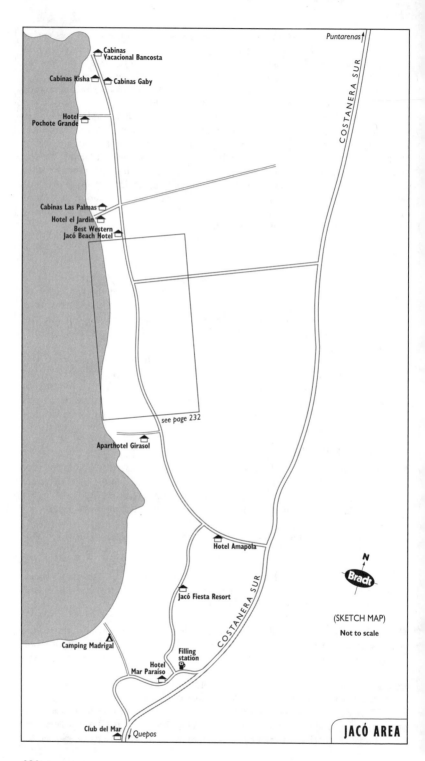

Puntarenas↑

COSTANERA SUR

Cabinas
Vacacional Bancosta

Cabinas Kisha ▭ ▭ Cabinas Gaby

Hotel
Pochote Grande

Cabinas Las Palmas
Hotel el Jardin
Best Western
Jacó Beach Hotel

see page 232

Aparthotel Girasol

Hotel Amapola

N

Bradt

(SKETCH MAP)
Not to scale

Jacó Fiesta Resort

COSTANERA SUR

Camping Madrigal

Filling
station
Hotel
Mar Paraíso

Club del Mar ↓ Quepos

JACÓ AREA

complete with kitchen, dining room and living room. There is a lovely pool, spa, bar, restaurant (although a bit pricey), conference rooms and secure parking. Honeymooners have been very happy staying at this hotel and I've yet to hear a bad word about the place. Those with a larger budget can't go wrong here. *Rates: rooms US$140; condos US$203–290.*

🏠 **Best Western Jacó Beach** (125 rooms) Across from bus station; ✆ 643 1000; f 643 3246; www.grupomarta.com. One of the largest hotels in Jacó, rooms are equipped with phones, safes, TV and either pool or garden views. The hotel is clean and spacious, with a large pool, a children's pool, tennis court, beach volleyball court, exercise room, conference room, restaurant, snack bar and a beachfront bar. A safe bet. *Rate US$132.*

🏠 **Hotel Amapola** (44 rooms) ✆ 643 2255; f 643 3668; www.hotelamapola.com. Formerly part of the Barceló hotel chain, this hotel changed hands in 2004 and is now a stand-alone resort. The junior suites and 3 villas are spacious and neat, with AC, satellite TV and phones. The resort has a pool with 2 jacuzzis and a swim-up bar and a popular casino. Guests can choose from either an all-inc package or rooms with b/fast only. *Rates US$96 pp dbl for all-inc, US$120–190 room with b/fast.*

🏠 **Apartotel Girasol** (17 rooms) South end of town; ✆ 643 1591; www.girasol.com. A well-managed complex featuring large apts with simple décor and lovely terraces or balconies, hot water, AC, cable TV, a large pool, colourful gardens, secure parking and direct beach access. Family-friendly and a good option for those who want a 'home away from home'. *Rate US$115.*

🏠 **Canciones del Mar** (11 rooms) Ca BriBri at the beach; ✆ 643 3273; f 643 3269; www.cancionesdelmar.com. An oasis of calm in the midst of the madness that can be Jacó. The walled beachside complex houses 1-bedroom suites, 1 honeymoon suite and 1 2-bedroom suite. All rooms have AC, TVs and a view of both the pool and the ocean. Rooms could use a new coat of paint and fixtures are looking a bit tired but overall, a good spot. B/fast inc. *Rate US$111.*

🏠 **Jacó Fiesta Resort** (80 AC rooms) South end of beach; ✆ 643 3147; f 643 3148; www.jacofiesta.net. Not to be confused with the Fiesta Resort in Puntarenas, this Fiesta is a non-inc hotel. The resort is clean, with rooms centred around 3 large pools. There are all the usual amenities one expects with a beach resort – tennis courts, sports bar, beach restaurant, conference centre, even a sports book for those who like a wager. *Rate US$105.*

🏠 **Hotel Copacabana** (35 rooms) Ca Anita; ✆ 643 1005; www.copacabanahotel.com. Suffered a fire in 2000 but has been rebuilt since. Choice of rooms or suites with AC, cable TV, balconies with ocean view, pool, bar, billiards, sports bar and lovely gardens. *Rates US$103–173.*

🏠 **Hotel & Casino Cocal** (43 rooms) On the beach; ✆ 643 3067; f 643 1201; e cocalcr@racsa.co.cr. A definite step up, this Spanish hacienda-style hotel has well-appointed rooms surrounding 2 pools. Two beachfront restaurants/bars offer gourmet food and there is a small casino for slot action. B/fast inc. *Rate US$95.*

🏠 **Hotel Poseidon** (15 rooms) Centre of town; ✆ 643 1642; f 643 3558; www.hotel-poseidon.com. Having changed ownership into American hands, this hotel has seen marked improvements. The rooms are small but are bright, clean and simply appointed with nicely tiled bathrooms. There is AC, minibar, cable TV, refrigerator, pool with swim-up bar and 2 bars. The showcase, though, is the hotel restaurant with its Asian-fusion creations. B/fast inc. *Rate US$76.*

🏠 **Hotel Pochote Grande** (24 rooms) From the town entrance heading to the beach; ✆ 643 3236; f 220 4979. Clean, beachfront rooms, AC, fridge, pool, restaurant and bar and is one of the better options in town. *Rates US$70–80.*

🏠 **Hotel Mar de Luz** (29 rooms) Behind the subway; ✆/f 643 3259; www.mardeluz.com. Recently remodelled, fully equipped apts with AC, kitchenette, microwave, cable TV, 2 pools, jacuzzi and a cheerful garden. Some cabins have lovely wood and river stone detailing. The Dutch family who own the hotel are multi-lingual and helpful. *Rate US$67.*

🏠 **Hotel & Cabins Tangeri** (14 rooms) In town; ✆ 643 3001; f 643 3636; e tangeri@racsa.co.cr. Well-maintained condos and cabins on the beach with AC, TV, refrigerator and balcony with ocean view. New condos and cabins were recently built that are nicer and include a kitchenette. 3 pools, playground, sports courts, bar and 2 restaurants. *Rates US$64–128.*

🏠 **Cabinas Centro Vacacional Bancosta** (34 rooms) Near the Tangeri; ✆ 643 3016. With large rooms, basketball, beachfront gardens and 3 pools aimed at keeping families busy and happy. A good deal. *Rate US$65 for up to 6 people.*

🏠 **Paradise Hotel** (6 rooms) In town; ✆ 643 2563. This place is the former Jacó Jungle Inn. Some rooms have cable TV and there is AC, a pool, jacuzzi, parking and a shared kitchen. *Rates US$60–82.*

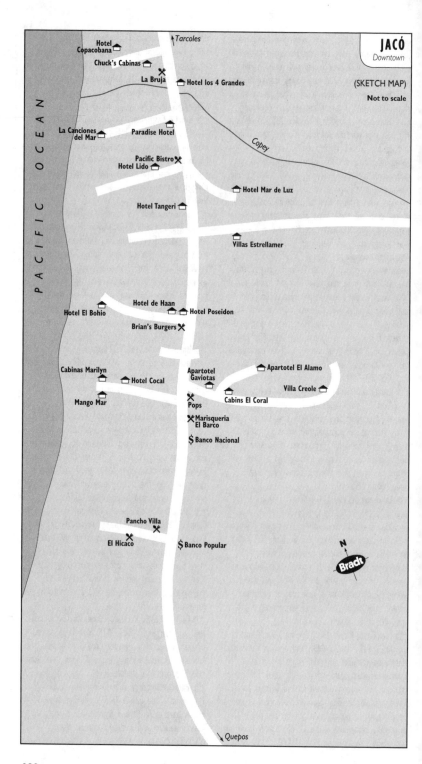

JACÓ
Downtown

(SKETCH MAP)
Not to scale

PACIFIC OCEAN

Tarcoles

Copey

Hotel Copacobana
Chuck's Cabinas
La Bruja
Hotel los 4 Grandes
La Canciones del Mar
Paradise Hotel
Pacific Bistro
Hotel Lido
Hotel Mar de Luz
Hotel Tangeri
Villas Estrellamer
Hotel El Bohio
Hotel de Haan
Hotel Poseidon
Brian's Burgers
Cabinas Marilyn
Hotel Cocal
Apartotel Gaviotas
Apartotel El Alamo
Villa Creole
Mango Mar
Cabins El Coral
Pops
Marisqueria El Barco
Banco Nacional
Pancho Villa
El Hicaco
Banco Popular

N

Bradt

Quepos

⌂ **Hotel Mar Paraiso** (24 rooms) South end of the beach; \/f 643 1947; www.hotelmarparaiso.com. Nothing special here, as the building could use an overhaul and rooms have plastic beach furniture as dining sets. But it's close to the beach, has 2 beds and a sofa bed in each room, cable TV, phones, AC, pool with jacuzzi, a kiddies' pool and a restaurant. A popular spot with Ticos and surfers, the hotel offers a variety of discounts to surfers, students and those staying Sun to Thu so be sure to enquire. B/fast and taxes inc. *Rates US$56 pp for all-inc option (no alcohol) or US$78 for a dbl.*

⌂ **Hotel Mango Mar** (14 rooms) On the road to the beach; \/f 643 3670. Clean rooms with kitchenette, balcony, TV and AC. There is a guitar-shaped pool with a jacuzzi, lounge, beach access and safe parking. *Rate US$55.*

⌂ **Villas Estrellamar** (29 rooms) Behind the subway; \ 643 3102; f 643 3453; www.hotel.co.cr/estrellamar. Offers the option of rooms, 1-, 2- or 3-bedroom bungalows and an all-inc meal option as well. Rooms have AC, phone, cable TV while the bungalows have a kitchen. There is a nice garden, pool and a restaurant. *Rates US$53–66.*

⌂ **Cabinas Gaby** (9 rooms) From the town entrance heading to the beach; \ 643 3080. Offers large rooms, fan, AC, kitchen, cable TV, safe parking and a pool. *Rate US$47.*

⌂ **Apartotel El Oasis** (10 rooms) Behind Pops; \/f 643 3915. Rooms for up to 4 people, cable TV and a children's pool. *Rates US$46–62.*

⌂ **Cabinas El Coral** (14 rooms) Behind Pops; \ 643 3133. Simple rooms with refrigerators, AC option, some with cable TV, facing a large pool. *Rates US$42–56.*

⌂ **Hotel El Jardin** (10 rooms) Near Cabinas Las Palmas; \ 643 3050. Clean, comfortable rooms, AC in some, very nice pool and a relaxing bar to chill out in. *Rate US$41.*

⌂ **Paraiso del Sol** (11 rooms) Behind Pops; \ 643 3250; f 643 3137; www.paraisodelsolcr.com. Large rooms with AC, kitchenette, pool and a bar. *Rate US$40.*

⌂ **Cabinas Kisha** (6 rooms) North end of main road; \/f 643 3126. Offering simple cabins with kitchen and a small pool. *Rate US$55 for up to 6 people.*

⌂ **Apartotel Gaviotas** (12 rooms) Behind Pops; \/f 643 3092. Cabins for 2 to 5 people, TV, pool, kitchen, secure parking and optional AC. *Rates US$35–45.*

⌂ **Cabinas Las Orquídeas** (10 rooms) Behind Pops; \ 643 4056. Offers rooms with coffee maker, refrigerator, cable TV and pool. *Rates US$35–45.*

⌂ **Hotel Los 4 Grandes** (14 rooms) Main road; \ 643 2215. A new addition to town with clean, fresh rooms, AC, pool and jacuzzi. *Rates US$25–50.*

⌂ **Hotel/Camping El Bohio** (14 rooms) \ 643 3017. Simple rooms, pool, bathrooms, a safe, tent rental as well as a bar and seafood restaurant on the beach. Great spot to hang out grab a beer and meet some people. *Rates: rooms US$24–40; camping US$3.50 pp.*

⌂ **Cabinas Marilyn** (7 rooms) On the road to the beach; \ 643 3215. With beachfront cabins, some with fridge and kitchen. *Rate US$20.*

⌂ **Hotel de Haan** (12 rooms) Across bridge heading towards the beach; \ 643 1795. Offers simple rooms, shared kitchen and a pool. *Rate US$8 pp.*

⌂ **Chuck's Cabinas and Board Repair** (9 rooms) Ca Anita towards the beach; \ 643 3328. Geared towards surfers and has simple cabins with shared bath, cold water. *Rate US$7 pp.*

⌂ **Camping Madrigal** Far south end of beach; \ 643 3230. Has a picnic area under shady trees, bathrooms and cold-water showers. *Rate US$2.50 pp.*

✦ WHERE TO EAT As Jacó is 'Party Central', restaurants are generally basic and affordable, although there are a few better dining establishments popping up.

✗ **La Bruja Bar & Restaurant** On the main road into Jacó; \ 643 3493. A charming place featuring great fondue (the owners are Swiss). If you hit it lucky, a live band might be playing. *Cheese fondue US$17 pp. Open 19.00–00.30; closed Mon.*

✗ **Pacific Bistro** In town next to Paradise Hotel; \ 643 3771. Jacó's most exciting new restaurant, offering salvation for taste buds tired of pedestrian seaside fare. The Asian-fusion menu changes daily with inventive combinations of fresh fish and local ingredients. Yum! *Meals average US$18. Open 06.00–22.00 Wed–Sun.*

✗ **Pops** Main road in town. Pops is the national ice cream chain and worthy of the line-ups stretching outside its doors. Great variety of flavours, rich milkshakes and sundaes at very affordable prices make it the perfect way to cool down at the beach.

✗ **Bar & Restaurant Marisquería El Barco** Next to Pops; \ 643 2831. Great service, great food and great prices, which explains why all the locals eat here. Pizza, seafood and steaks are guaranteed to please. *Main course US$7–25. Open daily 10.00–12.00.*

✗ **Bar & Restaurant Pancho Villa** Main road; ☎ 643 3571. This place has been around almost as long as Jacó has. A great spot to people watch and quell the late-night munchies, it's not a place for fine dining (especially with the strip joint upstairs). The building is in desperate need of a good cleaning and redecoration. Food is OK and portions are large but there are better spots for dinner. *Meals average US$16. Open 24hrs.*

✗ **Caliches Wishbone** Main road; ☎ 643 3406. Popular with the surfing crowd, the margaritas and Mexican food are extremely well done, making this a cut above the rest of the 'hang 10' hangouts. Pizza and seafood round out a relaxed menu that has something for everyone. *Meals average US$16. Open Thu–Tue 11.30–15.00, 17.30–22.00.*

✗ **Restaurant Marisqueria El Hicaco** Near Pancho Villa; ☎ 643 3226; e elhicaco@playajaco.com. Serves up Tico fare and seafood. Basic, affordable and good. *Everyday 'Wine festival' (20 differents types of wine) US$25. On Wed 'Lobster festival' US$56 (all you can eat and drink). Open daily 11.00–23.00.*

NIGHTLIFE Bars and discos line the streets but they open and shut in the blink of an eye, so don't be surprised if this section is out of date by the time you read it. **El Zarpe Sportsbar** (☎ *643 3473*) is at the bus station, for those who want to stay on top of the game. **Club Ole** (☎ *643 1576*) has a restaurant, disco, games room and a mechanical bull. **La Central** is a hopping disco. **La Bruja** is an institution of sorts and offers up live music from time to time. **Onyx Bar**, upstairs over the subway, plays classic rock, has pool tables and is usually packed. **Hotel Copacabana** has live music on weekends. **Hollywood Nightclub** on the main road is a strip club. Those wanting casino action can head to **Hotel Cocal**, **Jacó Fiesta** and **Hotel Amapola**.

PRACTICALITIES

Banks **Banco Nacional** (☎ *643 3072*) is in the town centre. There is also **Banco de Costa Rica** and **Banco Popular**, which has an ATM.

Medical **Centro Medico Bolaños** (☎ *643 2323*) is at the north end of town. Also **Centro Medico Integral** (☎ *643 3205*) 50m south of Banco Nacional and the **Pharmacy** (☎ *643 1127*).

Police There is one station on the beach and another in Garabito (☎ *643 3011*). **OIJ** (☎ *643 1723*) (OIJ is the Costa Rican equivalent of the CID in the UK or the FBI in the US).

Internet **Internet Café** (☎ *643 1959; open 08.00–21.00*) is in the town centre: international calls, stamps, faxes. **Mexican Joe's Internet Café** (☎ *643 2141*): international calls, faxes, scanning, PlayStation, Mexican food. **Jacocafe.com** (☎ *643 2601*), across from Mexican Joe's: international calls, digital photography, faxes.

Car rental **Budget** (☎ *643 2665*); **Zuma** (☎ *643 3207;* e *zumaway@hotmail.com*); **National** (☎ *643 1752*).

WHAT TO SEE AND DO Jacó and the surrounding area isn't just surfing and partying and there are some excellent nature areas to explore.

Butterflies **The Lighthouse** (☎ *643 3083*) is a 24-hour restaurant on the main road that also has a butterfly garden and an unofficial animal shelter for injured wildlife.

Canopy tours **Chiclets Tree Tour** (☎ *643 1880;* f *643 3509, www.jacowave.com; rate US$60 plus transportation, depending on where in the area you are being picked up from*) has eight platforms in the forests just outside of Jacó. They've been around since 1996 and provide an excellent tour.

Gym **Corpus Gym** (☎ 643 1476), above Happy Video, Main Street, has free-weight equipment, limited exercise equipment.

Horses **Jacó Equestrian Centre** (☎ 643 1569; *www.horsestour.com; tours US$65*) offers up a unique tour around Herradura Bay, finishing on the centre's 2,000-acre farm near Los Sueños Marriott. The 2½-hour jaunt on well cared-for horses includes snacks and drinks, with either a morning or sunset tour option. For those who want to learn more about horses, 'Horse Whispering' seminars are available to all levels of riders.

Jungle river cruise **JD's Watersports** (☎ 257 3857; *www.jdwatersports.com; rate US$49, includes lunch, guide and boat ride*) has a half-day cruise on a flat-bottomed boat through a mangrove forest and down the Tárcoles River, renowned for its crocodiles. I highly recommend this tour for its professional and knowledgeable guides who do not feed the crocodiles, a dangerous practice other tours often employ that not only endangers the guide but the families who live on the nearby riverbanks.

Kayak **Kayak Jacó** (☎/f 643 1233; *www.kayakjaco.com*) offers river adventures via kayak, sea kayaks, outrigger canoes (as seen in Hawaii) and snorkelling.

Sport fishing Some of the best fishing is in the Central Pacific area. **JD's Watersports** (☎ 257 3857; *www.jdwatersports.com; rates: US$1,200 private charter, US$250 per person non-charter*) has a 44ft Striker yacht with all the equipment. The full-day tour includes lunch, drinks, bait and tackle for up to six people. Fishing licences must be purchased at the dock.

Shopping The main street in Jacó is home to a number of lovely little boutiques featuring handicrafts, ceramics and handmade clothing. **La Heliconia Art Gallery** (☎ 643 3613) has paintings by local artists, jewellery and unique ceramics. **Guacamole** (☎ 643 1120) is one of my favourite spots to pick up fun, one-of-a-kind clothing that's handmade, hand-painted and perfect for the beach! **El Cofre del Tesoro** (☎ 643 1912) is a charming boutique, showcasing a plethora of imported goodies from the world over.

Spa **Serenity Spa** (*El Paso Mall;* ☎ 643 1624) offers massages, manicures, pedicures and facials in relaxing surroundings.

Surfing Not the easiest beach to surf – Tamarindo is the best beach for beginner surfers – but if you can learn to surf here, everywhere else will seem like a piece of cake. **Chosita del Surf** (☎/f 643 1308; e *chuck@racsa.co.cr*) is an institution in Jacó. Gringo Chuck, the owner, can set you up with boards to rent or buy as well as lessons. Other surf shops with gear, rentals and lessons include **Walter Surfboards** (☎ 643 1056), **Jacó Surf** (☎ 643 3574) and **El Surf Spot** (☎ 643 3533). **Vista Guapa Surf Camp** (☎/f 643 3242; *www.vistaguapa.com*) has week-long surf camps which include breakfast, dinner, transportation, room and lessons for US$1,050.

PLAYA HERMOSA TO QUEPOS

Continuing south down the Coastal Highway, a number of sleepy beach towns offer alternatives to the larger centres of Jacó and Quepos.

Playa Hermosa or 'Beautiful Beach' is located about 3km south of Jacó Beach. It is one of the most popular surfing spots on the Pacific coast of Costa Rica and often hotels will offer discounts on rooms to surfers. In fact, this is the location of Costa Rica's national surf contest every year. Not only is the surf activity high, but also there is a variety of exotic birds that hang around the beach. These include white herons, snowy egrets, jacanas, and black-bellied whistling ducks. Definitely a must-see for surfers.

Note: the riptides and surf here are incredibly strong and this beach is NOT recommended for swimming or beginning surfers. A number of unfortunate souls drown on this beach every year so take heed.

Continuing down the road is Esterillos, still an undeveloped gem (although land is being snatched up) and a great spot to beachcomb for sand dollars. Closer to Quepos is Playa Bejuco and then Playa Palo Seco, both beautiful beaches where tourists are few and far between.

WHERE TO STAY

Xandari By the Pacific (6 villas) On beach at Playa Esterillos Este; 443 2020; www.xandari.com. From the creators of the uniquely artistic Xandari Hotel in Alajuela, they've opened their magic paintbox to create the first luxury hotel on the beach in the central Pacific. At the time of writing, construction was being completed but the hotel boasts the same attention to detail, beautiful original artwork and thoughtful architecture of its sister hotel. Each private villa has a large terrace, private garden, sitting area, minibar, huge bathroom with hot water with a shower that opens on the garden as well as AC and a fan. There is an open-aired restaurant on site and a pool. A second pool, a spa and more villas are planned for 2007. Rates US$245–350, includes b/fast.

The Backyard Oceanfront Rooms & Suites (8 rooms) Last hotel on Playa Hermosa; 643 1311; www.costaricanet.net/backyard. Located right on the beach, this 2-storey structure has great views of the surf below. Each tidy and spacious room has a view, a balcony, AC, private bathrooms with hot water as well as a swimming pool and jacuzzi. There is a happening bar and restaurant where everyone hangs out in the evenings. Rates US$115–165.

Terraza del Pacifico (43 rooms) At the start of Playa Hermosa; 643 3222; www.terrazadelpacifico.com. Surfer's paradise found — this is a hotel for and by surfers, boasting the only night surfing in the country, thanks to the giant Klieg lights they have set up on the beach. Recent upgrades and renovations have made the rooms better than they were, with nicely appointed furnishings in the suites. All rooms are quite roomy and feature an ocean view with either a patio or a balcony. All rooms have dbl bed and 1 sgl bed, hot water, private bathroom, cable TV, telephone and AC while suites have a large sitting area and a kitchenette. There is a restaurant, 2 pools and a swim-up bar. Rates US$107–210.

Beso del Viento (4 apts) Playa Seco; 779 9674; f 779 9675; www.besodelviento.com. This is one of the secret spots I hate to share but I will with you, dear reader. Less than 30 mins' drive from Quepos/Manuel Antonio (you can see these towns from the beach here). Playa Palo Seco is a long, skinny stretch of beach backed by an estuary and river. Only a 5km jaunt behind the palm plantations in Parrita, Playa Palo Seco is a sleepy little beach spot that the rest of the world has seemingly forgotten about. Even during the crazy Christmas crush, I saw fewer than 10 other souls on the beach. There is little here but Beso del Viento is the perfect spot for those who want to be away from it all yet close enough to 'the action'. The charming French owners have added an artistic touch to each of the apts, which boast a kitchen, tiled bathroom with hot water, fan, living/dining room and a comfortable bed. There is a lovely oval pool and a huge expanse of lawn that has only a small dirt road separating it from the beach. Horses are available for rent and the owners also offer mangrove tours on their boat. Rate US$73.

Hotel Pelican (10 rooms) In Esterillos Este on the beach; \/f 778 8105; www.aubergepelican.com. Set amongst palm trees, just steps from the beach, this small but charming hotel is a great bargain for those seeking a laid-back beach holiday. Rooms are simply furnished but nicely finished with hardwood floors and ceilings. Each room has AC and a private bathroom with hot water. There is a pool, beach bar, pool table and a charming restaurant and bar out of wood. B/fast inc. Rate US$60.

Hotel del Fin (27 rooms) Playa Bejuco; 778 8054. This classic beachfront hotel has been recently renovated and reopened. Situated at the end of the beach, this quiet spot is quite stunning, with handsome woodwork and an impressive wooden staircase. Each room has giant windows, hot water and a fan. There is also a pool. Rates US$50–85.

Jungle Surf Café (5 rooms) On the main highway in Playa Hermosa; ☎ 643 1495. This place is famous for its Tex-Mex burgers and killer omelettes. Simple cabins. B/fast inc. *Rate US$15 pp.*

Cabinas Playa Hermosa (7 rooms) On the main road in Playa Hermosa; ☎ 643 2640. Recently built thatched-roofed and wooden cabins make for rustic yet comfortable lodgings, with fan, private bathroom, a kitchen in some units and a communal kitchen for all. There is a snack bar and a Pizza Express. This is truly a place for surfers by surfers, as the famous Fischer brothers are artisans with their surfboard creations. Got a ding? Bring it in and they'll fix it within 24hrs. Recommended. *Rate US$15 pp*

QUEPOS AND MANUEL ANTONIO

White-sand beaches, kissed by lush rainforests crowned by breathtaking sunsets – it's no wonder Manuel Antonio is the single most visited spot in Costa Rica, with over 25% of all tourists to the country making this a priority destination. Being the most popular, it is also the priciest area so be prepared to pay top dollar for food and lodging. The former banana port to the north, Quepos ('KAY-pos'), is the gateway to Manuel Antonio and those seeking budget digs will find them here.

The primary draw of this area is Manuel Antonio National Park, one of the first in the country but also one of the smallest at only 683ha – despite its diminutive size, it's certainly the gem of the national park system, boasting some of the best snorkelling, swimming and hiking trails in the area. The wildlife, though, is the star attraction and it's not unusual to see three species of monkeys (howler, white-faced and the tiny squirrel or 'mono titi' endemic to the area), two-toed sloths, coatimundis, and iguanas.

Besides the park, sport fishing, boating, rafting, hiking, canopy tours, horseriding, and exploring the beautiful beaches makes Manuel Antonio a popular destination. There are a few low-cost cabins located close to the beach but they are rather shabby. The first beach, Espadilla, is long and open to the sea with serious riptides and strong currents. Further down is Espadilla Sur and then you'll enter Manuel Antonio National Park, with seven exquisite white-sand beaches. Dining in the area is varied and, for the most part, excellent.

GETTING THERE AND AWAY
By air Both **Sansa** (☎ *221 9419*) and **NatureAir** (☎ *220 3054*) run numerous flights between San José and Quepos, lasting only 25 minutes.

By car The four-hour drive is one of the smoothest in the country, thanks to the paved roads that are in very good condition. There are a few bridges under repair so traffic must take turns crossing. Follow the Coastal Highway that snakes through La Garita to Jacó and then heads due south.

By bus Daily **Transportes Delio Morales** (☎ *223 5567*) buses leave from San José's Coca-Cola Terminal.

GETTING AROUND Quepos is small enough for you to walk almost everywhere. In Mauel Antonio, everything is spread out along the main road and there are no pavements. Buses run every 30 minutes along the main road between Quepos and the traffic circle by the park. Taxis have to come in from Quepos (☎ *777 0277*) and charge a minimum of US$4.

QUEPOS

The town of Quepos (pronounced 'KAY-pos') isn't a holiday destination – this is the 'meat and potatoes' fishing town (formerly a banana port) that services the surrounding area. It's rough around the edges, a little run down and lacking in 'picture postcard' charm. But it does have some good spots to eat, has the only supermarkets in the area and budget *cabinas* and hotels for those who don't want to pay the higher prices of its neighbour up the hill, Manuel Antonio.

WHERE TO STAY
Prices are based on double occupancy during high season (December–April) unless otherwise noted. Mandatory hotel tax of 16.39% must be added to prices unless noted.

Best Western Hotel Kamuk (35 rooms) Downtown Quepos, near the water; ☎ 777 0811; f 777 0258; e info@kamuk.co.cr. Straightforward hotel-chain rooms with AC, cable TV, hot water and a phone. Amenities include a nice pool, 2 restaurants and, the big draw here, a casino. For those who want a clean, American-style hotel room at a decent price, this is a good bet. B/fast inc. *Rates US$60–85.*

Hotel Sirena (14 rooms) On the first road heading from beach; ☎ 777 0528; www.lasirenahotel.com. One of the better options in town, with nice rooms, AC and a pool. *Rate US$69.*

Cabinas El Cisne (35 rooms) On the southeast outskirts near the football field; ☎ 777 0719. Acceptable rooms for up to 5 people with fan or AC option, private bath, hot water and some with a fridge and kitchenette. Ask for a newer room as

they are larger. *Rates US$35–45.*

Hotel Ceciliano (24 rooms) On the first road from beach; ☎ 777 0192. Very clean with spacious and sunny rooms, some with shared baths, AC option, very nice grounds with a small but pleasant garden. Recommended. *Rates US$15 shared bath, US$30 private bath.*

Hotel El Parque (12 rooms) Coastal road entering Quepos; ☎ 777 0063. Very basic, low-budget rooms. *Rate US$15.*

Hotel Melissa Second road from the beach; ☎ 777 0025. Simple, clean rooms with fans and private bathrooms. *Rate US$10 pp.*

Hotel Mar y Luna (17 rooms) Second road from beach; ☎ 777 0394. It may be very budget (small rooms, very basic) but it's very clean. Upper floor has shared baths and lower floor has private baths but no windows. *Rate US$8 pp.*

WHERE TO EAT
Café Milagro On main road across the bridge in front of beach; ☎ 777 0794; e 777 2272; www.cafemilagro.com. A great spot with in-house roasting of organic coffees – if you like dark, full-bodied beans, be sure to pick up a few bags. They offer excellent b/fasts, lunches and early dinners (the carrot cake has been called 'the best in the world' by many people I've met). They have another location up the hill by the turn-off for La Mariposa. Highly recommended. *Main course US$3–7. Open daily 06.00–18.00.*

El Gran Escape By Café Milagro; ☎ 777 0395; f 777 0765; e granescape@racsa.co.cr. A long-time sport fishing hangout offering excellent seafood, burgers and Mexican/Costa Rican fare. This is a place where the locals hang out, as the food is great, beer is cold and there's always someone interesting to talk to. *Meals average US$17. Open 07.00–22.30; closed Tue.*

Restaurant/Bar Dos Locos On the corner on the second road away from the beach; ☎ 777 1526. An open-air Mexican Cantina with live music. *Main course US$10–13. Open Mon–Sat 07.00–22.00, Sun 11.00–20.00.*

Restaurant/Bar Escalofria ☎ 777 0833. On the second road away from the beach. Another local haunt, renowned for great pasta, pizza and Italian ice cream. Recommended. *Pizza US$5–10, pasta US$5–12. Open Tue–Sun 14.30–22.30.*

Wacky Wanda's Bar Near the Escalofria; ☎ 777 2245. This is another institution in Quepos where everybody and anybody comes to chill out (being one of the only places around with AC). Even fitness guru Richard Simmons has paid a visit to the wacky owner! *Open for b/fast until late night. Main course US$4–7. Open daily 11.00–01.00.*

PRACTICALITIES Two banks, **Banco Nacional** and **Bando Popular**, are just off the football field.

Hospital Dr Max Teran (☎ 777 0020) is 3km south of Quepos, near the airstrip, while the **Red Cross** is 100m east of the bus station. The police station is 100m south of the football field.

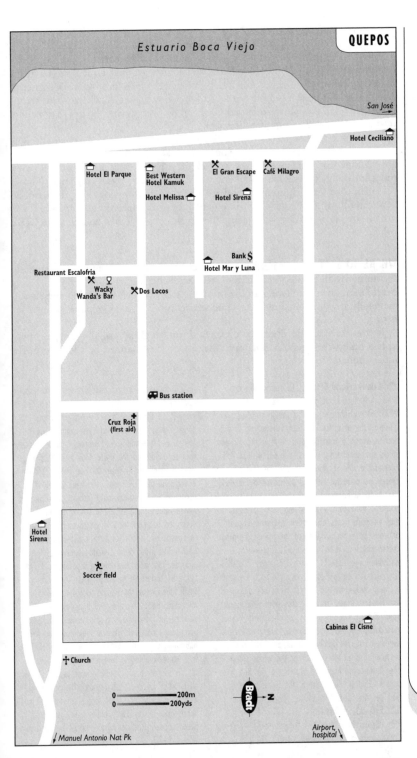

Estuario Boca Viejo

QUEPOS

San José →

Hotel Ceciliano

Hotel El Parque

Best Western
Hotel Kamuk

El Gran Escape

Café Milagro

Hotel Melissa

Hotel Sirena

Bank $

Hotel Mar y Luna

Restaurant Escalofria

Wacky
Wanda's Bar

Dos Locos

Bus station

Cruz Roja
(first aid)

Hotel
Sirena

Soccer field

Cabinas El Cisne

† Church

0 ———— 200m
0 ———— 200yds

Bradt

N

Airport,
hospital ↓

↓ Manuel Antonio Nat Pk

As mentioned, this is one of the most visited areas of the country and one of the first tourist areas to be built. Hotels and restaurants are spread out along the main road that leads from Quepos to a small traffic circle in front of the park entrance. As this is a rainforest, it is quite humid and the rainy season usually lasts from April to December, although the odd rain does pop up even during the dry season. The upside is the lushness engulfing the area.

If you have the budget, I strongly recommend renting a vehicle as everything is fairly spread out (unless you're staying at beach level). Taxis are scarce and, as they are stationed in Quepos, prepare to wait if you call one and expect to pay a minimum of 1,500 colones to get anywhere. The public buses run up and down the main road every 30 minutes and are a bargain. If you walk along the road, be very careful, as there aren't any pavements, there are many blind curves and the drivers are crazy. Always walk facing the traffic, in single file, and be aware at all times.

WHERE TO STAY Surprisingly, the hotels at beach level are the shabbiest of the accommodation you'll find in the area, with the better hotels on the cliffs overlooking the ocean (some of the most spectacular views you'll find anywhere). Generally, if you're looking for real budget accommodation, Quepos is your better bet.

Prices are based on double occupancy during high season (December–April) unless otherwise noted. Mandatory hotel tax of 16.39% must be added to prices unless noted.

Gaia Hotel and Reserve (16 rooms) On main road of Manuel Antonio; ☎ 777 2239; f 777 9125; www.gaiahr.com. By far the most luxurious hotel in the area, Gaia is cool, European chic nestled within a pristine forest reserve. Rooms and suites are atop a very steep hill but with a golf cart and driver at your beck and call, 24hrs, there's no need to worrying about having to tackle the climb. Architecture is very much of the Bauhaus movement — sleek lines, lots of angles and all white walls. Each room features original artwork, slate floors, high-end furnishings, Egyptian-cotton sheets and bath towels, AC, massive bathroom, mini-bar, TV, phone, CD player ... the list goes on and on (did I mention each room has its own butler, on call 24/7?). Views are mostly of the forest but still stunning. The pool is a marvel, spilling over 3 levels and is complete with waterfalls, a wheelchair accessible entry and a swim-up bar. The food is outstanding and the service is white glove (without the white gloves or the stuffiness). Imagine W Hotel and the Ritz have a love child in the midst of the rainforest and you get the idea. Outstanding. *Rates US$330–880, b/fast inc.*

Tulemar Bungalows* (14 bungalows, 12 villas) On the main road; ☎ 777 0580; e 777 1579; www.tulemar.com. Interspersed amongst 33 acres of rainforest, these bungalows and villas are secluded yet just off the main road. The octagon-shaped bungalows are spacious and have beautiful views. The villas are brand new, 2 storeys high and have a separate studio on the lower floor as well as a large balcony on the main level (if only 1 bedroom is required, the main level is rented). Beautifully decorated in a tropical motif (lots of palm trees in muted tones), these villas are among the best-decorated hotel spaces I've yet encountered. Both the bungalows and villas have a well-equipped kitchenette, living room, separate bedroom, TV, AC and fan. The villas also have a separate pool and bar area exclusively for villa guests' use while a small infinity pool by the restaurant is available to all guests. Both the villas and bungalows are situated on the hill and require some walking to get to so those with physical impairments might find them a bit challenging. At the base of the hill is a white-sand beach, complete with a beach bar that is touted as the hotel's private beach (although all beaches are technically public). The restaurant, with its million-dollar view, serves international fare but is quite pricey. Large buffet b/fast is inc. Recommended. *Rates: bungalow US$270; 2-bedroom villa US$420.*

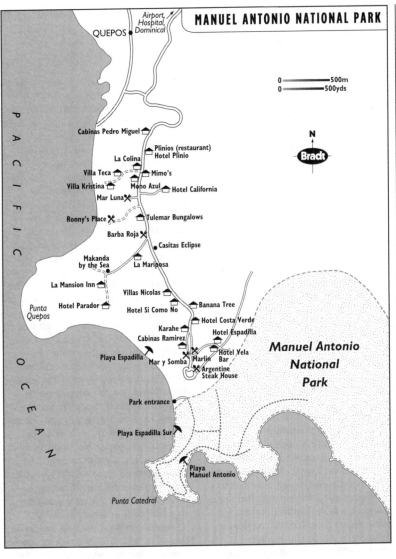

MANUEL ANTONIO NATIONAL PARK

QUEPOS

Airport,
Hospital,
Dominical

Cabinas Pedro Miguel

Plinios (restaurant)
Hotel Plinio

La Colina

Villa Teca

Mimo's

Villa Kristina

Mono Azul

Hotel California

Mar Luna

Ronny's Place

Tulemar Bungalows

Barba Roja

Casitas Eclipse

Makanda
by the Sea

La Mariposa

La Mansion Inn

Villas Nicolas

Hotel Parador

Banana Tree

Hotel Si Como No

Hotel Costa Verde

Karahe

Hotel Espadilla

Cabinas Ramirez

Hotel Yela

Playa Espadilla

Marlin Bar

Mar y Somba

Argentine
Steak House

Punta
Quepos

**Manuel Antonio
National
Park**

Park entrance

Playa Espadilla Sur

Playa
Manuel Antonio

Punta Catedral

PACIFIC OCEAN

0 ——— 500m
0 ——— 500yds

N

Bradt

🏠 **Makanda by the Sea** (11 rooms) On the same road as La Mariposa; 📞 777 0442; 📠 777 1032; www.makanda.com. No children under 16 years allowed. Without a doubt, the most romantic hotel in Manuel Antonio, thanks to its location, accommodation and service. Nestled in the rainforest, the villas and studios are spacious, airy and built to maximize the breezes blowing off the ocean (in fact, one villa has no windows or doors, with only mosquito netting to keep you from the critters). High vaulted ceilings with wooden beams house romantic canopied beds, kitchenettes, spacious bathrooms and comfortable sitting areas. The décor is a blend of Japanese Zen with Central American handicrafts with a bit of Santa Fe mixed in — the result is a soothing setting that has just the right amount of colour and zip. All have either a terrace or a balcony. The pool and jacuzzi are beautifully tiled and overlook the rainforest and ocean. The poolside Sunspot Grill is arguably one of the best restaurants in town and by far the best hotel restaurant in the lower Pacific. B/fast is delivered to your door every morning. Highly recommended. *Rates US$230–350.*

🏠 **La Mariposa** (56 rooms) On the turn-off at Café Milagro, halfway up the hill; ☎ 777 0355; e 777 0050; www.lamariposa.com. One of the first luxury hotels in the area, it still has the best view, perched on a cliff 550ft above the ocean, with over 270° of stunning ocean and rainforest vistas. While there have been additions of new suites, the standard and deluxe rooms (in the original building) are definitely in desperate need of an upgrade, as furnishings and décor are very dated and one gets the feeling that the hotel is coasting on its reputation won by past glories (the original rooms are scheduled for renovation at the time of writing). Beds are hard (a complaint voiced by many guests) and service runs the whole gamut from attentive to snarky. The restaurant has a commanding view but food is pedestrian and overpriced — best to head to the bar for the best sunset in town and quaff a cold one. There are 2 pools and the one at the bar (an infinity pool) is the idyllic spot to sip a drink and watch the last rays of the day streak across the sky. Junior suites have jacuzzis with incredible views while the penthouse suite has the hands-down best vantage point in all of Manuel Antonio (and the outdoor hot tub is total hedonism). Interestingly, the premiere suites are large but lack TVs. If you have trouble walking, ask for one of the older rooms in the main building. Free shuttle services to main beach and back throughout the day as it's a long walk otherwise. *Rates US$195–430.*

🏠 **La Mansion Inn** (11 rooms/suites) Just down the road from the Parador (see below); ☎ 777 0002; f 777 3489; www.lamansioninn.com. This small, boutique hotel is the creation of Harry Bodaan, the former partner of neighbouring property El Parador and long-time general manager of the Press Club in Washington — the hallways are a 'who's who' gallery, featuring photos of Bodaan and countless heads of state. His experience with 'high maintenance' VIPs certainly qualifies him as the benchmark of customer service in Costa Rica and his staff have been carefully trained in the fine art of keeping guests happy. Each of the rooms or suites has a balcony or patio affording a lovely view of the ocean and surrounding rainforests and the pool is only a few steps away. The restaurant, Jacques Cousteau, is pricey but has excellent food and the wine cellar is extremely well stocked with premium wines and vintages. The small 'Cave Bar' is really a cave (complete with bats — but no worries, as they are visible via a wall of Plexiglas) and is definitely worth a visit. Rooms are spacious and very well appointed and the over-the-top presidential suite (complete with 24-carat gold taps in the jacuzzi) was named one of the 'Most Decadent' by *Elite* magazine. Excellent European b/fast is inc. *Rates US$188–1,500.*

🏠 **Hotel Parador** (108 rooms and suites) On the turn-off at Café Milagro halfway up the hill; ☎ 777 1414; f 777 1437; www.hotelparador.com. Although they call themselves a 'boutique' hotel, as the largest hotel in the south of the country, it's actually quite sprawling. Decorated in the style of the Spanish Paradores, the hotel is filled with antiques, 17th-century Flemish and Dutch paintings, oriental rugs, gilded chandeliers — the overall feel is a bit ostentatious for my tastes but others find it the very lap of luxury. The infinity pool with swim-up bar is quite spacious and offers splendid vistas of the ocean. There is also a spa with an adults-only pool. There are 2 restaurants, a bar and a small private dining room (max 10 people) for those who seek a very formal dinner. The standard rooms are a bit on the small size, have a patio with views of the hotel's gardens (and are a fair distance from the main building) while deluxe rooms are a bit larger and some have partial ocean views. A new 3-storey building opened at the end of 2003 housing deluxe superior rooms, and is the closest building to the pool and restaurants. Premium rooms have 180° views from their balconies while the junior suites have living room, jacuzzi and private gardens — it's a long hike to these rooms but the hotel does offer a golf-cart shuttle service. The presidential suite, complete with 3 bedrooms, living room, dining room, jacuzzi, various antiques and private entrances, is just off the main building. Other amenities include tennis, mini-golf, steam room, outdoor gym and even a helicopter-landing pad. Large buffet b/fast inc. *Rates US$175–800.*

🏠 **Hotel Si Como No** (61 rooms) On the main road; ☎ 777 0777; f 777 1093; www.sicomono.com. A stylish Mediterranean hotel in 10 acres of rainforest, Si Como No is the largest eco-friendly resort in the area. The dream of former Hollywood producer/art director, Jim Damalas, the hotel combines the drama of a film set with the natural beauty of the jungle setting. The lobby is a spiralling cathedral of pointed angles, resplendent with stained-glass windows. There is a full-service spa, 2 restaurants, a gift shop, internet café, a small THX theatre, hiking trails, a butterfly garden, 30-acre nature refuge and 2 pools, both with swim-up bars and whirlpools — one is for adults only while the family pool has a 30ft waterslide and a waterfall. The rooms are surprisingly simple in furnishings and all have AC, a kitchenette or wet bar and a telephone. The superior rooms offer a balcony (for the extra US$25, I'd definitely upgrade myself from a standard). Superior rooms have higher ceilings and a panoramic view, the deluxe suites are double the size of a regular room, have a sitting area and balcony with a view while the honeymoon suites are the same as deluxe suites with the addition of a private jacuzzi with a small garden area in the bathroom. The hotel's commitment to the environment is to be applauded – apparently, only one tree was felled in building the original hotel (they have since purchased the adjoining hotel and converted it) and the resort uses solar power, grey-water recycling, composting and biodegradable cleaning products. In addition, guests are reminded to keep their electricity and AC usage to a minimum and to request new linens and towels only when necessary. If you're a TV junkie, this isn't the place for you as there are no sets in any of the rooms. B/fast inc. *Rates US$170–270.*

🏠 **Hotel Casitas Eclipse** (30 rooms) On the main road; ✆ 777 0408; f 777 1738; www.casitaseclipse.com. The blinding white *casitas* stand out against the dark green of the surrounding jungle, reminiscent of Greek villas along the Aegean Sea. Standard rooms are simply decorated (Spartan, even) with 11 featuring 1 dbl bed and 6 rooms with a queen and a sgl bed. The 9 suites are roomier, with sitting and dining areas and a kitchenette while the 2-storey *casita* has 2 bedrooms, 2 bathrooms, kitchenette, terrace and a balcony with a view. All rooms have fans, AC, hot water, safety box, cable TV, refrigerator and either a terrace or a balcony. The property features 3 pools and a small spa as well. While the views are mostly of the surrounding jungle, with a view of the ocean peeking through now and then, this is definitely one of the best value for money places in Manuel Antonio. B/fast inc. Recommended. *Rates US$112–275.*

🏠 **Hotel and Cabinas Espadilla** (16 rooms, 12 cabins) Up a side road at Marlins Restaurant near the beach; ✆ 777 2135; www.espadilla.com. The newer, 2-storey hotel is comfortable, clean and offers AC, mini-fridge and a kitchenette in some units. The restaurant is airy and spacious, with good food while the pool is clean. Also offered are a tennis court and a hiking path through the neighbouring reserve. The older cabins across the street are much more basic and are favoured by *Tico* families. The hotel is one of the nicer ones you'll find at beach

level. Includes buffet b/fast. *Rates: rooms US$108; cabins US$72.*

🏠 **Hotel California** (22 rooms, 1 suite) On a side road to left of main road heading up the hill; ✆ 777 1234; f 777 1062; www.hotel-california.com. The name may not be the most creative but the hotel is a comfortable spot to lay one's head. Standard rooms have a balcony and garden view while the deluxe rooms are larger with a balcony and ocean vies. There is also a villa with 2 bedrooms and bathrooms and a kitchen. All rooms have AC, hot water, telephone, cable TV, safety box and a minibar. Amenities include a small restaurant, a pool and a jacuzzi. Robbie Felix, the American owner, has a number of charitable efforts she spearheads in the community, specifically to help the schools in the area and the Robbie Felix Foundation for handicapped children. Guests are encouraged to bring school materials, books, etc for the local schools and if you'd like to get involved and volunteer a couple of hours, the staff at the hotel would be more than happy to set it up. B/fast buffet inc. *Rates US$105–125.*

🏠 **Villa Kristina** (5 apts) Up a side road near Villa Teca, close to Playa Macha; ✆/f 777 2134; e villa_kristina@hotmail.com. Overlooking the rainforest and ocean, this beautiful multi-level home is fully equipped and one of the best hideaway spots you'll find in the area. Very relaxed atmosphere that makes you instantly feel at home. Be warned, though, that the drive is a steep one and you MUST have a 4x4 vehicle in order to make it up and down the hill. Recommended. *Rate US$95.*

🏠 **Hotel Villa Teca** (40 rooms) On the first side road coming up the hill; ✆ 777 1117; f 777 1578; www.villatecahotel.com. Basic yet spacious rooms in 20 villas in a pleasant garden setting. The 2 pools are a bit worse for wear and there is an Italian restaurant and bar with less than stellar food. I was not impressed with my stay and I've heard of other guests who've had less than pleasant experiences (such as a sewer backing up, making the room uninhabitable). The Italian owners/staff seemed more interested in their own chitchat than tending to guests and the location makes it a bit remote if you don't have a car. B/fast inc. In my opinion, there are far better hotels for less money in the area. *Rate US$94.*

🏠 **Hotel Costa Verde** (43 rooms) On the main road heading towards the beach; ✆ 777 0584; f 777 0506; www.hotelcostaverde.com. One of the first hotels in the area and still one of the best deals in town. Over the years, they've built new rooms and buildings and presently, there is a wide variety of room types. It's a stunning location, situated on acres of rainforest, with the adults-only building and pool perched on a majestic cliff. All rooms include fans, kitchenettes, 2 beds, hot water, patio or balcony, cable TV and views of either the rainforest or ocean. The 14 efficiency units are the smallest offered but are still fairly spacious and have AC. In the older areas are 16 studios and 8 studio-plus (with ocean views) and both these units have AC. In the new, 5-storey Costa Verde II (the adult-only building), there is no AC but the rooms all feature huge, screened windows, with 8 studios (rainforest views) and 6 studio-plus with incredible views of the ocean. Crowning this building are 2 penthouses with spectacular views at an incredible price (only US$165 per night). Additionally, there are 2 bungalows (one a large studio with 3 beds, the other with 2 bedrooms and 2 baths) and the 3-bedroom Casa Quinta (which has apparently been upgraded since I complained to management after an acquaintance stayed there and was horrified by the poor state of the furniture in the house). Amenities on the grounds include 3 pools, hiking trails (I've had people swear they've seen more monkeys on the large grounds than they did in the park) and the Anaconda Restaurant, where monkeys make a regular morning and late-afternoon appearance in the neighbouring trees. Across the street, there is an internet café/BBQ restaurant/bar with live music every night. A couple of caveats, however – none of the rooms has a phone and some rooms are a good hike away from the main buildings (up or down hills) so those with walking impairments should be sure to ask for a room closest to the reception. *Rates US$89–165.*

🏠 **Villas Nicolas** (12 suites) On the main road next to Si Como No; ✆ 777 0481; f 777 1093; www.villasnicolas.com. One of the more interesting accommodation options in town, Villas Nicolas (with the weird but playful monster logo) is a collection of privately owned condos (6 with 1 bedroom and 6 with 2 bedrooms) so each one is decorated differently from the next. The cheapest units have a partial kitchenette and no balcony, the next level have a bar fridge and balcony and then the next levels come with full-size kitchens, living rooms and dining rooms and balconies with jungle or ocean views. AC is available in some units at an extra fee. An exterior staircase also connects some units, making them perfect for small families or 2 couples travelling together. There is a communal jacuzzi, a nice pool and garden area as well as a small

restaurant and bar. Note that children under 6 years of age are not permitted. Recommended. *Rates US$85–240.*

🏠 **Karahe** (24 rooms, 9 villas) On the main road towards the beach; ✆ 777 0170; www.karahe.com. One of the nicest beachfront hotels, Karahe offers 3 choices of accommodation types, with some marked differences between them. By far the best bet are the beachfront rooms (which are still about 75m from the beach), having been recently built. The 2-storey building features tiled floors, 2 dbl beds in each room, hot water, bathtub and a balcony. Across the street is reception and the first phase of the hotel, with the roadside standard rooms, housed in a 2-storey building in much the same fashion as the beachfront rooms. If you opt for one of the villas, be prepared for a very steep climb up 100-plus stairs. The view from the top is spectacular but the villas are showing their age. The surrounding gardens are quite lovely and are home to hummingbirds and lots of iguanas. There is a small pool, jacuzzi and restaurant/bar close to the beach. B/fast inc. *Rates US$80–110.*

🏠 **Hotel Plinio** (12 rooms, 1 house) On main road going up the hill; ✆ 777 0055; f 777 0558; www.hotelplinio.com. Tucked away in a private reserve, this small hotel has loads of charm, with gleaming hardwood and handiwork from Central America adorning the walls. There are basic standard rooms with fans while the suites have either 2 or 3 storeys, complete with sleeping lofts, living rooms and even an observation deck. There is also the appropriately named 'Jungle House' that is set back into the foliage, with 2 bedrooms. The pool and bar is a great spot to while away the day and the restaurant, with its Asian-fusion cooking, is one of the best in the area. Nature is close by, with 10km of hiking trails just behind the hotel and a 10m-high observation tower. The only drawback is the proximity to the road, which can be noisy especially during busy travel days. B/fast buffet inc. Rates decrease by half during low season when there is no b/fast inc. Recommended. *Rates US$70–150.*

🏠 **Mimo's Apartotel** (13 rooms/suites, 2 apts) On the main road coming up from Quepos; ✆ 777 0054; f 777 217; www.mimoshotel.com. Charming hotel run by an even more charming Italian couple. The older building has basic rooms that are nicely appointed (tiled sinks, teak furniture, terraces or balconies with hammocks) while the new, luxury building has even nicer suites and apts which can house upwards of 6 guests. All have fans, AC, cable TV, safes and either full kitchens or kitchenettes.

Both buildings have a pool and a jacuzzi. The Italian restaurant on the premises is quite good. One of the better deals in Manuel Antonio. B/fast inc. Highly recommended. *Rates US$65–230.*

🏠 **Banana Tree Hotel** (9 rooms) On the main road; ☎ 777 1585; www.banantreehotel.com. A new entry into the budget accommodation ranks, this small, cheery hotel is on the main road (so it's noisy) but the irreverent owners make sure guests have a good time regardless (there was a brouhaha shortly after it opened because of a 'NO CANADIANS' sign they posted outside, after a 'study' they did found Canucks ate the most food at the free b/fast out of all the nationalities). Canadians I know who've stayed here have had nothing but positive experiences so fear not, Great White Northers! The spotless 2-storey building has nicely appointed rooms, all bedecked in yellow paint, with bamboo furniture, original artwork, AC, cable TV, hot-water showers and ceiling fans. Standard rooms have 1 dbl bed and deluxe rooms have 2 and views of the rainforest. A 2-bedroom suite has a living room and a fully equipped kitchen for up to 8 people (undoubtedly the best deal going in town for a small group). There is also a pool, hammocks and a small restaurant. Recommended. *Rates US$65–145.*

🏠 **B&B La Colina** (11 rooms, 2 studios, 2 houses) The first hotel on your right coming up the hill from Quepos; ☎ 777 0231; f 777 1553; www.lacolina.com. Stunning views from the hillside location, this small hotel was originally a home turned B&B. The standard rooms are small but nicely decorated and have views of the gardens while the suites have ocean views and balconies and are quite spacious. In addition, there are 2 1-room flats — one with a full kitchen, the other with a refrigerator and a balcony. There are also 2 apts, both with 2 bedrooms, living room, kitchen and balconies with ocean views. All accommodation has fans, AC, cable TV and hot water. There is a small 2-level pool with swim-up bar and a restaurant that features live music throughout the week. Construction in many of the rooms is quite 'cheap' and the upkeep overall could be better — the hotel is presently for sale so hopefully, new owners with new energy will be more diligent in looking after the place. *Rates US$55–85.*

🏠 **Hotel El Mono Azul** (27 rooms) On the main road heading towards Manuel Antonio; ☎ 777 1548; f 777 1954; www.monoazul.com. Amiable hosts Jennifer and Chip make every guest feel at home and are eager to answer any question you might have. The standard and deluxe rooms are simple affairs, on the smallish side with 'suicide' (electric hot water shower heads found in cheaper hotels) showers, 2 or 3 beds (either sgls or dbls) and a fan, while the deluxe rooms have AC and cable TV. The villas are roomier and have a separate living room, kitchen and eating area, king bed, 2 pullout sofas, 2 bathrooms, cable TV, AC and patio. The 'tower', a 2-storey villa with 2 bathrooms, bedrooms and balconies, a sleeping loft, living and dining areas, AC and cable TV, has by far the best rooms in the house. There are 3 pools, an award-winning restaurant with great food and a gift shop run by Kids Saving the Rainforest, a non-profit society started by Jennifer's young daughter. *Rates US$50–125.*

🏠 **Hotel Vela Bar** (11 rooms) Last road on the left before hitting the park; ☎ 777 0413; f 777 1071; www.velabar.com. Small and just 100m from the beach, the rooms are small but breezy, with fans, optional AC, private bathrooms and a patio. There are also small apts with kitchenettes, hot water and a terrace. The hotel's restaurant has excellent international cuisine at very affordable prices. Only steps from the beaches and the park, this is definitely one of the best budget options in Manuel Antonio. *Rate US$45.*

🏠 **Cabinas Pedro Miguel** (16 rooms) Off the main road coming in from Quepos, across from Hotel Plinio; ☎ 777 0035; www.cabinaspedromiguel.com. Clean, basic but cheery and comfortable rooms set in the forest, this Sustainable Tourism award winner features a small pool, Spanish-language school and rooms with private bathroom, AC, cable TV and refrigerators. Some rooms also have a kitchen. The 2-storey building features a screened back wall, so all rooms gaze out into the adjoining trees. A quiet spot at a very good price. Recommended. *Rate US$35 inc tax.*

🏠 **Cabinas Ramirez** (16 cabins) On the beach by Mar y Sombra; ☎ 777 5044. Simple, cinder-block cabins with fans that are quite dark but clean, popular with young *Ticos* looking for a bargain. There is parking, shared kitchen and showers. As it's next to the popular night-time disco, Mar y Sombra, don't expect to turn in early and get a good night's sleep but if you plan on partying until the wee hours and just want a clean spot to sleep, you can't go wrong here. *Rates: cabins US$30; camping US$3.50 pp.*

🏠 **Rafiki Safari Lodge** (10 tents) 1hr northeast from Quepos on the Savegre River; ☎ 777 2250; www.rafikisafari.com. Truly one of the most interesting holiday spots in the country, this family-owned project brings a bit of South Africa to Costa

Rica. Owned and operated by the Boshoff family, the lodge is part of a grander plan to breed tapirs and reintroduce them into the wild, as they are currently one of the most endangered mammals in Central America. Using the South African model of utilising tourism capital to assist with conservation efforts, the lodge hopes to serve as a model to others. The luxury tents, all imported from South Africa, can sleep 4 and feature large windows, wood floors, patios, real bathrooms (complete with tiled flooring) and fire-heated spring water for the showers. The main buildings are constructed out of river stone, native woods and palm fronds. Most meals are cooked using the traditional South African BBQ method called 'Braai'. There is also a pool and one of the 5 fastest waterslides in the world, which uses only natural spring water without any chemicals, and also is a source of hydro-electric power for the lodge (going down it, you really feel like you're about to launch into the stratosphere!). Boredom is definitely not a problem here, with 700 acres of property for hiking, birdwatching, excellent horseriding and, being on the Savegre River, rafting and kayaking. Hanging out in a rocking chair, watching the beauty before you with a cold beverage at the end of a day is heavenly. I've heard nothing but rave reviews from other people who've stayed here and the hospitality extended to each guest is really quite amazing. If you have the chance, I highly recommend that you make time to stay at this remarkable piece of paradise. *Rates US$248 pp, inc 3 meals a day.*

✖ WHERE TO EAT

✖ **Restaurant Gato Negro** In front of Casitas Eclipse; ✎ 777 1728. Excellent Mediterranean and seafood with a spectacular view. The wine list is impressive and quite affordable. Dining on the open-air terrace, in the relaxed atmosphere, is the perfect way to end a day. Highly recommended. *Main course US$4–35. Open daily 18.30–22.00.*

✖ **Bar y Restaurante Marlin** Across from the main beach en route to the park; ✎ 777 1134. My favourite spot for sunset cocktails, this is one of the few restaurants at beach level in the area. With gleaming wood floors, tables and chairs, the setting is simple yet has a certain sense of elegance to it. Seafood is the speciality here and the tuna sashimi is some of the best I've ever had. The black bean soup was judged the best in all of Costa Rica by *La Nación's* very picky food critic (no small feat, considering black bean soup is as common as *gallo pinto* here). B/fast offerings include *Tico* and North American favourites such as pancakes and portions are huge. Highly recommended. *Main course US$4–7. Open daily 07.00–22.00.*

✖ **Bar and Restaurant Barba Roja** Main road; ✎ 777 0331. One of the first restaurants in Manuel Antonio, Barba Roja has been the stuff of legend for over 30 years. Unfortunately, a recent change in ownership has seen the restaurant slip in its quality while upping the prices. Numerous locals have confirmed my findings — while the view from the balcony is beautiful, there are better spots for dinner around. *Main course US$10–25. Open Tue–Sun 16.00–22.00.*

✖ **Plinio's Restaurant** At Hotel Plinio on the main road; ✎ 777 0055. A consistent favourite with locals and tourists alike, Plinio's delights with Thai and Asian food, using fresh organic ingredients grown in the hotel's garden. Check the blackboard outside for daily specials; vegetarians will find a cornucopia of offerings on the extensive menu. The climb up 3 sets of stairs can be a bit challenging for some but the final destination is worth it — in addition to great food, the service is prompt and the setting comfortable. Highly recommended. *Main course US$6–20. Open daily 17.00–22.00.*

✖ **Sunspot Bar & Grill** At Makanda by the Sea; ✎ 777 0442. Outstanding food expertly served at a poolside open-air restaurant with a stunning vista of the ocean and rainforest. Local ingredients such as rum and mango paired with fresh *mahi mahi* create a dinner alchemy. Open for lunch and dinner, no children under 16 years are allowed. Highly recommended. *Meals US$30–50 lunch, US$80–100 dinner. Open daily 11.00–22.00.*

✖ **Mar y Sombra** On the beach. A true institution, this open-air restaurant has been on the beach about as long as people have been coming to Manuel Antonio. Concrete tables and chairs underneath palm trees, just metres from the water, make for an idyllic beachside setting. The food here is simple and straightforward *Tico*, with seafood the speciality (naturally). Prices are very reasonable and it's a good deal for the money. At night, the tables in the restaurant are cleared away to make room for sweaty bodies moving to the latest tunes. This is the place for night-time action. *Meals average US$7. Open daily 08.00–22.00 (Fri–Sat to 02.00).*

✖ **Ronny's Place** Up the road at Amigos del Rio; ✎ 777 5120; www.ronnysplace.com, e milugar@ racsa.co.cr. This small, open-air restaurant has a commanding view of the ocean from its hilltop location. A ranching family privately owns the surrounding land so there isn't any construction to take away from the view. The beer is cold, the food is tasty and cheap and there's live music most nights of the week. It's a spot where the locals hang so you know it's good value. Recommended. *Main course US$10–12. Open daily 12.00–22.00.*

✗ **Bar & Restaurant Mar Luna** On the main road; ↘ 777 5107. This is one of those places that everyone raves about and I can't figure out why (maybe I've been there on off nights). The space is basically a long, rectangular box that overlooks the rainforest and ocean. Seafood is the main focus of the menu and overall, the food is fine. The atmosphere is a jumble of roadside fuzzy blankets, sarongs, bad art and fishing 'stuff'. It's OK but has never made me go 'wow' like other people. *Main course US$10–43. Open daily 15.30–22.30.*

WHAT TO SEE AND DO IN QUEPOS AND MANUEL ANTONIO

Manuel Antonio National Park (*Open 08.00–16.00; closed Mon; entrance US$6*) may be small but it is definitely worth a visit. There are only three main hiking trails that are easily negotiated on one's own, although a professional guide will be able to point out interesting flora and fauna one might miss otherwise. Most guides, with high-quality binoculars, charge around US$35 for a three-hour hike and your hotel can assist you in setting one up.

To enter the park, you have to cross through a low stream which becomes waist high during high tide (there are small rafts to ferry you across for a small fee). Once you've crossed the stream, you pay your entrance fee at the park ranger station and receive your map. Note that only 600 visitors are allowed each day, so make sure you arrive early during high season.

Hiking From Playa Espadilla Sur or Playa Manuel Antonio, there is an easy hike that will take about a half an hour to complete, with the high point (literally) being Punta Catedral, which offers a spectacular view down the coast all the way to Dominical (this is a bit of a steep hike). The inland trail from Playa Manuel Antonio is mostly uphill in a straight line but offers greater opportunities for wildlife encounters.

There is another trail, which can be tricky, and you should check the tide charts before embarking on it. Starting at Puerto Escondido, it takes you to Punta Surrucho where you can explore sea caves. While the hike itself is easy enough during low tide, it can be dangerous once the high-tide waters come in so make sure you don't allow yourself to get trapped.

Boat trips Planet Dolphin (↘ 777 2137; *www.planetdolphin.com*) offers daily tours for snorkelling, dolphin tours, catamaran and starlight dinner cruises. **Sunset Sails** (↘ 777 4304) offers dolphin watching, sailing and snorkelling.

Sport fishing One of the best areas in the world for sport fishing, where the action is great year round. Rates for a full day average around US$700. **Bluefin Sport Fishing** (↘ 777 2222; f 777 0674; *www.bluefinsportfishing.com*) is regarded as one of the best operations in the country, with three different boats. Highly recommended. **Flounder Sport Fishing** (↘ 777 1060; *www.floundersportfishing.com*) has been in business over ten years. **High Tec Fleet** (↘ 777 3465) has eight different boats. Other companies: **Costa Rican Dreams** (↘ 777 0593); **JP Tours** (↘ 235 3490); **Pacific Coast Charters** (↘ 777 1382); **Luna Tours Sport Fishing** (↘ 777 0725); **Sport Fishing Wahoo** (↘ 777 0832) and **Flamingo Bay Pacific Charters** (↘ 256 3222; *www.fishingcostarica.com*) who offer fly fishing along the Pacific coast.

Scuba diving Costa Rica Adventure Divers (↘ 777 0234; *www.costaricadiving.com*) offers boat dives, classes and island tours.

White-water rafting The Sevegre River offers Class IV action while the Naranjo is a shorter river with Class III rapids. **Ríos Tropicales** (↘ *233 6455; www.riostropicales.com*) offers trips to both rivers as does **Amigos del Río** (↘ *777 0082; www.amigosdelrio.com*).

Mangrove tours One of the nicer tours to do here is a gentle boat ride through the mangroves, teeming with interesting wildlife. Make sure to wear plenty of bug repellent. **Iguana Tours** (↘ *777 1262; www.iguanatours.com*) and **Cambute Tours** (↘ *777 3229;* e *cambutetour@terra.com*) both offer professionally guided, half-day tours.

Horseriding **Brisas del Nara** (↘ *779 1235;* f *779 1049; www.horsebacktour.com*) offers an excellent tour to rivers and a 300ft waterfall. **Equus Stables** (↘ *777 0001;* e *havefun@racsa.co.cr*) has rides on the beach.

Canopy tours **Canopy Safari** (↘ *777 0100; www.canopysafari.com*) is the largest operator in Costa Rica (which has led some clients to complain about the number of people on each tour, giving a 'cattle car' feel at times). Closer to town and less busy is **Titi Canopy Tour** (↘ *777 1020*).

4x4 tours If bombing around on noisy ATVs is your idea of fun, check out **Four Trax Adventure** (↘ *777 1829; www.fourtraxadventure.com*) with guided tours in the backcountry and to waterfalls. Just don't expect to see any wildlife as these noisy machines scare birds and animals away.

Nature tours **Villa Vanilla** (↘ *779 1155;* e *vanill@racsa.co.cr*) offer tours on an organic spice farm, with trails for hiking and waterfalls. **Pura Vida Jungle Safari** (↘ *777 1661*) has an eco-nursery near the Naranjo River where they offer horseriding, tours to waterfalls and through the rainforest. The proceeds aid conservation efforts. **Rainmaker Conservation Project** (↘ *777 3565; www.rainmakercostarica.com*) is 22km from Quepos, en route from Parrita to Quepos. Situated in the Fila Chonta mountain range, these 1,530 acres of virgin rainforest (well, 90% is) features suspension bridges attached to hardwood trees, allowing a bird's-eye view of the forest with minimal impact. There is also a walk along the Río Seco with handrails and observation platforms – a dip in the waterfall pool at the end of the hike is the perfect way to cool off.

Shopping For a popular tourist town, the shopping is amazingly limited. At the traffic circle by the park entrance you'll find a multitude of stands selling everything from sarongs to souvenirs. For higher-end goodies, check out the following.

La Buena Nota (↘ *777 1002;* f *777 1946;* e *buenanota@racsa.co.cr*) is on the road to the beach and is the oldest souvenir shop in town with the largest selection of beach, surf wear, jewellery, books, newspapers, tourist information and maps. For unique works of art, the best selection is at **Regaleme** (↘ *777 2640*), one branch being at Si Como No, the other in Quepos.

Spas A few excellent spas have appeared on the landscape and are a great way to pamper yourself. Prices for massages start at US$75 but therapists are qualified.

Sea Glass Spa (↘ *777 2607; www.seaglassspa.com*) reached from the turn-off by Karola's and through the gate on the right. The two-storeyed, all-glass structure looks out onto the lush rainforest surrounding you. Stepping across the threshold is like entering a cool, peaceful retreat. A variety of services is offered, including massage, facials, wraps, manicures and pedicures (excellent – they include a mini-facial). **Serenity Spa** (↘ 777 0777) is based in the Si Como No Hotel. Part of the Serenity Spa chain it offers the full range of spa services. Massage rooms open on to the rainforest outside. **Raindrop Spa** (↘ 777 2880; *www.raindropspa.com*) is in Manuel Antonio Estates. Brand new, featuring décor from Bali and Vichy hydro-massage, this is by far one of the best-looking spas in the country.

MATAPALO

Looking for a stretch of beach that seemingly goes on for ever without anyone else on it? Head to Matapalo, which is a bumpy 26km ride south of Quepos on the Constanera Sur, but well worth it once you discover the 45km stretch of grey-sand beach. There is little here other than a small village but that's part of the charm. The surf here is great but makes it a dangerous spot for swimming. There is a large European contingent here and French-, Austrian- and German-owned restaurants and hotels seem to be the norm.

As this is still a developing area, telephones are scarce so many places rely on email.

GETTING AROUND

By car Take the Constanera Sur and continue straight rather than turning right for Quepos. Follow for 26km (approx 1 hour).

By bus Take the Quepos–Dominical bus **Transportes Blanco** (↘ 771 4744) and get off at Matapalo.

WHERE TO STAY
Prices are based on double occupancy during high season (December–April) unless otherwise noted. Mandatory hotel tax of 16.39% must be added to prices unless noted.

⌂ **Jungle House** (6 rooms, 2 bungalows) On the beach; ↘/f 777 5005; www.junglehouse.com. Only steps from the beach, guests can stay in the 6-bedroom house, which features 3 bathrooms, 2 kitchens, 1 kitchenette, AC, cable TV, hot water and DVD players or one of 2 charming bungalows. Constructed out of gleaming woods and tiles, it's a comfortable spot to lay one's head. The ardilla bungalow is a cement affair, with 1 queen bed and 1 dbl bed, hot water, AC, cable TV, hot water, kitchenette and DVD player. The cane house is the honeymoon cabin, constructed completely out of teak, almond and cane, giving it an elegant yet rustic feel. There is a gym, pool table, pool, a 'hammock park' and massage hut. Recommended. *Rates US$65–250.*

⌂ **Bahari Beach Bungalows** (6 rooms) On the beach; ↘ 787 5057; www.baharibeach.com. New addition to the restaurant, this complex now features 4 'safari-tent' bungalows (soft-sided tent walls with tiled floors, full bathrooms, outdoor private shower and electricity) that can sleep up to 6. 2 small but cosy cabins in the main building have cable TV,

refrigerator and the option of AC. There is also a pool. The tents are an unusual but exotic way to spend a few nights being lulled to sleep by the sound of the ocean and the nocturnal jungle. Recommended. *Rates US$55–90.*

⌂ **El Coquito del Pacifico** (6 bungalows) On the beach; ↘ 787 5028; f 787 5029; www.elcoquito.com. Gleaming white tiled floors and walls, all neat as a pin, offer comfortable accommodation amidst 85 acres of lush gardens at the water's edge. There is a lovely kidney-shaped pool and open-air restaurant with good food. *Rates US$41 inc tax.*

⌂ **Oasis Cabinas** On the beach road. Offers simple cabins. *Rates US$15–20.*

⌂ **Cabinas Escala del Sur** Just before town on the right; ↘/f 787 5160. Simple rooms that are airy and spacious with communal kitchen. Hot water, fans, nice gardens and a pool table. *Rate US$10 pp.*

⌂ **El Ranchito** On the road to the beach. Features small but pleasant cabins and *Tico* food. *Rate US$10.*

WHERE TO EAT

✗ **Soda Chasa** In town. This is a simple, typical *soda* offering delicious Costa Rican food. Run by a *Tico* and his grandmother, it's good food at bargain prices. *Meals average US$5. Open 08.00–18.00.*

✗ **Restaurant Espresso del Pacifico** In town. Set in a charming garden, this French restaurant has the largest drink menu in town and where the European community congregates. Excellent food, with pizza and steak being the specialities. *Meals average US$10. Closed Sun.*

PRACTICALITIES Matapalo Beach Area Tourist Information Centre (↘ 787 5082) can help you with any questions. **Oasis Tour Information Centre** (✆f 777 1984; e *oasisame@racsa.co.cr*) is another good resource.

WHAT TO SEE AND DO The **Portalon Ecological Reserve**, near the Savegre River, has some lovely waterfalls you can hike to.

13

The South

In many ways, the south is the final frontier, a place where life moves at a much slower place and bad roads have kept the push of civilisation at bay. It's a place of contradictions, with ice on high mountaintops and humid jungles where jaguars still roam, grungy port towns and luxury nature lodges. For those who really want to get away from it all, to experience an adventure just in travelling to the destination, the south of Costa Rica beckons. Not surprisingly, this is the least-visited area of Costa Rica, on account of its distance, weather patterns and travelling challenges.

Being primarily a rainforest, the entire area sees much greater amounts of precipitation than the rest of the country.

Most travellers to the nature lodges in the Osa Peninsula choose to fly in. Even if you decide to take the bus and stay in the 'budget' lodges in the Osa, be prepared to pay more than you would in other parts of the country, as supplies (such as food, cleaning products, fuel) are all shipped in. The cost, however, is justified as it is one of the most magical spots on earth. The Golfo Dulce is the tenth-deepest gulf in the world (up to 200m) and one of only four tropical fjords on this big blue ball – resulting in a unique environment where whales teach their young to swim, 5,000-year-old coral is found and open water fish, such as tuna, dorado and swordfish pass through.

LOS SANTOS, CERRO DE LA MUERTE

The 'Route of the Saints' winds through a number of coffee plantations that produce some of the best coffee in the world and are recommended for serious javaholics – think of it as a 'wine country' tour for coffee lovers. A popular bumper sticker in these parts declares 'Juan Valdez Drinks Costa Rican Coffee' (and after a threatened law suit by the Colombian coffee growers, the Costa Rican coffee association found a *Tico* named Juan Valdez to sign a statement that he drank Pura Vida java, thus nipping the international coffee war in the bean). Most of the small villages along this route are named after saints (hence the name 'Los Santos') and still retain the typical ways of the *campesinos* (farmers). The mountains are often shrouded by fog that can make driving dangerous and night-time travel is strongly discouraged. Attempt these roads only with a good 4x4 vehicle. Cerro de la Muerte (Peak of Death) is an impressive 3,491m high and it's not unusual to see ice or a bit of snow during colder months. The name of doom comes from the many unlucky *boyeros* who perished on this curvy, steep road – one slip of an ox's hoof on an icy road was all it took to that coffee plantation in the sky.

This area also offers some of the best opportunities to see quetzals in the wild and there are a few lodges catering to the birding crowd.

Further down the highway is **San Isidro de El General Perez Zeledón**. The largest town in the area, San Isidro de El General is an important transportation

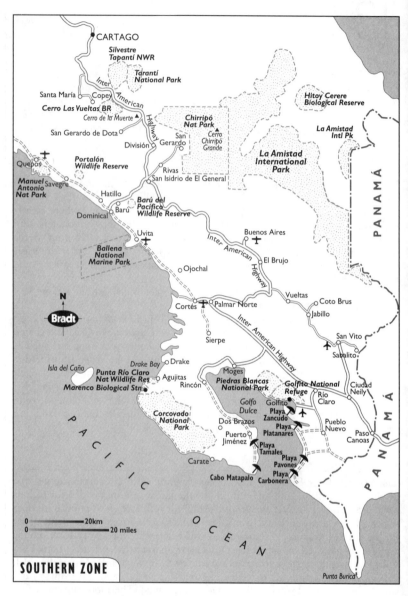

and marketing hub in addition to being a great place to stock up before exploring the Chirripó National Park or heading to the beach at Playa Dominical. Located in the foothills of the Talamanca Mountains, it's a beautiful location. Not much to do here though, other than hike Chirripó.

GETTING THERE AND AWAY

By car This is one of the most difficult stretches of road in Costa Rica, so be prepared for a long and winding trip. From San José, take the Inter-American Highway and brace yourself for the arduous (and chilly) climb up Cerro de la Muerte. Travel time is about three hours.

By bus MUSOC (✆ 222 2422) buses leave every hour from San José to San Isidro and Chirripótel. **Transportes Blanco** (✆ 771 4744) leave twice daily from south of the court building on the Inter-American Highway to San Isidro and Dominical.

⚑ WHERE TO STAY

🏠 **Albergue Mirador de Quetzales** (11 rooms) Off the highway; ✆/f 381 8456. This family-run lodge on 43ha with ancient oak trees has basic cabins with private bathrooms, hot water and fans (although it gets nippy up here). The focus here is on birds, not creature comforts so don't expect the Marriott but if you're into quetzals, check it out. *Rate US$47 pp includes meals and tours.*

Trogon Lodge (22 rooms) Off main road in San Gerardo de Dota; tel: 293 8181; fax: 239 7657; www.gruposmawamba.com. Basic accommodation on a 105-acre farm beside the Savegre River. Rooms have dbl beds, private baths and heating units. There are forests to explore and streams for trout fishing. Restaurant serves simple Costa Rican fare. *Rates US$68–120 dbl.*

🏠 **Savegre Hotel de Montaña** (35 rooms) 9km down a steep dirt road from the highway; ✆ 740 1029; f 740 1027; www.savegre.co.cr. Also known as Cabinas Chacon, this is one of the best spots to see the elusive quetzal. Over 150 bird species have been identified and the Quetzal Education Research Centre is housed here. Rooms are basic but comfortable and clean, with either a fireplace or small heating device and private bathrooms with hot water. There is a restaurant/bar, trout pond, river fishing, orchards, tours to waterfalls, forest trails, bilingual birding guides and horseriding. B/fast inc. *Rates US$79–101.*

🏠 **Hotel Iguazú** (21 rooms) Northwest of the park; ✆ 771 2571. Good clean, basic rooms. Some have private bathrooms and TVs. *Rates US$15–23.*

🏠 **Hotel y Restaurante Chirripó** (41 rooms) Downtown San Isidro; ✆ 771 0529. Basic rooms, some with shared baths. Ask to view the room first as quality varies (get a room that's not at the front, on account of the noise). Popular and affordable restaurant for good *Tico* fare. *Rates US$8–13.*

⚑ WHERE TO EAT
The area is off the beaten tourist path and is more of a business/transportation hub so accommodation is basic and food cheap. The following are in San Isidro.

✗ **Taqueria Mexico Lindo** South end of the shopping centre; ✆ 771 8222. Mexican and vegetarian food.

✗ **Kafe de la Casa** La Cascada, 500m west of the church; ✆ 771 6479. Coffees, pastries, lunches, art gallery, live music.

WHAT TO SEE AND DO
Birdwatching and climbing Mount Chirripó are the two activities in this area.

Refugio Genesis II Private Nature Reserve (✆ 381 0739; e genesis@yellowweb.co.cr) is a private 95-acre reserve in a cloudforest which has a reforestation project, four zip lines, trail tours and excellent birding. There are a limited number of rooms in a very basic lodging so call beforehand if you plan on overnighting. A good 4x4 is a necessity to make it down to the reserve.

COOPEDOTA (✆ 541 2828; *tours Mon–Fri*) is the local coffee co-operative and offers free coffee tours. A good place to stock up on the golden bean at bargain prices.

Las Quebradas Biological Centre (*7km from San Isidro*; ✆/f 771 4131). This 750ha private reserve is community run and offers almost 3km of trails through primary forest. It's a nice spot for birding and features a butterfly garden and a picturesque pond. *Rates: rooms US$6; camping US$3 pp.*

New Dawn Centre (*4km from San Isidro*; ✆ 833 1176; *www.thenewdawncenter.org*). A tropical/medicinal herb farm dedicated to ecological living and New Age healing, the centre offers courses on tropical medicinal plants, sustainability, ecological health gardens and Spanish language. Students can also do a work exchange for room and board. Tours of the gardens are available (*US$5*), organic meals (*US$5*) and overnight stays (*US$10*).

Chirripó National Park Lying 20km northeast of San Isidro, this park is named after the looming Cerro el Chirripó found in its centre. With its peak at a lofty 3,819m, Chirripó is the highest mountain in Central America south of Guatemala and on a clear day, both the Atlantic and Pacific oceans are visible from its summit. A favoured trip for the more adventurous, Chirripó offers a range of environments, from cloudforest to rocky mountain terrain. In between, you'll find an almost-Alpine setting, with rocky outcrops, small shrubs and hearty grasses. This *paramo* is similar to Andean plateaux, with muted browns, yellows and deep purples colouring the landscape. Chirripó is the only place in Costa Rica where traces of glaciers that once covered the land 30,000 years ago are visible, such as glacial lakes, moraines and crestones. Much of the land is boggy so hikers need to be careful where they step.

Weather here is wild and unpredictable, with temperatures dipping below 0°C at night while soaring to 20°C on sunny days. Usually, May to December sees humid and rainy conditions, improving in January to April (although rainstorms and clouds are common) with March and April seeing dry spells.

If you want to climb Cerro Chirripó, you must make reservations by calling 192 (in San José) in advance as only 40 hikers are allowed per day. Most hikers find two or three nights sufficient, as it is a long, slow ascent to the top. Although camping and fires are strictly prohibited, hikers can stay in the accommodation huts on the mountain. These communal huts feature 20 bunks, cold-water showers, a cooking area and washing tubs for laundry. Hikers must bring in their own food and drink although sleeping bags are available for rent. Make sure to pack warm clothing (such as a polar fleece jacket and gloves) as well as clothes that can be layered/removed depending upon the conditions mother nature dictates. It is not advised to deviate from the path as you run the risk of becoming lost and suffering hypothermia – the hike along the paths is strenuous and the scenery stunning enough to keep even the most advanced hiker challenged.

Herradura hot springs (*entrance US$2*) are a small, natural springs just a short walk along the footpath north of San Gerardo and you'll find the entrance about 1km past there, a further ten-minute walk.

Fiesta del Diablitos is the annual festival in February where the *Boruca* Indians perform traditional dances portraying the Spanish conquest of the Americas. Donning colourful hand-painted masks, for which this tribe is famous, it's a fascinating cultural experience. The dates vary so check with the ICT (Costa Rican Tourism Board).

DOMINICAL, UVITA, PLAYA TORTUGA

For a long time, this was the best-kept secret in Costa Rica but the word is out and Dominical could be another Manuel Antonio down the road. Attractive jungle and beaches make this as pretty as a postcard and a great spot for birdwatching but swimming isn't recommended – Dominical is blessed with both right and left breaks, making it a surfer's paradise. Swimmers are advised to head south to Dominicalito or Ballena for safer swimming.

Further south, Uvita and Playa Tortuga are basically undeveloped and here you'll find long stretches of secluded beaches. Uvita is close to Ballena National Park where snorkelling, fishing and birdwatching are the favoured activities. French-Canadians have settled in Ojochal and have set up a number of wonderful restaurants, creating a culinary paradise in the most unexpected of spots. Playa Tortuga is still almost deserted and isn't recommended for swimming.

GETTING THERE AND AWAY

By air The closest airstrips are in Quepos. Both **Sansa** (✆ 220 2414) and **NatureAir** (✆ 220 3054) fly from San José, and once in Quepos you can hire a taxi or pick up a rental car (which is a good option for this area).

By car Driving is recommended as the roads are in good shape and taxis aren't always easy to find. From San José, take the Inter-American Highway south (towards Cartago) to San Isidro de El General, then turn right and head towards the coast for approximately five hours. If you're in Quepos/Manuel Antonio, take the road for Dominical from Quepos (follow the signs) which should take about 1½ hours.

By bus **Transportes Blanco** (✆ 771 4744) leaves twice daily 300m south of the court building on the Inter-American Highway to San Isidro and Uvita.

WHERE TO STAY **Selva Mar** (✆ 771 4582) can assist with booking hotels and tours, as some places don't yet have phones.

⌂ **Cuna del Angel** (16 rooms) Dominical; ✆ 787 8012; www.cunadelangel.com. Newly opened in December of 2005, this cosy hotel is the most luxurious in the area. Each room is named after an angel and is nicely decorated with Asian influenced furniture and features wireless internet, AC, fan, private bath with hot water and bathtub, mini bar, safe, hairdryer, CD and DVD player, TV and beautiful ocean and jungle views. The spa on site is outstanding as is the restaurant. Careful attention to detail is evident throughout, with an emphasis on Heaven, Earth and keeping the positive energy flowing. As someone recently said, 'It's the perfect spot for a girl's weekend getaway.' *Rates US$153.*

⌂ **Villas Rio Mar** (48 rooms) Dominical; ✆ 787 0052; f 787 0054; www.villasriomar.com. Cabins are a lovely blend of stucco with hardwood construction and thatched roofs, with fan, AC, satellite TV, terrace, refrigerator and hammock. Junior suites can accommodate up to 4 people and some have bathtubs. There is a pool with wet bar, jacuzzi, tennis courts, gardens, spa, internet, conference centre and an elegant open-air restaurant/bar. Lovely setting with the mountains at the back, the river at the front and beaches 800m away. *Rates US$70–125.*

⌂ **Diuwak Hotel & Beach Resort** (18 rooms) On the main road in Dominical, 50m from the beach; ✆ 787 0087; www.diuwak.com. Family owned and operated. Guests can choose from 4 types of cabins. All have private bathrooms with hot water, a terrace and fans or AC — suites have kitchens. Amenities include pool, jacuzzi, gardens, mini-market, tours, kayaks, snorkelling and a restaurant/bar. Not much

in the way of character but it is a convenient locale. B/fast inc. *Rates US$92–110.*

⌂ **Villas Gaia** (12 rooms) Playa Tortuga; ✆ 244 0316; www.villasgaia.com. Small but quaint hotel is the best bet in this secluded area. Brightly painted wooden cabins are spacious, with either a queen and a sgl or 3 sgl beds and have fans, private bathrooms, verandas with jungle view and some have AC. The hilltop pool (specially designed for scuba instruction) and bar have great views. Excellent restaurant. They also rent out La Casa for up to 7 people. Recommended. *Rate US$75 per cabin.*

⌂ **Hacienda Baru** (6 rooms) 1km north of Dominical; ✆ 787 0003; f 787 0057; www.haciendabaru.com. Set amongst 815 acres, this is a great spot for birdwatching and hiking. The spacious cabins are clean and comfortable, with private bathrooms with hot water, fans and kitchenette. There is a canopy tour on site, butterfly and orchid gardens and an open-air restaurant. B/fast inc. *Rate US$60 inc.*

⌂ **Beachfront Cabinas & Restaurant Tortilla Flats** (18 rooms) On the main road; ✆/f 787 0033. Long-time surfers' hangout has a mixture of older and newer rooms — some with fans, some with AC. Newer rooms have skylights and carved wooden headboards. Typical seafood restaurant, tours, surf rentals. *Rates US$35–45.*

⌂ **Antorchas Campground** 25m from the beach; ✆ 787 0307. Safe spot to pitch your tent or lay your head. Basic rooms with fans and shared cold water bathrooms. There is a communal kitchen, parking, volleyball, basketball, ping-pong, dartboard, chess and hammocks. *Rates: rooms US$8; camping US$5 pp.*

✖ WHERE TO EAT

✖ **San Clemente Bar and Grill** Next to the football field; ℡ 787 0055; www.dominicalbeach.com. The local gathering spot in town. The food is fresh, filling and tasty, with mostly Mexican and fish offerings. *Main course US$5–8. Open daily 07.00–22.00.*

Additionally, there are a few *sodas* around town. If you have a car, head south to Ojochal where an enclave of French-Canadians have set up shop, with a number of great French-inspired restaurants.

✖ **La Parcela** Just south of town at Cabinas Punto Dominical; ℡ 787 0016, ℮ lapinfo@laparcela.net; www.laparcela.net. The daily changing menu features fresh seafood and fish cooked in a variety of flavours influenced by cuisine the world over. Chicken and meat dishes are also menu staples at this small restaurant with the stunning view overlooking the Pacific. *Main course US$8–12. Open daily 07.30–21.00.*

✖ **Coconut Spice** Plaza Pacifica; ℡ 829 8397; www.coconutspice.com. If searching for good Thai or Indian cooking, this is the place in the south to head to. Despite the utilitarian setting on the second floor of a strip mall, the food is surprisingly authentic, with Pad Thai, lemon-grass soup, samosas and a variety of curries. *Main course US$10–12.00. Open Tue–Sun 16.30–21.30.*

✖ **Roca Verde** South end of the beach; ℡ 787 0036. Located in the hotel of the same name, the bar is often a noisy spot with a lot of people drinking, dancing and enjoying a night out. The food is straight ahead meat, fish or chicken, either grilled or simply prepared. A good bet for dinner and a bit of partying afterwards. *Main course US$6. Open daily 07.30–21.00.*

✖ **Villas Gaia** 35km south of Dominical on the Costanera Sur; ℡ 363 3928; www.villasgaia.com. One of the joys of travelling is discovering good food in the middle of nowhere. This small restaurant in a small hotel is a little treasure in no-man's-land, where intrepid travellers will be rewarded with creative cuisine with flavours ranging from Italy to Mexico and points in between. *Main course US$8–11. Open daily 07.00–21.00.*

PRACTICALITIES There is a pharmacy, **Farmacia Dominical** (℡ 787 0404) at the Pueblo de Río shopping mall, as well as **Clinica Gonzalez Arrelano** (℡ 787 0129) which offers health and dental services. There are no banks.

WHAT TO SEE AND DO Surfing is the big thing in Dominical and if you head further south, towards Roca Verde, Dominicalito or Playa Hermosa, you'll find better swimming spots. At the small village of Uvita (16km south of Dominical), is the north end of Ballena National Park. Playa Uvita, a protected area, has good swimming.

There are some splendid waterfalls around Dominical, and the best is the **Santo Cristo** or **Nauyaca Waterfalls**, which has a great swimming hole. Most hotels in the area can arrange for tours to the falls. **Don Lulo's** (℡/f 787 0198) offers full-day tours by horse or foot. **Hacienda Baru** (℡ 787 0003; f 787 0057; *www.haciendabaru.com*) offers 7km of self-guided trails, guided rainforest hikes, birding, canopy tour, platform for wildlife viewing, tree climbing, butterfly garden, overnight beach and jungle excursions. **Skyline Ultra-Flight** (℡ 743 8037) has individual flights with an English/German-speaking pilot; also offers flying lessons. **Ballena National Marine Park** is one of the few maritime national parks. With 5,400ha, it is home to the Pacific coast's largest coral reef. Humpback whales with their calves are a common sight between December and April. At low tide, you can walk from Bahia Beach to a number of good snorkelling spots. **Selva Mar** (℡ 771 4582) offers snorkelling tours here.

DRAKE BAY

Sierpe, a small village, is the gateway to the Osa Peninsula and its river of the same name is home to 39,950 acres of mangrove. Sir Francis Drake, the notorious

British pirate, is said to have anchored in this bay at the northernmost tip of the peninsula in 1579 (hence the name) and rumoured to have buried treasure here, although it's yet to be found. Although roads and an airstrip were built here in 1997, development has been slow and miles of untamed jungle and deserted beaches are the norm – hopefully, it stays this way for many years to come.

Nearby **Caño Island** makes for an interesting trip and is one of the better areas of the country for diving and snorkelling. Make sure to take a guided hike on the island to see the mysterious stone spheres, which archaeologists are still befuddled by.

GETTING THERE AND AWAY Owing to its remote nature and isolation of the resorts, it's imperative that you have both reservations and transportation pre-arranged. Almost all the resorts will arrange transportation for you.

The older (and more adventurous) route is to fly to Palmar Sur (or take a bus there), take a 15-minute taxi ride to Sierpe past all of the banana plantations dotted with ancient stone spheres, and then board a small boat to sail down the river for 40km. The first bit of the trip is languorous, slipping past mangroves and canals – the end of the trip is where the adventure comes in when the small boat has to negotiate the breakers where the wide Sierpe empties into the Pacific. Not for the faint of heart! It's recommended that you use a resort boat, as they have large outboard motors, steered by highly experienced captains – regardless, it's still a wild ride.

By air Flying is the fastest and easiest way to get to this remote part of the world. Both **Sansa** (\ 220 2414) and **NatureAir** (\ 220 3054) fly from San José to Palmar Sur or Drake Bay (which is the easiest way to get here).

By car Driving is not recommended as the roads are in bad shape and you can't drive beyond the small village of Drake Bay, as most resorts here are only accessible by boat. If you insist, it should be undertaken only in a good-size 4x4 during the dry season. Take the Inter-American Highway south and take the turn-off at Chacarita for Puerto Jimenez, then drive 40km down very rough roads to Rincón and from there, the road to either Drake Bay or Agujitas (some hotels are accessible from here).

By bus Tracopa-Alfaro (\ 223 7685) leaves from Avenida 6, Calle 14 in San José at 05.00 to Palmar Sur. The journey takes about six hours, then take a taxi to catch the 12.00 boat from Sierpe or hire a boat.

WHERE TO STAY

⌂ **Aguila de Osa** (14 rooms) \/f 296 2190; www.aguiladeosa.com. The most luxurious option in Drake Bay, this resort also has the most accessible location, high on a hill overlooking the bay. Right across from Drake Bay Wilderness. Guests can walk down the beach to the village of Drake Bay. Rooms are large with stunning views from their porches, private baths with hot water, ceiling fans – but it's a hike up those stairs so people with mobility issues should reconsider. Fresh carafes of coffee are left on your porch every morning. The open-air restaurant and bar is located just a short walk up from the dock. Numerous tours are offered and the resort has its own sport fishing boat and diving boats. Guests have free use of kayaks. *Rate US$514 pp, based on dbl occupancy and includes 2 nights, transport from/to Palmar Sur, 2 tours and all meals and taxes.*

⌂ **La Paloma Lodge** (9 rooms) \ 239 2801; f 239 0954; www.lapalomalodge.com. Recently remodelled bungalows, built up on stilts, have beautiful views from their balconies and the 4 screened walls allow guests to be up close with nature. All have a private bathroom, ceiling fans and hammocks, as do the smaller, and less private, rooms. Meals are served in an open-air thatched rancho. It's a steep hike up the hill but the views of the ocean are worth it. Other amenities include lovely gardens, pool, free use of kayaks and a beach 10 mins down the hill. *Rates are pp, based on dbl occupancy and includes 3 nights, flight from San José, 2 tours, all meals and taxes: room US$880; deluxe room US$1,000; sunset-view room US$1,120.*

🏠 **Drake Bay Wilderness Resort** (7 tents, 20 rooms) Great location, where the Río Aguajitas meets the Pacific, right in Drake Bay; ✆/f 770 8012; www.drakebay.com. Rooms with dbl beds and shared communal baths are great for those who are on a budget. Those seeking more luxury find it in the private rooms with fans, decks and private bathrooms. Filling and tasty meals are inc. There is a small bar overlooking the saltwater pool (the beach in front is too rocky to swim), which is a nice spot to watch the sun set. One of the first resorts in the area, the owners were the movers and shakers behind the airstrip being built in Drake and all of their packages fly in to that strip. Guests have free use of canoes and same-day laundry service (pack light). In addition to the regular gamut of tours, the resort offers a jungle butterfly farm. *Rates are pp, based on dbl occupancy and includes 3 nights, transport from*

Drake Bay airport, 2 tours, all meals and taxes: cabinette US$560; cabin US$660.

🏠 **Poor Man's Paradise** (12 rooms) ✆/f 771 4582; www.mypoormansparadise.com. Rustic cabins have private baths with cold water while the *rancho* and tents have shared baths with cold water. Just steps from the beach, it's a great spot to fish, hike or just relax. Packages inc 3 nights' accommodation, all meals, transportation from/to Sierpe, tour of Corcovado Park, tour of either Caño Island or dolphin watching. *Rates are pp based on dbl occupancy: tent US$316; rancho US$334; cabina US$367 (inc taxes).*

🏠 **Marenco Beach & Rainforest Lodge** (25 rooms) ✆ 258 1919; f 258 1346; www.marencolodge.com. Sitting on a 1,500-acre private reserve, with 5km of beach, this former biological research station has great views of Caño Island and is only 5km north of Corcovado Park. The 17 bungalows are basic but comfortable affairs, with kitchenettes and the 8 rooms are bright and cheery. All have fans, private bathrooms and decks. There is a bar and restaurant where family-style meals are served 3 times a day. Numerous tours are available through the lodge and hiking through their reserve is always a great treat. The best value in the area. *Rates US$50–75 pp (inc taxes).*

✕ **WHERE TO EAT** The village of Drake Bay is nothing more than a few small shacks on the beach. Owing to the remote nature of the lodges, they all include three meals a day as part of their pricing as there simply is nowhere else to eat.

WHAT TO SEE AND DO Wildlife, deserted beaches and sport fishing are the draws here.

Osa Tours (*in Palmar Norte;* ✆ 786 7825; e catuosa@racsa.co.cr) organises various tours and the owner also runs the Osa Tourism Chamber. **The Bug Lady** (✆ 382 1619; *www.thenighttour.com*) is one of the more unusual tours in the country. Biologist Tracie Stice takes brave people into the forest around Drake for a night hike using high-tech night optics. Interesting, informative and fun. **Caño Island Biological Reserve**, accessible only via a one-hour boat ride from Drake, is an uninhabited island believed to be a pre-Columbian cemetery, possibly of the *Diquis* tribe. Only 3km by 2km, it's most likely the exposed top of an underground mountain. The island is like a table, almost completely flat after an initial hike, and at one time, one of the big fruit companies had cleared a landing strip on the island's top. Very few animals live on Caño but the big draw here is the mysterious stone spheres that are scattered throughout. Look carefully and you'll see bits of broken pottery on the ground.

Snorkelling and diving here are excellent, with clear visibility in the dry season, coral reefs and waters teeming with life. On my last trip there, I was snorkelling just 1m above a lazy white-tipped shark and a pod of dolphins playfully followed our boat's wake en route to the island. All the resorts listed here offer trips to Caño Island – which makes it surprisingly busy for such a wilderness location – and I highly recommend exploring this mystical spot.

This is the largest community in the Osa Peninsula, although it seems pretty sleepy at first glance (but don't let appearances fool you). Many travellers use this as their base before exploring the surrounding areas and parks while gold panners are always around, either buying supplies or whooping it up if they've hit pay dirt. Surfers have discovered the right break down the coast at Cabo Matapalo thus the resulting mix of visitors ranging from backpackers to the well-heeled eco-tourist.

The town itself is small, with the ubiquitous football field, some tour offices and budget accommodation. Those seeking more refined hotels should head to one of the outlying lodges.

GETTING THERE AND AWAY

By air Flying is the fastest and easiest way to get to this remote part of the world. Both **Sansa** (↖ *220 2414*) and **NatureAir** (↖ *220 3054*) fly from San José and NatureAir has flights from Quepos. Give yourself extra time, however, as these flights don't always operate like a Swiss watch and will often stop off for additional pickups. Also, make sure you arrive at the airstrip 30–45 minutes before your flight in case they are early (you don't want to be stuck in the middle of nowhere).

By car It's a looooong, slow drive that should only be undertaken in a good-size 4x4. Take the Inter-American Highway east from San José (via Cartago), then through San Isidro de El General (about three hours) and continue to La Palma (about another three hours). Follow the signs for Puerto Jimenez – the last 35km is on gravel roads so take it easy.

By bus **Transportes Blanco-Lobo** (↖ *771 4744*) leaves from Avenida 7/9, Calle 12 in San José to Puerto Jimenez. The journey takes about eight hours.

By boat A daily ferry leaves from Golfito at 11.30 and takes 1½ hours, costing 1,000 colones. The return from Puerto Jimenez leaves at 06.00. Private water taxis can also be chartered for around US$60.

WHERE TO STAY AND EAT IN TOWN
Accommodation in town tends to be basic and simple with higher-end lodges further south. The town is small enough that you can walk or hail a taxi. The Banco Nacional is 100m north of the petrol station.

⌂ **Cabinas y Restaurante Carolina** (15 rooms) On the main street; ↖ 735 5696. The restaurant is the real draw, with great seafood at low prices. Hangout for budget travellers. *Rates: rooms with private bathrooms US$10; newer rooms with AC US$35.*

⌂ **Cabinas Iguana Iguana** (10 rooms) North entrance of town; ↖/f 735 5158. Basic but clean rooms with fan, some private baths, cold water, pool and a restaurant/bar. One of the better bets for budget travellers. *Rate US$7 pp.*

WHERE TO STAY AND EAT AROUND OSA
If you are travelling all this way, you'd best relax and enjoy the spectacular views for at least three nights. Owing to the remote nature of this area, all the listed hotels include meals in their pricing and often have transportation as part of their packaging as well.

⌂ **Lapa Rios** (16 rooms) Between Matapalo and Carate; ↖ 735 5130; f 735 5179; www.laparios.com. Luxury at the ends of the earth is how to best describe this jungle hideaway. Bungalows are perched high above the ocean on a series of ridges, allowing for heart-stopping views but heart-pounding climbs to and from your room and restaurant. But the workout is worth it — open screened walls, mosquito netting-draped beds and open-air showers on a private deck are sure to

13

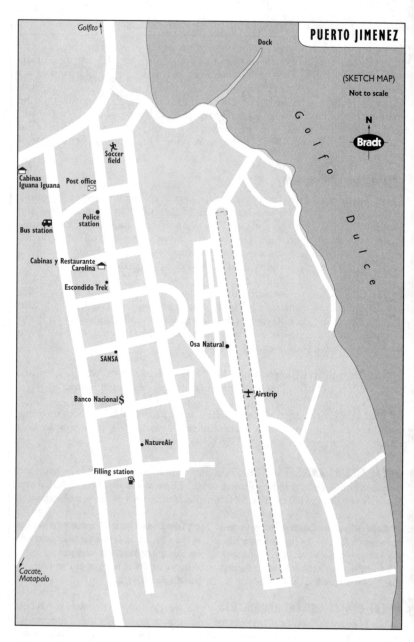

Golfito ↑

Dock

N

Bradt

Golfo Dulce

Soccer field

Cabinas Iguana Iguana

Post office

Police station

Bus station

Cabinas y Restaurante Carolina

Escondido Trek

Osa Natural

SANSA

Banco Nacional $

✈ Airstrip

NatureAir

Filling station

Cacate, Matapalo

kindle passion's sparks. Meals are served in the open-air restaurant, which houses a spiral staircase leading to the observation deck above. Situated on 1,000 acres of private reserve, you can spot macaws from the comfort of your own porch. Activities include surf lessons, massage, yoga, fishing, hiking through the forest reserve, with a naturalist

guide, marine turtle tour, horses, kayaking, swimming with dolphins and boat tours. There is no TV or AC (although the breezes are sufficient) and it's a 15-min hike down to the beach, which isn't swimmable. Relaxing, taking in the view and hiking the reserve area are the best activities and it's not surprising that this is a favoured honeymoon spot. The hotel has won numerous awards, including many for its commitment to sustainability, community building and true eco-tourism, for which it is to be congratulated. Recommended. *Rate US$242 pp, meals and taxes inc.*

🏠 **Villa Corcovado** (8 rooms) North tip of Golfo Dulce in Rincón; ☎ 817 6969; f 770 8061; www.villacorcovado.com. Gleaming hardwood villas with screened windows, are tucked into a hillside surrounded by fragrant ylang ylang trees. Spacious and beautifully appointed, these villas have splendid views of the gulf from their private porches. The open-air restaurant has an Argentinian flair and uses organic produce from the hotel's own gardens. There is a lovely bar, beachfront massage hut and the beach is just steps from the villas. In addition to sport fishing, hiking trails throughout their 70 acres, snorkelling, dolphin tours and kayaking, you can have a picnic on a deserted beach, sleep under the stars (under a mosquito net) on a balcony or take a tour of a neighbouring organic cocoa farm and then enjoy a meal of chocolate-based delicacies and even a chocolate massage. Recommended. *Rate US$188, all meals and taxes inc.*

🏠 **Bosque del Cabo** (12 rooms) Left from Lapa Rios; \f 735 5206. Sitting 500ft above the meeting point of the Pacific Ocean and the Golfo Dulce, this is one of the most spectacular spots to relax for a couple of days. Bungalows have private baths with outdoor garden showers, solar-powered electricity and porches with great views. Deluxe bungalows are larger. 2 rental houses are also on the grounds. Meals are served in the al fresco restaurant and are tasty. The beach is just a short stroll away as are the tidal pools and a waterfall. Other features include a pool, canopy tour, suspension bridge, daily yoga classes, massages, surfing, birding, trips to Corcovado and guided nature hikes in the private reserve. *Rates US$150–165 pp, meals and tax inc.*

🏠 **Iguana Lodge** (8 rooms) ☎ 829 5865; f 735 5436. Beautifully crafted wooden 'tree houses' have luxury rooms, complete with fans, Egyptian-cotton sheets on the beds, hot-water showers (some rooms with outdoor garden showers) with stone floors and large decks with hammocks and plush lounge chairs. Delicious meals are served on the second floor of the main *rancho*, the main level housing one of the largest libraries in the Osa. *Rate US$120 pp, all-inc.*

🏠 **Villa Villa Kula** Next door to Iguana Lodge. This 3-bedroom rental home architectural wonder looks like something Pippi herself would have created. All guests have the use of the new Japanese soaking tub, boogie boards and kayaks. *Rate US$330 per night (min 3 nights).*

🏠 **Cabinas and Restaurante Carate Jungle Camp** (6 rooms) In Carate (no phone). This is the only budget option outside of Puerto Jimenez and has rustic cabins set on 6ha, some with shared baths, cold water. There is a restaurant and horses. *Rates US$10–15 pp.*

WHAT TO SEE AND DO

Corcovado National Park (*office in Puerto Jimenez;* ☎ *735 5282;* f *735 5276; open daily 08.00–16.00; entrance US$8 pp*) Reservations through **Osa Natural** (☎ *735 5440; www.osanatural.com*). This huge park is the main reason for tourists to make the trek south. Covering 103,258 acres of land and 5,930 acres of marine habitat, the park encompasses most of the Osa Peninsula. Here, you'll find eight habitat types – the only personate forest (also known as tropical humid forest) of any size on the Pacific coast of Central America, cloudforest, alluvial plains forest, palm forest, mangrove, swamp and rocky as well as sandy vegetation. There are 500 species of trees, whose density and height have prompted comparisons to the Amazon Basin. Endangered mammals, like jaguars, ocelots and tapirs, make their homes here although few hikers are lucky enough to spot these elusive creatures. Regarded as the most biologically diverse region in the world, Corcovado has 400 species of birds, 6,000 species of insects, 116 species of amphibians and 114 species of mammals, most of which are more active at night.

Day hikes are available and many lodges offer day tours complete with guide and transport to and from the park (note that walking is the only means of transportation inside the park). There are many options for multi-day hikes but be forewarned – hiking here is a hot and very humid business. Distances are long between the four ranger stations and there are several natural threats, such as insects (repellent and mosquito netting, if camping, are requirements), sharks (no going for a quick dip to cool off) as well as herds of peccaries (a type of wild pig), which can be very aggressive. And don't forget the snakes, including the legendary bushmaster that will attack without provocation. Rainstorms can turn trails into mud bogs within minutes, making hiking even more arduous. Hiking along the beach from La Leona or San Pedrillo is an alternative, but then you have to time yourself with the tides, as the beach disappears at high tide. This is not an outing I would recommend for a young family.

If you're planning a multi-day hike, you must book space with the park in advance as you need reservations for camping, meals or lodging at one of the *puestos* as space is limited. Reservations are also a safety issue – if you do not show up, the ranger will go out to look for you.

There are four entry points to the park, all of which lead to ranger stations. From Puerto Jimenez, **La Leona** ranger station can be accessed by car or bus. If driving, take the road to Carate (at the end of the line), from which it's a 3km hike to the station. A bus also makes the trip twice a day but best to ask at the park office in town first for times.

El Tigre is 14km along the dirt road from Puerto Jimenez and **Los Patos** is accessible from the town of La Palma. From Los Patos, you can hike 19km through the middle of the park to the Sirena station, which is also home to research facilities and a small landing strip. The fourth entrance is at **San Pedrillo** at the northern end of the park and is accessible by boat from Drake Bay or Sierpe.

All stations permit camping (US$4 per person) as well as a simple *soda* offering a meals service (usually rice, beans and fish), available for US$5 or US$8 (in colones). La Leona and San Pedrillo have basic dormitory rooms (US$8 per person – bring your own bedding and mosquito netting) while Sirena has larger, more modern accommodation and a research facility. Make sure to stock up on food, water (you can fill up at the *puestos*) and other essentials before you enter the park as there aren't any mini-marts or stores. Do not drink water from the streams. And if you don't speak Spanish, be sure to have a phrasebook as the rangers generally don't speak any English. Most importantly, never hike alone as this is wild country.

Hikes Most hikers start out at the crack of dawn and stop at midday on account of the heat.

From **La Leona to Sirena** is a 15km trail almost entirely along the beach (about six hours in total) and is a hot one. Hats, sunscreen and at least five litres of water are advised.

Sirena to San Pedrillo is perhaps the most difficult, clocking in at 25km with a river that must be forded. Be careful as it's very strong and sees sharks at high tide – attempt only at low tide! This is a two-day hike and you must be comfortable setting up a tent in the rainforest. Many hikers will do the beach section either before dawn or after dark, as the danger of snakes on sand is nil. The jungle part of the trek will most likely take seven hours.

Los Patos to Sirena at 22km is another challenge as the first 8km are all uphill in humid, hot rainforest before 14km of very hot (think 26°C and higher) hiking along the lowlands – best left to experienced rainforest hikers and those really eager at the possibility of spotting mammals. The easiest and fastest routes are in the eastern area around **El Tigre**, which can be done in a morning.

Escondido Trek (☏ 735 5210) offers dolphin watching by kayak, night paddling, tree climbing, waterfall abseiling, snorkelling, fishing, mangrove exploration, horseriding and gold-mining hikes. **Osa Natural** (☏ 735 5440) has gold-mining tours, fresh and saltwater kayak tours, horses, tours to the Guaymi Indigenous Reserve and boat tours. **Everyday Adventure** (☏ 735 5138) offers waterfall abseiling and kayaking as well as tours with a naturalist guide.

There's a local joke that goes: 'Why do those destined for Hell stop off at Golfito first? That way, they're halfway there.' Needless to say, Golfito isn't a bustling tourist town, although its setting between the bay and lush, forested hills is gorgeous. Unfortunately, the town is run down and seedy with rubbish-strewn streets. At one point, this was a busy banana-port town until labour strife and falling market prices caused United Fruit to shut up shop here in 1985. Now, Golfito is a duty-free zone to which *Ticos* flock to purchase imported goods (December is a particularly busy time). Be warned that finding a room in Golfito can be difficult.

Most travellers use Golfito as a jumping-off point to the areas further south while fishermen come here for the outstanding marlin and sailfish found just outside of the bay. This is also a great spot for dolphin-watching tours while the nearby hills offer excellent birding opportunities.

GETTING THERE AND AWAY
By air Sansa (☏ *220 2414*) and **NatureAir** (☏ *220 3054*) have daily flights.

By car Prepare yourself for a long, rough 340km ride that is almost impassable during the rainy season. Follow the Inter-American Highway south from San José, take the Río Claro turn-off and follow the large signs for the 'Deposito Libre' (Duty Free).

By bus **Tracopa-Alfaro** buses leave from Avenida 5, Calle 14 in San José at 07.00 and 15.00 for the eight-hour trip to Golfito.

By ferry *La Lancha* makes the 1½-hour trip between Puerto Jimenez and Golfito at 06.00 and returns at 11.30 for 1,000 colones. Water taxis are also available.

WHERE TO STAY
⌂ **Esquinas Rainforest Lodge** (14 rooms) 10km north of Golfito on dirt road to La Gamba; ☏/f 775 0901; www.esquinaslodge.com. A gorgeous spot that is part of the Piedras Blancas National Park. Neat as a pin, this lodge is affectionately called the 'Rainforest of the Austrians'. The comfortable bungalows set among the pristine gardens have a fan and a fair bit of space. In the main house, you'll find the living room, library and restaurant/bar while the main grounds feature a pool with a jungle stream! Wonderful spot for hikes and birding. *Rate US$100 pp, all-inc.*

⌂ **Complejo Turistico Samoa del Sur** (13 rooms) Centre of town; ☏ 775 0233; f 775 0573; www.samoadelsur.com. Newly renovated, this popular hotel offers clean and spacious rooms, with modern bathrooms and comfortable beds. Waterfront rooms, newly remodelled, cable TV, AC, restaurant/bar, shell/handicraft museum/souvenir shop, gallery, new butterfly-shaped pool, pool table, sport fishing, kayaks, bikes. *Rates US$38–50.*

⌂ **Buena Vista Lodge** (4 rooms) 2km south of town; ☏/f 775 2065; e petergolfito@hotmail.com. This clean and pleasant lodge is on 22ha of rainforest and its 4 simple but shady rooms have fans, cable TV and mini-fridges in a couple of the rooms. There is a small pool and a bar and the staff can arrange area tours. B/fast inc. *Rates US$25–45.*

⌂ **Hotel/Restaurant Golfito Bay & Business Centre** (17 rooms) North of town on the waterfront; ☏ 775 0006; f 775 2189; e golfitobay@hotmail.com. This vintage, wooden hotel has been recently renovated and is a good option. Rooms are Spartan, with either a fan and cold water or with AC and hot water (the 'deluxe' rooms). All rooms have cable TV and private bathrooms. The café sports a very cool tiled floor and pretty good eats while the views are lovely. *Rates US$10–25.*

There are rooms available in the 'US Zone' where you find the old United Fruit houses but they are of varying quality and aimed primarily at *Ticos* shopping at the Deposito Libre.

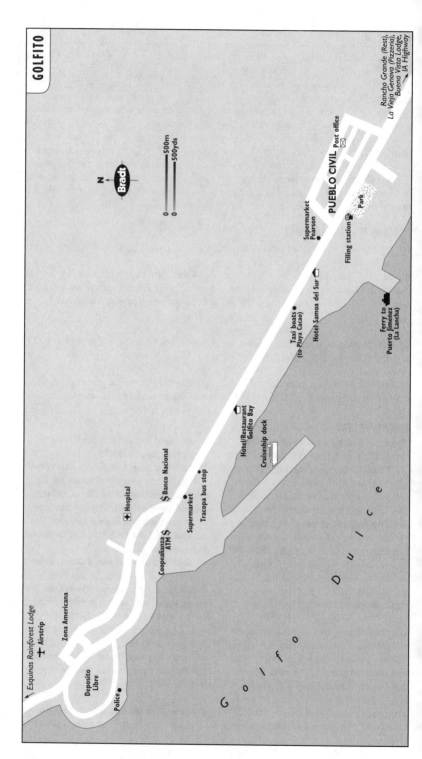
GOLFITO

500m
500yds

Esquinas Rainforest Lodge
Airstrip
Zona Americana
Deposito Libre
Police

Hospital
Banco Nacional
Coopealianza ATM
Supermarket
Tracopa bus stop

Hotel/Restaurant Golfito Bay
Cruiseship dock

Taxi boats (to Playa Cacao)
Hotel Samoa del Sur

Supermarket Pearson
PUEBLO CIVIL Post office
Filling station
Park

Ferry to Puerto Jimenez (La Lancha)

Rancho Grande (Rest),
La Vieja Genova (Pizzeria),
Buena Vista Lodge,
IA Highway

Golfo Dulce

WHERE TO EAT

Restaurante Rancho Grande On the road 8km south of Golfito centre; ☎ 775 1951. Offers seafood, steak and reputedly has the best *patacones* on the west coast. Recommended. *Main course averages US$8. Open 11.30–21.00 daily.*

Restaurant Mar & Luna On the waterfront: ☎ 775 0192. The most sophisticated place to dine, offers seafood and lovely views of the harbour. *Meals average US$14. Open 06.00–22.00; closed Mon.*

PRACTICALITIES Buses run from one end of town to the other. Three **banks** – Banco Nacional, Banco de Costa Rica and Banco Popular – are all found at the Deposito Libre. Banco Nacional is also found on on the main road in the Zona Americana. **Hospital de Golfito** (☎ 775 0011) is in the Zona Americana. The **police station** is in front of the Deposito Libre.

WHAT TO SEE AND DO

Casa de Orquideas is a private six-acre garden surrounded by primary rainforest in the Golfo Dulce, accessible by a 30-minute boat ride that most hotels can arrange. Tours are US$5 per person (four person minimum) for two hours and includes fruit drinks fresh from the garden.

Senderos y Cataratas Avellan (*6km north of Deposito Libre on the dirt road to Gambas;* ☎ *378 7895; www.waterfallsavellan.com; camping US$5 pp*). A pleasant 'back to nature' experience on a family farm turned eco-tourism. Here you'll find three lovely waterfalls, trails through primary and secondary forests, horseriding and some delicious home-cooked meals.

Sport fishing **King & Bartlett International Sport Fishing** (☎ 775 1624; *www.kingandbartlett.com*) features a 22-slip marina and three sport fishing boats for charter. **Froylan Lopez** (☎ 824 6571) captains a boat for up to seven fishermen. **Banana Bay Marina** (☎ 775 1624; f 775 0735; *www.bananabaymarina.com*) has a floating-dock marina and offers kayaks as well as charter fishing. **C-tales** (☎ 775 0062; *www.c-tales.com*) has its office at Hotel Las Gaviotas and is a non-profit foundation that offers charters with English-speaking captain and crew.

GOLFO DULCE

The 'Sweet Gulf' is home to remote beaches and stretches of virgin rainforest. There isn't much here, other than a handful of lodges, palm trees and sand.

The northeast shores are only accessible via boat and the hotels can pre-arrange your transportation.

GETTING THERE AND AWAY

By car Playa Cacao is accessible via a 10km stretch of road west of Golfito and passable most of the year.

By boat Water taxi (about a five-minute and US$3 ride).

WHERE TO STAY

🏠 **Rainbow Adventure Lodge** (4 rooms) From the US or Canada, ☎ 800 565 0722; www.rainbowcostarica.com. Undoubtedly, one of the most refined jungle lodges you'll ever encounter in the middle of nowhere. The 3-storey wooden lodge is appointed throughout with hand-woven rugs, fine antiques, stained glass and fresh flowers, giving an air of 'Age of Enlightenment Meets the Jungle'. The main floor houses the open-air dining area, lounge and AC library, home of the largest private collection of natural history books in Costa Rica (a bibliophile's heaven). Rooms are on the second floor

while the third-floor penthouse has incredible 360°
views of the ocean and surrounding rainforest.
Private cabins atop stilts, a few metres from the
lodge, have living rooms and private verandas. All
accommodation has a queen bed, private bath with
hot water, mosquito netting for the bed and partial
walls, allowing for unobstructed views of the jungle.
There are plenty of hammocks to laze in but if
you're feeling more active, there's hiking, kayaking,
snorkelling, dolphin watching, fishing tours as well as
swimming off the pebbly beach or in the freshwater
pools dotting the property. All-inc, with 3 meals,
snacks, beer, wine and soft drinks, transfer from
Golfito and one jungle tour. *Rates US$178–198 pp,
per day.*

🏠 **Playa Nicuesa Rainforest Lodge** (8 rooms) ✆ 735
5237; www.nicuesalodge.com. This beautiful lodge
offers 4 luxury cabins with either 1 or 2 bedrooms
and a gorgeous guesthouse with 4 rooms. All have

canopied beds, fans, private balconies from which
one can commune with nature, solar-heated water,
fans and romantic open-air showers. Delicious meals
showcase fruit from the many trees on the property
and wood-oven pizzas are a favourite. Everything
here is recycled and the emphasis is on being a
gentle guest of mother nature – candles are used
extensively for lighting, roof tiles were once plastic
bags used in banana production and even the
buildings themselves were constructed from fallen or
farmed trees. Guests can hike through neighbouring
Piedra Blancas Park, kayak, snorkel, fish or go
birding with resident naturalist guides. The attention
to detail, such as the stunning main house
chandelier made from glass and seashells, makes this
a first-class eco-lodge but at bargain rates.
Recommended. *Rates US$150–170 pp, 2-night min
stay, includes boat transfer, 3 meals and use of
sports equipment. Closed Oct.*

ZANCUDO

This 6km grey-sand beach is situated below the estuary of the Río Coto River and
edged by the mangroves of the Coto Swamps. Boasting one of the best swimming
beaches in Costa Rica, it is also known for its world-class sport fishing. The
southern end of the beach offers excellent surfing. This quiet, peaceful, and
secluded area boasts a number of inexpensive hotels and eateries making it a
popular destination for families from Golfito on weekends as well as backpackers
throughout the year. 'Zancudo' means 'mosquito' in Spanish and there are a
number of biting insects, thanks to the mangrove edging the beach, so pack plenty
of repellent.

GETTING THERE AND AWAY

By air The closest airstrip is in Golfito. From there, take either a water taxi or car.

By car A good 4x4 should be able to make the 1½-hour trip year round but double
check on road conditions before heading out. Take the Inter-American Highway
south from Golfito and turn right at Salon El Rodeo (about 4km) then drive 10km
to the car ferry (US$2 per vehicle) and then follow the signs along the dirt road for
25km.

By bus Buses leave from Golfito via Conte daily at 14.00. The total trip takes about
three hours so the water taxi is a much faster option.

By boat Boats are the fastest way to get to Zancudo. Launching out of Golfito, trips
and times depend upon the tides – high-tide routes go through the mangrove while
low-tide heads into the gulf, making for a sometimes rocky ride. The trip lasts about
15 minutes and costs US$10 per person (minimum US$20 charge). If planning
ahead, call **Zancudo Boat Tours** (✆ 776 0012) and they will meet you in Golfito.

🏠 **WHERE TO STAY** There are a number of simple, inexpensive cabins up and down
the beach, along the only road and many of these cabins also have small *sodas* or
restaurants.

Roy's Zancudo Lodge (20 rooms) 150m from police station on beach; ☏ 776 0008; f 776 0011; e fishroys@royszancudolodge.com; www.royszancudolodge.com. By fishermen, for fishermen, Roy's boasts 50 world sport fishing records, 11 fully stocked boats and the top fishing tackle and bait in the country. The bungalows all feature AC, fans, cable TV, phone, fridge and private bathrooms with hot water. 4 suites include a sitting area. There is also a pool, jacuzzi and a seafood restaurant where it's all you can eat and if you catch it, they'll cook it. Although the lodge is geared for the serious angler (they even include all tackle and gear in the package), non-fishing guests are welcome. *Rate is US$2,242 inc transfers from Golfito, 3 days of fishing, licence, tackle, meals and open bar. Non-fishing rate is US$120 pp, per day, all inc. Closed Oct.*

Oasis on the Beach (formerly Zancudo Beach Club) (5 rooms) 4km before town; ☏ 776 0087; f 776 0052; www.oasisonthebeach.com. This tiny, idyllic setting has 3 cabins with fans and a 2-storey villa with AC, all set just steps from the beach. All have private baths, hot water, refrigerator, coffee maker and either a porch or a balcony. The restaurant/bar features pizza and bread baked in a wood oven while the hotel's farm has a stable of 17 fine horses guests can ride. B/fast inc. *Rates US$60–75, taxes inc.*

Cabinas & Restaurante Sol y Mar (5 rooms) On the beach; ☏ 776 0014; www.zancudo.com. Basic, clean and comfy bungalows have fans, private baths with hot water and balconies. All but one have ocean views. The 2 oldest cabins have a unique platform shower surrounded by river rocks with sunroof while the newer cabins are larger but not as artistic. The open-air bar/restaurant is the local spot to hang and the fish burgers are a treat. *Rates US$25–41.*

La Jungla (no phone) On the road into town. The spot to party on Sat nights. *Camping US$3 pp.*

WHERE TO EAT

La Puerta Negra In front of *pulpería* Buen Precio; ☏ 776 0181. This is the place to head for excellent Italian food. Emphasis is on fresh — the herbs are grown in the garden, bread is homemade and they have an extensive wine list. Set in a beautiful beachside garden, this is one of the nicest restaurants on the coast. *Meals average US$12. Open daily 18.00 until last diner has gone.*

WHAT TO SEE AND DO Years ago, bananas used to wash ashore from the United Fruit Company in Golfito, giving rise to a healthy pig farm industry that used the leftover fruit for feed. Although the pigs have long since gone, Zancudo remains a spot without impetus, preferring to roll along with whatever washes up on the beach. Life seemingly stands still on this narrow strip of beach and folks don't do much of anything other than practise the fine art of relaxing (they've honed it to Olympic standards). Lying in a hammock, lying on the beach, playing dominoes or chatting with the locals are favoured pastimes here while the more adventurous will boogie board or surf a bit along the south part of the beach. Sport fishing is the other draw, with numerous record-setting catches having been pulled from the surrounding waters.

Arena Alta Sportfishing & Adventures (☏ 776 0115; f 776 0117; *www.cosaricasailfish.com*) offers sport fishing, customised packages, jungle tours, transfers and also rents golf carts. **Golfito Sportfishing** (☏ 776 0007; *www.costaricafishing.com*) is in Zancudo (despite the name) and offers packages as does **Sportfishing Unlimited Charters** (☏/f 776 0036; *www.sportfishing.co.cr*).

PAVONES

Surfing magazines publicise Pavones as having the longest rideable left break in the world – more than 1km long on a good day giving rides up to three minutes. The best surfing is during the rainy season (May–October) as it takes swells of 6ft or more to get the waves moving but surfing is pretty decent year round. The beach can become crowded and it's not recommended for swimming or body surfing. Non-surfers can enjoy birding, hiking or fishing for tarpon and snook. The town is tiny so services are limited.

Being so remote, Pavones has garnered a 'Wild West' reputation – surfers here are very possessive of their waves while fierce battles between landowners, speculators and squatters have raged for decades, turning bloody in 1997 when a gunfight left a squatter and landowner dead. Best advice is to be a respectful surfer (no wave hogging) and steer clear of real estate deals.

GETTING THERE AND AWAY

By air The closest airstrip is in Golfito. A private taxi can be hired to drive from the airstrip to Pavones (approx US$50).

By car A good 4x4 should be able to make the two-hour trip year round but double check on road conditions before heading out. Take the Inter-American Highway south from Golfito and turn right at Salon El Rodeo (about 4km) then drive 10km to the car ferry (US$2 per vehicle) and then follow the signs along the dirt road to Pavones.

By bus Two buses a day head out from Golfito but it's best to double check schedules beforehand.

WHERE TO STAY

Surfing is the focus of Pavones and accommodation is largely geared towards surfers looking for a cheap spot to crash. There are numerous *cabinas* around the town square, offering basic rooms and cold-water showers for US$8–15 a night. There are also several *sodas* in town for filling and cheap eats.

Tiskita Lodge (14 rooms) 6km south of Pavones; ☏ 296 8125; f 296 8133; www.tiskita-lodge.co.cr. Originally an experimental fruit farm, this nature reserve is a relaxing spot to really get away. Set on 550 acres of rainforest, almost half of the reserve is primary forest. Rooms are in hardwood cabins, with screen walls and porches, many with open-air bathrooms (you still have privacy). Homemade *Tico* meals are served family style, with most of the ingredients coming from the lodge's gardens and fruit trees. Guests can enjoy informative tours of the orchards by knowledgeable owner, Peter Aspinall. Other activities include birding (285 species identified to date), hiking to waterfalls, turtle watching, sport fishing, horseriding or swimming at the beach. Packages include all meals, tours, accommodation as well as flights from San José to their private airstrip. *Rate US$240 pp.*

Casa Siempre Domingo (4 rooms) On the road to Punta Banco on the hill; ☏ 820 4709; www.casa-domingo.com. Large, airy rooms have been built to maximise the cooling breezes, with details such as high ceilings and tiled floors. Meals are served family style, there is a sitting room with satellite TV and the ocean views from the porch are stunning. B/fast and dinner inc. *Rate US$120.*

Rancho Burica (7 rooms) At the end of the road; www.ranchoburica.com. These Dutch-owned simple wooden cabins sleep up to 3 people, some with shared baths and cold-water showers. Meals are served family style. Great spot for monkey and sloth spotting, exploring tide pools or hiking to the nearby waterfalls. The owners can also set up tours to the Guaymi Indigenous Reserve. *Rates US$5–15 pp.*

Cantina Esquina de Mar (9 rooms) In the centre of town and on the beach; ☏ 394 7676. Popular spot for surfers, with basic rooms, some with shared baths and a shared kitchen. The small *soda* serves up good *Tico* fare and the bar is filled with surfers. *Rate US$6 pp.*

WHERE TO EAT

La Manta Club In town (no phone). This seasonal bar/restaurant has laundry service, tourist information, maps, serves great Mediterranean food and offers free movie nights. *Meals average US$11.*

Café de la Suerte In town. Good vegetarian cuisine, smoothies and decadent brownies. *Meals average US$10. Open 08.00–18.00.*

LAS CRUCES BIOLOGICAL STATION

At the end of the country, bordering Panamá, is this 236ha reserve. Within the reserve is the 10ha Wilson Botanical Gardens, bursting with thousands of species of cacti, orchids, ferns, agave, lilies and heliconias. It is home to the largest fern collection in the world and is the repository for the Begonia Society and the Heliconia Society. A must-see for serious gardeners! (*Open 08.00–16.00, closed Mon.*)

Birdwatchers will also be richly rewarded as over 330 species have been recorded and animal lovers can spot monkeys, deer, pacas, anteaters, small cats, sloths, porcupines and over 35 species of bats. Run by the Organisation of Tropical Studies, it is a centre for research, scientific study (new plant species are propagated for horticulture) as well as having a focus on public education.

GETTING THERE From San José, take the Inter-American highway to the Río Terraba Bridge turn-off, 15km south of Buenos Aires at Paso Real. Follow signs for San Vito, then 6km further south.

WHERE TO STAY

Las Cruces (12 rooms) Located in the heart of the reserve; ☎ 773 4004; www.ots.ac.cr. The rooms are surprisingly elegant, with fans, private verandas, private baths with hot water and gleaming hardwood throughout. Wheelchair access. *Rates US$156 pp inc meals and tours.*

13

270

Appendix I

LANGUAGE

The official language of Costa Rica is Spanish. Costa Rican Spanish is spoken fairly slowly and without a thick accent, but the dialect is very idiomatic and full of jargon (known locally as *tiquismos*). Generally Spanish pronunciation and grammar are straightforward, with few irregularities. Words ending in a vowel, 'n' or 's' take the stress on the penultimate syllable; all words that end in other consonants take the stress on the last syllable. Irregular stresses are marked with an accent.

PRONUNCIATION
Consonants

c   As in 'cat', before 'a', 'o', or 'u', like 's' before 'e' or 'i'

d   as 'd' in 'dog', except between vowels, then like 'th' in 'that'

g   before 'e' or 'I', like the 'ch' in Scottish 'loch', elsewhere like 'g' in 'get'

h   always silent

j   like the English 'h' in 'hotel', but stronger

ll   like the 'y' in 'yellow'

ñ   like the 'ni' in 'onion'

r   always pronounced as strong 'r'

rr   trilled 'rr'

v   similar to the 'b' in 'boy' (not as English 'v')

y   similar to English, but with a slight 'j' sound. When y stands alone it is pronounced like the 'e' in 'me'.

z   like 's' in 'same'

b, f, k, l, m, n, p, q, s, t, w, x as in English

Vowels

a   as in 'father' but shorter

e   as in 'hen'

i   as in 'machine'

o   as in 'phone'

u   usually as in 'rule'; when it follows a 'q' the 'u' is silent; when it follows an 'h' or 'g' it's pronounced like 'w', except when it comes between 'g' and 'e' or 'i', when it's also silent

USEFUL WORDS AND PHRASES
Essentials

Hello	*hola*	How are you?	*¿Cómo está?*
Good morning	*buenos días*	Fine	*muy bien*
Good afternoon	*buenas tardes*	And you?	*¿y usted?* (formal)
Good evening	*buenas noches*		or *¿y vos?* (informal)

Thank you	*gracias*	less	*menos*
Thank you very much	*muchas gracias*	better	*major*
		much	*mucho*
You are very kind	*usted es muy amable*	a little	*un poco*
You are welcome	*con gusto*	large	*grande*
Yes	*sí*	small	*pequeño*
No	*no*	quick	*rápido*
I don't know	*yo no sé*	slowly	*despacio*
It's fine	*está bien*	good	*bueno*
Please	*por favor*	bad	*malo*
Pleased to meet you	*mucho gusto*	difficult	*difícil*
Excuse me	*discúlpeme* (physically)	easy	*fácil*
	perdóneme (figuratively)	I don't speak Spanish	*no hablo español*
I'm sorry	*lo siento*	I don't understand	*no entiendo*
Goodbye	*adiós*	Do you speak English?	*¿habla ingles?*
See you later	*hasta luego*		
more	*más*		

Numbers

0	*cero*	15	*quince*	300	*trescientos*
1	*uno* (masculine)	16	*dieciséis*	400	*cuatrocientos*
1	*una* (feminine)	17	*diecisiete*	500	*quinientos*
2	*dos*	18	*dieciocho*	600	*seiscientos*
3	*tres*	19	*diecinueve*	700	*setecientos*
4	*cuatro*	20	*veinte*	800	*ochocientos*
5	*cinco*	30	*treinta*	900	*novecientos*
6	*seis*	40	*cuarenta*	1,000	*mil*
7	*siete*	50	*cincuenta*	2,000	*dos mil*
8	*ocho*	60	*sesenta*	3,000	*tres mil*
9	*nueve*	70	*setenta*	4,000	*cuatro mil*
10	*diez*	80	*ochenta*	5,000	*cinco mil*
11	*once*	90	*noventa*	10,000	*diez mil*
12	*doce*	100	*cien*	15,000	*quince mil*
13	*trece*	101	*ciento uno*		
14	*catorce*	200	*doscientos*		

Days of the week

Sunday	*domingo*	Thursday	*jueves*
Monday	*lunes*	Friday	*viernes*
Tuesday	*martes*	Saturday	*sábado*
Wednesday	*miércoles*		

Time

What time is it?	*¿Qué hora es?*	tomorrow, morning	*mañana, la mañana*
one o'clock	*la una*	yesterday	*ayer*
two o'clock	*las dos*	week	*semana*
at two o'clock	*a las dos*	month	*mes*
ten past three	*las tres y diez*	year	*año*
06.00	*las seis de la mañana*	last night	*anoche*
18.00	*las seis de la tarde*	next day	*al día siguiente*
today	*hoy*		

Terms of address

I	*yo*	wife	*esposa*
you (formal)	*usted*	husband	*esposo* or *marido*
you (informal)	*vos, tu*	friend	*amigo* (male)
he/him	*él*		*amiga* (female)
she/her	*ella*	girlfriend	*novia*
we/us	*nosotros*	boyfriend	*novio*
you (plural)	*ustedes*	father	*padre*
they/them (males		mother	*madre*
or mixed gender)	*ellos*	son	*hijo*
they/them (females)	*ellas*	daughter	*hija*
Mr, Sir	*señor*	brother	*hermano*
Mrs, Ms, Madam	*señora*	sister	*hermana*
Miss, young lady	*señorita*		

Getting around

Where is …?	*¿Dónde está …?*	north	*norte*
How far is …?	*¿Qué tan lejos está …?*	south	*sur*
From … to	*De … a*	west	*oeste*
highway	*la carretera*	east	*este*
road	*el camino*	straight ahead	*adelante*
street	*la calle*	to the right	*a la derecha*
block	*la cuadra*	to the left	*a la izquierda*
kilometre	*kilómetro*		

Accommodation

Can I see a room?	*¿Puedo ver una habitación?*	hot water	*agua caliente*
		cold water	*agua fría*
What is the rate?	*¿Cuál es el precio?*	towel	*toalla*
a single room	*una habitación sencilla*	soap	*jabón*
a double room	*una habitación doble*	toilet paper	*papel higiénico*
key	*llave*	air conditioning	*aire acondicionado*
bathroom	*baño*	blanket	*cobija* or *manta*

Public transport

bus stop	*parada de bus*	Here, please	*Aquí, por favor*
airport	*aeropuerto*	Where is this bus	
ferry terminal	*terminal de ferry*	going?	*¿Dónde va este bus?*
I want a ticket to …	*Quiero un pasaje/tiquete a …*	round trip	*ida y vuelta*
		What do I owe?	*¿Cuánto le debo?*
I want to get off at …	*Quiero bajar en …*		

Food and drink

menu	*menu*	tea	*té*
glass	*vaso*	sugar	*azúcar*
mug	*taza*	drinking water	*agua potable*
fork	*tenedor*	beer	*cerveza*
knife	*cuchillo*	wine	*vino*
spoon	*cuchara*	milk	*leche*
napkin	*servilleta*	juice	*jugo*
soft drink	*gaseosa*	eggs	*huevos*
coffee	*café*	bread	*pan*
cream	*crema*	watermelon	*sandía*

banana	*banano*	fried	*frito*
apple	*manzana*	roasted	*asado*
orange	*naranja*	barbecue	*a la parilla*
meat (without)	*(sin) carne*	breakfast	*desayuno*
chicken	*pollo*	lunch	*almuerzo*
fish	*pescado*	dinner	*cena*
shellfish	*camarones, mariscos*	the bill	*la cuenta*

Making purchases

I need …	*necesito …*	I'm just looking	*Estoy buscando*
I want …	*quiero…*	Can I see …?	*¿Puedo ver …?*
I would like …	*quisiera…*	This one	*ésto/ésta*
How much does it cost?	*¿Cuánto cuesta?*	expensive	*caro*
		cheap	*barato*
What is the exchange rate?	*¿Cuál es el tipo de cambio?*	cheaper	*más barato*
		too much	*demasiado*

Health

Help me, please	*ayúdeme, por favor*	diarrhoea	*diarrea*
I am ill	*estoy enfermo*	chemist	*farmacia*
pain	*dolor*	medicine	*medicina*
fever	*fiebre*	pill, tablet	*pastilla*
stomach ache	*dolor de estómago*	birth control pills	*pastillas anticonceptivas*
vomiting	*vomitar*	condoms	*preservativos*

LANGUAGE SCHOOLS

San José

Centro de Idiomas Berlitz ☏ 204 7555; f 204 7444; www.berlitz.com
Conversa ☏ 221 7649; f 233 2418; www.conversa.net
Costa Rican–North American Cultural Centre ☏ 207 7500; f 224 1480; www.cccncr.com

COSI – Costa Rica Spanish Institute ☏ 234 1001; f 253 2117; www.cosi.co.cr
CRLA – Costa Rican Language Academy ☏ 280 1685; f 280 2548; www.spanishandmore.com
INTENSA ☏ 281 1818; f 253 4337; www.intensa.com

Beach schools

COSI – Costa Rica Spanish Institute Manuel Antonio; ☏ 777 0021; f 777 3507; e office@cosi.co.cr
Escuela de Idiomas D'Amore Manuel Antonio; ☏/f 777 1143; www.escueladamore.com
Horizontes de Montezuma Montezuma Beach; ☏ 642 0534; f 642 0625; www.horizontesmontezuma.com

Intercultura Language School Samara Beach; ☏/f 656 0127; e samaracampos@racsa.co.cr
Santa Teresa Beach Spanish School ☏ 640 0049; f 221 5238; www.spanishandsurf.com
Wayra Spanish Institute Tamarindo; ☏ 653 0617; f 653 0359; www.spanish-wayra.co.cr

Rural schools

Spanish Language and Cross Cultural School (CPH) Santa Ana; ☏/f 282 9920; www.spanishincostarica.com
SEPA San Isidro de El General; ☏ 770 1457; f 771 5586; e sabalo@racsa.co.cr

Centro Panamericano de Idiomas (CPI) San Joaquin de Flores; ☏ 265 6306; f 265 6866; www.cpiedu.com. In Monteverde; ☏ 645 5448 and in Flamingo; ☏ 654 5001.

Appendix 2

FURTHER INFORMATION

You may have a hard time finding some of these books outside of Costa Rica but any bookshop in San José should have copies.

CULTURAL REFERENCE

Biesanz, Mavis, Richard and Karen *The Ticos: Culture and Social Change in Costa Rica* 1998.

Nystrom, Gail *The Moon is a Woman's Thing* 2000. Beautifully illustrated by artist Patricia Erickson.

Ras, Barbara (ed) *Costa Rica: A Traveller's Literary Companion* 1994. Compendium of 26 short stories by Costa Rica's most famous authors.

Salazar, Rodrigo *The Costa Rican Indigenous People: An Ethnographic Overview* 2002.

FOOD AND COOKING

Campabadal, Isabel *The New Costa Rican Cuisine* 1999.

Chavarria, Oscar *A Bit of Costa Rica or How We Costa Ricans Eat* 1999.

de Musmanni, Carmen and de Weilar, Lupita *Costa Rican Typical Foods* 1994.

HISTORY

Christensen, Daryl Cole *A Place in the Rainforest: Settling the Costa Rican Frontier* 1997.

Honey, Martha *Hostile Acts: U.S. Policy in Costa Rica in the 1980s* 1994.

Leboucq, Fabrice and Molina, Ivan *Stuffing the Ballot Box: Fraud, Electoral Reform and Democratization in Costa Rica* 2002.

Leitinger, Ilse Abshagen *The Costa Rican Women's Movement: A Reader* 1997.

Molina, Ivan and Palmer, Steven *The History of Costa Rica* 2001.

NATURE

Agace, Lucy *Diving and Snorkelling Guide to Cocos Island* 1997.

Alvarado, Guillermo *Costa Rica: Land of Volcanoes* 1993.

Amel, Barry *Costa Rica Native Ornamental Plants* 1999.

Barrientos, Zaidett and Monge, Julian *The Biodiversity of Costa Rica: An Ecological Guide* 1997.

Carrillo, Eduardo *Costa Rica Mammals* 1999.

de Vries, Philip *Butterflies of Costa Rica and Their Natural History* (Volumes I and II) 2000.

Ewing, Jack *Monkeys are Made of Chocolate* 2003.

Franke, Joseph *Costa Rica's National Parks and Reserves* 1999.

Hermanos, Trejos (ed) *Birds of the Rainforest* 2000. Great illustrations.

Kanda, Kimio *Costa Rica: The Bird's Paradise* 1999.

Morales, Francisco *Bromeliads of Costa Rica* 2000.

Robles, Rafael *A Field Guide to the Common Plants of the Caribbean Coast of Costa Rica* 1997.

Stiles, Gary and Skutch, Alexander *A Guide to the Birds of Costa Rica* 1990. The birder's bible.

PHOTO BOOKS

Boza, Mario *Costa Rica: National Parks* 2002.
Calderon, Gloria *The Life of Costa Rica* 2001.
Schafer, Kevin and Ugalde, Alvaro *Costa Rica: The Forests of Eden* 2000.
Weston, Christopher *Cocos Island* 1992.

BUSINESS: MOVING TO COSTA RICA

Borner, Tessa *Potholes to Paradise* 2001.
Brooks, Guy and Victoria *Costa Rica: A Kick Start Guide for Business Travellers* 1996.
Howard, Christopher *The New Golden Door to Retirement and Living in Costa Rica* 2002.
Howells, John *Choose Costa Rica: Travel, Investment and Living Opportunities for Every Budget* 2002.

DRIVING TO COSTA RICA

Weisbecker, Allan *In Search of Captain Zero* 2002.
Westler, Dawna Rae *You Can Drive to Costa Rica in 8 Days* 2000.

WIN £100 CASH!

READER QUESTIONNAIRE

**Send in your completed questionnaire for the chance to win
£100 cash in our regular draw**

All respondents may order a Bradt guide at half the UK retail price – please
complete the order form overleaf.

(Entries may be posted or faxed to us, or scanned and emailed.)

We are interested in getting feedback from our readers to help us plan future Bradt
guides. Please answer ALL the questions below and return the form to us in order
to qualify for an entry in our regular draw.

Have you used any other Bradt guides? If so, which titles? . . . .
. . . .

What other publishers' travel guides do you use regularly? . . . .
. . . .

Where did you buy this guidebook? . . . .

What was the main purpose of your trip to Costa Rica (or for what other reason
did you read our guide)? eg: holiday/business/charity etc. . . . .
. . . .

What other destinations would you like to see covered by a Bradt guide?
. . . .

Would you like to receive our catalogue/newsletters?

YES / NO (If yes, please complete details on reverse)

If yes – by post or email? . . . .

Age (circle relevant category) 16–25 26–45 46–60 60+

Male/Female (delete as appropriate)

Home country . . . .

Please send us any comments about our guide to Costa Rica or other Bradt Travel
Guides. . . . .
. . . .
. . . .
. . . .

Bradt Travel Guides

23 High Street, Chalfont St Peter, Bucks SL9 9QE, UK
☏ +44 (0)1753 893444 **f** +44 (0)1753 892333
e info@bradtguides.com
www.bradtguides.com

CLAIM YOUR HALF-PRICE BRADT GUIDE!

Order Form

To order your half-price copy of a Bradt guide, and to enter our prize draw to win £100 (see overleaf), please fill in the order form below, complete the questionnaire overleaf, and send it to Bradt Travel Guides by post, fax or email.

Please send me one copy of the following guide at half the UK retail price

Title		Retail price	Half price
...	....	....	......

Please send the following additional guides at full UK retail price

No	Title		Retail price	Total
...	....		....	....
...	....		....	....
...	....		....	....

Sub total	....
Post & packing	....
(£1 per book UK; £2 per book Europe; £3 per book rest of world)	
Total	....

Name ....

Address...

Tel .... Email ....

☐ I enclose a cheque for £........ made payable to Bradt Travel Guides Ltd

☐ I would like to pay by credit card. Number: ....

    Expiry date: ... / ...   3-digit security code (on reverse of card) .....

☐ Please add my name to your catalogue mailing list.

☐ I would be happy for you to use my name and comments in Bradt marketing material.

Send your order on this form, with the completed questionnaire, to:

Bradt Travel Guides COS/1
23 High Street, Chalfont St Peter, Bucks SL9 9QE
☎ +44 (0)1753 893444   f +44 (0)1753 892333
e info@bradtguides.com   www.bradtguides.com

Bradt Travel Guides

www.bradtguides.com

Africa

Africa Overland	£15.99
Benin	£14.99
Botswana: Okavango, Chobe, Northern Kalahari	£15.99
Burkina Faso	£14.99
Cape Verde Islands	£13.99
Canary Islands	£13.95
Cameroon	£13.95
Eritrea	£12.95
Ethiopia	£15.99
Gabon, São Tomé, Príncipe	£13.95
Gambia, The	£13.99
Ghana	£13.95
Johannesburg	£6.99
Kenya	£14.95
Madagascar	£14.95
Malawi	£13.99
Mali	£13.95
Mauritius, Rodrigues & Réunion	£13.99
Mozambique	£12.95
Namibia	£14.95
Niger	£14.99
Nigeria	£15.99
Rwanda	£14.99
Seychelles	£14.99
Sudan	£13.95
Tanzania, Northern	£13.99
Tanzania	£16.99
Uganda	£13.95
Zambia	£15.95
Zanzibar	£12.99

Britain and Europe

Albania	£13.99
Armenia, Nagorno Karabagh	£13.99
Azores	£12.99
Baltic Capitals: Tallinn, Riga, Vilnius, Kaliningrad	£12.99
Belgrade	£6.99
Bosnia & Herzegovina	£13.99
Bratislava	£6.99
Budapest	£7.95
Cork	£6.95
Croatia	£12.95
Cyprus see North Cyprus	
Czech Republic	£13.99
Dubrovnik	£6.95
Eccentric Britain	£13.99
Eccentric Cambridge	£6.99
Eccentric Edinburgh	£5.95
Eccentric France	£12.95
Eccentric London	£12.95
Eccentric Oxford	£5.95
Estonia	£12.95
Faroe Islands	£13.95
Hungary	£14.99
Kiev	£7.95
Latvia	£13.99
Lille	£6.99

Lithuania	£13.99
Ljubljana	£6.99
Macedonia	£13.95
Montenegro	£13.99
North Cyprus	£12.99
Paris, Lille & Brussels	£11.95
Riga	£6.95
River Thames, In the Footsteps of the Famous	£10.95
Serbia	£13.99
Slovenia	£12.99
Spitsbergen	£14.99
Switzerland: Rail, Road, Lake	£13.99
Tallinn	£6.99
Ukraine	£13.95
Vilnius	£6.99

Middle East, Asia and Australasia

Georgia	£13.95
Great Wall of China	£13.99
Iran	£14.99
Iraq	£14.95
Kabul	£9.95
Maldives	£13.99
Mongolia	£14.95
North Korea	£13.95
Oman	£13.99
Palestine, Jerusalem	£12.95
Sri Lanka	£13.99
Syria	£13.99
Tasmania	£12.95
Tibet	£13.99
Turkmenistan	£14.99

The Americas and the Caribbean

Amazon, The	£14.95
Argentina	£15.99
Bolivia	£14.99
Cayman Islands	£12.95
Costa Rica	£13.99
Chile	£16.95
Chile & Argentina: Trekking	£12.95
Eccentric America	£13.95
Eccentric California	£13.99
Falkland Islands	£13.95
Peru & Bolivia: Backpacking and Trekking	£12.95
Panama	£13.95
St Helena, Ascension, Tristan da Cunha	£14.95
USA by Rail	£13.99

Wildlife

Antarctica: Guide to the Wildlife	£14.95
Arctic: Guide to the Wildlife	£15.99
British Isles: Wildlife of Coastal Waters	£14.95
Galápagos Wildlife	£15.99
Madagascar Wildlife	£14.95
Southern African Wildlife	£18.95
Sri Lankan Wildlife	£15.99

Health

Your Child Abroad: A Travel Health Guide	£10.95

Index

Page numbers in bold indicate major entries; those in italic indicate maps